Women and Children in the Factory

Women and Children in the Factory

A Life of
Adelaide Anderson
(1863–1936)

Anne Spurgeon

Women and Children in the Factory: A Life of Adelaide Anderson (1863–1936)
Anne Spurgeon

Published by Aspect Design, 2016

Designed, printed and bound by Aspect Design
89 Newtown Road, Malvern, Worcs. WR14 1PD
United Kingdom
Tel: 01684 561567
E-mail: allan@aspect-design.net
Website: www.aspect-design.net

ISBN 978-1-908832-93-1

Dedicated to the memory of
Barbara Blanche Anderson (1922–2015)

CONTENTS

ILLUSTRATIONS

ACKNOWLEDGEMENTS

This biography grew out of a thesis, completed in 2012, which explored the work of the Women's Factory Inspectorate. My first acknowledgement, therefore, is to the University of Worcester and particularly to my tutors there, Sue Johnson, Maggie Andrews and Frank Crompton.

The book would not have been possible without the help of many people, notably a number of archivists and librarians, especially those at the Women's Library, now part of the Library of the London School of Economics. My thanks go to the staff there, first for their agreement to catalogue Adelaide's mountain of papers, a considerable and expensive task without which I would not have been able to progress at all, and second for their unfailing help and support throughout the many weeks I spent in the library's earlier home in Old Castle Street, Whitechapel, London.

Thanks also go to staff of the National Archives and the British Library, and to those many organisations who at various times have provided me with important pieces of information, or with photographs, namely Aberdeen City Archives, the Caird Library, the Dudley Archives and Local History Service, the Guildhall Library, the Hull History Centre, the Imperial War Museum, the Modern Records Centre of the University of Warwick, Nottinghamshire Archives, the Plymouth Record

Office, the Salvation Army International Heritage Centre, Smethwick Heritage Centre, the Wellcome Institute, and Wolverhampton Archives and Local Studies Department. I am also extremely grateful to the staff at the headquarters of the Health and Safety Executive in Liverpool who allowed me a long loan of some early copies of Factory Inspectors' Reports. Special thanks go to Archivist Hannah Westall at Girton College who helped me to piece together Adelaide's time at Cambridge.

My partner Tim has supported this project with unfailing enthusiasm, accompanying me on numerous interesting explorations (and correcting my unreliable geography) as we attempted to 'walk Adelaide's patch'. His comments on various drafts of the book have been invaluable.

Finally and most significantly, I owe a great debt of gratitude to Barbara Blanche Anderson, Adelaide's niece; and to Shelagh Molloy, who introduced me to Barbara after a chance meeting several years ago. Barbara made available to me a huge and precious resource of family letters, papers and photographs which, together with her own personal memories of her aunt, have provided me with countless insights into Adelaide's life beyond the official persona of the factory inspector. There have been many happy hours spent with Barbara and other members of her family 'talking Adelaide'.

Adelaide Anderson, Principal Lady Factory Inspector

Chapter One
INTRODUCING ADELAIDE

Early in the morning of the 5 May 1936 the Ellerman Line steamship *City of Exeter* slipped quietly into Plymouth Sound. Anchoring inside the breakwater she awaited the arrival of the tenders that would transport most of her passengers and their assorted luggage to Millbay dockside and the waiting Pullman railway carriages. Plymouth in those days was a popular disembarkation point for London bound passengers keen to 'cut the corner' by joining a fast train to Paddington. Large elegant ships arrived daily from across the Atlantic and rather less often from more distant places around the globe. The voyage of the *City of Exeter* had begun three weeks earlier in the East African port of Lourenço Marques in Portuguese Mozambique. Amongst those assembling along the ship's rail that day was the diminutive figure of an elderly lady carrying, as always on these occasions, an overflowing travelling bag and a sturdy umbrella. She had joined the ship in Durban following a visit to her much-loved brother Ralf and his family in South Africa and was now heading home to her pretty cottage on the edge of Kew Gardens in West London. The transfer from ship to tender and from there to the quayside could be a precarious experience in the 1930s and the fragility of this lady's appearance would have provoked numerous offers of assistance. Almost certainly these would have been received with the most gracious appreciation. Equally certainly, however, they would have been quite unnecessary, for this particular passenger was a robust and highly experienced traveller. Her name was Miss Adelaide Mary Anderson, CBE, Dame of the British Empire and formerly His Majesty's Principal Lady Inspector of Factories and Workshops. Her retirement from the Factory Inspectorate, fifteen years earlier, had provided her with many opportunities to sail the world, sometimes for business, sometimes for pleasure, and most often for both. Ralf's last letter, which had reached her during the ship's brief stop in Cape Town, was full of entreaties to return soon, a prospect that would have filled her with delight. She loved travelling, relishing the going, the arriving and the return in equal measure, and Ralf's family held a special place in her heart. Sadly, however, this was not to be. At the age of seventy-three Miss Anderson had completed her last voyage. Less than four months later, on 29 August, a stark headline appeared on an inside page of *The Times*. Dame Adelaide, it declared, was dead.

Her death, from pneumonia, which had taken place the previous day in a Chelsea nursing home, was perhaps unexceptional in a lady of her years. In 1936, however, the name Dame Adelaide would have been familiar to large sections of the British public and her passing would not have gone unnoticed. *The Times* was the first to carry the news, for Dame Adelaide was well connected to those in high places and merited an obituary which extended over several paragraphs.[1] This was not, however, a simple case of the rich and powerful honouring one of their own. A sense of sadness, it seems, was as keenly felt on the legendary Clapham omnibus as amongst the more illustrious sections of society and tributes soon began to appear in newspapers of every social and political complexion up and down the land. Letters of condolence, both formal and personal, arrived from people in Australia, China, South Africa and Egypt, from the League of Nations and Save the Children, and from a catalogue of organisations sufficiently eclectic to include both the National Institute of Industrial Psychology[2] and the rather more eccentric Grith Fyrd Boys Club.[3] The common factor that had secured for Dame Adelaide a place in the affections of such a disparate group was her lifelong commitment to the reform of unsafe and unhealthy conditions in the workplace, particularly those which affected the lives of thousands of women and children.

Appointed in 1894 as one of the first female factory inspectors, Adelaide Anderson had rapidly moved into the position of 'Principal Lady Inspector', heading the small but growing section of the British Factory Department devoted specifically to the needs of women workers. She was to lead this section through the next twenty-five years. It was a period marked by significant advances in factory reform, fuelled by a growing political acceptance that the state had a duty to intervene in the conditions under which people were employed. 'Sanitary science', based on new models of disease causation and prevention, had already begun to inform the introduction of public health measures designed to provide clean water, efficient sewerage systems and generally better living conditions in the densely populated industrial cities. Increasingly, at the end of the nineteenth century, this new medical and scientific knowledge was applied to the policies and practices of industrial health and safety. As the first women to gain entry into the British Factory Department the 'lady factory inspectors', as they were invariably known, were central players in this process.

The abuses visited on workers during the first quarter of the twentieth century have received rather less historical attention than the compelling horrors of the nineteenth, a result perhaps of the particular prism through which, apparently, we prefer to view the years that immediately preceded the First World War. Despite the attempts of revisionist historians to prise our national psyche away from its balmy notions of a golden

Edwardian age there seems to be a stubborn resistance to engage with a less comfortable reality. Thus we prefer to focus on a small section of society which, in the popular imagination at least, basked confidently in the fruits of the Empire, enjoying a world of long hot summers, teas and tennis parties. This mythical view of the Edwardians not only misrepresents the lives of many in the wealthier sections of society but also largely ignores the majority of the population. For the world in which Adelaide Anderson moved during her most productive years in the Factory Department was an increasingly uneasy one. Here, in a shifting political landscape, an emergent labour movement was beginning to flex its muscles and attention was turning gradually but ever more insistently to the unacceptable conditions in which thousands of people worked. Today, we are inclined to associate violent protest in the Edwardian age with the fire-raising and window smashing of the militant suffragettes rather than with the widespread industrial unrest which repeatedly beset the nation. Yet during this period many more women were preoccupied with the immediate need to put food on the table than ever marched shoulder to shoulder under the 'widely blowing banner', or furtively bought teacups decorated in suffragist purple, white and green.[4] A huge and increasingly discontented industrial workforce, composed of men, women, and what we would now define as children, existed simply to supply the burgeoning middle classes with the goods and services demanded by a growing consumer society.

The factories and workshops in which so many of these workers spent their days, and often their nights, were dangerous, insanitary places where industrial accidents and disease occurred with alarming regularity. With the arrival of the Great War ordinary working women enjoyed a brief period of historical visibility as they moved in their thousands to fill the jobs left vacant when their menfolk boarded troop ships for France. Once more, however, it seems our attention has been drawn almost exclusively to one particular section of this population, the munition girls, the so-called 'canaries',[5] who risked illness or death from toxic jaundice as they filled shells with the yellow powder containing trinitrotoluene (TNT). Yet, in some ways, these were the lucky ones. Mindful of their importance to the nation and the need to encourage recruitment into the industry, the government was particularly assiduous in its protection of the health of those who produced its armaments. Stringent safety regulations, routine medical checks and elaborate welfare facilities succeeded in reducing the incidence of jaundice to only a handful of cases within two years. The iconic status of the women in the munitions factories, however, has tended to obscure the fate of thousands of other women who struggled to operate unfamiliar machinery, often with disastrous results, who soldered millions of metal provision boxes in badly equipped Black Country workshops or worked sixteen hour days to produce everything from bronzed field glasses and thermometers to army uniforms and nose-bags for horses. The essential accoutrements of war extended well beyond the immediate requirement for munitions.

Adelaide Anderson and her colleagues were exclusively drawn from the middle classes of society and entered this industrial world with no personal experience of manual labour. Historically, therefore, it is tempting to place them either as philanthropically motivated social reformers or, alternatively, as successful representatives of the late Victorian feminist movement in pursuit of equal educational and professional employment opportunities for women. Neither picture, however, is entirely appropriate for, unlike other contemporary reformists whose names may be more familiar to us, the Pankhursts, the Webbs and the Fawcetts for example, the factory inspectors did not organise protest meetings, make rousing speeches or write provocative letters to the newspapers. Nor did they base their activities on a model of charitable giving, despite an undeniable commitment to improving the lot of the less fortunate. Rather they carried out their work within the constraints of government service, as paid officials of the state that so many of their radical contemporaries sought to attack. The story of Adelaide Anderson is thus a story of a woman who operated rather differently from the more celebrated proponents of social reform. Civil servants are rarely colourful or heroic figures in the public imagination and it is easy to underestimate their importance, not only as advocates for improvement, but also as highly effective agents of change. Adelaide Anderson, the directing mind of the women's inspectorate, was a perfect exemplar of the breed, a curious mixture of conformist and reformist who quietly manoeuvred rather than strode across the national stage. To her could be attributed that ultimate civil service accolade, 'a safe pair of hands' for she remained consistently, one might say obsessively, firm on the requirement to disassociate herself from political parties or radical movements of any complexion. Indeed this particular Civil Service maxim often seemed to provide her with a handy defence against unwelcome demands to join such organisations, for she personally abhorred violent direct action and had little enthusiasm for other forms of demonstration. Instead she chose to work through official channels, relentlessly identifying abuses, gathering unpalatable statistics and pressing for legislative change. Prominent trade union leader and Labour MP, Margaret Bondfield, 'came gladly' to Adelaide's memorial service in 1937, 'to pay homage to her life and work . . . on behalf of millions of working women whose lives have been made more bearable because Dame Adelaide Anderson has lived.'[6]

For many years Adelaide Anderson occupied the highest rank of any woman in the British Civil Service, operating in a sphere previously occupied exclusively by men. During this period women were entirely absent from the party political arena and largely excluded from the state apparatus. She had, therefore, breached one of the strongest bastions of nineteenth century male supremacy and it was with some justification that she claimed for herself the label of female pioneer. More controversially, however, she also considered herself a feminist. Yet this is a more complex, multifaceted label and not everyone agreed. The very nature of her work put her at odds with one particular strand of contemporary feminism, provoking the wrath of campaigners for women's rights. The position of those who supported total occupational equality between men and women was an uncompromising one, encompassing equal access to jobs, equal pay and, importantly, equal working conditions. The introduction of protective factory legislation, selectively targeted at female workers, was thus regarded by many feminist activists of the period as a direct attack on women's employment rights. It opened the way, for example, to the imposition of shorter working hours for women and possibly even exclusion from certain jobs. In the early twentieth century industrial health and safety was a stage on which fierce feminist battles were fought. Adelaide Anderson was by no means oblivious to such concerns but she was, above all, a practitioner of the art of the possible, an advocate of the pragmatic over the ideological. How, for example, should equality of opportunity be interpreted in the face of jobs that presented a disproportionate risk to women workers or even to their unborn children? In many ways, therefore, her position in the women's movement of the period is an ambiguous one. Most often her approach allied her with more moderate 'social feminists' who embraced the concept of female parity, best described as 'equality with difference'.

In 1921 the work of the women's section brought Adelaide Anderson the title of Dame of the British Empire, but also, to her bitter dismay, her removal from her post and forced retirement from the Factory Department. For that year marked the amalgamation of the male and female factory inspectorates into a single organisation, a development to which she was strongly opposed. Unexpectedly, however, this unlooked for turn of events marked the beginning of an entirely new chapter in her life that took her, at the age of fifty-eight, across the world and into contact with the most terrible child labour conditions she had ever seen. It was here, in China, and later in Egypt that she carried out investigations at the behest of various organisations including the emergent League of Nations. Her work overseas occupied her until a few years before her death, involving her in attempts to establish factory regulations and factory inspectorates in countries where children as young as five laboured in cotton mills, and where attempts to introduce basic safeguards were frequently thwarted by the advent of floods, famine and war.

In 1879 Alexander Redgrave, then Chief Inspector of Factories, had outlined his objections to the appointment of women as factory inspectors. 'The general and multifarious duties of an inspector of factories', he said, 'would really be incompatible with the gentle and home-loving character of a woman. Factory inspecting requires activity and acumen and the stern authority of a man to enforce obedience to his interrogatories.'[7] Adelaide Anderson's quiet manner would not have impressed him, and her physical appearance would probably have reinforced his misgivings, for she was small and slight with an air of delicacy and refinement. Always respectably well dressed, she had a conspicuous attachment to extravagant hats which persisted long after they ceased to be *de rigeur* for the fashionably well-to-do. The hems of her skirts may have risen very slightly over the years but throughout her life she retained the persona of an entirely proper Victorian lady. Invariably calm and courteous she was also undeniably prim. Many who worked for her were dismayed by her unrelenting formality, her exacting standards and her tenacious hold over the work of her staff. Her behaviour, above all, seems to have been underpinned by a fierce attachment to the concept of duty, something which no doubt owed much to the values of nineteenth-century middle-class

England. This image was genuine but also perhaps carefully cultivated in pursuit of her aims. Employers, she once said, were often taken off-guard by her arrival in a factory, assuming her to be the mission lady who had come to hand out religious tracts to the workers. Long-term friend and colleague, Hilda Martindale, who published a pen portrait of Adelaide in 1948, emphasised above all her indomitable determination, a feature that, in different ways, seems to emerge in numerous aspects of her life. Her ostensibly mild manner, it seemed, masked a single-minded and largely unsentimental determination to get her way. She was, as we shall see, a rather successful organiser of other people's lives.

Adelaide Anderson was essentially a private person whose reluctance to discuss her own motivations and feelings was matched only by her refusal to discuss those of her friends, relatives and colleagues. Unlike some other characters in this story she rarely gives vent to her opinions about the behaviour of others. Part of this, no doubt, reflects her strong belief in the value of discretion and personal control, features that dictated both the conduct of her life and the clues to that life which she chose to leave behind. Her archive contains a mountain of papers for, as a diligent civil servant, she carefully filed away each official and semi-official letter she received, noting the date of its reception and acknowledgement and making a hand written copy of her reply. She continued this practice throughout her life. Yet in many ways this biographical embarrassment of riches tends to obscure rather than illuminate the personality behind the official façade. Her correspondence provides only rare glimpses of her emotional response to the employers and workers with whom she came into contact. And yet it is difficult to reconcile her steadfastly optimistic view of human nature with the cruelty, suffering and official indifference she would have encountered on a regular basis. In many of the letters of condolence her family received at her death there is more than a suggestion of saintliness, even allowing for the hagiography that tends to accompany bereavement. One suspects that this is what she would have wanted, for she seems to have set herself very high standards of personal behaviour. In her family letters as well as in her official correspondence there is rarely any digression from that unexcitable control which she, and no doubt others of her generation, viewed as indicative of personal strength. It perhaps comes as no surprise, therefore, that her papers contain no hints of love affairs of any complexion. This is not to deny their existence. It is known for example, that she received at least one proposal of marriage, confided only to her sister-in-law Margaret, and resolutely turned down. Margaret, however, kept her counsel, and the rejected suitor must, at least for now, remain a mystery. This is entirely in keeping with the discretion which Dame Adelaide always exercised over personal matters and the curious reader will look in vain for tales of love, tempestuous, unrequited or otherwise. Rather this is a story set against a background of apparently contented singledom. Adelaide's passion, it seems, was for her work.

Today Dame Adelaide Anderson is no longer a household name. Ironically the work that, in earlier in times, had turned her into a public luminary now seems to condemn her to historical obscurity. When she was first appointed Principal Lady Inspector the spectacle of occupationally related accidents and disease was a *cause célèbre*, trumpeted in the sensation seeking new media and embraced enthusiastically by activists determined to shock a voyeuristic public and embarrass the government of the day. As a legacy of the actions taken in those years many of us in Britain today enjoy the luxury of relatively safe and healthy workplaces where industrial accidents and disease are considered scandalous anomalies rather than the norm. Somewhat perversely, however, the successors of that early popular press are now more inclined to snigger at the supposed excesses of that much maligned and unfashionable activity 'health and safety'. Such comfortable complacency is not new. In 1923, John Murray published Adelaide Anderson's first book entitled *Women in the Factory*,[8] an account of her twenty-seven years as an inspector. It was, she said, a story of 'sufferings and trials . . . of which no responsible thinker, or leader in the nation's affairs should ever be allowed to remain ignorant.'[9] But in many ways, of course, they did remain ignorant, and they undoubtedly forgot, especially in a post-war world immersed in collective grief for those who had suffered and died in even more terrible circumstances. The book did not sell well. Indeed John Murray was at pains to point out that the firm had made a loss on the publication and would not be printing a second edition. A few years later they rejected her second book which described her work in China.[10] Health and safety ennui, it seems, had already taken a firm hold. Yet by the middle of the 1930s, Dame Adelaide herself was still a well-known and well-respected figure. Shortly before her death she had been approached by another publisher with the suggestion that she write her memoirs. It was a proposal that Adelaide actively considered, for she had always maintained that her existing books represented, not so much her own personal story, but rather the story of women workers and the conditions in which they were employed. However, as she herself seems to have discovered, it is difficult to separate the two narratives or indeed to separate the British story from the one she subsequently encountered in other parts of the world. This second portrayal of *Women in the Factory*, therefore, is primarily a biography of Adelaide Anderson, but it also offers a window on working conditions during the period, both in Britain and elsewhere. It is perhaps interesting to speculate how Adelaide would have responded to some of the uncomfortable truths about working conditions today, in countries from which Britain sources many of its material goods.

Chapter Two
HOW SHE CAME TO BE

'My dear mother, congratulate me on the birth of a daughter who is now more than a fortnight old having been born on the 8th.' So wrote Alexander Gavin Anderson, manager of the Melbourne branch of the Oriental Banking Corporation, on 25 April 1863. The baby, he said, was thriving and her mother, Blanche Emily, was 'fast getting strong again.' Four names had been tried but none so far had 'stuck.'[1] Alexander's mother, Mary Gavin Anderson, received the letter nearly three months later at her home in Aberdeen where his father, Alexander senior, was headmaster of the Chanonry House Boys' School. In the event, the name that 'stuck' was Adelaide, not as might be supposed in recognition of the baby's Australian birth, but rather because her parent's favourite song was a Beethoven cantata based on Friedrich von Matthisson's eighteenth-century poem of that name. The Adelaide of this lyrical fantasy was an idealised woman, the symbol of love, for Blanche Emily and Alexander Gavin were a happy young couple who delighted in their growing family. They had met and married in New Zealand where Alexander Gavin had been manager of the Dunedin branch of the Oriental. Shortly afterwards they had moved to Australia where Adelaide and her older brother, Maxwell Gavin, were born. Melbourne, in 1863, was a busy, bustling town, pioneering in its spirit and irreverently informal in its manners. It was not only physical geography that separated this young territory from the stifling social conventions of Victorian Britain. Since the 1850s the gold rush had been in full swing and hopeful prospectors of every creed and class had poured into the surrounding area rubbing shoulders in ways that would have been unthinkable back home. Like most of their neighbours, therefore, Adelaide's parents were relative newcomers to this environment with family roots planted firmly elsewhere, and in their case elsewhere was in Scotland.

The Anderson family into which Adelaide was born was a large and enterprising one, ambitious in its aspirations and increasingly international in outlook. From modest rural beginnings numerous Andersons had responded energetically to the opportunities offered by the nineteenth century, developing highly successful careers in business and the professions. The family was also a close one, for there was much intermarriage between its various branches, forming a wide-ranging network of useful and supportive contacts. From the perspective of Adelaide's position in this intricate web the single most influential figure seems to have been her paternal grandfather, Alexander 'Govie' Anderson, the 'Governor' of the Chanonry House School. Govie had originally been a Presbyterian Minister in the small rural Parish of Boyndie in Aberdeenshire where he and his wife, naval surgeon's daughter Mary Gavin, had twelve children. Alexander Gavin, Adelaide's father, was the eldest of the eleven who survived into adulthood. As well as providing a large supply of useful relatives Govie's life story had, by the time Adelaide was born, formed the basis of a powerful family legend that was to exert an important moral influence over his descendants. In the early 1840s Govie had been part of the Great Disruption when over one third of Scottish clergymen had walked out of the church's General Assembly and abandoned their Presbyterian livings to form the new Free Church of Scotland. The 'Disruptors' were protesting against the system of patronage in the selection of church ministers, a system which both restricted entry into the

Ministry and reinforced the social divide between an invariably wealthy clergy and their impoverished flocks. Govie's role in this story was an especially colourful one, for he had in fact left his own church in a somewhat dramatic fashion twelve months before the official Disruption. Family history records that, on a freezing night in the middle of the severe winter of 1842/3, he had ceremoniously closed and locked the front door of the large well-appointed Manse in Boyndie and set off, on foot, along the narrow track out of the village. He took with him two devoted servants, a dutiful but no doubt extremely uneasy Mary Gavin, and his current family of six young children. Poor Mary, clutching a few belongings and the smallest baby, is reputed to have surveyed the snow, banked up in the surrounding fields, and enquired anxiously as to where exactly the family were now to live. Her husband, no doubt warmed from within by the strength of his convictions, delivered a lofty rebuke. The Lord, he said, would provide. 'Butter we might not get, but God will make us sure of bread.'[2] In the event, the instrument of this providence turned out to be Govie's Uncle Sandy, a popular and wealthy sea captain known locally as 'Tarrybreeks'. Uncle Sandy, brother to Govie's father, John Ford Anderson, was a wealthy man. He had been a naval officer during the Napoleonic Wars and in 1815 he had purchased a ship, a French prize, setting himself up as a successful West Indian sugar trader. For many years he had assumed responsibility for Govie and his three siblings after their father, a physician, had died as a young man, apparently as a result of typhus contracted from one of his patients.[3] Now, in 1843, Uncle Sandy once more stepped into the breach, supporting Govie and his family in two small fisherman's cottages in the nearby coastal village of Whitehills. Complete destitution had been avoided but life was now cramped and uncomfortable and the necessities of life reduced to their most basic.

This tale, alone, was sufficient to provide Govie's descendants with a salutary lesson in the virtues of moral integrity and

principled self-sacrifice. It was, however, only the beginning
of a much longer story. In 1846 Govie was invited to take up
the position of minister to a recently formed Free Church
congregation in Aberdeen's central medieval district known
as the Old Machar. The church, which operated from a large
wooden hut, provocatively situated next door to the old
fourteenth-century cathedral, represented a constant source of
irritation to the Presbyterian clergy. With its associated evening
schools for poor children it was popular amongst large sections
of the local community and Govie acquired a considerable
reputation as a charismatic minister and a gifted teacher. But
barely had Mary Gavin settled thankfully into this new and
infinitely more comfortable life than her husband engineered
yet another spiritually inspired domestic disruption. Following
an intensive study of early Christian documents in the British
Museum he told an exasperated group of church elders that he
felt compelled to reject various aspects of church teaching and,
in particular, that of infant baptism. This practice, he informed
them, had been introduced into the church at a relatively late
stage, in 1311. Only adult baptism had been ordained by Christ.
Govie's steadfast refusal to compromise on this central tenet of
ecclesiastical doctrine resulted in his excommunication from the
new Free Church and the loss, once more, of his family home.
This time, however, rescue came in the form of a group of wealthy
Aberdeen merchants and philanthropists who had embarked on
a project to establish a new school in the city. As representatives
of the rising business community in Aberdeen this 'Council of
Gentlemen' (which fortuitously and unsurprisingly contained
several members of the Anderson family) had long despaired of
traditional Scottish grammar schools, with their heavy emphasis
on classical scholarship. They looked instead for a curriculum
that would prepare young men for useful careers in trade and
commerce. For inspiration they turned to the enlightened
'Gymnasium' schools in Germany which offered instruction in

Adelaide's grandfather, Alexander 'Govie' Anderson

modern foreign languages, mathematics, science and the arts.
In January 1848, therefore, with financial assistance from the
ever helpful Uncle Sandy, the new Chanonry House School, or
'Gym' as it was often known, opened in Aberdeen, with Govie
as it new headmaster. The school was situated, once more,

alongside the old cathedral, taking its name from the medieval street known as the Chanonry, where the Cannons of the old cathedral had once lived. Under Govie's inspired leadership the Gym soon acquired an academic reputation that went well beyond the immediate confines of Aberdeen. Within a few years its classrooms, dormitories and science laboratories had advanced with lightening speed along the Chanonry, and its playing fields occupied a large swathe of land behind the street's old stone houses. Today the site enjoys, according to a local historian, 'a fair and fragrant burial'[4] beneath the University's botanical gardens, but the school functioned more or less successfully for over forty years. Three of Adelaide's brothers were to be pupils there and she, herself, owed her own enlightened education to the influence of her grandfather, not only in terms of its content but also in the very fact that, as a girl, she received it at all. The young Adelaide and her siblings were all well acquainted with Govie's story and grew up with a degree of reverence for their paternal grandfather. They appear to have been not only respectful but also inordinately fond of him. It was an admiration seemingly uncontaminated by the undoubted trials he had inflicted upon his immediate dependants for, despite his uncompromising opinions, he was, by all accounts, a gentle and kindly man, particularly in his relationships with children.

Adelaide's father, Alexander Gavin, was born in Boyndie in 1833, a year that perhaps rather presciently marked the passage of the first British Factory Act, an initial if rather limited attempt to address some of the appalling conditions under which thousands of young children slaved in the great urban textile mills of Northern England. Under the terms of this Act the first four British factory inspectors were appointed and thus the Factory Inspectorate itself was born. None of this, of course, would have crossed the consciousness of Govie's young family, for Boyndie was a small rural village in Eastern Scotland, remote from the thumping of steam engines and the palls of black smoke which hung over so many industrial towns. The comfort and security of early life here, however, would have made the abrupt severance from the Manse and the years of uncertainty which followed, particularly difficult for Govie's children. Alexander Gavin, the eldest, would have had the clearest memories of a more agreeable existence, an experience that seems to have left him with a strong instinct for self-preservation and a fierce determination to avoid the deprivations of poverty. In 1849, therefore, the year after the Gym opened, he enrolled at nearby King's College, the forerunner of Aberdeen University. Here, amongst its grandiose buildings and monastically inspired quadrangles, he studied the traditional syllabus of Greek, Latin, Theology and Moral Philosophy, a curriculum designed primarily to prepare young men for a career in the established church. Alexander Gavin had no such ambitions but he nevertheless emerged from Kings with a passion for classical literature, a love of religious music and, it seems, a leaning towards a more traditional faith. It was something he would share with his wife and subsequently pass on to his children, for by the time he left Scotland for New Zealand he had largely shed the Free Church influences that had engendered such a precarious childhood. Thus in 1863, when Adelaide was just two months old, he casually informed his father that the absence of the usual letter from Blanche Emily was due to her preoccupation with various social arrangements surrounding the baby's christening. It was a pointed reminder to his family of a significant shift in his religious allegiance.

Alexander Gavin's career aspirations lay in the direction of banking and particularly overseas banking. Economic migration was popular among ambitious young Scots of the late nineteenth century and like many of his contemporaries he was keen to venture out into the Empire. In 1850 he obtained a junior post in Aberdeen's North of Scotland Banking Company, but six months later he moved to London, where he joined the newly established Oriental Banking Corporation. It was a stepping-stone to Britain's newest territories for the bank had established a network of branches across the Indian and Pacific Oceans as well as a successful operation in Australia where it had invested in the gold trade. Alexander Gavin seems to have been an able young man for when the bank decided to expand further, into New Zealand, he was selected to be its new manager in Dunedin, the centre of the Scottish settlement in South Island. However, these were uncertain times in Britain's newest territory. Relationships with the indigenous Māori population in South Island, although much less fraught than in the volatile North, were nevertheless uneasy and prone to erupt into open conflict. And the bank's operation into the country proved to be much less successful than had been hoped. In the years since 1850 many other banks had entered this financial arena and competition was now very fierce. Moreover trade in the South Island was still relatively underdeveloped and New Zealand's gold rush was much smaller in scale than that currently engulfing Australia. Perhaps Dunedin's new manager was unsuited to the challenges presented by overseas banking, or perhaps the expectations of the company had always been hopelessly unrealistic. Whatever the reasons, the Oriental began to consider the closure of the branch within months of its opening, finally handing over its operations in August 1861 to the Bank of New South Wales. Thus when Alexander Gavin met Blanche Emily Campbell, the daughter of the British Land Commissioner in Christchurch, he was twenty-eight years old and a man of uncertain prospects.

Adelaide's numerous paternal relations would remain central to her life for many years. Her mother's family, by contrast, would be almost entirely absent for, by the time Adelaide was born, most were already deceased. Blanche Emily's life had been marked by a series of tragedies which by 1861 had left her living alone in Christchurch, New Zealand, with only one remaining close relative, a brother Francis. She had spent her early childhood in a large country house on the Isle of Man, the youngest of seven children of Scottish military veteran Lieutenant-Colonel James Campbell and his Irish born wife Charlotte. As a young man James had served under Wellington during the Peninsular War, commanding a brigade at the victorious battle of Salamanca in 1812. The family were wealthy and well connected and the future seemed promising. At Christmas 1836, however, when Blanche Emily was just two years old, the area had been visited by an epidemic of whooping cough which, over a period of seven days, killed three of her siblings. This devastated household had been further depleted ten years later, with the early deaths, in successive years, of eighteen-year-old Charlotte and twenty-three-year-old Jane. The death of James's wife, Charlotte, is unrecorded in the family bible, but it had certainly occurred by 1851 when James made the decision to embark on a new life overseas for himself and his remaining daughter, seventeen-year-old Blanche Emily. To this end he attached himself to the Canterbury Association, a group of high-ranking Anglican churchmen and wealthy British aristocrats who proposed to establish an agrarian settlement in New Zealand. James's particular attraction to New Zealand had been considerably enhanced by enthusiastic reports about the country and its opportunities emanating from his remaining son Francis, now serving there with the Royal Welsh Fusiliers.[5] Later that year, therefore, James and Blanche Emily arrived in the port of Lyttelton, South Island. Apparently James had hoped to be appointed as the land agent for the Canterbury Association but was disappointed on arrival to discover that this position had already been allocated to one of the organisation's founders, William Godley. James seem to have fallen out with the Association at this point and accepted instead the colonial post of Crown Land Commissioner offered to him by New Zealand's Governor, Sir George Grey. Unfortunately, however, this was a move that placed him on a direct collision course with the Association, for the Canterbury Pilgrims were inspired by a particular utopian vision of English rural life. The settlement

Adelaide's father, Alexander Gavin Anderson

they proposed would be characterised by landowning gentry, served by respectable tenants 'of good character and the Christian religion'. They were anxious to maintain a high price for the land to ensure that it fell into 'civilised hands'. James, by contrast, was willing to sell it 'cheaply to all and sundry', a factor which,

the Association considered, contributed in no small measure
to their own growing financial difficulties.[6] The next few years
were marked by a series of increasingly acrimonious disputes as
the Canterbury dreams of a rural nirvana began to ebb away.
The whole situation seems to have taken its toll on James's
health for he died only a few years later, in 1858, leaving his
daughter alone in a decidedly hostile and uncomfortable world.

Blanche Emily had been seventeen years old when she left her
wealthy surroundings in Britain and embarked on the hazardous
voyage to New Zealand. Stepping ashore in Lyttelton in 1851 she
would have seen, clustered around the port area, a few wooden
houses, a couple of grocery stores, and a single basic 'hotel'. Beyond
this was a bare expanse of plain punctuated by a few primitive
dwellings. She spent the following ten years in a timber-framed
bungalow, relying for her basic household goods on a solitary
sailing ship, the *Mountain Maid* which periodically arrived from
Sydney in Australia. It carried, it was said, 'everything from a
needle to an anchor',[7] but this bounty probably included little
that appealed to a young girl who had previously been poised
on the threshold of fashionable British society. Yet despite these
deprivations, or perhaps because of them, Blanche Emily seems to
have emerged as a determined, resilient young woman, speaking
little of her unhappy experiences in New Zealand and bringing up
her children to be extremely proud of their maternal grandfather.
When she met Alexander Gavin she was twenty-seven years
old, two years after her father's death and, in the Victorian
age, probably considered well beyond any realistic prospect of
marriage. Photographs around that time, however, show a slim,
elegant young woman with fine features and glossy dark hair
and it is clear that she and Alexander Gavin fell immediately
in love. Their brief courtship speaks of a carefree impetuosity,
happily unencumbered by such Victorian niceties as financial
security, parental consent or respectably long engagements.
Thus, on 25 May 1861, less than a year after Alexander's arrival in

New Zealand, the couple made their vows in the small wooden building that served as the church of St Michael and All Angels in Christchurch. This first church was, in truth, little more than a shed. In 1861 its only redeeming feature was a quaint wooden bell tower, constructed by Canterbury pilgrim Benjamin Mountfort who based his design on the timber belfries he had seen in Essex and Sussex. James Fitzgerald, the first Superintendent of Canterbury Province, considered the little tower to be an example of 'architectural insanity', but it is all that now remains of that first St Michael's, having withstood both the test of time and a major twenty-first-century earthquake. In 1861 it had no bell to ring out in celebration of the wedding of Blanche Emily and Alexander Gavin, for that would not arrive on a ship from England until the following September. The young minister who conducted the ceremony, the Reverend Charles Alabaster, had come to New Zealand only a year earlier in a last attempt to stem the progress of the tuberculosis that would kill him a few months later. There could have been few guests and, with the exception of Francis, no family members to offer their congratulations. None of this, however, would have dampened the spirits of this ardent young couple who delighted in each other's company and in the prospect of a new and infinitely better life together.

A few weeks after the wedding Alexander Gavin managed to secure a position as a temporary replacement for the manager of the bank's Melbourne branch, a man with failing health of uncertain prognosis. The happy couple, therefore, packed up their belongings and boarded one of the steamers which by now plied between Christchurch's port of Lyttelton and Melbourne. Blanche Emily was already pregnant with their first child and Adelaide's older brother Maxwell Gavin would be born early the following February, a little less than nine months after the wedding. The couple's first sight of Melbourne must have warmed their hearts for this was a thriving town, its harbour full of ships and its port bustling with merchants, horses, wagons, and all

the other accoutrements of trade. Comfortable transport to the
heart of Melbourne was available every half hour by courtesy of
the Melbourne and Hobson Bay Railway Company and a choice
of smart hotels, lit by gas and supplied with piped water, awaited
new arrivals. Fuelled by the gold trade Melbourne had money to
spare in the 1860s and the town was experiencing extraordinary
development. Its wide streets and ornamental gardens, laid out in
an ever-expanding parallelogram, were lined with elegant stone
buildings. Prominent amongst these was the headquarters of the
Oriental Banking Company standing proudly on Queen Street.
This mini Parthenon with its Corinthian pillars and elaborate
portico sporting a rampant lion and unicorn was undoubtedly
designed to impress upon its customers the solidity of the bank.

The couple set up home in a large wooden house on the newly
developed east side of the city and settled down to enjoy life
in this thriving sociable environment. Max, as he was always
known, proved to be a robust and lively child and Blanche Emily
was soon pregnant again. Adelaide Mary arrived just fourteen
months after her brother. The new daughter was, according to
her delighted father, 'a beauty with a clear brown complexion
and brown hair.'[8] Blanche Emily and Alexander Gavin seem
to have been warm, indulgent parents who revelled in their
children's antics and achievements sending regular reports to the
Anderson family back home. Alexander's letters, in particular,
exude a joyful and uninhibited enthusiasm for the little details
of his children's development. Max was reported to have
twelve teeth, to be 'running about the house quite freely and
becoming bold, fighting with his mother several times a day and
establishing complete dominion over his nurse.'[9] Blanche Emily
wrote in similar vein to Alexander Gavin's mother, Mary Gavin.
In the absence of a mother or older sisters with which to share
her joys and worries, she seems to have established a warm and
chatty relationship with the mother-in-law she was yet to meet, a
correspondence which was all the more satisfying since Alexander

Adelaide's mother, Blanche Emily Campbell

Gavin's sister Frances had two young children of similar ages to Max and Adelaide. The opportunity to compare notes was irresistible. 'You make me feel quite jealous about Frances's boy. He must have greatly the start of Max in talking,' she wrote in September 1864, adding however, 'I defy Alex Edward to beat him in manly accomplishments – he rides his hobby horse and cracks his whip in a most independent manner. Each day he astonishes us with some new achievement.'[10]

In the midst of the family's obvious happiness, however, there remained the unresolved question of Alexander Gavin's future at the Oriental. The absent bank manager, 'the mysterious Mr

Masson', was, it seemed, half expected to return to Melbourne
on each arriving steamer and Alexander Gavin viewed the
unresolved situation with growing resentment, not least
because he had received neither the salary nor the official rank
of manager since arriving in Australia, both of which he had
apparently been promised. Wryly comparing his situation to that
of the ill-fated King Charles in 1641 he would, he told his father,
be issuing 'Grand Remonstrances' to the Head Office of the
Oriental. These protestations, however, like their parliamentary
forerunners, seem to have fallen on deaf ears and his instinct
for self-preservation began to assert itself. 'I think I am quite
able to take care of myself,' he wrote to his father in September
that year. 'I have good grounds for believing I would have no
difficulty acquiring a post at another equally stable bank and at
nearly the same pay.'[11] Thus in October, Blanche Emily wrote to
Mary Gavin describing her preparations for the family's return
to Scotland. Alexander Gavin had resigned from his position. It
was a principled stance, for he had no obvious plans for future
employment, but the principles in question were rather different
to those that had inspired his father's actions some twenty years
earlier. And it is unlikely that Alexander Gavin shared Govie's
trust in the beneficence of divine intervention. Blanche Emily's
letters show that she was well aware of the family's precarious
situation and the real extent of Alexander's anxiety, but she was,
of course, well used to making the best of things. And she was a
loyal and loving wife. 'Despite everything,' she told Mary Gavin,
'I have a large amount of confidence in my husband.'[12]

Alexander Gavin booked their passage on the sailing
clipper *Essex*, which provided a fast, although not a particularly
comfortable service between Melbourne and London. 'I mean to
try and nurse baby until I arrive in England if possible,'[13] Blanche
Emily told her mother-in-law, anxious no doubt about the quality
of provisions on board and what might be lurking in the ship's
water supply. Thus Adelaide, at the age of just nine months, set

off on her first voyage. It would be nearly sixty years before she visited her birthplace again and by then the journey would be significantly more comfortable and considerably shorter. In the absence of the Suez Canal, a construction which lay five years in the future, this voyage, beginning in January 1865, would last nearly three months and take her across the South Pacific and round the notoriously tempestuous Cape Horn. The *Essex*, however, proved to be a sturdy little ship and by early April she had delivered the family safely to London. Several days later they had their first sight of Aberdeen as the coastal steamer passed the recently constructed military fort on Torry Point.

In January the *Essex* had left behind a city sweltering in steamy humidity, for Melbourne had a particularly hot summer that year. The old granite city of Aberdeen, by contrast, was braced against the rigours of a typical Scottish spring. It must have looked and felt distinctly chilly to the wide-eyed children peering over the ship's rail. Warmly wrapped against the cold they would have been bundled into a carriage and driven the four miles north along the coast to the Medieval district of Old Machar. Here they would have clattered along the rectangle of narrow cobbled streets which comprised the Chanonry, passing the ancient sandstone cathedral, its twin spires rosy pink in an otherwise severe granite landscape. Amongst the grey stone buildings which lined these streets were those of the Chanonry House School, including the home of the headmaster and his family. This square, four-storied residence standing behind a sweeping semi-circular drive was by no means dissimilar in appearance to that despised and abandoned Manse in Boyndie but, unlike the Manse, this was the centre of an enterprise much more attuned to Govie's moral sensitivities. It was an establishment providing a liberal education for boys, many from poor backgrounds and supported by charitable bursaries.

Adelaide was to spend the next five years in and around Aberdeen, a city to which she developed a lifelong attachment.

Like Melbourne, it was undergoing huge commercial growth
in the 1860s. There was a new port, new roads and a new
railway, all essential components of a developing centre of
trade. Old buildings were rapidly being torn down to be
replaced with new more prestigious constructions, each faced
with the polished granite that was so much the hallmark of the
new city. For if Melbourne was built on gold, Aberdeen was
built on granite. By the time Adelaide arrived, over seventy
thousand tons of this sought after commodity, cut, polished
and sculpted, was exported each year, much of it to the United
States of America. The city was also an important gateway
for the products of Scottish farming and fishing. Upwards of
eleven thousand live cattle a year were crammed into coastal
steamers bound for London and eight thousand tons of beef
went the same way by rail. And each spring a long line of herring
boats set off for their traditional North Sea fishing grounds,
returning to Aberdeen laden with 'silver darlings' destined
for London's Billingsgate market. Thousands of fisher lassies
worked at a frantic pace, filleting and packing the fish into ice
laden casks. In later years Adelaide would be much exercised
by the conditions under which these women and girls worked
at the dockside. Meanwhile the rising prosperity of Aberdeen's
expanding entrepreneurial class fuelled both the demand
and the wherewithal for improved public amenities, a new
water and sewerage system, gas lighting, parks and gardens,
libraries and art galleries and of course new schools offering
progressive education. Chanonry House was the first of many.
The prominent cities of nineteenth century Scotland buzzed
with scientific progress and new learning, and Aberdeen,
the acknowledged capital of the North, embraced it all with
unbridled enthusiasm. Meanwhile the wider family to which
Blanche Emily was now introduced was primarily engaged in
business and in mercantile activities. There was, it seemed,
no hankering amongst the Andersons for a lost rural idyll

such as that which drove the aspirations of the Canterbury Association. The future lay in production and trade.

Blanche Emily was pregnant again when she arrived in Scotland and was probably looking forward eagerly to meeting the mother-in-law with whom she had been corresponding so warmly for so long. Adelaide's mother was, after all, badly in need of a friend. The environment in which she found herself, so familiar to her husband, would have been somewhat disconcerting for a young woman who had left Scotland more than a decade earlier. Victorian Britain with its manners and conventions was now a distant memory and this strictly religious household was fraught with social pitfalls for the novitiate. Sadly her acquaintance with her mother-in-law was to be a short one, for Mary Gavin's health was rapidly deteriorating. Repeated child bearing and the other undoubted challenges of her thirty-three years with Govie had finally taken their toll on this reputedly saintly woman. That spring, when the boarders returned from their Easter vacation, there was no motherly presence in the form of Mary Gavin to welcome them, and in June they gathered to mourn her loss. She was buried, aged just fifty-seven, in the churchyard of the old cathedral.

Shortly after the funeral Alexander Gavin and Blanche Emily moved out of the family accommodation at the school. They elected to rent a house in Cults, a few miles outside Aberdeen. Situated high above a picturesque stretch of the River Dee, Cults was a pretty village largely composed of a line of large granite houses strung along its main street. It had recently acquired that much-valued facility, a railway station. The journey to Aberdeen could now be accomplished in only twelve minutes. For Alexander Gavin, however, any prospect of enjoying these agreeable surroundings was immediately subverted by the necessity of earning a living. On returning to Scotland he had obtained employment as a banking inspector with a London merchant house, Redfern, Alexander & Company. The firm had links with several major businesses in Australia and New Zealand and shortly after settling the family in Cults he found himself once more en route to the other side of the world. His absence was to last over three years. It is difficult to reconcile this development with the close loving attachment which clearly existed between Blanche Emily and Alexander Gavin and the decision must have been a difficult one for both parties. Blanche Emily, pregnant and alone with a young family in an unfamiliar environment, was again required to draw on her emotional reserves. She seems to have rapidly discovered that a Scottish country village was a lonely and dull environment compared to Melbourne, where she would have enjoyed a much more relaxed and informal style of life. In the early autumn, therefore, she moved back into central Aberdeen renting a large terraced house in one of the most attractive parts of the city. Rubislaw Place, a row of elegant stone villas, was home to a number of Aberdeen's growing professional and business classes and provided much more stimulating and agreeable company than that available in Cults. It was also just round the corner from an urban garden, a green space with trees, flowers and boulevards, providing ideal walks for the young children and their nurse. Despite her obvious resilience, however, this period of separation, so soon in her marriage, must have been an emotional struggle for Blanche Emily, particularly in the early months. At Christmas that year Govie, himself so recently bereaved, reached out to his forlorn daughter-in-law in the way he knew best. Presenting her with a bible he inscribed it with the message 'from your most affectionate father', adding, 'Psalm CXXI',[14] the traditional psalm of comfort for those in distress. Blanche Emily, a fastidiously religious young woman, would have been touched and encouraged by this simple gesture. For the children, too, Govie seems to have provided an influential father figure in those early years, filling the gap left by their own absent parent. Alexander Gavin never seems to have fully recovered the ground lost with his two eldest children during this period, for both Max and Adelaide maintained a strong attachment to their grandfather. In Max's case this was soon to be strengthened further when he enrolled as a boarder at Chanonry House. Adelaide meanwhile developed an equally strong bond with her mother during these early years. All the Anderson children regarded 'the mother', as she was known, as the lynch pin of the family. While several grew up to pursue careers in different parts of the world, they remained a remarkably close knit unit, maintained by an extensive network of letter writing which Blanche Emily both initiated and insisted upon.

By the time she was eighteen months old Adelaide had a sister as well as a brother. Isobel Campbell was born at Rubislaw Place in late October 1864. Adelaide's middle name of Mary had been chosen to honour Mary Gavin but now Blanche Emily reverted to the old Scottish custom of attaching her own maiden name to that of her daughter. In the summer of 1867 she moved again, this time closer to the Chanonry and the family. She rented a mellow old Georgian house called Bridgefield on the far side of a green space called Seaton Park which stretched away behind the old cathedral. The house stood high above a deep gorge carved out by the River Don at the Old Bridge of Balgownie. It was a beautiful spot and one to which Adelaide would return repeatedly during the course of her life. In the 1860s Bridgefield was owned by John Forbes White, a wealthy local flour producer and an enthusiastic patron of the arts. He had recently commissioned the architect Daniel Cottier to install a drawing room on the eastern side of the house and its large bow window provided long uninterrupted views of the sea from which the children could glimpse the sailing ships as they raced along the coast. John White's own home, Seaton Cottage, where he lived with his wife and four young children, was further up the river, next door to his flour mills. The two families became firm friends, the children moving back and forth between the two houses to play together. Adelaide and

John White's younger daughter Alice forged a friendship here that was to endure for the rest of their lives. Nearly seventy years later Alice recalled nostalgically how the two little girls spent many happy hours together playing 'housies' under an iron stair leading from the cottage dining room to the garden. Alice, who grew up to marry merchant William Macdonnell, spent much of her married life in India but, on William's death, she returned to live at Bridgefield with her son Archie. Adelaide was always a frequent guest there for she loved the old stone house which seemed to contain some of her happiest childhood memories. And it was invariably to Alice's hearthside that she would retreat in periods of anxiety or sadness. Both women treasured the friendship. 'It was,' as Alice recalled, 'one of the best things life brought us.'[15]

Adelaide always considered herself to be a 'Scotch'[16] woman, by virtue of her origins and her early years, but the summer of 1867 was the last time she was to live in Scotland. In the autumn, Alexander Gavin finally returned to Aberdeen and resumed his family life. For Blanche Emily the reunion immediately brought another pregnancy, and another change of residence. This time the move was to London. By the time a new Blanche Emily, always known as Blanchie, was born in May 1869 the family had moved into Church Buildings, Clapham, a large and elegant Georgian terrace overlooking the Common. Clapham of the 1860s was an exclusive suburb, well-separated from the outer reaches of South West London and inhabited by wealthy business people. It is clear that Alexander Gavin's position with Redfern, Alexander & Company was paying well and the undoubted sacrifices of the previous three years had brought dividends in terms of the family's prosperity. This improved still further in 1870 when he joined the family firm of shipping agents, Anderson, Anderson & Company. This highly successful firm had grown out of the activities of Govie's brother James, who, like Govie, had received timely assistance from Tarrybreeks. In James's case this help had come in the form of a position in the firm of James Thompson & Company the agents for Uncle Sandy's ship. James Anderson had done exceedingly well, acquiring a partnership in the firm in 1842 such that it became Anderson, Thompson & Company. When its founder, James Thompson, died another Anderson, Alexander Gavin's younger brother James Skelton, also become a partner. By 1870, therefore, when Alexander Gavin joined the firm, it was trading under the name of Anderson, Anderson & Company, and a few years later it would transmute once more, into a highly successful shipping line, the Orient Steam Navigation Company.

The next few years, therefore, were prosperous and happy times for Alexander Gavin and Blanche Emily. There were lots of outings and social events involving the large extended Anderson family which, it seemed, was progressively migrating south from Aberdeen to London. One such event was the marriage of James Skelton to pioneering woman doctor Elizabeth Garrett[17] in February 1871. Visiting Clapham before the wedding Elizabeth was delighted to meet the children whom she found to be 'specially gracious to me.'[18] Meanwhile the adults at Clapham were engaged in vigorous family discussions about the remarkable independence of mind of the bride to be. Elizabeth's reluctance to utter the word 'obey' in the forthcoming marriage ceremony was of particular interest. Elizabeth had apparently rejected James Skelton's choice of clergyman and demanded a replacement who could be persuaded to accept her omission of the offending word. Her bridegroom was relaxed about the matter. No-one, he said, ever attended to the form of words and he did not, therefore, care 'how he was married.' Alexander Gavin agreed. Casting his mind back to his own carefree nuptials a world away in New Zealand, he could remember nothing of what he promised. For her part Blanche Emily was conciliatory. A woman should give in to her husband, she remarked archly, but only 'at the *very* last.'[19]

Predictably, James Skelton found a compliant clergyman from within the ranks of the family to officiate at the ceremony. Govie's

cousin, the Reverend James Anderson, was the Presbyterian
Minister of Morpeth, and married to the sister of Mary Gavin.
The 'high priest of Morpeth' as the Reverend James was known
(he was exceedingly tall) seems to have been rather uneasy about
Elizabeth's demands however. Govie apparently disapproved
thoroughly, and with his long and bitter experience of church
authorities considered that tampering with the established
wording of the marriage ceremony was likely to invite severe
censure. The argument erupted again on the eve of the wedding.
Blanche Emily accused the reverend of 'letting Elizabeth off
cheaper than other women if he did not make her promise to
obey.'[20] Elizabeth, clearly irritated and alarmed, threatened that
he would be 'packed right off to Morpeth again if there was
anything of that sort at the ceremony.'[21] Eventually, however, an
acceptable form of words was found with the, by now, extremely
prickly bride promising to be 'a dutiful wife'. It was, according
to Govie, 'a corrupt compromise.'[22]

Blanche Emily was clearly intrigued by this marriage,
describing the arguments and the generally unconventional
behaviour of James and Elizabeth in a letter to Alexander Gavin's
sister, Mary.[23] Elizabeth, it seemed, was keen to minimise the fuss
normally associated with middle-class weddings, particularly the
rituals and conventions surrounding the bride. It was another way
of rejecting the traditional role of women in Victorian society and
emphasising the centrality of her professional life as a doctor. She
had spent the day before the wedding at a meeting of the School
Board followed by a patient consultation in Wimbledon. The
ceremony was arranged to take place at 8.30 the following morning
and she had arrived at the church wearing a grey walking dress,
'very nice in itself, but scarcely the dress for a bride,'[24] Blanche
Emily observed. The sober dress of the Garrett party as a whole,
it seems, was in marked contrast to that of the Andersons who
looked 'quite a vision of magnificence.'[25] Elizabeth had also worn
her wedding ring for several days before the wedding, only passing

it to James Skelton at the appropriate moment in the ceremony. They were, Blanche Emily concluded, 'an original couple'.[26] The goals of female autonomy and emancipation promulgated by members of the radical women's group the Langham Place Set,[27] were beginning to permeate the thoughts of many in the middle classes during this period. Prominent members of the group such as Emily Davies, one of Elizabeth's closest friends, campaigned, in particular, for women's rights in terms of higher education and access to professional careers. Elizabeth Garrett had brought this debate directly into the heart of the Anderson family and it was by no means an unreceptive environment. James Skelton had, after all, been attracted to Elizabeth by the very independence which the family were now discussing. The young Adelaide and her siblings were not, of course, party to any of these discussions but the tone of Blanche Emily's letter to Mary was far from critical. Rather she appeared amused and not a little admiring of Elizabeth's behaviour. Significantly Adelaide would be one of the early beneficiaries of the education provided by Girton College, founded by Emily Davies.

Shortly after James Skelton's wedding, Alexander Gavin decided to move his branch of the family again, probably to be nearer his relatives but also, it seems, to find a more agreeable residence. For some reason 'that wretched house on Clapham Common',[28] as another younger brother Andrew called it, appears to have been generally disliked. Everyone, it seemed, thought Blanche Emily and Alexander Gavin should move somewhere else. The choice was the developing north London suburb of Hampstead where various other members of the extended family were already installed. Govie's brother James, original partner in Anderson, Anderson & Co, now lived in some style at Frognal Park, with his wife, Eliza, and their eleven children. The house was generally acknowledged to be the grandest in the area. John Ford, another brother of Alexander Gavin, and great nephew of that first John Ford, also lived in Hampstead. Perhaps inspired by the name conferred upon him, this John Ford had similarly chosen to become a doctor, qualifying in Edinburgh in 1863 and thus providing another useful professional to look after the family. Following a spell with the newly formed Red Cross he had been caught up in the siege of Paris in 1871, during which time he had met his French wife Gabrielle Coudron. The two had returned to England in 1872 where John Ford had set up a successful practice in a large white stucco fronted house in Buckland Crescent.

Meanwhile, Alexander Gavin moved his family into a more modest residence in nearby Lyndhurst Road, a tree lined street which climbed gently upwards on the west side of the town. It was less than a mile from Buckland Crescent and equidistant from two stations situated along the newly constructed North London Railway line. As ever the railway line, opened in 1865, was an important feature in Hampstead's growing popularity and Alexander Gavin could travel daily into town. The Anderson house was a dignified if rather dull construction, consisting of three stories of plain brick and plain windows set behind iron railings and a small front garden. Its austere appearance was relieved only by a rather fussy Greek portico which sat somewhat incongruously over the front door. The house's rather forbidding facade however would have masked a hive of happy, noisy activity within, for over the next ten years it rapidly filled up with more children, and with servants to cater for the family's needs. Walter Archibald was born here in 1873, followed by Mary Charlotte in 1874. Ralf William arrived in 1877 and finally Alexander James, (Alex) was born in 1879.

In September 1870, a few months before James Skelton's wedding, Blanche Emily had also given birth to another child, her fifth. George Wallace Douglas Campbell, or Douglas as he was known, was born at the house of John Ford. It was clear from the start that Douglas was unlike his healthy siblings. He was a sickly child, slow to develop and his head was unusually large. It is likely that Douglas was suffering from hydrocephaly, although his condition appears to have been relatively mild for, in the absence of any available treatment in the nineteenth century, he survived into early adulthood. During his babyhood and early childhood the problem seems to have been successfully absorbed within the immediate family, although in later years Blanche Emily and Alexander Gavin arranged a series of protected environments for their handicapped son, mainly in the homes of clergymen's families in remote parts of Scotland. However, Douglas's condition seemed to be the only cloud in an otherwise uniformly blue sky. The shipping agency was thriving and well able to support several members of the Anderson family for two more brothers had by now joined the firm. In 1877 Uncle James of Frognal Park finally acceded to the trials of his uncertain health and handed over at least some of the reins of the company to James Skelton. Always the most adventurous and entrepreneurial of the brothers, James Skelton immediately embarked upon a daring expansion plan. In the 1870s the shipping industry as a whole was hovering uncertainly between steam and sail and, although large companies such as P&O used auxiliary steam, none so far had dared to abandon sail completely. James Skelton, however, had no doubts about where the future lay. Entering into partnership with established London shipbuilders, Frank Green & Company, he set up the first steam-only service between England and Australia. It was an immediate success, shaving ten days off previous schedules and providing unprecedented reliability in terms of arrival times. The Orient Steam Navigation Company, a predominantly family affair, was officially established in November 1877. During the next ten years more ships were built and the Anderson brothers settled down to enjoy a period of uninterrupted prosperity.

At home Adelaide's family were now pursuing the typical life of the wealthy middle classes. After the birth of Alexander James in 1879 Blanche Emily seems to have at last been freed

Left to right, Isobel, Max and Adelaide Anderson in 1880.

from the trials of repeated pregnancies. She and Alexander Gavin
delighted in this time of relative ease making frequent trips to the
Continent, especially to Italy, indulging their shared passion for
painting and sculpture, often bringing back little presents for the
children. The boys went away to school, including Douglas who
spent a few years at Chanonry House under the watchful eye of
Govie. Max was also a pupil there, from 1873, followed by Walter

Adelaide's younger siblings. *Left to right*, Mary, Ralf, Blanchie holding Alex, Douglas and Walter.

a few years later and, like their father before them, both moved on to Kings College, Aberdeen. In 1876 Govie retired and the school continued for a further decade under the headship of Govie's successor, Dr James Clarke. By now, however, there were many similar schools in Aberdeen competing for pupils and Chanonry House was running into increasing financial difficulties. Perhaps anticipating the school's eventual closure in 1887, Adelaide's youngest brothers were dispatched instead to a small preparatory school, Norton Hall in Northamptonshire, and from there to Marlborough College. Adelaide and her sisters meanwhile, progressed from nurse to governess as befitted the daughters of their class, pursuing the usual activities of well brought up young ladies. Adelaide became an accomplished performer on the piano and developed a well-honed appreciation of classical music and fine art. Other aspects of her education, however, departed significantly from that offered to most girls of the period. Under the advisory influence of Govie she and her sisters also studied a curriculum which included French and German, history, science and mathematics. Adelaide seems to have been an overly serious little girl, mindful of her supervisory responsibilities towards her younger siblings and earnestly preoccupied with intellectual pursuits. Taking her cue from Govie, her interests centred on weighty subjects such as medieval history and scriptural doctrine and, like her father and grandfather, she was fascinated by moral philosophy. Within the family she soon acquired the title of 'Sissy', designating her position as the eldest sister. She had no particular occupational ambitions in mind, and there are no indications that she harboured any desire to become involved in any of the prominent issues of the late nineteenth century. While the minds of other well-educated and rather more restless young woman were turning increasingly to matters such as equal employment rights, female suffrage and social reform, Adelaide, it seems, was largely content with life as it was. Her childhood was happy, comfortable and secure.

Chapter Three
FROM STUDENT TO LECTURER

In the spring of 1879, when Adelaide had just turned sixteen, Alexander Gavin decided that his two eldest daughters should attend a girls' day school in London. His choice was Queen's College in Harley Street where Aunt Elizabeth Garrett had been a pupil thirty years earlier. Accompanied by their governess, therefore, Adelaide and Isobel travelled each morning to school, and each evening the governess returned to check that hats and gloves were in impeccable order before escorting her charges home. Adelaide seems to have been ideally suited to the atmosphere at Queen's for, as fellow pupil Jessie Barratt remembered, it was certainly not a place for the frivolous. Girls felt proud and privileged to be there. 'We worked because we *wanted* to, and weren't just schoolgirls being made to.'[1] Another former pupil recalled the stillness in the classroom, unbroken, she said, 'except for the scratching of pens' and the sound of the lecturer's voice.[2] Proper behaviour was maintained at all times with lady chaperones installed in the corner of each classroom whenever, as was usual, lectures were conducted by men. Divinity classes alone, conducted by clergymen, were exempted from this requirement. Queen's College had been founded in the 1840s with the original objective of providing proper training for young ladies destined to become governesses. By the late 1870s, however, it had set its sights rather higher, aiming to prepare its older pupils for university entrance. London University had begun to admit women in 1878 and two women's colleges, Girton and Newnham had already been established in Cambridge, the former by Aunt Elizabeth Garrett's friend, Emily Davies. The transformation of the curriculum at Queen's College had taken place largely under the leadership of Emily's brother the Reverend John Llewelyn–Davies who introduced a range of courses suitable for older pupils. Adelaide would no doubt have been pleased by the inclusion in 1879 of one such course 'The Moral Philosophy of Hume and Mills', a subject which this rather intense young lady elected to study a few years later at Girton.

Despite the strong links between Queen's and Girton neither Adelaide nor Isobel sat a university entrance examination at the end of their twelve months at the school. One suspects that Isobel, lively, creative and less conformist than her elder sister, would have left Queen's College with a certain amount of relief. A promising artist, she subsequently enrolled at the newly established Female School of Art in London, part of a group of colleges known collectively as the National Art Training School or, more informally, the South Kensington Schools. Here the emphasis was on art as a profession rather than an accomplishment, and training in fine art, design and industrial application received equal weight. John Ruskin noted with approval the attention paid to science in the development of industrial design and to anatomical knowledge in the execution of life drawing. Moreover students were strongly encouraged to explore the relationships between art and the political and economic concerns of the day and the school became an important development centre for those campaigning for women's rights. Prominent suffragist Sylvia Pankhurst would be a student there some ten years later, devoting much of her art to industrial scenes which depicted women workers, while another early student was art critic and patron Emilia Dilke who would later become President of the Women's Trade Union League (WTUL) which spearheaded the establishment of the Women's Factory Inspectorate. Thus it was not Adelaide but her younger sister who, during this period, seemed to be destined to participate in the social and feminist activism of the day. The lively, radical atmosphere at South Kensington seems to have suited Isobel considerably better than the rigid conformity prevailing at Queen's College and her artistic talents developed and prospered accordingly. Adelaide, meanwhile, followed a very different path. Serious, reserved and entirely conventional she pursued the course of the ladies finishing school, going first to Strasbourg and then to Dresden, to improve her French and German. Her ambitions, however, appeared to extend little beyond a desire for personal intellectual development. Thus in the spring of 1883, just one day after her twentieth birthday her father sent off her application for a place at Girton College, Cambridge.

Adelaide's acceptance at Girton was likely to have been a mere formality for her references from her teachers at Queen's were impeccable, as of course were her connections, and there was little doubt that sufficient funds were available. In the autumn, therefore, she travelled to Cambridge to begin the Michaelmas Term. She would also have said good-bye to her childhood home, for the rest of the family were once more on the move, relocating to a brand new house round the corner in Fitzjohn's Avenue. By now there were nine Anderson children, four domestic servants and a governess, and the house in Lyndhurst Road must have struggled to accommodate them all. The new home was considerably more spacious and seems to have represented the zenith of the family fortunes. Fitzjohn's Avenue was part of an extensive development plan which, in the late nineteenth century, aimed to sweep away the dark alleys and slums which had previously housed Hampstead's poor and complete the town's transformation into a fashionable residential area. Largely insulated from the problems of the working classes, Adelaide was probably unaware that the road was built on land that reformer Octavia Hill had struggled to acquire for social housing. Launching a mighty campaign to raise the purchase price, Octavia had come within a whisker of success but had ultimately failed to accumulate sufficient capital in time to realise her dream. Instead the land was acquired by a wealthy property developer who set about creating a very different type of housing. Behind a line of ornamental trees which graced each side of the road there arose a parade of towering Victorian residences. By 1883, Fitzjohn's Avenue was the most fashionable street in Hampstead, popular with artists and writers as well as prosperous businessmen and politicians. With a degree of hyperbole, Harpers magazine of the day described it as one of the noblest streets in the world, comparable to the boulevards of Paris.[3] Number One, the new Anderson residence, was designed by Scottish architect John James Stevenson, a nephew by marriage of Alexander Gavin's sister, Mary. Two years earlier Stevenson, who had a penchant for Dutch revivalism, had designed the offices of the Orient Steam Navigation Company in London's Fenchurch Street and there was more than a passing resemblance between the two buildings. Built in warm pink and red brick and adorned with curly porticos the house, which is now part of a girl's school, rambled over a large corner plot, its various wings jutting out at odd angles. Classics enthusiast Alexander Gavin chose to decorate the front wall with a plaque containing a quotation from Horace, a caution against luxurious living and the assumption of permanence in property ownership.[4] It would turn out to be a highly prescient inscription for the Anderson family.

Adelaide would have confronted yet another new building as she alighted from her fly at the front entrance of Girton. The college, established in 1869 to provide higher education for women, had begun with just four resident students in a small country mansion, Benslow House in Hitchin, Hertfordshire. Three years later, following a rapid increase in student numbers, a new site had been purchased in the village of Girton, about a mile and a half from Cambridge. Building work had commenced immediately and the newly named Girton College moved to its partially constructed home the following year. Students of the 1880s would have been well acquainted with the colourful story of wealthy heiress Jane Catherine Gamble who left £19,000 to Girton in 1885, and thus provided much of the money for the college's expansion. In 1851, at the age of forty-three, Jane had travelled to Italy, during which time she had reputedly been pursued and seduced by a fortune hunter. Opinion is divided about Jane's level of complicity in this adventure but, by all accounts, it ended with her abduction and subsequent imprisonment in a Genoese palace. Having been rescued a few weeks later by her distraught relations, she had, it seems, emerged from the experience with an enduring distrust of men, resolving to leave her considerable fortune solely for the benefit of women. Following the expansion of Girton, her memory was enshrined in the Gamble Essay Prize created in 1888. Somewhat ironically male and female students now compete equally for this award, but she would, no doubt, have approved of one of its first recipients, Adelaide Anderson.

The college that greeted Adelaide in 1883 was thus a much smaller building than that which exists today, although due to the beneficence of Miss Gamble it was definitely a work in progress. During the next three years the existing first wing would be joined by two more, forming three sides of a quadrangle that surrounded a grassy area for tennis and other recreation. A library, given by wealthy benefactor, Lady Stanley, was added in 1884 and in 1886 the distinctive Gatehouse Tower topped by its observation platform rose to dominate the entrance to the college. Resident students, close to one hundred in Adelaide's day, were delighted to discover themselves accommodated in single rooms, some with adjoining sitting rooms and balconies that overlooked the central quadrangle. The surrounding grounds were tranquil spaces carpeted with aconites and celandines in the spring where girls could wander, think and talk. And later in the year there were picnics and flower dances on the lawns during summer evenings. Students gathered in each other's rooms after supper to gossip and drink cocoa, their practical needs catered for by college servants, known, like their

Adelaide (second from right, middle row) with fellow students at Girton, 1883. (Reproduced with the permission of Girton College, Cambridge.)

counterparts in the men's colleges, as 'gyps'. Most girls took part in theatrical productions or joined choral and debating societies. Others played cricket and tennis, and there was even the occasional ball, predictably popular with male students who arrived in droves to compete for partners. As one student remarked, one could on these occasions become engaged twice over during every dance.

There was much that was idyllic about Girton, at least to retrospective eyes, and contemporary accounts by Adelaide's fellow students certainly seem to endorse this picture of an intellectual Elysium.⁵ Helena Swanwick, later a prominent suffragist and labour activist who, like Adelaide, studied Moral Sciences there in the early 1880s, found the social life of Girton 'intoxicating'. 'I was too excited to eat or sleep properly,' she recounted, contrasting college life with the closeted, highly supervised existence she had been used to at home.⁶ Adelaide's response to such agreeable surroundings, however, can best be described as cool. She was, it seems, a rather solitary unsociable student, dedicated to her work and with an apparent aversion to any activities that might be described as 'fun'. Other students considered her pompous and dull. Adela Kensington, a future teacher of classics and mother of social reformer Barbara Wooten, was kinder, although she clearly struggled to understand this gravely reserved young lady with her 'air of great respectability'. 'Her rather prim and unyouthfully serious demeanour at college and her preoccupation with high philosophy, art and music sometimes oppressed a more frivolous junior,' she said.⁷ To invite such a comment Adelaide must indeed have been a noticeable puritan, for most other students at Girton during this period were, in fact, far from frivolous. Conscious of their pioneering status and also their good fortune, Girton girls were keen to prove the intellectual worth of women and worked extremely hard. Many, like Rosalind Shore Smith, a cousin of Florence Nightingale, were strongly committed to social and political reform. In later years it would be Rosalind who would first bring Adelaide face to face with ordinary working women. Other students pursued higher education in the context of aspirations for sexual equality in academic life or in the professions.

Adelaide, however, seems to have been motivated solely by a love of learning for its own sake, her choice of subjects informed by academic rather than practical aspirations, and more than a little influenced by the intellectual leanings of her father and grandfather. Her failure to engage with the social side of college life seems to have been driven to some extent by an inwardly focussed preoccupation with weighty philosophical and theological issues, which increasingly separated her from the everyday interests of her fellow students. Her choice of subject for an extended essay, for which she was later awarded the Gamble gold medal, is revealing, not only in terms of her intellectual intensity but also in terms of her philosophical and religious leanings. Entitled 'Joannes Scotus, called Erigena, A backwater in the history of philosophical thought', this treatise seems to have excited a modicum of intellectual excitement among contemporary philosophers at Cambridge. The ideas of Erigena, a ninth-century Irish monk, largely neglected for several hundred years, had recently re-entered the consciousness of late nineteenth century philosophers, particularly followers of Hegel whose central ideas could, it was considered, be traced back to the thinking of Scotus. Adelaide's ability to read, without translation, the work of German scholars who were at the forefront of this revival, provided her with a distinct advantage. It was a process which introduced her to earlier forms of spirituality, at variance with much of contemporary Christian practice, and which also seems to have encouraged her to examine the relationships between religion and different forms of social organisation. Her own faith appeared to deepen as a result of this exploration incorporating, as perhaps Govie had done before her, the early history of the church into an integrated set of beliefs to which she would adhere tenaciously for the rest of her life. If her faith in God remained intact, however, her attitudes to society seem to have undergone considerable change. In her essays at Girton, including those she produced for meetings of the Girton Moral Science Club, the only club she seemed inclined to join, she explored definitions of 'Socialism' and 'Communism', and the consequences of different social systems. She described the 'revolting extremes of wealth and poverty which arise in societies where competition is the fundamental principle' and maintained that 'socialism' offered a way in which capitalism and the accumulation of wealth might exist alongside certain essential functions of the state.[8] All this was essentially theoretical intellectual activity but there are hints here of the beginning of a social unease and an engagement with issues of social reform, notably the extent to which the state should 'manage the resources of a community.'[9] The intensity of her focus at Girton was always on the high ground of moral philosophy but at least some elements of what she studied seemed to influence her subsequent thinking in very practical ways. When, in later years, she herself became a servant of the state she was forced to confront uncomfortable conflicts between ideology and pragmatism and to defend government intervention against those who would leave matters either to market forces or, alternatively, to the uncertainties of labour activism.

Other parts of her courses at Cambridge were to provide more direct background material for her future career. Moral Sciences dealt not only with mental philosophy, psychology and metaphysics, but also with logic, and scientific method. She emerged from Girton with a sound grasp of the concepts of definition, classification, scientific inference and the rules of evidence, all significant tools in determining the extent of specific industrial diseases and their relationship with particular working conditions. Significantly she also studied 'political economy' exploring forms of industrial organisation, trade and exchange and the production and consumption of commodities. Like their male counterparts in other Cambridge colleges, students at Girton were taught by many of the prominent academics of the day, many of whom had distinctly socialist leanings. Edith Read Mumford, who in the early 1890s

would work with Adelaide as a précis writer on the Labour
Commission, recalled in particular the teaching provided
by Alfred Marshall, probably the most influential British
economist of the period. His book the *Principles of Economics*
published in 1890, dominated economic thinking for many
years.[10] Professor Marshall was, by all accounts, a provocative
teacher, given to acerbic and hurtful criticism of his students'
work, particular that produced by women. He apparently
disapproved of female students. There were, he considered, too
many of them in his lectures and he was dubious about their
abilities, often subjecting their efforts to caustic comments. 'He
said the amount I had written was in reverse proportion to the
importance of the subject matter,' said one aggrieved student,
and to another he observed, 'your writing takes longer to read
than anyone else's, and the result is not worth it.'[11] Despite these
sensitivities, however, he seems to have been a popular, or at least
well-respected figure amongst most of the Girton girls. Edith
noted how Professor Marshall's presentation of the subject was
'very human, the living application of theoretical knowledge to
the economic and industrial problems of the day.'[12] 'The walrus'
as he was known (he had a large straggly moustache) regarded
practical knowledge as equal in value to his own theoretical
considerations and invited prominent labour leaders, referred
to as 'comrades', up to Cambridge to discuss their first hand
experiences. Often students were invited to meet these 'working
men' at dinners held at the Marshall's home or to visit factories
and workshops. Student Hertha Ayrton, later a mathematician
and prize winning electrical engineer, remembers a visit to a
mill where her own interest in the machinery was completely
subverted by her shock at the plight of the mill girls. Having
extolled the magnificence of the machine as 'one of the most
wonderful sights I have ever seen', she added, 'When I saw the
mill girls standing in those great hot fluffy rooms, or sitting on
forms without backs, slaving, it struck me that no-one who had

not lived the life could understand its peculiar hardships.'[13] It was something Hertha never forgot and it is hard to imagine that Adelaide was completely unaffected by such experiences.

There were also lectures from economist John Neville Keynes, father of the more famous John Maynard, and from Henry Sidgwick who taught ethics and politics, expounding the utilitarian philosophies of John Stuart Mill and Jeremy Bentham. Adelaide seems to have been particularly drawn to the study of psychology, a subject in which she did particularly well in her final examinations. In the 1880s students at Girton were taught psychology by Dr James Ward, a series of lectures described by Edith Mumford, as 'stimulating to thought' but not easy to follow . . . for he thought very deeply.'[14] Helena Swanwick was more forthright. '. . . of Dr Ward's [lectures] I may have understood one sentence in ten. My philosophical vocabulary was still so childish . . . I remember puzzling over the question as to what on earth "discreet" [sic] points could be . . . I rather wish now that I had had the nerve to get up and go out.'[15] Her comments may have reflected the fact that British psychology was rather slow to emerge from the tradition of 'mental philosophy' which in continental Europe and the United States was rapidly being replaced by psychophysical experimentation and psychometric testing. Helena recalled that at Girton, psychology was treated largely as an 'abstract' subject, lacking the 'floods of light thrown on the primary instincts of the herd' by 'the use of children and animals.'[16] Thus Adelaide's final examination paper in the subject invited students to 'Discuss from a philosophic standpoint the relation between Mind and Body', and 'how you would distinguish between Feeling and Sensation'.[17] It was all rather difficult to distinguish from philosophy as an academic discipline, the reason, no doubt, for its special appeal to students like Adelaide.

Adela, alone, seems to have seen glimmers of a different Adelaide from the awkward, unsociable young woman she

knew at Girton. She recalled how she had once been invited to
a dance at Fitzjohn's Avenue and had marvelled at the sight of
her fellow student, 'prettily attired in a pink dress and white
sash', busily organising the party to ensure that all the guests
enjoyed themselves. And yet she could be forgiven for her
assumption that her 'frail little friend' was 'destined for life
as a valetudinarian.'[18] Accustomed to Adelaide's fragile health
Adela was unsurprised when, in 1886 as Easter approached, her
friend became sufficiently ill to request a term's leave. In the
absence of any specific diagnosis it is difficult to judge how far
this 'illness' was driven by psychological as opposed to strictly
physical symptoms. There are strong indications that Adelaide
was far from happy at Girton. Solemn, aloof and seemingly
unable to make friends, she was christened 'the widow' by
other girls who teased her mercilessly. Whether her attitudes
represented a genuine belief in her own personal moral or
intellectual superiority, or whether she was simply struggling
with excessive shyness borne of an overprotected childhood is
uncertain. When her leave was granted, however, there was no
indication of any specific incapacitating physical illness, for
she neither returned home to Hampstead, nor adjourned to a
resort on the South Coast, the traditional retreat for invalids in
need of recuperation. Instead, she obtained, through the good
offices of Adela's sister, a post as governess to the daughters of
Sir Courtney Ilbert, a distinguished lawyer and Counsel to Her
Majesty's Treasury, who had recently returned from service in
India. The move seems to have been a considerable restorative
success. Adelaide felt instantly at home with the Ilberts and
loved the surroundings of Sir Courtney's house, Troutwells,
in Penn, Buckinghamshire. It was the beginning of another
lifelong friendship, with Sir Courtenay's eldest daughter,
twelve-year-old Lettice, who in later years would become the
first Chair of the National Council for the Unmarried Mother
and Child, subsequently known as 'Gingerbread'. Adelaide

would contribute financially to this organisation for most of her life. How far the Ilberts were instrumental in introducing some elements of wider social concern into Adelaide's thinking during the 1880s is difficult to know. It is clear, however, that they restored, or perhaps first engendered in her a degree of confidence, as well as some of the social skills that were conspicuously lacking when she went to Girton.

This rehabilitation, however, was insufficient to persuade Adelaide to return to Cambridge. When the time came for her to resume her studies a further term's leave was requested, and granted, despite there being no obvious evidence of significant illness. Eventually arrangements were made for her to return at the end of the Easter term 1887, simply to complete her Moral Sciences Tripos examinations. Effectively, therefore, she had abandoned Girton. In July of that year she learned that she had gained a creditable second class honours. A letter from one of her lecturers suggests that she may have been a little disappointed with this result. She might have hoped for a first. 'I hope you were not dissatisfied with your place,' he said. 'We were very much pleased with some of your work. The Ancient philosophy turned out best: but some of the psychology was very good indeed.'[20] Women were not, of course, formally awarded degrees during this period. Cambridge would turn out to be particularly tardy in this respect[21] and in 1906 Adelaide would become one of the 'steamboat ladies' who travelled over to Dublin for one night only, to take advantage of Trinity College's practice of awarding *ad eundem* degrees to graduates of Cambridge who 'took up residence in the city'.[22] It was a loophole that lasted for only three years, for in 1907 Trinity began to insist that women kept terms in order to qualify for such an award. In 1887, however, there was no degree of any sort to be had and the women had to be content with seeing their results reported in *The Times*. At least one fellow student, significantly a philosopher, was delighted to read of Adelaide's success. Future classics lecturer, Maud Daniel, wrote to her immediately. 'I have been very impatient for the lists. A thousand congratulations. I cannot tell you how glad I am. I knew you would do it but that does not mean the merit is any less.' Clearly well aware of how difficult Cambridge had been for Adelaide, however, the kindly Maud added a postscript. 'Now *at last* you can say goodbye to Girton for good!'[23] It had, in many ways, been an unhappy period in Adelaide's life but one that she herself seems to have recast in a somewhat different mould in later years. As 'Dame Adelaide' in the 1930s she responded eagerly to invitations to speak about the history of Girton to current students and contributed generously to appeals for funds. On these occasions she appeared inordinately proud of her connection with the college and full of praise for its ethos and achievements. Significantly, however, few of her fellow students remembered her as anything other than an unremarkable and somewhat reclusive figure, if indeed they remembered her at all.

Whatever her feelings, in the summer of 1887 Adelaide had little time to bask in the afterglow of her academic success or, as things turned out, to pursue her personal occupational ambitions. She had by now settled on the idea of becoming a private teacher of philosophy, something which fellow student Hermia Durham, a future inspector at the Department of Employment, described disparagingly as 'Plato for Duchesses'.[24] However, individual tuition would play to her intellectual strengths, Adelaide decided, and would also make fewer demands on her social reserve. Unlike her younger sister Blanchie, now pursuing a promising career as a schoolteacher, Adelaide would always dislike addressing large gatherings and would avoid it wherever possible. In September 1887, therefore, she set about obtaining a collection of references from her tutors at Cambridge. Her referees were unanimous in their praise of her intellectual ability, her clarity of expression, her painstaking approach and her 'readiness and capacity for independent investigation'.[25] James Ward observed her 'genuine liking for philosophical studies' and the 'thoughtful originality' of her work. She could, he was sure, 'render valuable assistance to those engaged in the private study of psychology, metaphysics and kindred subjects.'[26] By October she had assembled all she needed to embark upon her chosen path. These carefully made plans, however, were about to be derailed. A month later came the upheaval that would ultimately lead Adela's 'frail little friend' into a life of 'knocking about on trains and dirty factories of the north.'[27]

The events of November 1887, which were to have such a pivotal effect on Adelaide's life, are surrounded by a certain amount of mystery. Adela seems to have known more than most but even that, it seems, was rather little and relayed with reluctance. 'Possibly Adelaide might not like the financial crash being so explicitly emphasized here,' she said hesitantly at her friend's memorial service some fifty years later. 'However,' she conceded, 'it is so long ago I hardly think anyone can be hurt.'[28] There had, she said, been a 'disagreement' between Alexander Gavin and other partners in the Orient Steam Navigation Company, specifically with James Skelton and Uncle James of Frognal Park. This 'disagreement' was, in fact, a serious and irretrievable falling out. When Alexander had joined the firm in 1870 his previous banking experience had made him the obvious choice to oversee the company finances. This arrangement had, it seems, proceeded quite happily for the next seventeen years. In 1887, however, the Orient Line underwent major restructuring on the advice of a specially appointed panel of prominent ship owners, commissioned by the brothers to advise on the most economically profitable way forward. The report of this panel, which appeared that autumn, made a number of recommendations which seemed to have been accepted by everyone except Adelaide's father. When the list

of signatories to the new agreement appeared in the November
edition of the *Shipping Gazette* Alexander Gavin's name was
conspicuously absent.[29] It seems a major family row had erupted
with James Skelton and Uncle James of Frognal Park accusing
Alexander Gavin of using the firm's money to finance the
building of the house in Fitzjohn's Avenue. The precise details
of this affair are extremely unclear, securely wrapped, as they
were, in a cloak of Victorian discretion. Even in later life the
children, it seems, were never informed of the circumstances of
their father's departure from the company. He had, so it was
reported in all official references to the matter, simply 'retired'.
Although he retained his position on the Boards of two other
companies, his main source of income was effectively cut off,
as was his relationship with most of his brothers. John Ford,
alone, appears to have taken Alexander Gavin's side in the
argument and, with his wife Gabrielle, continued to defend
his brother's position, but the response of the others seems
to have remained hostile. Whatever the rights and wrongs
of the situation, however, the effect on Adelaide's family was
profound. At Fitzjohn's Avenue the situation provoked an acute
financial crisis, felt most immediately by the youngest children,
Ralf and Alex, who were hurriedly brought home from school.
In the longer term, however, it was the lives of Adelaide and
her sisters that were most permanently affected. For Adelaide,
in particular, the eldest child still at home, there was a terrible
sense of shock followed by an awakening fear of the future.
Adela was clear in her recollection that 'on Adelaide descended
the full weight of the misfortune', and that her immediate
response had been to 'set about earning money to support
her small brothers and sisters.'[30] Hermia Durham noted how
Adelaide began delivering a series of lectures at Hampstead
library and other places of middle class education. For the
young Adelaide who, even in later life, remained extremely
reluctant to speak in public, these lectures must have been a

considerable ordeal. Her agreement to take them on provided, perhaps, a first glimpse of the courage and determination that lurked beneath the delicate exterior. Yet her assumption that her own employment as a lecturer could support the current Anderson lifestyle was testament not only to her fortitude but also to her naivety. Well-protected middle class girls had little acquaintance with financial realities.

In the event, Alexander Gavin, himself, seems to have staved off complete financial ruin by operating as a London agent for a cousin called George Yuill, a successful exporter of Australian frozen meat. George had originally established his business as a co-operative venture with the Orient Line but, from the first, his relationship with the Anderson brothers seems to have been extremely volatile. There are tales of violent arguments in George's office in Sydney where George and William Anderson could be heard 'hurling abuse and heavy objects at one another.'[31] Ultimately, therefore, George had left the Orient and set up independently. By 1887 his business, now a significant rival to the Anderson operation, was doing extremely well and it clearly offered an opening for Alexander Gavin when he too parted company with his brothers. It was, however, a move that widened the gulf between Adelaide's father and the rest of the family. Moreover Alexander Gavin's relationship with his eldest son may also have been under some strain at this point for Max, who always retained the respect of the rest of the family, became one of the Orient Line's Australian agents shortly after his father's departure from the firm. Alexander Gavin's options, however, appear to have been rather limited and his association with George seems to have made sufficient money to maintain at least some aspects of the family's earlier life. Walter, for example, went to Kings College, Aberdeen, to complete his education and the younger boys returned to school. Yet it would have become clear to Adelaide and her sisters that, in the future, they could not hope to be maintained by 'independent means'. Nor was there any reconciliation between Alexander Gavin and James Skelton, a point underlined a few months later when James removed Alexander's name from a document appointing him as trustee for Elizabeth Garrett's marriage settlement. The replacement signature was that of younger brother William, now a partner in the reconstituted Orient Line.[32]

As 1888 turned into 1889 Adelaide began to draw on her contacts from Cambridge to secure further lecturing work. Former fellow student, Rosalind Shore Smith, now engrossed in radical politics, had embarked on a career as a journalist, writing on questions of women's suffrage and labour conditions for the popular liberal newspaper the *Daily Chronicle*. Rosalind was also heavily involved in the work of the Women's Co-operative Guild. Founded in 1883, initially as part of the Co-operative Wholesale Society (CWS), the Guild had established itself as a separate women's organisation dedicated to the improvement of health and education among women in poor neighbourhoods. Its new General Secretary was a niece of Emily Davies, former Queen's and Girton girl, Margaret Llewelyn-Davies, and under her leadership the organisation was expanding rapidly. By the late 1880s it had over fifty branches and a membership close to 1,700. Rosalind recruited Adelaide to give a series of lectures to members of the Guild. Initially these meetings were held at rented rooms on the King's Road in Chelsea, but later they moved to East London's Toynbee Hall, which, said Rosalind, was 'making a start at educating people.'[33] Toynbee Hall's founders, Samuel and Henrietta Barnett had established it as a residential settlement where socially conscious middle class men could spend periods living and working in the East End.[34] The provision of education, as the key to lifting people out of poverty, had become an important part of the settlement's work. The Barnetts established an immediate rapport with the 'Co-operators' whom they regarded as the aristocracy of labour, people who would transmit education to the masses, forming a bridge between the privileged middle classes and those deprived of even the most basic opportunities for learning. When, in 1885, the large London boardroom of the CWS was destroyed by fire, Samuel and Henrietta immediately offered Toynbee Hall as accommodation for the Society's meetings and lectures, including those of the Guild. It was an arrangement that cemented the relationship between the two organisations, and their collaboration continued long after the CWS had rebuilt its own premises.

Rosalind was impressed by Toynbee Hall and the standard of its educational aspirations, and particularly impressed by one of the settlement's current residents, a radical journalist called Vaughan Nash whom she would marry in 1892. Thus inspired, she was determined that Guild meetings should not degenerate into 'sewing sessions' or mere social events but should be focussed on serious education. Her new lecturer, however, while undoubtedly well qualified, was rather ill equipped to cross the social divide. Adelaide's proposed syllabus which covered the essential elements of a capitalist system, the organisation of production, the division of labour and the distribution of wealth was, no doubt, theoretically impeccable. But to those who had left school on completion of Elementary Standard IV it was largely impenetrable. Rosalind was tactful but clearly rather worried. 'I fear that the lectures might be *too* good for an audience of this class,' she advised,[35] suggesting that it might be best to avoid publishing the subjects in advance. 'I am afraid the subject is so alarming that, if made so prominent, it would keep many away who might come for the sake of the social evening.' Opting for pragmatism over principal, she suggested advertising the evening as a social event, with just an outline syllabus hung up in the room. 'Once in, they will see that it is not too dreadful and be induced to come regularly.'[36] Given the heavyweight nature of the subject matter

and Adelaide's inexperience it is unlikely that these lectures
went down particularly well with her audience at Toynbee Hall.
Fortunately, however, the Barnetts had also offered the Guild
the services of its tea-room and here there were refreshments
and the opportunity for informal chatter. Music was popular
when a provider could be found and Adelaide, of course, was
a useful pianist. Much to her own surprise she began to enjoy
the company of these wives of working men. Toynbee Hall
offered a space where she could get to know them and learn
about their lives. In these encounters she appears to have found
a new energy, the first inklings of an extension of ambition,
beyond the simple desire to maintain her own comfortable,
middle class lifestyle.

It was not only events inside the Hall that occupied
Adelaide's attention during this period. Even by the standards
of the East End, notorious for its crime and social problems, this
was a turbulent time for the local inhabitants for in the autumn
of 1888 Jack the Ripper stalked the streets of Whitechapel.
Arriving at Aldgate East station and making her way through
the maze of allies that lay behind the High Street, Adelaide
would have been fully aware of the horror unfolding in the
newspapers. The mutilated corpse of one of Jack's victims was
found only a few hundred yards from Toynbee Hall. It was
not until November that this particular killing spree came
to an end, although, in truth, murderous assault was always
a frequent event in Whitechapel. There were many other
incidents, both before and after the Ripper murders, which
gained much less prominence in the popular press. In Charles
Booth's poverty map of London compiled in 1889, much of the
area was coloured in the black or dark blue ink which signified
his categories of 'vicious and semi-criminal' and 'very poor'.
It is hard to imagine what Blanche Emily and Alexander
Gavin thought of their eldest daughter's new enthusiasm
for this environment. Her activities must have provoked

considerable surprise and not a little anxiety at home. Their worries, however, were about to increase. A few months later, as Adelaide chatted to the Co-operative wives inside the Hall, the surrounding streets of the East End began to pulsate with militant labour demonstrations. For 1889 was the high point of New Unionism when, for the first time, workers excluded from traditional craft based organisations began to band together to form their own Trade Unions. Since the beginning of 1888 there had been scattered strikes across the country as miners, steelworkers, boilermen and brewery workers took to the streets to demand higher wages and better employment conditions. Other prominent players in this growing movement had been the women chainmakers of Cradley Heath in Staffordshire and the matchmakers of London's Bryant and May. Now numerous other women's groups were joining the cause, the laundresses, the seamstresses, the jam and biscuit makers and the producers of a thousand and one small items.

The laundresses were particularly active, forming their own union in 1889. Within a year The Amalgamated Society of Laundresses had over three thousand members. One of their champions was a pretty young Irish girl called May Abraham, recently arrived from Rathgar in County Dublin. A few years later May and Adelaide would work closely together, first on a government appointed Labour Commission and then during the early formative years of the Women's Factory Inspectorate. In 1889 twenty-year-old May was already full of reformist zeal. She had left Ireland in 1887 on the death of her barrister father, arriving in London with little money but a clutch of letters of introduction. One of these was addressed to Lady Emilia Dilke, formerly Emilia Strong and erstwhile student at the Kensington School of Art. Emilia was by now a well-known and much discussed figure in London society. In 1861 she had entered into an apparently inexplicable marriage with an elderly Oxford academic who had seriously cramped her radical style. Trapped in these circumstances for several years, Emilia was widely considered to be the model for the frustrated and desperate Dorothea in George Elliot's *Middlemarch*. Like Dorothea, however, Emilia was eventually released from this unfulfilling relationship by the demise of her husband. Almost immediately she had found a much more exciting partner. Liberal MP, Sir Charles Dilke, second Baronet Wentworth, was a colourful character, the subject of a scandalous divorce case in 1885 and surrounded by prurient rumours about his sexual behaviour. Neither the loss of his reputation nor his Parliamentary seat, however, deterred Emilia who married him the same year. Newly liberated to resume her labour reform activities she became President of the Women's Trade Union League (WTUL) in 1886, establishing its headquarters at her home in fashionable Sloane Street. The League was an umbrella organisation which promoted and organised the establishment of women's trade unions. May, on her arrival from Ireland, was appointed as Emilia's secretary, moving into a top floor flat in nearby Tite Street with Emilia's niece, Gertrude Tuckwell. In the late Victorian age this was a bold move for two respectable middle class women particularly since, during 1888 and 1889, they played host to many of the prominent male activists of the day. In order to calm the worries of Gertrude's mother, they were forced to employ a housekeeper to act as a chaperone. Amongst those prepared to climb the 104 steps to their top-floor flat were Kier Hardie, founder of the Independent Labour Party; Sydney and Beatrice Webb of the Fabian Society; textile trade union leader James Maudsley; and numerous journalists including Rosalind, Vaughan Nash, Norman McCaul (editor of the *Athenaeum*), and Joseph Knight of *Notes and Queries*. Other frequent visitors were Tom Mann and Ben Tillett, who in August 1889 would lead the celebrated London Dock Strike. This was the high point of New Unionism, which would bring the Port of London to a complete standstill. By the end of August the number on strike was estimated to be in excess of 130,000. Some fifty years later Ernest Bevin described the events of that year as 'a new political awakening . . . virtually a revolution against poverty, tyranny and intolerable conditions . . . laying the foundation of a great industrial movement.'[37]

For Adelaide, too, this was an awakening, the completion of an irreversible change in her thinking about the world that had begun at Girton. At Toynbee Hall she met many of the same people who frequented Tite Street, including Emilia and May who were regular visitors to the settlement. It had become a popular meeting place for the numerous strike committees, now forming in the East End. Residents helped to organise relief for striking dockers and their families and wrote letters to the newspapers to persuade readers of the justice of their cause. Surrounded, as she was, by these activities and conversations, she was forced to reappraise her own position, and her ambitions. The Dock Strike was particularly unsettling. Hitherto she had experienced the shipping industry from the perspective of its owners and managers. Rarely, if ever, had she considered the conditions of those who manned the vessels, unloaded the goods or maintained the ships in port. For the first time she was confronted by the long hours, low pay and hazardous conditions of so many. And there lingered the memory of Govie, now lying beside his wife in the Old Machar churchyard,[38] his uncompromising principles and concern for the poor inextricably bound up with his Christian faith. As Adelaide encountered the reality of life for many in the working classes, her steadfast religious commitment seems to have combined with another of her enduring characteristics, a deep-rooted belief in the requirements of duty. The result, it seems, was a powerful sense of mission, sustained by a personality which, like that of her grandfather, was uncompromising, single-minded and doggedly determined. Years later when asked by her sister-in-law, Ralf's wife Margaret, if she ever regretted the course she had chosen in life she would reply that she had not, in fact, chosen it. Perhaps this was a simple admission of the family circumstances that had required her to take up paid employment. Perhaps, however, it also reflected her sense of vocation, a deeply held belief that she was engaged in work sent to her by God.

Yet Adelaide was no revolutionary. She believed implicitly in the British way of life, sharing, no doubt, the fear of French revolutionary terrors, which still lurked at the back of many middle class minds. For Adelaide any societal change could and should be effected through the mechanisms of government. It was within existing structures, supported by official authority, that she felt most comfortable. Similarly, there was no place in her make-up for impulsive decisions. Given her earnest and serious nature she would have pondered long and hard on the direction of her future. Her experiences at Toynbee Hall had convinced her that she wished to pursue the cause of better employment conditions, but there remained her deeply conformist nature, her desire for an organised framework within which to work, and, not least, her need for a regular income. There was no family fortune to fund her activities and there would be no feather bed to return to if life became difficult.

This last problem was brought into sharp focus in the late autumn of 1892 when Alexander Gavin, whose health had been deteriorating for some time, became extremely unwell. The eldest of the Anderson brothers, he was still only fifty-nine, but the last few years had been difficult and unhappy ones. Struggling with financial worries and alienated from much of his wider family, he was also suffering from the symptoms of heart disease. John Ford, prescribing bed rest and administering doses of digitalis, was losing the battle to treat his brother's symptoms. Alexander Gavin's pain and breathlessness had increased over the past few months and now he was suffering from 'dropsy',[39] his swollen legs and ankles making it difficult for him to walk. As Christmas approached, his condition rapidly worsened, and on the morning of 6 December, John Ford was hastily summoned from Buckland Crescent. But there was nothing he could do. Alexander Gavin had suffered a final fatal attack, and later that day John Ford sadly signed his brother's death certificate. No more than a bystander in the quarrels surrounding the Orient Line, he had always remained close to the family, trying unsuccessfully to heal the breach between Alexander Gavin and his other brothers. Now, in the absence of their support, he took charge of the funeral organisation. London's increasingly overcrowded churchyards were by now largely closed to local populations but, fortunately, a family burial plot had been purchased at the Brookwood Cemetery twenty miles away in Surrey. Three days later, therefore, as other Londoners prepared for their seasonal celebrations, Blanche Emily and the children accompanied Alexander Gavin's coffin on the special train which ran from Waterloo's purpose-built 'Necropolis Station'. It would have been a cold and comfortless journey. The almost indecent haste with which the funeral was arranged suggested that few other relatives were either expected or wanted. And the bare surroundings of Brookwood would have felt bleak, particularly in winter. Even forty years after its opening, the huge cemetery was still sparsely populated with memorials and largely devoid of vegetation. Bereft of the familiar comforts of St John's church in Hampstead, the funeral must have been a particular ordeal for Blanche Emily. And it would have been a joyless Christmas that year, so unlike the happy family gatherings of earlier times. The advent of the New Year did not present a hopeful prospect. And yet, for Adelaide at least, life was about to expand considerably beyond the confines of the immediate family.

Chapter Four
TOWARDS THE FACTORY INSPECTORATE

For many in the middle classes the events of the late 1880s were not so much a political awakening as an unwelcome social convulsion that threatened to destabilise society. 'Something' must be done. In 1890, amidst increasing labour unrest, the Conservative government formulated its response, establishing, under the direction of the Home Office, a Royal Commission on Labour to investigate employment conditions among the poor. At the end of 1891, under pressure from the WTUL, a special group to investigate women's work was established. Emilia's influence in the formation of this Women's Employment Commission was clear. May, of course, was one of the four Commissioners, as was Clara Collet, a graduate of London University who had worked with Charles Booth on his survey of London's poor. Like Adelaide, Clara had become all too familiar with the desperate situation in and around Whitechapel. The others were Margaret Irwin, active in the Scottish labour movement and Eliza Orme, the first woman lawyer to practise in Britain. This overtly cohesive group was, in fact, beset by conflicts born of differing convictions. Eliza was probably the clearest in terms of her ideological position. A passionate advocate of women's rights she was a strong opponent of protective employment legislation. For Eliza the way forward was trade union membership, representation and negotiation, not state protection which seemed to classify women with children as needful of government care. Eliza, the official chair of the group, was determined that any recommendations should reflect these views. Clara, with her background in social survey work was less sure. Her primary concern was that the report should be soundly based on statistical evidence and the results of systematic interviews. Margaret and May presented a different problem. Both had been active supporters of organised labour and yet, strangely to Eliza's way of thinking, neither seemed to oppose the development of protective legislation. Yet theirs was a position that reflected new thinking within the WTUL, now dominated by Emilia and closely allied to contemporary Liberal politics. Originally formed as the Women's Protective and Provident League, the WTUL had earlier espoused Eliza's position, that ultimately protective legislation was degrading to women, undermining their position as free independent agents. Under their founding president, Emma Paterson,[1] the organisation had worked hard to establish women's trade unions to fight for employment rights. By the late 1880s, however, it was obvious that the maintenance of women's unions was going to be an uphill struggle. Most women were simply too preoccupied with holding down a job and looking after their children to expend their energies on union activities. Even the initially successful Amalgamated Society of Laundresses,[2] which at its height had achieved a membership close to three thousand, had lost support following an initial defeat of its campaign for shorter hours. Most female union members emanated from the traditionally well-organised areas of the Lancashire textile industry. Elsewhere membership was patchy at best. In the face of these realities, the position of the League had softened by the late 1880s, embracing what came to be known as 'social feminism', gender equality which also acknowledged the possibility of differences between the sexes in terms of aptitudes, aspirations and, importantly, employment risks. Moreover legislative protection was beginning to be seen as a right of both male and female workers. The hard line 'total equality' stance of an earlier generation of feminists such as the Langham Place Set that had inspired Emily Davies and Elizabeth Garrett, was now being supplanted by a more moderate ideology.

For many, including Eliza, this development represented a significant betrayal, but for others it was a constructive move, recognising practical realities and also drawing the teeth of male dominated unions who had felt threatened by women's demands for equal jobs and pay. When Emma Paterson died in 1886, a victim of diabetes, her replacement by Emilia as WTUL President strongly reflected these new trends in feminist thinking. Thus, as the Women's Employment Commissioners returned to London with the results of their investigations, fierce arguments broke out over the content and wording of the final report. The job of reconciling these differences fell in no small measure to another important participant in the exercise, the précis writer. The job of classifying and summarising information into a readable form was one that had presented Adelaide with an ideal employment opportunity, newly energised as she was by her experiences at Toynbee Hall. The government had already shown its enthusiasm for Girton girls as government scribes, carrying out a recruitment drive at the college when Adelaide was still a student there. By the end of March 1892, therefore, she had secured this important and, as it turned out, distinctly challenging position. It was her first real job, and an important step towards her new career. The Labour Commission had been assigned government offices at 44 Parliament Street, one half of a pair of eighteenth-century houses that still featured the handsomely carved furnishings and sculpted ceilings of an earlier gracious age. Installed in one corner of these elegant if rather faded surroundings, she began the task of reducing hundreds of pages of information into a digestible report, and one to which all four of these determined and opinionated women could sign up. She could not have anticipated how difficult and daunting the task would be, and yet it was one at which she excelled. Sharply analytical, clear in expression and painstaking in approach, her Cambridge referees had been accurate in their appraisal of her work. At the end of this two-year appointment she had acquired a reputation in the Home Office as a diligent employee, one who could be trusted with the impartial presentation of government information. Along the way she had also absorbed a detailed knowledge of the circumstances in which many other, less fortunate women spent their working hours. And, of course, she had become thoroughly acquainted with the ideological arguments now swirling around women's employment issues. Presumably, by 1894, when her time as a précis writer came to an end, she had a well-formed idea of exactly where she stood on this particular feminist battleground.

Across London in Kensington, Emilia Dilke had set her sights on a new important goal. The findings of the Women's Employment Commission, she argued, had made an overwhelming case for the appointment of women factory inspectors. By the mid 1890s there were almost one and a half million women in the industrial workforce. Just over sixty thousand were employed in the well-established textile mills of the North of England, but the rest worked in factories and workshops up and down the land, making a huge variety of products for the new consumer age. Women workers, she concluded, needed the protection of state regulation, but such regulation should be negotiated and enforced by women, for women. It was a proviso that she hoped offered a degree of compromise to those who espoused 'equality feminism'. Fortuitously, around the same time, two potent sources of opposition to the appointment of women factory inspectors had dissolved in quick succession. The first was that of the Chief

Inspector of Factories, Sir Alexander Redgrave. His oft quoted and quaintly expressed objections, published in his Annual Report for 1879 had enraged feminists of the day. Not only did he feel that the 'gentle and home-loving character of a woman' was incompatible with the duties of a factory inspector, but also that it was 'seldom necessary to put a question to a woman.' He 'failed to see what advantage might be gained by such an approach.'[3] In 1891, however, after forty-seven years in the Factory Department, Sir Alexander had reached retirement age. He had been succeeded by another long serving Superintending Inspector called Frederick Whymper, whose views seemed likely to mirror those of his former superior. But this was a short-lived appointment, dramatically cut short by ill health only three months later. When, Whymper was replaced by yet another contemporary of Sir Alexander, Richard Sprague Oram, Emilia had initially begun to despair. Oram was a round, bewhiskered little man who, at the age of sixty-one, was himself nearing retirement. He wrote with an enormous quill pen and his tendency to wave this about excitedly left the floor and walls of his office spattered with multi-coloured ink. Such old-fashioned eccentricity did not augur well for the modern feminist cause. Yet Sprague Oram was to prove a surprise. He was, it seemed, a staunch and determined supporter of women inspectors. Waving aside opposition, no doubt with an accompanying shower of ink, he persuaded a doubtful Home Secretary and reluctant senior inspectors to think the unthinkable.

The second dissolution was that of Parliament in 1892, and the subsequent ousting of the Conservative government by an alliance of Gladstone's Liberals with what *The Times* called 'the multifarious elements of the motley majority'.[4] The new Home Secretary, in whose Department resided the Factory Inspectorate, was Liberal MP Herbert Asquith, a man with a particular interest in employment conditions. He was already persuaded of the need for women inspectors, not least because of his personal friendship with a network of Liberal social reformers who espoused the cause. Prominent among these were Sir Charles and Emilia Dilke and his own private secretary and brother-in-law, Harold (Jack) Tennant, son of Baronet, Sir Charles Tennant. Jack was a passionate advocate of labour reform. He was currently chairing the Dangerous Trades Committee, set up in the wake of the Labour Commission to identify and address significant industrial risks. He was also a strong supporter of women inspectors. Asquith faced considerable opposition in government circles. 'State officials', he noted in his memoirs, 'considered women factory inspectors to be a terrible proposition. They shook their heads and did not sleep at night.'[5] Appealing to the very attitudes that underpinned this opposition, however, Asquith decided to emphasise the presumed emotional differences between the sexes. He talked of 'the peculiar knowledge, the intuitive and instinctive knowledge . . . which a woman necessarily had as to the wants of her own sex.' Thus, 'there could not be free and frank communication between female operatives on the one side and a male inspector on the other.'[6] And he had another useful card to play. In December 1892 the popular press was alive with shocking stories about the plight of women who worked in the white lead industries. 'White cemeteries: massacre of the innocents', screamed the headlines.[7] Rosalind's new husband, Vaughan Nash of the *Daily Chronicle*, led the charge. Women without any other means of support, he claimed, were forced into a form of employment which frequently resulted in lead poisoning. Many suffered from paralysis and convulsions. Others died or faced the loss of their unborn children.[8] There was a need for extensive improvements in the white lead factories, including the introduction of proper ventilation equipment. Perhaps unsurprisingly, the employers took a different view. Such costly modifications to the process would ruin the British trade, they argued, for it would become prohibitively expensive and move abroad. Everyone would suffer, not least the women workers themselves who depended on it for their very livelihoods.[9] The Home Office was thus embroiled in its first significant industrial health dispute, confronting a conflict of interests and a well-rehearsed series of arguments that would feature in many future scenarios. And this one involved women. What the government needed, Asquith argued, were women factory inspectors. Such women would be indispensable allies in the negotiations surrounding this highly charged issue.

A window of opportunity, it seemed, had opened. Moreover, the male dominated Trades Union Congress (TUC), formerly lukewarm in its attitude to sexual equality and the demands of women's unions, was now willing to offer its support. Traditionally male unionists had tended to dismiss the concerns of women workers as a trivial distraction from the wider labour struggles of the time. And middle class women campaigners were often viewed as ill-informed do-gooders.[10] Meanwhile, noted feminist writer, Ray Strachey, 'The men's very genuine fears were put aside by the feminists as plain sex selfishness.'[11] By the 1890s, however, the attitudes of some of the larger unions were beginning to change. Those currently lobbying for the appointment of more male inspectors, and particularly the recruitment of more 'working men' into the Factory Department, saw no inherent conflict between the aspirations of the men and the women for improved state protection. There would be more arguments in the future about the middle class composition of the women's factory inspectorate, but for the moment, at least, the major unions were willing to throw their weight behind the campaign.

In 1892, therefore, the TUC joined the WTUL in a large promotional meeting at London's Assembly Hall in the Mile End Road. And early in 1893 Emilia led a deputation to the Home Office which included not only members of various women's organisation but also representatives of male dominated unions. 'Several hundred people of both sexes', *The Times* reported, 'waited upon Mr Asquith for the purpose of requesting him to appoint women as factory inspectors, and generally increase the numbers of inspectors so as to secure more efficient supervision of workshops and factories.'[12] The Home Office rooms were apparently too small to receive the deputation which had to adjourn to the much larger rooms of the Foreign Office. The meeting was a great success with Mr Asquith agreeing to an initial appointment of fifteen 'working men' as assistant inspectors and two women inspectors. He had, he said, already obtained the agreement of the Treasury. By early 1893, therefore, the question was no longer whether there should be women inspectors, but who should be appointed.

From her desk in Parliament Street Adelaide followed these developments with a keen interest. There were, apparently, to be two women inspectors initially, one based in London and one in Scotland. In the nineteenth century recruitment to the Civil Service was still largely dependent on personal recommendation and she knew that the first hurdle to be overcome was that of securing a nomination. Only then would she be able to take the qualifying Civil Service examination. She also knew that a nomination would depend on the support of influential friends. At the end of January 1893, therefore, she wrote two letters. The first was to Asquith indicating that she would like to apply for the Scottish post, citing her academic qualifications, her work on the Labour Commission, her lectures to the Co-operative Guild and finally her Scottish background. The second letter was to Anthony Mundella MP, President of the Board of Trade and initiator of the Factory Act of 1875, the so-called 'Ten Hours Act' which had guaranteed a ten-hour day for women and children in textile factories. The tone of her letters to Asquith and Mundella suggests that, by 1893, she was able to count both men as personal acquaintances to whom she could confidently appeal. The need

for friends in high places was perhaps one reason why, a few
months earlier, she had taken up the opportunity to be presented
at Court. This traditional entrée into polite society was a curious
step for Adelaide, both in its nature and its timing. Undoubtedly
her family had travelled a considerable social distance since their
early days in New Zealand but they were essentially part of the
merchant and business class. They might even be described as
'trade', hardly the usual pedigree for those seeking an audience
with the Queen. And pressure to partake of the traditional
'coming out' ceremony usually emanated from ambitious mothers,
anxious to secure for their daughters a favourable position in
the marriage market. This seems to sit uneasily with Blanche
Emily and with the Liberal traditions of the wider Anderson
family and Adelaide was, in any case, well past conventional
marriageable age. Was it, therefore, that she wished to secure
for herself a badge of social respectability that might enhance
her professional prospects? Or was the decision motivated by
a lingering attachment to her comfortable former life that was
by now slipping away? Whatever the reason, in May 1892, she
attended the traditional ceremony in the Queen's Drawing
Room, making the formal, well-practiced curtsy that signalled
her acceptance into higher social circles. Her photograph shows
her resplendent in a luxurious white brocade gown, encircled
by a train of enormous length and carrying the obligatory fan
composed of three Prince of Wales ostrich feathers. She looked,
as ever, solemn and inscrutable. Whether she participated in
the subsequent round of promotional social engagements which
comprised 'The Season' is questionable. She needed to make
useful acquaintances but she had little enthusiasm for balls and
parties or, it seems, for their primary objective, the acquisition
of a suitable husband. The dress, however, seems to have been
treasured and preserved, for nearly thirty years later it would
be brought out to serve another unexpected and very different
purpose.

Adelaide's presentation at court

On receiving Adelaide's letter, Mundella was initially cautious. He would see the Home Secretary on her behalf and do what he could, but he noted there was a considerable lobby for the selection of women with factory experience. Feelings on this point were running very high and he feared the government would have to appoint someone from the working classes. 'Feelings', in this case, were emanating from male trade unionists, who were themselves pressing for the appointment of more working class men as factory inspectors. The appointment of middle class ladies would, they felt, undermine their own case. Emilia had little sympathy for this view. Typically confident of her own influence and her own judgment, she had already interviewed several working class women as prospective candidates and found them to be 'lacking in tact, discretion and self control.' They had no knowledge of 'how to take the initiative or responsibility and no experience of office work.'[13] Emilia, of course, had already decided who was to be appointed as the first woman factory inspector, her own secretary and protégée, May Abraham. Asquith eventually agreed, appeasing trade unionists with the appointment of fifteen new male inspectors' 'assistants' who were working men, although officially these were training posts, with no powers of inspection or law enforcement. In Scotland the second post of 'Lady Inspector' was filled by Mary Muriel Paterson, the daughter of a prosperous Glasgow boot manufacturer. The nature of the social connections that secured for Mary her nomination as a candidate are obscure, but her background was strong in Liberal politics and her uncle, medical doctor Henry Muirhead, was a noted champion of professional education for women. He had donated a considerable amount of money to Queen Margaret's Women's College in Glasgow, where Mary received her university education.

On hearing of these appointments, Adelaide was disappointed but undeterred. She had, after all, said she would be unavailable to apply for the Factory Inspectorate until the completion of her work on the Women's Employment Commission. She was aware that there would be further appointments and her papers were now firmly on file. Mundella had written to Asquith on her behalf, enclosing a glowing testimonial from Mr Dwyer, her immediate manager on the

Commission. Adelaide was by now in charge of a whole office of précis writers. She was, according to Dwyer, 'accurate, trustworthy and competent . . . possessed of great tact and power of management . . . good judgement and an unbiased mind . . . and able to present dry statistics in a readable form.'[14] Her attempt to acquire a reference from the eminent Henry Sidgwick, her former lecturer at Cambridge, was less successful. Clearly bewildered at the route she had chosen, he had refused to provide a testimonial. Any information he could provide on her ability to write thoughtful essays on philosophical subjects would not, he assumed, be relevant to the post in question.[15] In March 1894, however, came good news. There were to be two more appointments and she was to be offered a nomination. The post would be subject to her fulfilment of the requirements of the Civil Service examination. May and Mary had avoided this particular hurdle but pressure was growing for women applicants to be treated in the same way as their male counterparts. Certain aspects of the existing examination, however, with its emphasis on 'physical mechanics' were not considered appropriate for women and the subjects, Adelaide was told, were still to be decided. She would be informed of these by Mr Tennant in due course. By the end of March she had completed her work on the Commission and, having heard nothing further, she decided on a week's holiday in the Harz Mountains of Northern Germany. It was almost a fateful decision. On arrival on the Continent she was horrified to find a forwarded letter waiting for her. She was to present herself at the Home Office in two days time for her examination. Failure to arrive would result in the forfeiture of her nomination. Rushing to catch the first steamer back home she was dismayed to find the English Channel enveloped in fog. Her ship finally found its way back to Dover at 2 a.m. on the day of the examination.

Arriving at the Home Office in a state of anxious exhaustion

Adelaide found a fellow candidate waiting nervously outside the examination room. Lucy Deane was a London sanitary inspector who had long coveted a nomination for the post of factory inspector. Over the previous eighteen months she had made several abortive attempts to gain influential supporters, writing first to Margot Asquith, Jack Tennant's sister and wife to the Home Secretary, who 'had promised to do all she could.' 'In other words *nothing*!'[16] Lucy remarked ruefully in her diary a few weeks later. She had also managed to have tea with Sir Alexander Redgrave for his niece was a personal friend. It was, of course, an ill-advised visit. 'A very kindly old man but he does not approve of women inspectors and cannot, or rather *will not* help me.'[17] At some stage, however, her persistence had brought her to the notice of Emilia who invited her to lunch. Emilia was once more fighting off suggestions that a working class candidate should be put forward. Lucy recounted the conversation at Sloane Street with a certain amount of glee. 'Lady D told me that TUs and labour organisations would be very angry at me being appointed – a lady! I heard a great deal about Miss Heaton (the factory girl genius!) – their labour candidate, strong and talented but conceited and aggressive and only working for her own ends.'[18] Lucy had become Emilia's second protégée, introduced to the inner circle of influence and schooled by May in the requirements of the job. She was also given 'invaluable counsel'[19] by Eliza Orme who was keen to alert her to Home Office attitudes. 'Keep clear of public speaking or sympathy with anything political or Trade Unions etc.,' she advised, 'because the government can't employ a party woman strongly connected with any cause in a matter requiring such tact as a factory inspector in touch with employers and employees.'[20] In the event, competition for the second nomination came not from the much maligned Miss Heaton but from a Miss Peasehill, an impeccably connected member of the aristocracy. Asquith had already abandoned all notions of appointing a factory worker for there remained a sizeable opposition to women factory inspectors within the Home Office and he knew that the appointment of working class women would have been a bridge too far. The government was already open to charges of trade union appeasement. The choice between Miss Deane and Miss Peasehill, however, was a difficult one. Asquith's father and Miss Peasehill's uncle were old friends. Moreover the Queen's daughter-in-law, the Duchess of Albany, had supported her nomination. As usual, however, Asquith consulted Emilia and, somewhat against the odds, Lucy emerged as the nominee.

With previous experience in nursing as well as in sanitary inspection, Lucy was, in fact, rather well-suited to the post of factory inspector. Nevertheless, she professed herself rather daunted to find her fellow examinee was a 'Girton girl'. Although the two were not in competition, she worried that her own performance would appear poor in comparison. When the examination was followed by an unaccountably long silence from the Home Office she feared the worst. With increasing anxiety she pursued her contacts inside the Civil Service and discovered, unofficially, that there was 'a difficulty' with the results.[21] Lucy, a self acknowledged dunce at mathematics, assumed that she had failed this particular paper, only to discover with some amazement that it was Adelaide's results that were in question. Adelaide herself was informed of the news by Mr Dwyer. It was apparently her knowledge of the 'Principal Provisions of the Factory and Workshop Acts' which had been found wanting. Adelaide's response was unhesitating. She wrote immediately to the Home Secretary, recounting the circumstances of her arrival in the examination room, her forty-eight hours of constant travel, her lack of sleep and the fact that she had not received the promised list of subjects from Mr Tennant. This, in particular, had prevented her from carrying out adequate preparation. She respectfully requested an opportunity to take the examination again.[22] It is fairly clear that Asquith wanted very much to appoint Adelaide. But there had to be a justification for another chance, something that would spike the guns of opponents in the Home Office, ever ready to attack the abilities of women. Her reference to Jack Tennant's omission provided Asquith with exactly what he needed. Jack was instructed to write a conciliatory *mea culpa* letter, confessing his own oversight and apologizing to Adelaide for any trouble and annoyance she had been caused. The Home Secretary, he said, wished to know when it would suit her to attend again. She would only need to re-take one paper. On 27 April 1894, therefore, Lucy was appointed as the third Lady Factory Inspector and on the 30th Adelaide presented herself once more for the examination. This time there were no mistakes. On 20 June she finally received her official appointment letter from Permanent Secretary, Geoffrey Lushington. She was to be the fourth appointee. It had been an inauspicious start to her career but, no matter, she was now officially installed in government service. James Bryce, newly appointed President of the Board of Trade, wrote to offer his congratulations. He expressed his complete confidence in Adelaide's ability to carry out her duties. Typically deceived by her appearance, however, he added a proviso. He 'just hoped her health and strength would keep up.'[23]

Fortunately Adelaide was indeed stronger than she looked, for her early experiences as a factory inspector would take place against a background of new, unexpected turmoil at home. The last few years, had already been disruptive and difficult. The disappearance of the family security, the anxiety surrounding Alexander Gavin's mysterious quarrel with his brothers and departure from the Orient Line, and finally his illness and death, had left the family feeling isolated and in low spirits. Adelaide's transition into the world of work had been accomplished without the encouragement of a strong supportive network of relatives. Almost as soon as she received news of her appointment as a factory inspector, however, she found herself confronting a new unfolding family tragedy, this time involving her younger sister Isobel. Spirited and strikingly pretty, Adelaide's closest sibling had indisputable creative talents. At the National Art School she had trained in art printing, hoping to build a career in a field now increasingly open to women. She was also an accomplished fine artist, her subjects ranging from rural landscapes and townscapes of her native Hampstead and beyond, to portraits of her friends and relatives. In the summer of 1894 her delicate and sensitively executed likeness of her sister Blanchie was selected for exhibition at the Royal Academy. Coinciding, as it did, with Adelaide's appointment as a factory inspector this event would have been a cause of much needed pride and joy in the Anderson house. And Blanchie was also doing well. By now she was assistant headmistress at a girl's school in Bolton, Lancashire.

Shortly after the Academy exhibition, however, Isobel began to behave in a strange and frightening manner. She heard voices that no-one else could hear and suffered from delusions about her identity. Sometimes she was Eve, living in the Garden of Eden. Other times she was 'Mrs Asquith', or 'a married lady with children'.[24] Increasingly, her conversation was rambling and irrational. It was the first attack of an illness, probably schizophrenia, from which there would be no recovery. Coming after Douglas's mental and physical difficulties, this would have been a crushing blow to the family, for in the Victorian period mental disability in all its forms was a significant social stigma. The role of inheritance in such conditions was a presumption that threatened to taint the lives and prospects of the sufferer's relatives, particularly those of her siblings.

Over the following two years the family would embark on a prolonged struggle to contain and conceal Isobel's symptoms. The strain on the recently widowed Blanche Emily during this

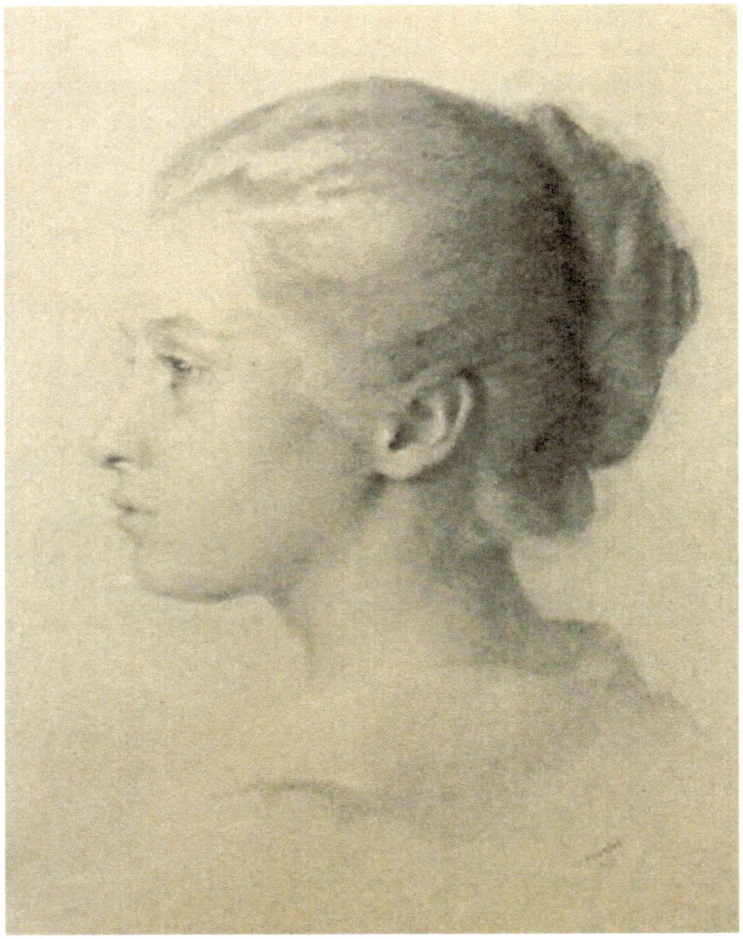

Isobel's portrait of Blanchie, exhibited at the Royal Academy in 1894.

period would have been immense, especially as Adelaide, the newly appointed factory inspector, was so often away and out of contact. Adelaide herself must have been plagued with worry, and with guilt, as she attempted to focus on her new job. As the eldest daughter, her pursuit of a professional career at a time of obvious family need would have raised some disapproving eyebrows. The requirement of unmarried women to devote themselves to family concerns in such circumstances was, for many households, a non-negotiable matter. The expectations of sons, by contrast, were much less exacting and, in any case, both Max and Walter were by now pursuing careers abroad. Max had remained in Australia, operating as an increasingly successful shipping agent while Walter had travelled to Canada, where he was attempting to build up a business in the canned fish export trade. It was probably a relief that Douglas was also elsewhere. For some time he had boarded with a clergyman and his family in the remote rural village of Kilcamonell in Argyleshire. It seemed to be a happy arrangement and this problem, at least, was under control. Alex was still at school in 1894, but Ralf, barely seventeen, was just embarking on his own first job. This was a post with the London based shipping company, the Blue Anchor Line, which carried passengers to Australia. Ralf was keen to follow his father into the international shipping business, but Alexander Gavin's dispute with the Orient Line seems to have left his sons with little prospect of a helping hand from influential relatives. An appointment letter from his new employer, Mr Lund, in November 1894, shows that Ralf was beginning his working life on the very bottom rung of the ladder. He was, apparently, expected to start work without any pay and, as the office junior, to make sure that he was the first to arrive in the morning and the last to leave at night. If he had any difficulty with these arrangements then he was advised not to turn up at all. 'How soon you receive some pay,' continued Mr Lund, 'rests entirely with yourself.'[25] Struggling to make headway against these Scrooge-like terms and conditions Ralf, like Adelaide, would have had little time and space to cope with upheavals at home. As a result, therefore, much of the burden of supporting 'the mother' whilst dealing with Isobel's increasingly bizarre behaviour would have fallen on poor Mary, the youngest sister, only twenty years old and significantly short on life experience. Mary seems to have had no obvious career in mind, a factor that would effectively seal her fate as the unpaid help on the home front. Adelaide would later organise a practical solution to the problem of Isobel, but for the moment she could only watch and hope while Mary took the strain.

Amidst these difficulties there was yet another family disruption to be faced, the departure from the much loved Anderson home. The truth of Horace's words, placed so prophetically on the front wall, was about to be realized. Alexander Gavin's will, written in May 1888 shortly after his break with the Orient Line, showed that Number One Fitzjohn's Avenue was no longer his to bequeath to Blanche Emily and the children, presumably one more unwelcome outcome of the quarrel with his brothers. It was, in any case, becoming increasingly clear that without the main breadwinner the luxurious life the family had previously enjoyed in Hampstead could no longer be sustained. Alexander Gavin's monetary estate, just over £7,000, was a considerable sum in 1892, but inadequate for the long-term upkeep of a widow and several dependent children. There were still Alex's school fees to pay, together with a regular contribution to Douglas's upkeep in Scotland. And, of the five children remaining at home, only Adelaide was earning money. Increasingly, therefore, it was she who began to assume the mantle of responsibility for financial matters on the domestic front. Regularly acquainted through her work with the problems of the poor, she was now forced to confront those in her own family. Trivial they might be by comparison, but the spectre of gradually increasing poverty, however genteel, would not have been an easy one to contemplate. The answer, she decided, was a much smaller house in a less expensive area. Hadley Wood, north of London, was a fast expanding part of the municipal borough of Enfield, close to open countryside and enjoying a regular train service to central

London. Adelaide's acquaintance with these facts was almost certainly due to another much more welcome development. Alice, her childhood friend from Aberdeen days, had recently returned from India and had settled in Hadley Wood with her husband, William, and their two young children. For Adelaide, the prospect of renewing her friendship with Alice would have seemed a heaven sent opportunity. Here, at least, was a source of comfort and moral support. Thus the sale of much of the contents of Number One Fitzjohn's Avenue was put into effect and Blanche Emily, accompanied by Adelaide, Mary, Isobel and the younger boys said good-bye to the area that had been their home for over twenty years. The precise timing of the move is unclear, but it had certainly been completed by November 1894. Isobel's illness may well have been a precipitating factor, not only because of the financial difficulties it threatened to provoke, but also because of the need to conceal the shame of her condition. The children had grown up in Hampstead and the Anderson family as a whole was well-known and well-respected in the area. In Hadley Wood, by contrast, they were strangers to their immediate neighbours. Much of the village was a recent development, inhabited by aspiring newcomers. The new Anderson home, Woodlands was one half of a large semi-detached villa, part of a recently constructed line of similar houses in a road called The Crescent. There is little doubt that Adelaide was the primary force behind this move, so satisfactory from her own point of view but rather less so for her mother. Uprooted from her familiar environment and deposited amongst strangers, Blanche Emily had now lost both husband and home. Although she was to remain at Hadley Wood for the remainder of her life, she never seems to have been fully reconciled to Woodlands. Much of the period that followed seems to have been spent in abortive attempts to find a more agreeable residence as, one by one, her children flew the nest.

Chapter Five
THE LADY INSPECTOR

Monday 2 July 1894 was a hot, uncomfortable day in London. The heat wave and drought of the last several weeks had left the city dustier and grubbier than usual and Adelaide, tightly contained in respectable Victorian dress, would have felt less than coolly prepared for her first day as a factory inspector. Emerging at Moorgate station from the smoke and steam of the underground, she would have been relieved to turn the corner and discover the green oasis that was Finsbury Circus. Number eight, shaded by the lime trees which encircled this urban garden, was yet another declining Georgian townhouse. A few years later it would be demolished for Edwardian redevelopment but, for the moment, it offered an agreeable home for the Factory Department. Ushered into the Chief Inspector's office, she encountered Sprague Oram, kindly, affable and welcoming. Perched, elf-like, behind a large oak desk he explained to her the details of inspectors' report forms, the importance of record keeping and of the 'abstracts' required to be posted on the walls of factories and workshops. These outlined the principle provisions of the Factory Acts. Her role, like that of the other three lady inspectors, was to be peripatetic, carrying out duties assigned by the Chief Inspector and reporting directly to him. Mary Paterson was based in Glasgow but Adelaide was to share an already cramped office with May and Lucy here in Finsbury

Circus. This hardly mattered, however. Much of her time, like theirs, would be spent travelling around the country. These arrangements contrasted sharply with those governing the work of their male counterparts who were attached to specific districts, working out of local Factory Department offices under the supervision of District Superintendents.

Women inspectors were to focus their attention specifically on the employment conditions of women and young persons (those under the age of eighteen). This, however, did not exclude the possibility that they might sometimes encounter problems affecting adult male workers and any such matters were to be referred to the Chief Inspector. The position of the lady inspectors within the existing structure of the Factory Inspectorate was thus highly unusual and somewhat ambiguous. Faced with a novel and unpredictable situation Oram, it seems, had elected to keep a close and somewhat protective eye on his new recruits. It was a situation which many male inspectors found both disconcerting and threatening. Some District Superintendents regarded the women inspectors as an annoyance and even as spies for the Chief Inspector. And junior inspectors feared territorial conflicts and duplications of work that might generate confusion and undermine their own authority. The responses to these perceived threats varied from the directly hostile to the deviously subversive. Lucy recorded several such difficult encounters in her diary. Captain Bevan, the District Inspector for Nottingham, was outraged at the introduction of women into the Factory Department. Over dinner one evening, this former army officer had 'burst into a furious tirade' accusing the lady inspectors of finding faults in workplaces where he considered there were none and conducting completely unnecessary prosecutions. All this interfered with the management of his district and hurt his own reputation.[1] Other inspectors seemed intent on undermining the authority of their new female colleagues. 'When a woman is sent to help them, they will send her to those places visited shortly before them, thus wasting her time and rendering her position ridiculous.'[2] Mr Arnold, District Inspector for Worcestershire and Gloucestershire, a man apparently 'in a terrible state lest I should tell tales to the Home Office', was rather more subtle in his approach. 'Very nice, but evidently wants to hoodwink me and keep me harmless,'[3] Lucy concluded. Accompanying him to Greenings clothing factory in Stroud she felt he did not wish her to hear the 'grievous complaints about sanitary matters' expressed by the women workers. And Lucy disapproved thoroughly of his 'devotion' to Cavendish House in Cheltenham.[4] This pioneering department store was the first to be established outside London and an essential destination for the fashionable of Gloucestershire. Like the London stores on which it was modelled, however, it worked its young assistants extremely hard. Retail establishments could legally employ young persons for no more than seventy-four hours per week, but even this restriction was frequently ignored and the new large department stores were some of the worst offenders. Lucy concluded that the relationship between Mr Arnold and the owners of Cavendish House was of a type that precluded any prospect of prosecution.

And yet the fears and objections of the men were not entirely unfounded. It is clear that Oram's attitude to his new lady inspectors was, from the first, supportive, defensive and undeniably partisan. Emilia considered him to be 'nice and loyal'. He will, she said, 'tell you if there is anything done or said against you in the Inspectorate and will warn you.'[5] Thus, on her first day, Lucy had been advised that Mr Dawkins-Cramp, Superintending Inspector in the Midlands, particularly disliked women inspectors and that she was to be careful in her dealings with him.[6] And, taking her cue from Oram's 'large and friendly feeling' towards the women, Lucy had been more than happy to report to him on the behaviour of Captain Bevan. 'I told him

[Bevan] that I was *not* his assistant and had in no way exceeded my instructions,' she complained. From Oram she received an immediate reassurance. She had, he said, behaved 'entirely correctly'.[7] May was equally supportive. 'The men inspectors are very jealous of us,' she declared. 'Many of them have been lax in their work through probably want of enthusiasm and through having been appointed merely as a means of livelihood.' May, it seems, considered that for a job to be done properly it should be nothing less than a vocation. 'When a woman is sent to inspect in their district', she continued, 'and by her energy brings to light the bad state resulting from their laxness, and challenges comparisons unfavourable to them by her better work, they are angry at what virtually amounts to an inspection of their inspecting work.'[8] Thus inspired, and bolstered by middle-class self-assurance, May and Lucy appear to have adopted a critical and condescending attitude towards their male colleagues. Their confidence, however, was hardly warranted by their current level of experience and expertise, and the exercise of their new found powers was perhaps too often informed by a somewhat simplistic approach to the enforcement of every letter of the law. Mr Arnold's district, they were to discover later, was particularly well managed, notable for its good working conditions and small number of accidents. The women had much to learn about the art of negotiated compliance when attempting to extract the best from hostile, grudging employers, or about the strong deterrent effect of more limited, carefully selected prosecutions. Failing to recognise that her training attachment to Mr Arnold was an indication of Oram's confidence in this particular inspector, Lucy was dismissive. 'I should think,' she declared loftily, 'that Mr Arnold is fairly useless as to the detection of illegality.'[9]

Early in July Oram arranged for Adelaide to accompany May around London for a few days to see how things were done. Lucy had experienced the same form of initiation two months earlier. She, however, had already been fully acquainted with the sweatshops[10] which supported the capital's burgeoning retail trade. She had trudged the same dingy back streets and encountered the same horrors and hostilities when she worked as a Kensington sanitary inspector. For Adelaide the experience would have been entirely new and not a little unnerving. May, who marched into workshops 'without ringing', faced down employers with barely concealed contempt and issued instructions with an imperious abruptness, had surprised even the streetwise Lucy.[11] For Adelaide it would have been a brutal beginning. Her experiences in London would soon be followed by visits around the country meeting District Superintendents and accompanying them to a wide variety of workplaces. There is no record of her thoughts during this period but it is hard to imagine that she indulged in the critical personal attacks that were so prominent in Lucy's diaries. It was simply not her style. More conservative and restrained than either of her two colleagues, her first report, delivered six months after her appointment, contained some significant pointers to her future approach. Making repeat visits to employers, (something for which she acquired a certain notoriety) she had, she said, been heartened to find that 'in almost every case' her instructions had been carried out.[12] It was almost certainly a naïve and over optimistic assessment, but it set the tone for all her dealings with workers and employers during the years that followed. Invariably polite, she favoured co-operation over confrontation and praise over censure. She was, it seems, always prepared to be encouraged by the faintest glimmer of improvement. At the beginning of August, Lucy met Adelaide for the first time since they had encountered each other in the examination room. The two had lunch together and swapped notes. The Girton girl, Lucy observed in her diary was '*very* capable, much more so than I expected.'[13]

During her first six months Adelaide also attended court

to observe May conducting prosecutions. For the inherently reserved Adelaide this was perhaps the worst of all the terrors presented by her new job, The situation had no precedence in nineteenth-century Britain, for although a woman might be required to attend court as a defendant or a witness her appearance in an official capacity was virtually unheard of. If the lady inspectors were unnerved by their role as prosecutors, however, many magistrates were equally disconcerted by the situation, their responses ranging from the overly solicitous to the sarcastically patronising. Those cases which progressed to appeal and hence to the higher court were particularly terrifying. Invariably the women found themselves pitted against eminent barristers enlisted by employers. Yet court cases were important, both to maintain the authority of the Factory Inspectorate and to act as a deterrent to miscreant employers. Fines, when they were imposed, were invariably rather limited, but publicity was not. For this reason alone it was important to win. And, of course, there was the on-going need to demonstrate a degree of competence to their male colleagues.

The women inspectors conducted 128 prosecutions in 1895 and achieved a conviction in all but three.[14] How many of these were conducted by Adelaide is unknown but by this stage she would have been playing her full part in this aspect of the work. Early in December that year, however, she was confronted with a particularly frightening legal experience when she, herself, was summoned to answer a charge of assault brought by a young girl called Annie Mitchell. Annie was an employee at a Leeds clothing factory who claimed that Miss Anderson, the Factory Inspector, had taken her by the shoulders and shaken her while asking how old she was. It was a charge which, if proven, could have spelled the end of her career. Fortunately for Adelaide, the magistrate was unimpressed by the ill-assorted group of workmates who appeared as prosecution witnesses and who 'contradicted one another in material particulars.'

Perhaps he also found it difficult to imagine a scene in which this meekly diminutive figure had assaulted a young worker. It was, he said, preposterous to bring such a charge to the court and dismissed the case without even calling the defence.[15] The 'assault' was almost certainly fictitious, concocted by resentful local employers in an attempt to discourage the activities of the women inspectors. Adelaide had been particularly active in the area during previous weeks, collecting evidence to prosecute the owners of clothing factories for excessive working hours and employing under age children. Despite the satisfactory outcome, however, the female inspectors were dismayed at the lengths to which employers would apparently go to undermine their work, and the extent to which workers were prepared to collude with this. 'What a miserable condition the poor women must be in to do such a thing to please their employers,' Lucy wrote in her diary.[16] A week after her 'trial', however, Adelaide returned to the scene of her ordeal, bringing cases against two more Leeds tailors. But it was an uphill struggle. Frightened youngsters, in fear of losing their jobs or worse, invoking ostracism from their fellow workers, first signed statements at the behest of the government inspector, and then repeatedly withdrew their evidence in court. The magistrate was again supportive. Concluding that witnesses had been intimidated he imposed a fine of forty shillings. It was a high penalty by the standards of the day but, in terms of winning hearts and minds, it was a sober reminder of the difficulties that lay ahead.[17]

By far the majority of cases taken by the women inspectors in the early days were concerned with the illegal employment of under age children or infringements of the restrictions on working hours. Just two concerned incidents where children had been allowed 'to clean machinery while in motion', a practice responsible for numerous child fatalities. Women inspectors were inexperienced in matters relating to factory machinery and this, to some extent, explains their primary focus on matters less directly concerned with health and safety. However it also reflected the types of workplaces they habitually visited and the limits of their powers. The reach of factory legislation into the lives of women workers during this period was, in fact, rather limited, largely as a result of the terms of the existing Factory Acts. Most legislation applied only to factories and workshops which employed at least fifty workers and which used some form of 'motive power'. This seemingly arbitrary restriction was perhaps understandable when viewed in the light of the concerns that had dominated much of nineteenth-century thinking. For the primary focus had always been on safety rather than health. Medical knowledge about industrial disease, although increasing, was still rather limited. The effects of exposure to poisonous dusts and fumes were rarely visible in the workplace, for they developed insidiously over time, wreaking their greatest injury weeks, months or even years after the victim had quietly withdrawn, ill and incapacitated, from employment. Accidents, by contrast, were more immediate, more obvious and certainly more graphic. It was difficult to ignore a body on the floor.

Over the years since 1833 the installation of machinery guarding had begun to provide some protection from the steam driven belts and pulleys that had drawn so many workers to their deaths. Despite undoubted improvements, however, weavers and spinners were still, on too many occasions, being mangled in the machinery of the great northern textile mills. In Lancashire and Yorkshire Adelaide soon faced the daunting prospect of entering these huge establishments presided over by despotic owners and unsympathetic managers. Hard-headed and hard-hearted, these men were, at best, amused and intrigued at the arrival of the lady inspector with her prim manner and large hat. More often they were scornful and dismissive. And on the factory floor the deafening rhythmic clatter of the machinery offered little opportunity to talk with any of the hundreds of workers who scurried busily between the looms, conducting their conversations in an exaggerated form of lip reading. Mesmerized by the action of a thousand belts and pulleys whirring above her head she could only look on in awe at this spectacle of mass endeavour. For the moment she needed to watch and learn, and the first lesson was not long in coming. Entering a factory early in 1895 she found a girl of fourteen about to be taken to the local infirmary with a compound fracture of the leg and 'other injuries'. Her skirt had been caught in the driving band of the machine on which she was working. It was, Adelaide said, 'lamentable to think of how many cases of scalping will occur in one year', a sobering reminder of the dangers of full skirts and loose hair. And in other ways it was a humbling experience for the new factory inspector. The girl who remained 'perfectly clear and conscious under her injuries' was 'chiefly concerned that no-one should alarm her mother who was ill at home.'[18]

The tragedy of this small girl was only the first of many Adelaide would witness, for the industrial development of the nineteenth century had introduced a whole range of new devices with the capacity to crush, burn, lacerate or amputate the body parts of the unwary operative. In the small industrial town of Walsall alone there were 193 such accidents in 1895, including six fatalities.[19] Circular saws, lathes, drills, hoists, presses, steam hammers, and numerous other forms of power driven equipment were now common features of the industrial workplace. Steam engines, with their relentless motion were useful servants but ruthless masters. No-one could bring them to an immediate halt by the flick of a switch. Adelaide was particularly worried by the vulnerability of children in these circumstances, watching in horror as small boys and girls dived under moving machinery to remove accumulating fluff and dust. In 1901 the women inspectors reported on a sadly typical accident in a cardboard box factory where a young girl of fourteen had been scalped when her hair had been caught in the revolving spindle of a card bending machine. This dying child was 'a mere wreck of humanity . . . the whole of her scalp was gone and of her face merely one eye and one ear and the mangled nose and torn mouth remained.' 'In this terrible plight,' reported Adelaide, 'the little girl lingered for three months', while the employer, whose foreman had ordered the child under the machine, received a nominal fine.[20] In Lancashire she saw young boys jump onto steam driven hoists to travel from one floor of the factory to another, timing their leap on to the

A textile factory in Blackburn, Lancashire, early twentieth century. (From *More Pictures of British History*, Elizabeth L. Hoskyn, 1914.)

platform to avoid the vertically barred gates which lifted and fell automatically as the hoist approached each floor. In Yorkshire she saw girls of thirteen using power driven hand looms and sharp edged cutting equipment in clothing workshops, and in Wales a boy of fifteen was killed when his clothing was caught in the cogs of a key compressing machine. By the 1890s the law required the reporting of all fatal accidents occurring in the workplace, and all non-fatal accidents resulting in at least three days absence from work. In 1896 there were almost fourteen thousand such accidents recorded by the Factory Inspectorate, including 496 fatalities and many more limb amputations. The most frequent victims were men, for it was they who most often operated heavy industrial machinery, but over two thousand of these accidents involved women and children, and three women and ninety young persons under the age of eighteen died.[21]

Most factory legislation applied equally to male and female workers but there was, of course, a suite of regulations concerned with restrictions on age and working hours which was directed specifically at women and young persons. By the early 1890s, employment under the age of eleven years was prohibited, but between eleven and thirteen most children became 'half-timers' permitted to work for up to six and a half hours each day as long as three hours had been spent in school. By 1890 there were just under one hundred thousand half-timers employed in British factories and workshops, roughly equal numbers of boys and girls.[22] Officially these children were supposed to be examined by a certifying surgeon to determine their age and their fitness for work. But as Adelaide soon discovered, abuse of both the system and the children was widespread. One child she suspended from employment was a small twelve-year-old girl called Annie whose appearance had attracted her attention. 'Deformed, undersized, knock-kneed, her feet turned inwards, thin and pale-faced, she seemed quite unfit for factory work,' Adelaide noted. 'It transpired that this piteous-looking little creature had been subjected – together with the other little half-timers in that room – to brutal treatment at the hands of the bullying overlooker;[23] she had not only been repeatedly cuffed, but on one occasion struck down by him. He did not deny it, but looked extremely shame-faced when I left him,'[24] she reported. Visiting this child at home a month later she was pleased to find her much better. 'What she seemed to appreciate most was not being obliged to get up at five o'clock in the morning; often when she first got up she could hardly stand, and could scarcely crawl to the mill.'[25] Many parents, however, looked forward to their children's thirteenth birthday when they could begin full-time work, provided, of course, they could produce a certificate showing successful completion of Educational Standard IV or, failing that, a five year attendance certificate. The latter was popularly known as the 'dunce's certificate' since it provided no evidence of any sort of educational progress. At fourteen even these restrictions disappeared, although those under the age of eighteen were still classified as 'young persons', a designation that attracted some limitations on their daily working hours and the jobs they could do. Unlike men, women were restricted to a maximum of fifty-six hours per week, and night work was prohibited for both women and children. This last provision appeared to rest largely on moral rather than health grounds. The risks posed by hours of darkness, particularly when males were present, could not, it seemed, be controlled within the confines of the workplace. And both women and children had been excluded completely from underground mines since 1842, when widely circulated illustrations of semi-naked men, women and children, working side by side in the heat of the coal seams, had shocked Victorian sensibilities.

Aside from the obvious difficulty of ascertaining the age of many a stunted, undernourished child, the apparently clear waters of working hours regulations were considerably muddied by a complex set of exemptions relating to overtime. This could, for example, be granted to dressmakers when 'the business is liable to a sudden press of orders arising from unforeseen events.'[26] As May wryly observed in her Annual Report for 1894, such concessions were usually granted for events that were, in fact, entirely foreseeable, such as the Queen's Drawing Rooms (presentations at court), Ascot, the Eton and Harrow cricket match and the Dublin Horse Show.[27] One wonders if Adelaide recalled her own presentation, two years earlier, with a new appreciation of the hours of labour that had gone into that beautiful white brocade gown. Certainly in future reports she would draw attention to the thoughtlessness of wealthy women who placed their orders for a new gown only a few days before an event and expected it to be delivered on time. The restrictions on working hours had always been central to feminist opposition to protective factory legislation for, it was argued, the regulations grouped women with children in terms of employment conditions and disadvantaged them in the labour market. Feminists dedicated to total equality were inclined to see the women factory inspectors as complicit in this form of oppression which they felt reaffirmed women as a weaker sex in need of special protection. By the 1890s, however, it was social feminism that was in ascendance and it was pragmatism that held sway amongst many prominent labour activists. Adelaide, herself, had clearly decided that principle could not be allowed to stand in the way of improving the desperate conditions of so many women. And in any case, she would always argue, better conditions for women were an important prerequisite for better conditions for men. They provided an example of how employment could and should be, for all workers.

In the early days, therefore, much of the energy of the women inspectors was expended on seeking out illegally employed young seamstresses and milliners hidden in obscure back workrooms, damp cellars and cramped attics. A great deal of this activity took place in central London where a subterranean workforce of thin, pale-faced girls slaved beneath the elegant showrooms of fashionable stores in places like Sloane Street, many just a few hundred yards from Emilia's luxurious six story residence. Here individual gowns were made to order for the wealthy and fashionable of London society. However, sweatshop conditions could also be found elsewhere, particularly in large cities. In Leeds, for example, tailoring had long been a traditional trade and, even after the introduction of mass produced clothing in the late nineteenth century, low skilled workers continued to be employed to carry out finishing work such as sewing on buttons and making pockets.

Somewhat paradoxically, the inspectors' own working hours would have frequently contravened the regulations they sought to enforce, for many of these hours were filled with provincial travel. The report of the Lady Inspectors for 1895 records that, between them, these four women visited a total of 2,358 factories and 4,599 workshops over the course of the year. In the process they covered over fifty-five thousand miles.[28] Travelling around alone, 'knocking about on trains' as Adela styled it, as well as staying in a series of unpredictable and indifferent hotels brought its own challenges to a young woman who, a few years earlier, had been prohibited from attending a lecture without the presence of a chaperone. Once more, it is Lucy's lively diary entries that give us a window on these experiences. Her first weeks had been spent in the relatively agreeable surroundings of the rural South Midlands where she had visited a succession of country towns, such as Hereford, Ledbury, Gloucester and Stroud. Here women factory inspectors were clearly considered to be of sufficient social standing to merit entry into the homes of the local gentry. It was a privilege that offered some respite from the hours spent in grimy factories and claustrophobic workshops. Based in the fashionable spa town of Malvern in Worcestershire, Lucy had been invited to tea with Lady Howard de Walden at her luxurious mansion, St James House, ('a palace!' Lucy noted). The other guests included a duchess (unspecified) and a Colonel Amerley. Leaving before dinner 'as I had no good clothes for the evening' Lucy was pleased to find that the local Imperial Hotel was 'gorgeous', which indeed it was. Seated amongst the luxuriant ferns of the residents' lounge she wrote of her pleasure when a band had played during the previous night's *table de hôte*, with a concert to follow.[29] For professional women of the period it was clearly useful to be socially comfortable amongst the rich and influential members of society. Adelaide was similarly at home in such an environment, always careful to cultivate her connections and mixing freely with the middle and upper classes. The rejected Miss Heaton, 'the factory girl genius', would presumably have struggled with the social demands of Victorian Malvern.

More typical, however, were Lucy's experiences in Stoke-on-Trent, 'a hideous town with no shops'[30] where the available accommodation was rather less extravagant. Like Lucy, Adelaide would have grown used to long uncomfortable railway journeys and dismal solitary dinners. Travelling northwards she encountered town after grimy town, whole districts where the sun struggled to penetrate the dense smoke from a thousand chimneys and where the dreary ugliness of it all threatened to overwhelm her. There were no lawns here carpeted with spring flowers, and the conversation and behaviour of the inhabitants was completely alien to a well brought up young lady from Hampstead. As she criss-crossed the country she met some of Sherard's *White Slaves of England*,[31] the women chainmakers of the Black Country, the nailmakers of Bromsgrove and the slipper makers of Leeds. In Macclesfield she found the child silk weavers and in Peterborough the women who loaded bricks into furnaces. She visited the hosiery knitters of Leicestershire where women were employed as teazle brushers, raising the nap of stockings and fleecy underwear and in Luton she chatted with those who sewed the linings and ribbons of straw hats for twelve hours each day. The industries about which she had written so carefully in the Labour Commission report now sprung all too vividly to life.

Back amongst the seamstresses and milliners in London, her inspection visits were frequently made after midnight to catch employers who forced their workers to continue beyond the statutory time limit, or infringed the prohibition on female night work. Sometimes Adelaide would wait outside small backstreet workshops and question workers as they emerged wearily in the early hours of the morning while on other occasions she would find workers strategically placed on watch at street corners, workshop doors or even railway stations. 'Fly, fly, inspectors,' they would cry as she was spotted hurrying round the corner. The elaborate game of cat and mouse would often descend into farce as youngsters, toiling by candlelight, were hurriedly put into beds to support the pretence that such children were not workers but simply inhabitants.[32] Sometimes whole families depended on the meagre wages of these young seamstresses. They were unlikely to betray the hand that fed them. Saturdays were particularly busy inspection days for this was supposed to be a half holiday but, in reality, for many workers, Saturday 'afternoon' began at 4.00 p.m. or even later. The rules governing the granting of overtime were a constant preoccupation. Too often, it seemed, the application of various exemptions meant regular fourteen-hour days, even for children. In this respect, at least, the northern mills were compliant with the law. Here Adelaide had observed that most young weavers and spinners could be sure of their complete half holiday on a Saturday. The textile trade, however, was an old, well-established and well-organised industry where many of the women were members of strong trade unions. Adelaide invariably maintained a suitable distance from such activity, but in the future she would occasionally express her approval of unions, particularly women's trade unions, as allies in the battle for social progress. Towards the end of her book *Women in the Factory* she would write of her hope that, increasingly, women would be 'empowered to act together to improve their own working lives' and that their 'share in self-government' would grow.[33] In the basements and attics of London during the 1890s, however, this prospect seemed remote.

In several countries on the continent of Europe, Adelaide noticed, hours of labour were much more limited than in

Britain. Even in 'more distant Hungary'[34] they had, since 1872, been reduced to ten per day. She was probably well aware that the presence of a law did not necessarily translate into action on the ground, but it was a start. Her command of detail was always unassailable. 'I may be permitted to hope that our law may not long remain behind the French law of 1892 (Section 1, Articles 3 and 4) which forbids overtime for persons under eighteen,' she observed, politely but pointedly in her Annual Report.[35] And in France the term 'industrial establishment' encompassed a much wider range of occupations than was the case in Britain. Many more French men and women appeared to enjoy protection under the law than did their British counterparts. Even menageries and infirmaries for dogs were subject to factory legislation! And then there was the question of fire regulations. Under French law there were extensive requirements for wide corridors between machinery, adequate numbers of exits and stairways, outward opening doors and external fire escapes on all floors. No such provisions existed in Britain, a situation compounded by the common practice of locking factory doors as soon as work began. Sadly the morning of the 11 January 1895 provided Adelaide with the opportunity to underline her point. When fire broke out in a large textile mill in Burnley, Lancashire, four hundred workers had rushed to the single exit and found the doors locked. Most had attempted to escape either by jumping from the roof or into the canal alongside the building. The official death toll was five, with two charred bodies taken from the rubble and three others never found, but many more suffered severe injuries that ended their working lives. There were, noted Adelaide, several other mills in the area where there were no fire escapes, where exits were inadequate and where the looms were so close together it was impossible to pass between them without turning sideways.[36]

As a fluent French and German speaker Adelaide's capacity for drawing attention to apparently superior legislation elsewhere was probably unequalled in the Factory Department and it was a skill she drew on frequently, producing detailed translations of foreign regulations for inclusion in her reports. In addition she published thoughtful pieces on the development of laws in Britain and in other countries, alluding to some of the legal and cultural differences which underpinned their contrasting approaches to similar problems. In 1902, for example, she wrote the introductory chapter to Thomas Oliver's comprehensive volume *Dangerous Trades*,[37] a compilation of all that was currently known about industrial diseases. The book would remain the most influential British work on the subject for many years. And a few years later, in 1911, she would be commissioned to write a piece for the latest edition of the *Encyclopaedia Britannica* which, over thirty four pages, covered the development of labour legislation from its early beginnings in the fifteenth century to its adoption in the nineteenth century, not only in Britain but in other countries across Europe and in the United States.[38] To some extent these endeavours provided an outlet for her considerable historical and philosophical inclinations, but they also had some very practical objectives. Industrial health and safety was increasingly the subject of international communication during the late Victorian and Edwardian periods. Meetings and conferences were attended by a growing cadre of experts keen to demonstrate the success of their new policies and techniques. Unfavourable international comparisons, particularly when they involved France, were always prone to provoke unease in the Home Office. Oram would have been well aware of the potency of this weapon as a driver for reform. In 1894 he noted in his Annual Report that he was 'indebted to Miss Anderson for a most interesting précis, attached to her report, of the regulations under factory laws in France.'[39] Adelaide had drawn attention, among other things, to the French prohibition on young persons operating power driven machinery. The importance of this, she commented, could be appreciated if one watched young girls of thirteen operating steam driven cutting equipment in British clothing factories. She was, however, equally impressed that the French did not allow young persons of either sex to participate in activity that threatened to 'injure their morals'.[40] The peculiar potency of the moral argument during this period had led to a French prohibition on the employment of youngsters in the 'preparation of writings, prints and bills', presumably liable to contain material unsuitable for young eyes. Adelaide clearly approved wholeheartedly. In Britain too, health, safety and morality, at least where women and children were concerned, had always been inextricably intertwined, and would continue to be so for many years.

At the end of 1895 Oram found himself once more indebted to Miss Anderson when a delegation arrived from the German government to discuss points of commonality in factory legislation. Her subsequent translation of German factory regulations, typically exhaustive in its detail, ran to fifty pages.[41] One factor to emerge from this impressive, if somewhat overwhelming document was the more advanced state of German legislation in relation to workplace ventilation. It was a subject Adelaide was keen to pursue. In Britain the conditions in which many women and girls worked were seriously overcrowded, cold in winter, overheated in summer and generally pervaded by foul, smelly air. Few dressmakers would allow open windows that might admit sooty particles, spelling disaster for new shirts and gowns. Open fires created a similar problem such that many employers opted for flueless gas stoves that emitted carbonic oxide (carbon monoxide), sometimes with tragic consequences. It was an opportune moment to raise the subject of ventilation, for the importance of clean air was a growing public concern. Steeped in medical notions of oxygen-starved 'vitiated' atmosphere, which harboured all kinds of threatening impurities, the better parts of society were increasingly worried. Towns were full of smoke and suffocating fogs and there was sewer gas arising from pavement drains, or worse, from the newly fashionable indoor water closets. Now the noxious vapours emanating from the seething masses could actually enter their own homes. In London travellers were subject to yet more threatening fumes if they ventured on to the recently constructed underground railways. The combination of steam trains and tunnels could make for an unpleasant journey. The fact that impurities in the air could now be measured, far from providing reassurance, tended to increase anxiety. Eminent scientist John Scott Haldane, who had developed his techniques in the coal mines of Lancashire and Yorkshire, was now turning his attention to other forms of noxious gas. A few years later he would be asked to produce a report on ventilation in underground workshops.

Sanitation was another subject close to Adelaide's heart. By sanitation she meant lavatories, specifically female lavatories. She was amazed and disgusted by the complete absence of such facilities for women and girls in many factories and workshops. Again, moral matters were to the fore. The low standard of decency, she said, where both sexes congregated together and where there was a marked absence of privy doors, inflicted injury on the moral character of children and young persons. Many such lavatories faced directly on to yards where men were at work. One of her first prosecutions involved a textile factory in Wigan where the owner had repeatedly ignored her instructions to remedy this situation and to deal with the problem of escaping 'effluvia'. The mill owner not only received a substantial fine but found himself required to reconstruct part of his factory to improve sanitary arrangements and to provide suitable female accommodation. Many employers considered that the preoccupation of the lady factory inspectors with lavatories represented an attempt to impose middle class sensibilities on a largely unconcerned workforce. Conditions, as one such employer was keen to point out, were much the same as those the workers experienced at home. Mary Paterson was unimpressed by this argument. 'The existence of one evil, though greatly to be deplored, seems hardly a good excuse for the toleration of another,' she observed succinctly.[42] And, more often than not, complaints about a lack of female facilities and privacy emanated from the workers themselves. In each of their early reports the lady inspectors were careful to list the number and the nature of the enquiries about working conditions they had received. Interestingly many of those investigated by Adelaide came via her contacts within the Women's Co-operative Guild. Those afternoon tea parties in Toynbee Hall were now paying social dividends and Rosalind was proving a staunch ally, producing a stream of Guild pamphlets which explained, in plain language, the terms of the factory regulations and urging women to take their complaints to the lady inspectors. Asquith's contention that women workers would feel more able to approach other women with their concerns had, it seems, been vindicated.

The actions, or rather the inactions, of another local government agency, the Sanitary Department, which operated under Public Health regulations, were a further source of frustration. Seriously overworked, the sanitary inspectors who patrolled each town and city were responsible for a huge range of 'public nuisances' including water quality, waste disposal, the cleanliness of houses and streets and, importantly, the sanitary and ventilation arrangements in small workshops. Factory inspectors were required to report any such defects, a responsibility they undertook with considerable enthusiasm, bombarding the Sanitary Department with an ever-increasing mountain of reports. But here their involvement in the matter effectively came to an end. The failure of the Public Health authorities to act on their reports represented a constant source of irritation to the Factory Department while the preoccupation of factory inspectors with apparently trivial matters was equally provoking to many an over worked sanitary inspector. It was a gulf that could sometimes be bridged by co-operative effort in some of the smaller districts, but in large cities it was a black hole into which many a pressing matter disappeared never to resurface. Adelaide, with her special interest in 'sanitary matters' became convinced that the interests of women workers were not well served by these current arrangements. In time she would manage to wrestle the responsibility for ventilation and sanitation in small workshops away from the Public Health Department and into the Factory Department, where she considered it belonged.

Many women workers were worried about another source of 'moral injury' to young persons, the objectionable and abusive language and 'immoral' behaviour of factory overlookers. Explicit evidence of sexual abuse or exploitation is difficult to find but the frequent references to 'moral injury' in the reports of the women inspectors may well have masked some more disturbing complaints which could not be mentioned in official reports. There was however no such taboo on the reporting of straightforward physical violence. On a cold March day in 1895 Adelaide encountered an employer who had turned a fire hose on a group of forty young weavers as a disciplinary measure. The filthy water drawn from the mill pond had been directed over a partition into a narrow vestibule where the workers were trapped, having taken refuge there following some kind of dispute and angry exchange with the foreman. Adelaide arrived to find these young girls soaked and freezing, many of them with several miles to walk home. She does not mention the source of the 'angry exchange' but she reported that she secured an apology from the foreman, and the provision of facilities to dry the girls' clothes.[43] She was, however, forced to admit that she could do nothing further within the limits of the law. The inadequacy of existing regulations, particularly as they applied to women, was something Adelaide encountered with increasing regularity during her early days as a factory inspector. She was particularly preoccupied with what she termed 'welfare', a field largely unregulated by the state during this period and thus neglected by the factory inspectorate. Matters such as sanitation, washing facilities and comfortable places for workers to eat their meals had never been the territory of male inspectors and Adelaide's focus on such matters seemed to imply a belief that women's occupational needs were different to those of men. She undoubtedly considered that a major role of the women inspectors was to make factories and workshops fit places for women to work. It was a position that invited criticism from both trade unions and 'equality' feminists who resented any suggestion that women were being branded as 'the weaker sex'. Adelaide would always counter this with her belief that welfare for women simply provided a model for the type of conditions that should exist for both sexes in all workplaces. But for the moment it was the women who commanded her attention. She would continue to worry away at 'welfare matters', throughout her tenure as an inspector but her aspirations in this field would only be fully realised during the First World War, and then for rather different reasons.

In the meantime, other matters were coming to the fore in the more traditional hunting grounds of the Factory Inspectorate. Increasingly, attention was turning to the consequences of the various forms of industrial poisoning such that industrial diseases, as well as industrial accidents, were now becoming the concern of the state. The Factory Act of 1895 had identified six such diseases as requiring notification to the Home Office. The list, consisting of ankylostomiasis,[44] anthrax, and poisoning by lead, arsenic, mercury and phosphorus, was a short and curious one, determined more by considerations of diagnostic certainty than any ambition to be comprehensive in its coverage of industrial disease. However, with the exception of ankylostomiasis, all of these 'notifiable' diseases, were liable to occur in places where women worked. In her first year as an inspector Adelaide had largely avoided the kind of premises where workers' health was affected by poisonous dust or fumes, despite being instructed by Oram to include these in her schedule. She cited lack of time. Probably, however, she also felt inadequate in the face of industrial processes she barely understood. By the end of 1895, however, she had begun to make some initial forays into this unfamiliar territory. Her first encounters were to be with dust, the scourge of so many industrial workers, and most particularly with that most ubiquitous of poisons, lead.

Chapter Six
THE SUFFERING OF SISTERS

Dust seemed to be everywhere in the 'lighter' work carried out by women. It choked their respiratory passages as they laboured at occupations like fur pulling, rag sorting, flock mattress stuffing and coal sorting. Significantly the women inspectors were the first to highlight the potential dangers of asbestos exposure when, in 1898, they encountered girls of fourteen carrying out the work of sifting, mixing and carding, 'without the least possible attempt to subdue the dust.' 'A microscopic examination of this mineral dust,'[1] Lucy observed, 'shows the sharp glass-like, jagged nature of the particles, and when they are allowed to rise and to remain suspended in the air of a room, in any quantity, the effects have been found to be injurious.' Somewhat prophetically she added that 'the worker falls into ill-health and sinks away out of sight in no sudden or sensational manner so that attention is seldom attracted to the ultimate source of the trouble.'[2] The propensity of the women inspectors to visit workers in their own homes made them uniquely sensitive to the potential long-term effects of poisonous dust. They could not have known the true scale of the insidious, lethal effects of asbestos exposure and the terrible death toll yet to come. But a few years later, in 1906, after Adelaide had found one asbestos works where 'the atmosphere is of a thick whitey-yellow consistency with larger particles floating about therein', inspector Hilda Martindale reported that several of the workers there were 'very hoarse' and 'suffered from a bad cough.'[3] Visiting the home of one woman who had died at the age of twenty-four from 'consumption', she found that this particular worker had been employed for six years as an asbestos spinner and had been too ill to work for ten months immediately before her death. It was rather curious, Hilda mused, that no other member of the family suffered from 'consumption'. In terms of the long-term epidemiological investigations that would finally identify 'the ultimate source of the trouble', Hilda's subsequent comment was perhaps even more prophetic. 'Much time for patient research among workers who have dropped out of this employment is necessary before any true idea can be formed of the effect of the process.'[4]

There were of course numerous other poisonous dusts which occupied the attention of the women inspectors during this period. Adelaide watched young girls 'bronzing' in lithographic printing works, dusting the borders of prints with fine metallic powder to create the effect of gold, silver or lustrous red and green. In Blackburn, Lancashire, young children were employed in this process to produce Christmas cards, using 'rough and ready methods' and working long hours for low pay. Elsewhere young workers were employed to decorate metal items. The lips and faces of the girls were coated with powder and their hair was full of it. Many workers suffered from diarrhoea and vomiting, anaemia and eruptions of the skin. After the death of one girl who had been illuminating tin plate boxes and the admission to Guy's Hospital of another, May sent off some samples of the powder for analysis. This revealed the presence of copper, zinc, aluminium and an aniline dye. Red bronze contained sulphide of mercury while gold and silver bronzes contained antimony. 'In France the employment of persons under sixteen at bronzing is prohibited, as it is in tinfoil works,' Adelaide remarked, quoting for good measure 'the French Decree of May

13, 1893, Schedule C.'[5] More directly, however, she wanted to know why such industries were not covered by 'Special Rules'. These were supplementary requirements intended to provide special protection for workers employed in high-risk industries. They were already applied, for example, in the use of the popular and poisonous pigment Scheele's Green, a colourant for fabrics and wallpapers that contained arsenic. In this case employers and managers were bound to supply workers with overalls, capable of being closed at the neck and wrists, as well as masks, moistened sponges and canvas working gloves, all of which must be frequently washed. Special Rules, however, remained somewhat limited in their application. They had first been introduced under the Factory Act of 1891 following the recommendations of the Dangerous Trades Committees. But under the Act interested parties, and most notably employers, retained the right to lodge objections to any proposed new Rules prior to their implementation and to enter into a process of arbitration over their scope and content. It was a right that would soon be swept away by the Factory Act of 1901, but in the late 1890s such objections invariably resulted in a prolonged period of negotiation, a wearisome, time-consuming process, widely abused by those wishing to delay the introduction of the new Rules.

Adelaide was learning that the introduction of factory regulations to reduce the toll of industrial disease was a far from straightforward process. Invariably it involved a long struggle with numerous interested parties. Nowhere was this more evident than in the case of lead. There were 1,030 reported cases of lead poisoning in 1897 of which just over four hundred were in women.[6] This was the first year in which industrial disease registers, compiled from the recently introduced notification system, were fully available. There were, no doubt, numerous shortcomings in the collection and recording of these data for this was an untried system, but even allowing for such difficulties it is clear from the figures that lead poisoning effectively eclipsed everything else as a source of industrial ill health. The number of cases of anthrax, the next highest figure, numbered only twenty-three that year.[7] Lead poisoning was hardly a new disease. Its symptoms had been described by Hippocrates in 370 BC, and four hundred years later Pliny observed the same condition in Roman ship painters who used lead-based paint. They suffered from colic and anaemia, blindness and neurological problems and experienced convulsions that were sometimes fatal. So pervasive was the use of lead in cooking pots and wine vessels it has even been suggested that this pernicious metal was partially responsible for the decline of the Roman Empire. Lead was equally ubiquitous in Victorian society. Most obviously it provided roofing materials and water pipes, but it was also an essential ingredient in the manufacture of paints and dyes, printing materials, pottery, tiles, ceramic insulators, glassware, tin boxes and a host of other metal and decorative goods. Most recently it had become an essential ingredient in the development of the electrical battery or 'accumulator'. For the industrial worker, lead was increasingly difficult to avoid.

One place where women workers encountered lead was in the white lead works of London and the North East of England. It was the problems in this industry that had finally persuaded the Home Office of the need for women inspectors. White lead, otherwise known as lead carbonate, was a pigment added to paint to increase its durability and covering power. For hundreds of years it had been produced using a technique known as the 'Dutch method', developed in the Netherlands and brought to England in the late eighteenth century by a lead merchant in Hull called John Picard. The process made use of a simple chemical reaction which took place when coils of bluish coloured metallic lead were stacked over pots containing vinegar (acetic acid) and placed on a bed of tanbark. In the presence of carbon dioxide emitted by the fermenting tanbark

Inside a white lead works in 1897. (From The White Slaves of England, Robert Sherard, 1910.)

a reaction between the lead and the vinegar produced lead carbonate. Over a period of weeks, therefore, the so-called 'blue beds' became 'white beds', a metamorphosis that created a significant industrial hazard. White lead, now encrusting the metallic coils, was in the form of a powder that was shovelled out of the 'white beds', after which it was crushed between rollers, washed, dried, emptied out of the stoves and put into sacks. The women workers who carried out these processes inhaled vast quantities of lead-laden dust and took home still more in their hair and the folds of their clothes. Unsurprisingly large numbers succumbed to lead poisoning, a disease manifested in symptoms ranging in severity from intestinal colic to convulsions and coma. Victims suffered from neurological problems such as tremor or palsy, most commonly affecting the hands and known as 'wrist drop'. And from a woman's point of view there was another, special problem. Lead was a foetal poison which all too often resulted in spontaneous abortions, stillbirths, or sickly children who died young.

For much of the nineteenth century the plight of these workers had excited little public interest. Lead work was dirty, unpleasant and badly paid. According to a contemporary pamphlet produced by the Humanitarian League[8] in 1893 the industry was 'the preserve of women of the very poorest and roughest class', a group which apparently included 'the widow who has a family to support, the wife of a drunken husband and the girl whose character will not bear scrutiny.'[9] White lead production was a miserable business, totally invisible to those who enjoyed the aesthetic appeal of sparkling white paint. It seemed an unlikely setting for the development of new innovative approaches to the practice of industrial health. Yet in the 1890s this unreformed industry became the centre of a public storm. Initial concerns about white lead production had been raised by Poor Law officials, worried about the numbers of seriously ill and destitute lead workers seeking shelter in the workhouse. Adelaide had first become acquainted with the problem when she had summarised the results of investigations undertaken for the Labour Commission. Regulations introduced in 1885, which required the watering down of the 'white beds' and the temporary suspension of workers showing symptoms of illness, seem to have made little impact on the toll of sickness and death. She had been shocked by the stories of women who suffered from paralysis, epileptic fits and blindness. Particularly dreadful were the tales of dead or dying children. Rosalind's husband, Vaughan Nash, had launched a savage attack on the industry in successive editions of the *Daily Chronicle* in December 1892, describing how lead was 'unavoidably gasped into the lungs, swallowed in the saliva, and absorbed through the skin.'[10]

In September 1893, while Adelaide was working for the Labour Commission, she had read the report submitted by May to the East London Coroner on the death of Annie Case, aged nineteenth, a worker at the Millwall White Lead Company.[11] Annie's death, which had occurred on the 9 August, was by no means the first fatality from this cause, but the public was by now highly sensitized to the plight of female lead workers. During the previous twelve months Annie had been medically suspended from work twice. Each time she had returned to work, the doctor had reported her to be 'pale but well'. When she died, four weeks after her last suspension, she was reported to be suffering from colic, anaemia, and severe brain damage. The doctor called to certify her death reported a classic sign of high exposure to lead, a marked blue-coloured line along her gums.[12] The Reverend Frederick Newland, who ran the Canning Town Settlement and Home for Working Girls where Annie had lived was also called to the stand. Many of the girls employed at the works were often ill, he said. Annie's sister was currently suspended from work on medical grounds.[13] She, however, had gained a temporary respite from the poisonous dust. She had 'gone hoppin'' in Kent.[14]

May's report found no evidence that the firm had flouted the existing regulations but, she concluded, the regulations themselves were inadequate to protect women from lead poisoning. In her opinion female workers must be completely excluded from employment in the dustier parts of the works. Dr Thomas Oliver, Consultant Physician at the Newcastle Infirmary and widely considered to be the foremost expert on lead poisoning, agreed. Women, he believed, were clearly more susceptible to all forms of lead poisoning than were men and, moreover, lead exposure specifically threatened the health of pregnant women and their unborn children. In the former conclusion he was ultimately to be proved wrong, but the latter at least was an incontrovertible truth, sadly well-known to many desperate Victorian women who resorted to the ingestion of lead in the form of diachylon to end unwanted pregnancies.[15]

Following Annie's inquest, Oram had detailed May and Mary Paterson to investigate the number of cases of lead poisoning in six of the larger white lead works. Finding that 70 per cent of female workers and only 9 per cent of males, succumbed to the disease, May considered that the results of this investigation showed 'in a remarkable manner the greater susceptibility of women' to lead poisoning.[16] It was perhaps a questionable conclusion for men were invariably employed in much less dusty work such as loading sacks on to carts. But her findings were more than sufficient to convince officials at the Home Office. Moreover, Dr Oliver had provided her with information about ten cases of women lead workers who had suffered numerous miscarriages or the early deaths of their children. Later that year, therefore, further Special Rules were drafted and submitted to white lead manufacturers. One aspect of these Rules, the selective prohibition of women and girls from employment in parts of the works, was to become the subject of a bitter and long fought battle. Home Office Permanent Secretary Edward Troup was probably well prepared for the onslaught that followed this particular proposal. Employers were, of course, convinced they would be ruined. Samuel Tudor, lead and paint manufacturer of Hull, whose grandfather had established the first British white lead works with John Picard, gave vent to a familiar raft of concerns. He complained that the exclusion of women would add immensely to the cost of manufacture. The industry would then move abroad. It would become extinct in Britain. The foreign manufacturer, unhampered by legislation, could obtain cheaper labour, had cheaper transport costs, and there was no tariff against his goods. Ultimately, he concluded, the greatest loss would be to the women themselves.[17] At least some of the women seemed to agree. Five hundred of those employed in the North East added their names, or at least their mark, to a petition that arrived on the desk of the Home Secretary in 1896. 'Many of us are widows,' it said, 'with large families to support – others have no means of getting a living except by this kind of work.'[18]

The proposal also provoked outrage amongst 'equality' feminists. Not since the Mines Act of 1842 had women been legally excluded from any form of employment. What would be the fate of those vulnerable workers turned out of the only work available to them? How far was this policy driven by middle class opinion that women should not work at all? Dr Oliver, whose medical views had been so influential was also, it seems, a leading exponent of the view that a woman's place was most definitely in the home. The nation, he argued, needed women to fulfil their natural domestic role, to produce and rear strong healthy children. The Home Office decision had also been taken against a background of popular opinion that the needs of the worker were, for the most part, subordinate to those of production. Many people continued to believe that the onus was on the worker to withstand the exigencies of working conditions, rather than on the employer to provide a fit place to work. In 1893, for example, when a potter called Edward Dunn wrote to the local factory inspector to express his concerns about the health of kiln men exposed to high levels of lead, he received a distinctly unsympathetic reply. Mr Dawkins-Cramp, Superintending Inspector for the Midlands region, begged to inform him that enamel kiln men were *adult males* (Dawkins-Cramp's emphasis) and therefore well able to take care of themselves. In this context the exclusion of women from parts of the white lead industry was a highly unusual step, and one that seemed to reveal an assumption that women needed a degree of protection that men did not. The guns of 'equality feminists' were now turned with considerable ferocity, not only on Dr Oliver but also on the Home Office and more particularly on the women inspectors. Here was a vindication of feminist misgivings about protective legislation aimed selectively at women. In their view May's report, the product of a Civil Servant but more particularly a woman Civil Servant, had provided the Home Office with the official justification for this iniquitous policy. Newly appointed lady factory inspectors currently enjoying their own professional advancement should, they argued, consider the employment rights of their 'sisters' in the industrial workplace. Invited to a meeting of the Women's Emancipation Union,[19] Lucy and Adelaide were left in no doubt about the views of its members. Only regulation that applied equally to men and women could be endorsed by members of the Union they were told. The white lead regulations threatened to create a precedent that would regulate women out of their jobs as well as their freedom. Women needed the vote and an equal footing with men in the workplace, not protection. Suffrage leader Jane Brownlow, was uncompromising. 'Any law which places full-grown women in the position of a helpless, irresponsible child, who must be legislated for, has the effect of creating and fostering an opinion that women are helpless, irresponsible beings, incapable of taking care of their own interests.'[20]

It was a difficult beginning for an inexperienced inspector and a sobering introduction to the complex nature of industrial health regulation. Adelaide and her colleagues had by now become the target of both employer hostility and feminist fury. Lucy was predictably angry, giving vent in her diary to her helpless exasperation at the official embargo on their right to reply. Adelaide's attitude meanwhile can probably be discerned by the brief contents of a note she wrote to Beatrice Webb in 1896. Beatrice was preoccupied with similar issues to those which concerned the Emancipation Union and was seeking Adelaide's opinion on a paper she had written on the subject of working hours regulations, aimed specifically at women. Adelaide, rushing to catch a train for her next inspection appointment, apologised for turning down Beatrice's accompanying invitation to afternoon tea and wrote a rather hurried reply. Defending the need for legislation in its current form, she concluded 'The case for factory legislation rests quite as much on what has been done – Do you not think so? – as on what might be done'. In other words, she seemed to be saying, we have to deal with things as they are, not as they might be or ought to be.[21]

Adelaide was also, of course, unswervingly loyal to her masters in the Home Office. She considered it was her duty to implement their decisions, whatever her private thoughts. However, it is more than likely that she did indeed agree with the exclusion of women from parts of the white lead industry. The decision was informed by current medical beliefs about the special susceptibility of women to lead poisoning, beliefs shared by Adelaide and the other women inspectors. In this context exclusion can be seen simply as a practical solution to an immediate problem. While Adelaide and her colleagues saw themselves as acting in the interests of their suffering sisters, therefore, supporters of the Emancipation Union considered the action to be an infringement of women's right to choose. Meanwhile, amidst the hail of criticism directed at the lady inspectors some support did arrive, from an unexpected quarter. Prominent women's trade union leader, Mary MacArthur was, naturally enough, a strong supporter of women's employment rights and of the pre-eminent role of union organisation as a driver for labour reform. But, like Emilia, she saw no inherent contradiction between union influence and state intervention in the form of protective legislation. It was not regulation *per se* that posed a problem, just the nature of that regulation. And in this case she was more than prepared to accept pragmatism over principal and, exceptionally, support the policy of exclusion. Her decision rested largely on the grounds that lead exposure threatened the lives of unborn children. For everyone involved, especially officials at the Home Office, the furore that developed over the white lead regulations proved to be an early lesson in the complexities of industrial health regulation. It was an area of policy development that would present significantly different challenges to that relating to industrial safety and accident prevention. And at this particular juncture the economic interests of the employers continued to hold considerable sway. The owners of white lead works managed to fight off the implementation of the exclusion policy for nearly three years. One firm, in particular, was granted a period of grace on the grounds of the costs involved. This was Locke, Lancaster and Johnson Ltd, owners of the Millwall works where Annie Case had been employed.

In the long run, exclusion proved to be as unsuccessful as it was unpopular. Far from being controlled, the risk from lead exposure was simply transferred to other groups of workers. Thus, in the years that followed, scores of male Italian immigrants, who took the place of women in the lead works of the East End, succumbed to lead poisoning.[22] It was not, after all, just a woman's problem. Women were not of course prohibited from working in every part of the white lead works, just the notorious whitebeds and drying stoves and amidst the outcry over this exclusion other aspects of the Special Rules were somehow forgotten. If the exclusion policy had seemed to some to be a regressive one, the measures which accompanied it were much more forward looking, a taste of things to come. Each employer was now required to install a hood connected to a fan in areas where lead was packed and stored. And these women of 'the very poorest and roughest class' found themselves provided with overalls and head coverings as well as new shoes and stockings, exclusively to wear at work. They were also required to wear 'respirators', cambric bags which covered the nose and mouth, to eat their meals in separate dining rooms, wash their hands regularly and take weekly baths. And it was the employer who was responsible for providing all these facilities.

During Adelaide's second year as an inspector, she was dispatched first to Millwall and then to the North East to enforce these regulations. It was to be a significant learning experience. Tramping through the grime of the leadworks, her own long skirts a considerable inconvenience, she expected to meet hostility or, at best, sullen resentment from the women. For a previous report by a male inspector had described them as 'degraded' and 'dissipated', careless of their own safety and unwilling to help themselves.[23] What she found was a workforce highly concerned about the risk of this industrial disease and anxious to talk about the difficulties of keeping clean in such a dirty environment. A few were indeed reluctant to consider their own safety and their fellow workers knew exactly who they were. Most, however, were ready and willing to take advantage of the new regulations. Adelaide listened as they described the discomfort of ill fitting face masks and their personal revulsion at wearing those worn, unwashed, by another worker the day before. She talked to employers about these problems and how they might be addressed. She identified deficiencies in record keeping. How did the manager monitor the number of baths, the timing of medical inspections, suspensions and re-employment, and how did they prevent desperate poverty stricken women, suspended from one works, simply walking down the road and gaining employment at another? It is difficult to know where she gained the experience to carry out these inspections. In her book of 1921 she would confess that it was a lack of insight into her own ignorance and the 'idealising power of youth' which carried her through these early days.[24]

Lead poisoning had occupied much of the women inspectors' time during the years since their appointment, but by 1900 there were of course five other notifiable industrial diseases that claimed the attention of the Factory Department. If lead was everywhere in Victorian society, then so were matches. During the nineteenth century everything associated with lighting, heating and cooking, not to mention smoking, required the application of a match. The match of choice was the 'lucifer'. Tipped with white phosphorus[25] it could be struck on any available surface, instantly producing a fluorescent glow. The dominant matchmaking firm in the country was Bryant and May, occupying an enormous site in the East End of London. It was the largest employer of female labour in the area, with women and girls accounting for more than three quarters of its two thousand workers. In the summer of 1888 the factory had acquired a celebrated place in labour history when it played host to the first industrial action by British women workers. Many of the women employed at Bryant and May were of Irish descent with familial links to another major employment group, the London dockers. As a precursor to the London Dock Strike the action of the matchgirls would have provided Adelaide, lecturing at Toynbee Hall, with her first taste of the anger and resentment simmering amongst the impoverished labouring classes.

The strike of the matchgirls, however, had been provoked not by the unhealthy conditions in the workplace, but by exceptionally low wages and an unjust system of deductions from pay. Nevertheless, it brought to the public's attention another, significantly more horrific aspect of employment in the match factory, a particularly nasty industrial disease called phosphorus necrosis. Known locally as 'phossy jaw' this condition developed over weeks or months among workers who inhaled fumes of white phosphorus as the tips of matches were dipped into vats of heated phosphorus paste. Once absorbed into the body, phosphorus rendered parts of the bone, particularly the jawbone, susceptible to infection. Those already suffering from dental decay were especially vulnerable. It was a horrible disease, beginning with severe toothache and swelling of the jaw and progressing to putrid, evil smelling abscesses of the cheeks and gums. The prolonged untreatable infection led to loss of

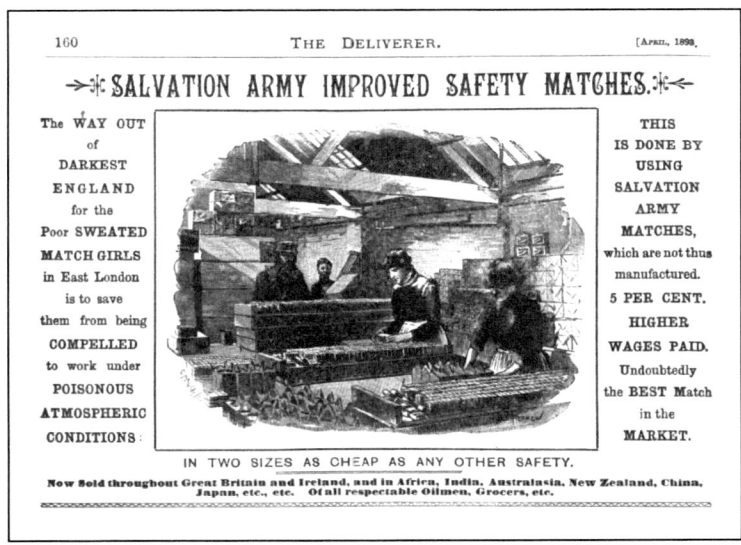

Advert for 'Lights in Darkest England', 1893, showing the Box Room at the Salvation Army Factory. (Reproduced with the permission of the Salvation Army International Heritage Centre.)

parts of the jawbone such that that the victims suffered an inability to eat and increasing disfigurement, often retreating from view to face a lonely and painful death.

The dangers inherent in the use of white phosphorus, if imperfectly understood,[26] had been known at least since the 1850s. Charles Dickens had published a popular account of the problem in *Household Words* in 1852, which was based on a number of articles in medical journals.[27] In 1891, the Salvation Army had set up its own match factory in the East End of London in an attempt to protect the workers' health. Here they produced 'Lights in Darkest England' paying their workers more than those employed at Bryant and May and using red rather than white phosphorus, a safe substitute. The factory managed to continue functioning for ten years, in the process saving numerous workers from the horrors of phossy jaw, but red phosphorus was significantly more expensive than white phosphorus and rather less inclined to ignite, and thus their matches proved less popular with the public. By 1901 the factory was forced to close, ironically being taken over by Bryant and May the following year.

The Home Office meanwhile was in difficulties. As a result of the strike the matchmakers were now highly visible on the national stage. Newspaper coverage, this time emanating from the increasingly popular *Star*, was unrelenting. In 1894 representatives of a number of European countries met in Berne, Switzerland, to consider a complete ban on the use of white phosphorus. Most agreed but the British government, closely focussed on the profits of Bryant and May's shareholders, (which included a number of prominent clergy and Liberal MPs) was reluctant to go down such a route. Their commitment to alleviating the problem remained distinctly lukewarm. The number of cases of 'phossy jaw', they argued, was really quite small. This unsupported assertion was based, apparently, on the very few gruesomely disfigured people prepared to wander about the streets and testify to the cause of their condition. Adelaide and her colleagues in the factory inspectorate, who had toured the workers' homes seeking out these victims, knew a different story.

For the British government, however, the solution lay in the application of more Special Rules. Thus, in 1895, Adelaide was dispatched on another of her first enforcement missions.

It proved to be a similarly instructive introduction to the practice of factory inspection and the frustrations inherent in confronting influential employers. The Rules required the provision of ventilation and the separation of dipping rooms from the boxing area where most of the women worked. May had already discovered the reason why so many women were victims of 'phossy jaw', despite the fact that they were rarely employed in the dipping process itself. Most factories had placed the dipping baths on the ground floor such that fumes rose to fill the rooms above where women packed the matches. Here ventilation appeared to be completely inadequate. In one factory it consisted simply of opening the top part of windows down one side of the room.

Adelaide's somewhat pedantic nature was in many ways ideally suited to the task of explaining the niceties of the law. Not only did she consult the official 'Blue Books', which contained the details of factory regulations and inspections but also, it seems, the latest edition of the *Oxford English Dictionary*. Thus armed she was always ready to confront employers with unassailable detail. In this case, she concluded 'No employer in England could possibly object' to the installation of mechanical ventilation. The Special Rules required 'effectual' and 'efficient' means, 'both natural and mechanical', to be taken 'to prevent the fumes from penetrating to parts of the factory distinct from where they arise.'[28] She was careful to acquaint employers with the precise definition of all of these words. She would discover, of course, that employers could and did object and that it was often the biggest employers, conscious of their power and influence, who were the worst offenders. During the next three years she struggled unsuccessfully to enforce what she considered to be the obvious requirements of the Special Rules. However, in 1898 Bryant and May was discovered to be systematically concealing cases of 'phossy jaw' that should have been notified to the Home Office. Journalists at the

Daily Chronicle and the *Star* identified fifty-one cases that had occurred during a period when the company had claimed there were none. More cases were discovered at Morelands in Gloucestershire, the makers of 'England's Glory' matches. One had necessitated the surgical removal of part of the victim's jawbone. Henry Cunynghame, an assistant under secretary at the Home Office noted that:

> Bryant and May in London and Mssrs Moreland of Gloucester, appear to have adopted a systematic method of concealing necrosis cases, by having them treated by their own doctor, omitting to report them and giving the work people pensions contingent upon their keeping their illness secret.[29]

Morelands was fined the somewhat paltry sum of 10*s.*, plus costs of £2 6*s. 6d.*[30] Bryant and May meanwhile was prosecuted in a highly publicised case and fined £20. This was the highest penalty available to the courts at the time although many thought it inadequate. The *Daily Telegraph* considered that the owners of Bryant and May deserved to go to prison[31] while the *Westminster Gazette* argued that the case demonstrated the need for more inspectors, and in particular 'a much larger proportion of women inspectors.'[32] By contrast a prominent article in *The Times* maintained that the government should resist 'hasty and sweeping legislation', and 'avoid the expense of increasing the already vast army of government inspectors.' White phosphorus 'was not necessarily dangerous to health,' they argued. It could be rendered virtually safe by 'personal cleanliness' and adherence to a few simple rules.[33] Much to the disappointment of the Factory Department it was this opinion that held sway. The scandal at Bryant and May failed to move the government's position and it would be another ten years before Britain would finally fall into line with countries on the Continent of Europe and institute a total ban on the use of white phosphorus. For

Adelaide it was a hard lesson in the politics of industrial health and safety. And, strangely, Aunt Elizabeth Garrett's sister, Millicent Fawcett, a strident campaigner for women's rights, strongly defended Bryant and May. After touring the factory she wrote a long letter to *The Standard,* and a few days later another one to *The Times*, describing conditions there as good. It was clean and airy, she said. Bryant and May were good employers who had simply made a mistake in breaching the Factory Acts.[34] Millicent, however, was a shareholder in Bryant and May. It was not, perhaps, her finest hour.

Elsewhere in the country there were more concerns over dust. Over two thousand women and young girls were employed in the flax mills of Ireland, Scotland and the North of England, most in the process of 'hackling', which involved pulling the flax through a large comb to split and straighten the fibres. Hackling produced a prodigious amount of dust and Special Rules, proposed in 1894, required the workers to wear respirators. In this case the subversive tactics of employers seem to have been aided and abetted by a somewhat ineffective factory inspector. Mr Osborne, a superintending inspector, had visited all three flax processing areas to review the situation and secure the support of manufacturers in the provision of masks. Returning to London he declared himself fully satisfied and rather pleased. Meeting with employers' representatives in each area he had found that they all 'approached the subject with great breadth of mind and public spirit.'[35] Virtually every firm in the United Kingdom had initially lodged objections but now most firms were in complete agreement, he reported. They just needed more time to implement the Special Rules and a few modifications, which in no way impaired the scope of the Rules. Most had, in any case, already introduced face masks, he added, some even anticipating the new Rules and others buying the most expensive masks at 3s. 6d. each.

The report of the Lady Inspectors, some twelve months

later, painted a less optimistic picture of the situation on the ground. The women inspectors were generally of the opinion that guileless young children made more reliable witnesses than either older workers or those in charge. Employers or their representatives, meanwhile, were the least likely to give a full and frank account. Visiting one mill, May enquired of a small girl why she was not wearing a respirator. 'I did not know the inspector was coming,' the child replied innocently. At another mill the manager claimed that respirators had been in use for many months. Here Lucy found small girls struggling with 'brilliantly new ones . . . as with a mysterious object, uncertain upon which part of their person to wear it.' It was, said one, 'given to me five minutes ago Miss.' Mary Paterson, visiting flax mills in Forfarshire, provided a bleak assessment of the situation there. She had not found respirators worn in any of the factories she had visited, nor had she found any attempt on the part of those in authority to secure the wearing of them. 'Children and young persons seldom appear to have even heard of such things,' she remarked tersely.[36] Adelaide decided on a systematic survey in one area to supplement these narratives. Careful to avoid any accusations of bias she noted that she had selected children at random in the chosen factory, following which she made a meticulous record. AB, for example, aged fourteen, 'thought she had worn a respirator for half an hour once but could not remember when'; CD, aged thirteen, without a respirator, never told to wear one; EF, aged eleven,without a respirator, never given one nor asked to wear one; GH, aged eleven, at work in the factory a week, never saw a respirator; IK, aged thirteen, at work two years, never given a respirator, and so on. In general, managers were defensive. The wearing of a respirator was the child's 'own look out', they said. None of them wanted to wear them and the foremen were powerless to insist. Lucy was unimpressed by this 'particularly callous disregard of the youngsters' welfare.' She had, she declared

scathingly, 'been solemnly advised by more than one mill
owner and his managers and the foreman, that their united will
was powerless to cope with the inclinations of a tiny child of
twelve years.' This, she remarked was 'all the more noteworthy
when it is remembered how strict is the discipline, and how
instant the obedience required from these children on other
points respecting their work in the mill.'[37]

The question of respirators, not only in the flax mills but
elsewhere in industry provided something of a dilemma for
the conscientious factory inspector. It highlighted both the
principles that had originally underpinned the introduction of
Special Rules, and the apparent shift in those principles that
would soon begin to inform protective legislation. Initially
the concept of Special Rules had been borrowed from earlier
mining regulations formulated in the middle of the nineteenth
century. These early Special Rules, however, were primarily
concerned with defining the safety obligations placed, not on
the owner or employer, but on the worker. As the response to
pottery worker Edward Dunn had shown, the assumption that
it was the worker, as an independent agent, who was primarily
responsible for his own safety was a pervasive one throughout
the nineteenth century. By the 1890s, however, the balance of
responsibility between employer and worker was starting to
shift and the Special Rules that emerged from the Dangerous
Trades Committees frequently specified the respective duties of
both employer and employee. But in many cases the distinction
remained somewhat blurred and, when it came to the question
of respirators, many employers argued emphatically that their
duty was simply to provide them. It was, they maintained, the
duty of the workers to actually wear them. Whether or not
workers could be said to be in breach of their obligations when
they were not aware of their existence or, more significantly,
were too young to understand their importance, were somewhat
moot points however.

Just as in the white lead works the inspectors had discovered some very good reasons why women did not wear respirators, still less recommend them to children. The masks were ill-fitting, uncomfortable and largely ineffective. Once more the women were forced to leave them, unwashed, at the works overnight, and to wear a dirty respirator, previously worn by another worker, the next day. As far as the inspectors were concerned the solutions were obvious. Managers needed to purchase better respirators, pleasanter to wear and more efficient in preventing the inhalation of dust. And they needed to devise a system whereby respirators were regularly washed and were assigned to individual workers. The sympathies of Superintending Inspector Mr Osborne, however, remained firmly with the employer. In 1894 he had proposed his own alternative solution to the problem, simultaneously laying the blame at the door of the workers and undermining the professional position of the women inspectors. The enlistment of charitable ladies, he considered, could persuade the ill-educated and ungrateful hacklers of the error of their ways. 'It is surprising,' he opined 'that the women seem unaware that by use of a respirator their lives would be longer and pleasanter and ailments and medical expenses less. One cannot help thinking that something might be done to disseminate knowledge on these important factors in life among these poor sisters by women of leisure in manufacturing towns.'[38]

Adelaide's visit to the flax mills in 1895 involved a trip to Scotland, travelling first to Dundee, then further north to Montrose in Forfarshire and finally to her old childhood home of Aberdeen. It was a long journey and not untypical, underlining the extent to which her work took her away from home. The following year, in addition to numerous districts of London, she visited eighteen different towns in Lancashire, nine in Yorkshire and seven other towns scattered across England and Wales from Bournemouth to Llandudno. Back at

Hadley Wood, meanwhile, matters were getting progressively more difficult. Unlike her colleagues Adelaide could rarely look forward to peaceful periods with her family as a respite from the challenges of her work. It was clear that Isobel's condition was deteriorating and each time Adelaide returned home she must have dreaded what she might find. One day, early in July 1896, events took a terrible turn for the worse. Isobel took a knife from the kitchen and attacked her mother. No serious injury was caused but it was suddenly clear to everyone that this illness could no longer be contained. The event precipitated an application to the local Justice of the Peace for a 'reception order', the authorisation to compulsorily detain Isobel in an asylum. This procedure, established only a few years earlier under the Lunacy Act of 1890, was an attempt to address widespread public fears about the incarceration of those exhibiting mental disturbance. Tales of inconvenient family members being permanently spirited away by unscrupulous relatives appeared periodically in the popular press, and such horror stories were a popular genre in Victorian fiction. A reception order was valid for only a year and required a further examination and a medical report to the Lunacy Commission for its renewal.

Isobel as a young woman

There is no record of where Isobel spent the first year of her detention, but it is clear that by July 1897 her condition had failed to improve. On the twenty-second, therefore, the order was renewed and she was admitted to the Coppice Hospital in Nottingham. Here she would spend the rest of her life, her condition gradually deteriorating and her paints and brushes abandoned. Unlike the County Lunatic Asylum, however, which housed the mentally ill poor, the Coppice was a private hospital, a comfortable environment intended for wealthier psychiatric patients. Set in extensive grounds and with an imposing front entrance, it had been designed intentionally to resemble a large country house. The staff prided themselves on the delivery of pioneering treatment based on the notion that tranquillity and beautiful surroundings offered patients the best chance of recovery. It seems to have been Adelaide, perhaps assisted by Uncle John Ford, who found this hospital and arranged for Isobel's admission. But the decision would have been a heartbreaking one for Isobel was her closest sister. The two girls had grown up together in the happy confines of the Hampstead home, shared their nursery days, their schoolroom and their governess. They had enjoyed their walks together on the Heath, organised family parties, and travelled daily together to Queen's College in London. In choosing the Coppice, Adelaide would have entertained strong, if ultimately vain hopes of a recovery. There was, therefore, no intention that her sister should be put away and forgotten. She would visit her regularly for the next thirty-eight years, endlessly checking on her condition and looking, ever hopefully, for signs of improvement. The hospital Superintendent and his wife would become her close friends. The immediate problem, therefore, had been addressed, but it came at a considerable emotional cost, and the financial implications were also significant. It seems to have been Max and Walter who initially bore the brunt of these, agreeing to take equal shares in the cost of Isobel's incarceration. Later Alex and Ralf would also begin to contribute.

There was no question of Adelaide discussing any of these family difficulties with her colleagues at work. It was imperative that women demonstrated an ability to focus completely on their professional role. Any sign of emotion might be construed as feminine weakness, and they must offer no ammunition to opponents in the Home Office. While Lucy poured out the contents of her heart into the pages of her diary Adelaide left no such document during this period and most probably it did not exist. Iron control seems to have been a characteristic for which she had a particular talent. Thus at the beginning of 1895, with her mother settling only reluctantly into the new home, Ralf struggling unhappily with the demands of Mr Lund and Isobel's behaviour becoming ever more frightening, Adelaide seems to have effected an air of undisturbed composure at work. She did, however, have her sources of support. There was the listening ear of her childhood friend, Alice Macdonnell, totally ignorant of the world of factory inspection, but always kind and sympathetic. And, most importantly, there was also the appointment of a fifth lady inspector, Rose Squire, who arrived at Finsbury Circus in December 1895. Rose was the daughter of a Harley Street physician and public health specialist, William Squire. Influenced by the work of her father she had followed a similar path, becoming the first woman to gain a certificate as a sanitary inspector in 1893. Initially she had worked with Lucy in Kensington but she too came to feel that the Factory Inspectorate offered more opportunities to advance the reforms that were so badly needed.

There were some similarities between Rose and Adelaide but some important differences too. Rose was, if anything, even more attached to the arcane details of factory law, freely admitting that the so-called Blue Books which contained these details held an enduring fascination for her. Unlike Adelaide, however, she seems to have combined an obsessive attention to detail with a mischievous sense of humour, and an entertaining theatrical flair in the courtroom. Adelaide's career in the courts had got off to a shaky start and it was never an environment where she felt at ease. Rose, however, seemed to thoroughly enjoy the prosecution experience taking a delight in outwitting employers and disarming magistrates. Thus, when the owners of an elegant Regent Street store appealed to the High Court against a fine imposed for illegal overtime they were surprised to find one of their beautifully decorated boxes of chocolates presented as an exhibit. Their young shop assistants regularly worked more than twelve hours a day and were required to live on the premises, leaving them vulnerable to even more exploitation. Frequently they would be required to work after hours, organising goods and displays for the next day. In this particular case Rose had conducted a midnight raid on the shop. She had taken evidence from 'the smart but wearied young ladies whose pleasure at being caught was very evident!' Several had been required to stay until well after midnight, assembling chocolates in a fancy box, each chocolate delicately and separately wrapped in coloured tissue paper, the box adorned with intricately tied decorative ribbons. It was not arduous work, the defence claimed. It was no different from putting groceries into a sack and could easily be carried out between serving customers during the normal working day. In reply Rose embarked on an elaborate and extremely prolonged demonstration of chocolate box assembly. Lord Chief Justice Alverstone was clearly impressed, agreeing that the process constituted 'adapting goods for sale' (and therefore came under the terms of the Factory Act) and should not therefore be carried on after hours. Back at the office, these 'costly high-class chocolates' were gleefully shared out amongst the other inspectors.[39] Adelaide developed a strong friendship with Rose, admiring her relaxed sociability and her facility for making life fun. In later years Rose would provide a useful counterbalance to the forbidding air of formality that tended to pervade the office of the Principal Lady Inspector, for even Adelaide's staunchest friends were forced to concede that she struggled to find a sense of humour.

The year 1895 brought a General Election, a minority Conservative government and a new Home Secretary, Sir Matthew Ridley. Asquith, the champion of the women inspectors, was no longer there to provide a shield from the attacks of their opponents. The year also marked the retirement of the elderly Sprague Oram. Almost his last act as Chief Inspector was to elevate May Abraham to the post of Superintending Inspector, in charge of her colleagues. It was a development suggested by the women inspectors themselves and intended to stabilise their position as a separate section of the Factory Inspectorate. It provided a basis on which they could progressively build in terms of their numbers and their administrative structure. It also gave May a degree of autonomy, most importantly in terms of her authority to approve the women's decisions to prosecute, without recourse to the consent of the Chief Inspector. The Home Office agreed to the new arrangement, on condition, of course, that no increase in salary was contemplated.[40] It was, Lucy reported with a certain amount of relish, a development that infuriated senior male inspectors, already anxious about the increasing power of the women. The men would have much preferred the women to be assigned to specific districts, essentially putting them under the control of male District Superintendents.

For the men there was a further affront on the horizon. Later that year, Ridley selected a medical doctor to replace Sprague Oram, ignoring eligible senior male inspectors. Arthur Whitelegge was an eminent specialist in public health, but he had no previous experience as a factory inspector. His appointment reflected a new direction in the Factory Department, an intention to develop industrial health policy, incorporating some of the new medical findings and scientific approaches already embraced by experts in public health. But the decision was predictably unpopular amongst those with long careers in the Factory Inspectorate. Oram's successor, they felt, should have been selected from their own ranks. Meanwhile, the women inspectors were about to experience their own period of upheaval and uncertainty, for in the spring of 1896 May Abraham announced her engagement to Jack Tennant.

Chapter Seven
PRINCIPAL LADY INSPECTOR

May's announcement provoked a mixed reaction amongst her friends and colleagues, but it was hardly one of unanimous congratulation. Gertrude Tuckwell in Tite Street was the first to know and summed up the general mood, 'I was sorry and glad but not surprised.'[1] Lucy was less accommodating. 'Such is woman! Its no good their trying to do any kind of public work unless they are ugly and old, or unhappy,' adding rather more waspishly 'however, she's in love and poor, and a clever ambitious woman.'[2] Marriage, with its repeated hazardous pregnancies and its interference with career aspirations, was regarded as an unattractive proposition by many middle class feminists. But in an insecure world, where well-paid employment for women was rare, it could be an expedient option, offering a shelter from poverty for those of uncertain means. If you were also in love, then this was bonus. May, it seems, was indeed in love and Jack certainly was. It was generally acknowledged that May was beautiful and highly intelligent, with a radical heart in exactly the right place. Harold Tennant, always known as Jack, was rich and well-connected, the younger son of a Baronet. During the Liberal government of 1892–95 he had served as assistant permanent secretary to Home Secretary Asquith, who also happened to be his brother-in-law. Jack had an undeniable commitment to social reform, especially the improvement of industrial conditions. It was a passion he shared with May and the two had worked together on the Dangerous Trades Committees. Within Emilia's circle, however, there were some unflattering mutterings about Jack's abilities. May, it was generally agreed, was much the brighter of the two. He was just not good enough for her. It was a judgement perhaps coloured to some extent by bitter disappointment at May's decision. There would have been an assumption amongst her colleagues that it would spell the end of her career, for resignation on marriage was written into the employment contracts of women in the Civil Service. Initially, however, May managed to slip through an administrative loophole, similar to the one that had enabled Elizabeth Garrett to gain a medical qualification a generation earlier. In the 1850s it had been assumed that no woman would ever wish to pursue a career in medicine. Thus it had simply not occurred to the Society of Apothecaries to stipulate that women were barred from its examinations. By the time this particular door was closed the horse had already bolted and England had its first qualified woman doctor. Women of this period needed to be alert to such useful gaps in the regulations and now such an oversight enabled May to stay in post. Other women in the Civil Service were employed almost exclusively as low-grade clerks and it was to these women that the marriage bar applied. No such regulation existed in the terms and conditions of the higher grades for it was assumed that only men would hold such positions. In July, therefore, May and Jack were married at that most fashionable of wedding venues, St George's, Hanover Square, and despite the obvious disapproval of her new husband's family May determined to carry on working.

The event, however, was soon to have major repercussions for Adelaide's career. By the end of the year May's resolve to combine employment with marriage was beginning to waver. She was now pregnant and Lucy's prediction that 'social duties, her husband's friends and relatives – and babies, will all crowd in' were proving accurate.[3] It was a second marriage for Jack. His first wife had died tragically young in 1892 at the age of only twenty-five and in March 1897 the single child of that marriage, seven-year-old Charles, also died. The shock and sadness in the family brought with it a renewed focus on the impending birth of May's own child, and the pressure to withdraw from work in the interests of a safe pregnancy was something she found impossible to resist. Almost immediately after the funeral of little Charles, therefore, she submitted her resignation to the Home Office. In June she gave birth to a much-loved son, Henry, sadly destined to die in the First World War some twenty years later.

At Finsbury Circus, meanwhile, the future of the women's inspectorate was suddenly in jeopardy. The post of 'Superintending Inspector' had been a short-lived one, apparently disappearing with its incumbent. Mary Paterson, now the most senior of the women, was based too far from London to take May's place. Lucy Deane, the next in line, had been absent from work for several weeks the previous year due to typhoid that she had contracted while working in Ireland. She had now returned to duty but, even before this episode, there had been concerns about her general health. In her first weeks as an inspector she had suffered badly with her 'months' confiding her worries to a sympathetic Lady Howard in Malvern, who had arranged for her to see her own personal physician and offered to pay for any necessary treatment. Lucy, having been informed by a previous doctor that her womb was 'misplaced and malformed from birth' and that she would need an operation 'if I were not to spend a greater part of my time on the sofa' had fervently hoped for surgery to cure her woes. Lady Howard's physician, however, had been cautious. Instead he had prescribed an iron tonic and 'fenacitin' for the pain. Now she must 'drag on or worse!'[4] Lucy, stoical by nature and fiercely committed to her work, did struggle on, but increasingly she was finding her punishing schedule a considerable strain.

Conservative Home Secretary, Matthew Ridley, meanwhile, had long been alarmed by the radical zeal of the women inspectors, particularly those closely allied to Liberal politics and more specifically to the Dilkes. He pondered the way forward for several months. Finally, in August, he announced that Adelaide, an apparently calmer and more neutral pair of hands, was to be appointed to replace May. Lucy seems to have been disappointed. 'Today', she noted in her diary, 'I received the sad news that Miss Anderson is to be Principal Lady Inspector.'[5] May, too, was upset, but it was the change of name and function that seemed to concern her most. The title 'Principal Lady Inspector', she wrote in the influential Liberal magazine *The Fortnightly Review*, sounded more like the leading character in a comic opera than the name of a government official. It had 'the taint of amateurism' about it.[6] More importantly, however, the autonomy granted to her as 'Superintending Inspector' had been stripped away. Adelaide would have no power to authorise prosecutions or to require the owners of small workshops to make structural alterations in the interests of health and safety. Now such recommendations would have to be submitted to District Inspectors for approval.

Freed from the constraints of government service, May launched a furious public attack on the Home Secretary and the Chief Factory Inspector. The action, she said, was a blatant appeasement of the male inspectors by Ridley and Whitelegge, a move calculated to undermine the authority of the women. Now the ability of the women inspectors to act 'with their known love of thoroughness' was dependent on the co-operation of men. The result she argued would be 'loss of time, loss of energy, the wear and tear of uncertainty and diminished administrative force.' The original purpose of appointing women inspectors, she concluded with colourful hyperbole, had been 'violated'.[7] Adelaide would have read this tirade with dismay. It was not her way of going about things and it could only make her own position in the inspectorate more difficult. Typically, however, she passed no public comment and quietly accepted the position. Perhaps she had some sympathy with Whitelegge, struggling to establish himself in a new post and besieged by angry senior inspectors who doubted his ability and resented his presence. There were, after all, some similarities between the situation of the new Chief Inspector and her own. An undoubted outsider to the Dilke's inner circle, Adelaide would not have been the obvious choice of those who had previously wielded influence in the women's inspectorate. Her appointment seemed to represent a sharp reminder to the acolytes circulating around Asquith that the political power base had shifted. As it turned out, Adelaide's apparently meek acquiescence with the limits placed on her new role paid off. Twelve months later, Whitelegge quietly asked Ridley to restore to the 'Principal Lady Inspector' the powers that the previous Superintending Woman Inspector had enjoyed. Now more firmly ensconced in his new position he presumably felt better able to withstand accusations of capitulation to the feminist lobby. And, it seems, he had developed a healthy respect for this quietly efficient woman. As he explained to doubtful male inspectors, he had seen enough of Miss Anderson's work to satisfy himself that she was trustworthy. The endless requirement to rubber stamp her decisions, he had decided, simply created unnecessary bothersome paperwork.

Adelaide's appointment also coincided with a physical move, a development that must have added considerable fuel to May's fire. Now the lady inspectors were accommodated in a crumbling terrace in Great George Street. Approaching the end of its lease and soon to be demolished it represented the typical home offered to less prestigious government departments. May would have seen this as further evidence that the women inspectors were being downgraded and sidelined. Committed as she was to industrial reform, May was also driven by a parallel, equally important agenda, the cause of feminine advancement. Any suggestion that this was being subverted must be resisted at all costs. Adelaide, however, professed herself pleased with her new surroundings. She now had two rooms instead of one and her office was more central, more convenient for conferences and meetings with workers and employers. Great George Street was, in any case, only temporary. A further move to Abbey Mansions in Victoria Street was proposed for the following year. Most importantly, she had also been promised the services of a clerk to help with record keeping, filing and correspondence. This would free up more time for the proper business of inspection. It was a response that underlined an important difference between Adelaide and many of her contemporaries in the women's movement of the period. While her appointment undoubtedly marked a significant step in the progression towards sexual equality in the managerial and professional classes, this never seems to have been a central objective of her ambitions. Motivated by an overarching sense of duty, the primary focus of her endeavours was always the mission itself, the reform of labour conditions for women and children. Her relentless refusal to recognise perceived slights against the cause of womanhood, or indeed against herself, was something that would frequently provoke frustration amongst her more radical feminist colleagues.

Adelaide's primary preoccupation during 1897 was, in any case, the various demands of her new post. After only two years in the Inspectorate she would now be expected to organise and direct the work of an expanding staff. May's conviction that Ridley was bent on the destruction of the fledging women's inspectorate seems to have been somewhat overblown. Although the section would never be large it experienced steady growth from 1897 averaging one new recruit each year. In October, therefore, with little experience of her own to draw on Adelaide found herself 'training' the first of these new recruits. Anna Tracey, the daughter of a West Country Vicar, had, like Adelaide, previously worked as a clerk to the Labour Commission. She rapidly proved herself a capable addition to the inspectorate, focussing in particular on conditions in steam powered laundries that were now springing up all over the country. The following year saw the appointment of Emily Sadler, granddaughter of Michael Sadler, who as MP for Leeds had been active in child labour reform. Emily began by taking on the endless round of sweatshops which proliferated in the back streets and basements of West London. These continued to occupy large amounts of the inspectors' time and Emily's energetic pursuit of the miscreants of Kensington and Chelsea allowed Adelaide to concentrate more fully on the 'dangerous and unhealthy industries', as they were categorised in her report, where workers were exposed to poisonous dusts and fumes. Prominent among these, as always, were those involving the use of lead. It was a problem that would dominate her first year as Principal Lady Inspector but one that would also prove to be a catalyst for the development of new approaches to the prevention of occupational disease.

By 1896, as the white lead arbitration process continued along its unhurried path, another potent source of lead poisoning had forced its way onto the social and political agenda. In the six towns of the Staffordshire Potteries[8] the disease had for many years contributed to a hugely inflated mortality rate, particularly amongst women. Female workers were employed largely in the decorative areas of manufacture, painting, gilding and burnishing the pots. Here lead could readily be inhaled in the dust which filled the air or ingested from the hands during mealtimes. The earthenware and ceramics industry had been designated a Dangerous Trade in 1892, attracting the requirement for Special Rules governing matters of ventilation, protective clothing, washing facilities and separate eating areas. But the road to effective regulation in the Potteries was proving to be even more tortuous than that in the white lead works. The Special Rules, proposed in 1894, had contained so many amendments and had been so poorly drafted that even Asquith had been forced to concede that 'in practice they were entirely inoperative.'[9] Vaughan Nash had lost no time in pointing this out to his readers in the *Daily Chronicle*. 'The poison was diluted', he observed witheringly, 'just a trifle watered down, but not enough to bring the employer to his right mind, not enough to stop the monumental waste of life which stands recorded in the death registers of the Potteries.'[10]

In 1897 during the months immediately preceding Adelaide's appointment as Principal Lady Inspector there had been a series of recommendations, revisions, committees and arbitration meetings that had left the workers largely unprotected and the manufacturers angry and uncooperative. Employers objected to persistent suggestions from medical men that women and children should be excluded from parts of the process and replaced by more expensive male workers. The government itself was reluctant to pursue this option, in part because of the controversy surrounding the exclusion policy in the white lead industry, but also for economic reasons. White lead production was a relatively small industry employing only a few hundred people. The Potteries, by contrast, employed over twenty-three thousand women and children and British earthenware and ceramics were famous all over the world. The industry made a huge contribution to the national economy.[11] The employers also resented government officials who proposed a raft of costly modifications to their premises and work practices. If workers would only acquaint themselves with soap and water, they argued, the problem would be solved. Worst of all, from the manufacturers' point of view, a head of steam was forming behind the proposal that they should begin using 'fritted' lead,[12] or even a completely leadless glaze. It was an idea the employers considered to be technologically unworkable. It had been dreamed up, they fumed, by ill-informed busy bodies in the drawing rooms of London, people like Emilia Dilke, Gertrude Tuckwell and, most recently, the imperiously vocal Lady Millicent Leveson-Gower, Duchess of Sutherland, or 'meddlesome Millie' as she was dubbed in Staffordshire. Emilia, meanwhile, had proposed a new solution. A woman inspector permanently resident in the Potteries would, she maintained, ensure that at least the existing regulations were rigidly enforced. Mustering her contacts in the newspaper industry to provide the necessary publicity she arranged for several blind workers, victims of lead-induced optic neuritis, to be brought to London by train to meet the Home Secretary. A woman inspector, she told him, would deal with such suffering. Matthew Ridley was polite but non-committal. He knew such a move would be an anathema to the manufacturers, but more particularly to the male inspectors who viewed the prospect of a woman tramping all over their territory with horror. For Mr Dawkins-Cramp, Superintending Inspector in the Midlands, the onward march of the women inspectors was a scenario he had grimly predicted, and dreaded. Senior civil servants in the Home Office were equally unenthusiastic. When a petition, purportedly from women pottery workers, requesting the appointment of a dedicated woman inspector, arrived on the desk of Permanent Secretary, Edward Troup, he was clearly irritated. The document, he considered, bore the unmistakeable stamp of the WTUL. 'I suppose this may be taken as indicating the direction in which the friends of the Lady Inspectors' Department propose now to agitate for the extension of their powers,' he observed icily.[13]

By early 1897, under attack from all sides, Ridley opted for that time-honoured diffuser of difficult situations, the Special Enquiry. Anxious to put an end to such 'petticoat pestering'[14] he decided to award this particular poison chalice to the lady inspectors. It was the first of many Special Enquiries they would undertake. Indeed these would become a major part of their work. But this first one, carried out in the eye of an extremely public storm and under the critical gaze of cynical government officials, was a hard training ground. Watched suspiciously by manufacturers on the one hand and feminist campaigners on the other, they could hardly be expected to please everyone. Whitelegge elected to hand the lion's share of the work to Lucy who was now something of a veteran of the six towns. She had visited them on several occasions during the interminable meetings with employers in the previous year. Arriving once more at the North Stafford Hotel in Stoke-on-Trent she found few changes to this 'hideous little town'. In the more agreeable parts of England pink and white blossom was bursting forth in the spring sunshine but the atmosphere of this district was, as novelist Arnold Bennett noted, 'as black as its mud'.[15] The manufacture of earthenware and china was a traditional industry, largely devoid of sophisticated technological developments and holding fast to its complex hierarchical patterns of labour. The six towns were similarly unreformed. In 1897 over forty-five thousand workers and their families were packed within a small radius of narrow dark streets, overshadowed by nearly three hundred giant potbanks. Day and night these towering structures belched out sparks and thick black smoke, enveloping the houses and depositing grimy smuts on every available surface. The emergence from this environment of an array of fine china and exquisite porcelain which graced the homes of the wealthy and discerning all over Europe was something of a paradox. More prosaically, and perhaps more usefully, Staffordshire also produced the nations' sinks and elaborately decorated water closets. Each town had its own speciality, its own workers and its own way of doing things. What they all had in common, however, was lead poisoning.

Over a period of three months Lucy, sometimes accompanied by Mary Paterson, visited 132 factories and combed the records of the North Staffordshire Infirmary and the nearby Haywood Hospital. According to their findings there had been a total of 404 confirmed cases of lead poisoning in the six towns during the previous year, fifty-six under the age of eighteen, and 233 in female workers. Nine patients had died.[16] Visiting the homes of the sick and deceased they uncovered some poignant personal details behind these figures: 'A boy of thirteen, a delicate lad who, after five months employed in the dipping house, died in convulsions induced by lead; a woman of twenty-one, a majolica paintress[17] who had had two previous attacks but had persisted

Potteries landscape, early twentieth century. (Reproduced with the permission of the Wellcome Library, London.)

in returning to work, died in convulsions due to lead; a woman of forty-six, a colour duster[18] on printed ware, had worked many years, seized with paralysis and died in convulsions; a single woman of twenty-three years, worked five years at majolica painting, continued to work though ill from time to time and in her last fatal attack became paralysed and blind.'[19] Mary and Lucy found themselves filled with both sadness and admiration as they tramped the dark streets.

Over and over again we were struck by instances of the generosity and kindness of the poor to each other, as when the deceased had been nursed and cared for by next door neighbours, who had cheerfully burdened themselves with the entire charge of the tiny orphans whom they had adopted, or when during months of weary death-sickness, the sufferer, debarred from earning her living, had depended for support on the unfailing generosity of a fellow lodger. The patient only rarely became an inmate of a hospital or workhouse infirmary, generally fading away in her own or a neighbour's house.[20]

They did, however, find cases of blindness in the infirmary, as well as examples of 'wrist drop',[21] the classic neurological symptom of lead poisoning. And then there was the matter of foetal poisoning. Miscarriages, stillbirths and infant deaths were all too common in heavily industrialised areas, for here life was a daily struggle against malnourishment and disease. But in Staffordshire the tales of grief and loss were more than usually harrowing. A woman aged thirty-five had experienced repeated attacks of poisoning and several miscarriages. Her last child was born dead and she herself, returning to work partially paralysed a month after her confinement, became seriously ill and died. Another woman had three stillborn children and four miscarriages, her one living child had been born during a year in which she was absent from work. Another woman, aged twenty-nine, had five children stillborn, three miscarriages, and one child born alive who died in convulsions when a few weeks old. The stories kept on coming.[22]

When Adelaide took up her position as Principal Lady Inspector in August she was confronted by a huge pile of information on the six towns, and the requirement to condense this into a formal report. Fortunately it was a situation that played exactly to her strengths and to her experience as a précis writer several years before. Combining dry statistics with

tragic personal stories, she produced a telling account of the
situation in Staffordshire, adding some thoughts of her own to
supplement the picture presented by Lucy and Mary. Some of
these thoughts were based on their extra notes. Of seventy-seven
women interviewed, for example, she noted that thirty-five
had experienced, between them, a total of ninety miscarriages
and eight had given birth to stillborn children.[23] It is clear,
however, that she had also personally visited the Potteries and
was unimpressed by the conditions she found. Little more than
lip service was paid to Special Rules in this district. The failure
of women to wash, she suggested, could perhaps be 'directly
traceable to the employer, whose zeal to carry out his share of
duty in this matter is limited to the provision of three basins
for each twenty-five workers.' In 'lamenting the carelessness of
young workers who fail to use this imposing array of "washing
conveniences,"' she continued, 'it is strange that they [the
employers] ignored the lack of soap and towels and the fact that,
to be of any use, each basin had to be carried away, emptied and
refilled on the other side of the factory.'[24] And then there was the
question of the designated 'mealrooms' provided in a draughty
corner of the works or in a cold warehouse which 'struck an
icy chill even on my well-nourished and warmly clad person.'[25]
There was, she concluded, clear evidence that lead poisoning
was increasing and that this was 'an unsatisfactory result which
appears to be due mainly to the superficiality of the regulations
and the difficulty, under the present arrangements, of fixing
responsibility for the due observance of these rules.'[26] While
there was no explicit recommendation for the appointment of
a resident woman inspector it was an easy suggestion to infer if
the Home Secretary wished to do so. It seems, however, that he
did not. For the moment at least, Mr Dawkins-Cramp was to
be spared further intrusions into his territory.

Instead the Home Office engaged in a prolonged negotiation
with employers over a further revision of the Special Rules,

the first draft of which was produced in the spring of 1898. This time the proposal was for a minimum age of fourteen for those working with lead, and monthly medical examinations for women and for young persons below the age of twenty-one. There was to be mandatory suspension of anyone found to be suffering from lead poisoning. For hard line feminists this was yet another form of discrimination against women, grouping them with children and placing them, but not men, at risk of losing their jobs. They need not have worried, however. Unlikely allies appeared in the form of the employers, of whom approximately one third refused to agree. The North Staffordshire Hotel, already doing good business that year, now played host to another prolonged round of arbitration talks. Although producing only minor modifications to the Rules this process resulted, by October, in a situation whereby those more compliant employers who had agreed to the earlier Rules were now, it seems, bound by a stricter code than those who had demanded arbitration. The situation deteriorated still further when the Home Office appointed two expert advisors, medical doctor Thomas Oliver, previously involved in the white lead negotiations, and chemist Edward Thorpe, the Principal of the Government Laboratories. When Oliver and Thorpe proposed just one way forward, the introduction of a lead-free glaze,[27] the employers were incensed, particularly as the Home Office, on receipt of their report, now proposed that only those using lead-free glazes were to be exempt from the regulations regarding medical examinations. Moreover, these regulations were now to be extended to all adult males, something which offered a degree of solace to equality seeking feminists, but none at all to employers. The manufacturers now dug in their heels, focussing their fury on the looming prospect of reductions in the lead content of the glaze. As fierce arguments continued over the precise percentage of lead allowable in the dipping tub a further 457 cases of lead poisoning were confirmed in the

Potteries, nearly 40 per cent of all cases reported throughout the country that year.[28] Meanwhile public concern, ably stoked up by the *Daily Chronicle* and the WTUL, grew rapidly.

From the beginning of 1899 Adelaide began to experience an ever-increasing tide of complaints from women workers in the Staffordshire Potteries and in the spring of 1900 she decided to make a return visit. Always optimistic and eager to find improvements she was, nevertheless, horrified by what she found in the six towns. There were no washing facilities, no meal rooms and few lavatories, with males and females crowded together in narrow, filthy places which many women found too objectionable to use. There were no caps and overalls provided, no respirators and no cleaning down of places where lead-laden dust collected. Record keeping of medical examinations was largely absent resulting in frequent redeployment of women who had been suspended with symptoms of poisoning. And there were other concerns surrounding the medical examinations. Women were, she noted, 'examined under very unsuitable conditions . . . on such lines as to offend the refined feelings.'[29] It is not hard to imagine the humiliation and lack of privacy attendant on these experiences. She was hardly surprised to find that young girls, in particular, shrank from the ordeal and simply stayed away from the factory when they felt ill, seeking 'treatment' at home. Thus many women with symptoms of lead poisoning rarely came to the attention of the certifying surgeon.[30] Adelaide found them at home, ill and frightened, but still reluctant to seek medical help. The terrible conditions in Staffordshire stood out in stark contrast to those in other areas where ceramics were produced. In Worcestershire, for example, conditions were much better and lead poisoning was rare. Given the appalling situation she encountered in Staffordshire she had no option but to embark on a number of prosecutions of 'the worst and most typical cases.'[31] Convictions and considerable penalties followed, but it was a sad sort of triumph, made worse by the fact that she felt compelled by pressure of work to abandon plans to spend more time in the district. Increasingly she was becoming aware of the size of the task before her and her own limited resources.

Pretty things and dense black smoke invariably seemed to go together in manufacturing areas. The Lancashire cotton industry was centred on the great city of Manchester with much of its cloth spun and woven in the towns and villages dotted around its northern hinterland. There was, of course, plenty here to occupy a factory inspector. There were forty-three fatalities in the various textile industries in 1897 and eighteen of these occurred in the cotton industry, all involving women. In most of these the victim had been dragged by her hair or by her clothes into steam powered machinery. Over a thousand other women were seriously injured in similar, non-fatal accidents.[32] However, supplementary to the central business of weaving and spinning, there were other, less well-known workplaces that provided yet one more potent source of lead poisoning. Lurking in back alleys behind the grandiose Victorian buildings of 'Cottonopolis', Adelaide found scores of small dyeworks. Stripes were popular during the 1890s, not only for bright summer clothes but also for the 'Grandrille shirtings'[33] worn by so many working men. Orange and yellow were the preferred colours, an effect achieved by the use of lead chromate, a pigment widely referred to as 'chrome yellow'. Somewhat unexpectedly, few cases of lead poisoning seemed to occur in the men who carried out the dying process. But men encountered the lead in solution, in the great vats of water containing lead nitrate where the cloth was stirred and squeezed. The women, by contrast, worked with the dry yarn. Following the application of the dye, they were employed in the 'lighter' work, as 'noddlers' and 'headers of yarn'. Looping the fibre over a metal frame they prepared the hanks of yarn for the weavers, straightening and stretching it and finally twisting one end into a knot or 'head'. As they pulled and shook the fibre, tiny fragments of lead chromate left on the surface of the yarn filled the air, and the nostrils of the workers. The results, Adelaide observed in her report, were the same as in other cases of lead poisoning.

Once more Special Rules had been introduced with requirements for ventilation, respirators, protective overalls and washing facilities and once more the problem lay in enforcement. The local male inspector was optimistic. The problem, he concluded, had been largely eliminated by the application of Special Rules and he had seen no cases of lead poisoning in the previous twelve months. Adelaide, however, had recently visited a worker in the Royal Infirmary who was still confined to bed after eighteen weeks of treatment for lead poisoning. Her 'long interview' with this woman seemed to tell a different story. In most dyeworks she found the Special Rules virtually ignored and a number of women in poor health struggling with symptoms of poisoning. Once more this familiar dismal picture was confirmed by visits to some of the workers' homes and to local doctors. Talking with the employers, however, Adelaide elected to avoid immediate prosecution. Here, she judged, more might be achieved by employer education. It was a decision encouraged by the continuing presence of Mary Paterson, still on secondment from Scotland. Mary was proving to be a highly effective colleague. Another outsider to the Dilke's inner circle she was, like Adelaide, pragmatic rather than ideological and, unlike Adelaide, deeply cynical in her attitude to employers. While Adelaide's approach was always ostensibly mild and tempered with a degree of encouragement, there was invariably a distinctly caustic edge to Mary's comments. Adelaide's strength was well hidden, an inner steel beneath a gentle exterior. Mary's, by contrast, was there for all to see, and to fear. Strongly focussed on the matter in hand she determined to make a difference in the dye works, a task she achieved within a few short months. Subsequent visits by Adelaide showed that 'ventilation was improved, missing overalls and caps and sanitary drinks[34] supplied, a good lavatory with hot and cold taps to each basin and other necessary appliances provided and, surprisingly, beyond the requirements of the Rules, a dining room was fitted up.' She was greatly impressed and encouraged by these developments. It went some way towards mitigating her severe disappointment with the situation in the Potteries.

In 1894 yet another source of lead poisoning had found its way on to the agenda of the women inspectors. The Quarries Act of that year had transferred the inspection of clay pits from the Factory Inspectorate to the Mines Inspectorate, but the brickworks often attached to these clay pits were to remain the responsibility of the Factory Department. It was Rose who first visited a brickworks and once more encountered the dreaded dust. Like the earthenware pots, bricks were dipped in a leaded glaze. Women and girls were primarily employed to smooth the bricks' surfaces and edges, scraping off the superfluous material. It was a process carried out in a dry state creating huge amounts of lead-laden dust. The girls, most of whom were between eighteen and twenty years old, then carried the bricks to the kiln, an operation which itself placed them under considerable physical strain. The story was by now a very familiar one. Virtually all these workers were either suffering from the symptoms of lead poisoning, or had done so in the past, many of them repeatedly. Many displayed the typical blue line on the gums, an indicator of high exposure to lead. One woman remarked that when the girls were carried down to the mess room 'struggling in the fits' she 'cleared out' because she could not bear to see them. It happened almost every day, she said. Most of them thought nothing of it, and when they were well enough, went back to work.[35] Rose decided on the course of action that was by now the lady inspectors' stock in trade, a programme of home visiting. She followed this up with visits to the premises of local doctors. It was a sobering experience. Symptoms of lead poisoning were, it seems, a normal part of these women's lives, and deaths. The employer, meanwhile, assured her that no cases of lead poisoning had occurred for a long time. The colic, he said, was due to natural causes and the fits to hysteria.

The result of Rose's investigations and Adelaide's subsequent report was the addition of the industry to the schedule of dangerous industries requiring Special Rules, broadly in line with those nominally in force in the Potteries. It looked like this was going to be another difficult and time-consuming issue of enforcement, requiring repeated visits and interminable discussions with reluctant employers. On this occasion, however, Adelaide found another way forward, one that was untenable in the Potteries but might just gain some traction in the brickworks. Making enquiries of technological experts Adelaide concluded that, owing to the particular type of clay used, it seemed unnecessary to use lead in the glaze. Unlike the earthenware manufacturers the brick makers, when confronted with this suggestion, seemed more than happy to comply. It would, after all, save them money and reduce the amount of regulation they would have to confront, not to mention the amount of 'hysteria' present in their workforce. By the end of 1899, therefore, Adelaide was happy to report that only fritted lead was used, and that in very small quantities.

Another industry provided its own solution to the problem of lead poisoning, although not one which would have appealed to those agitating for women's employment rights. The production of electrical accumulators was a new venture in the 1890s. It was part of the growing enthusiasm for electrical power and in particular for that latest exciting invention, the motor vehicle. Small factories were springing up in every industrial town and thus it was not long before lead poisoning also reared its head. This was another case where the victims were largely women.

Visiting one small manufactory in London Adelaide found young unskilled girls 'rough handling of oxide of lead in its loose form, preparatory to it being pressed by hand as a paste into the accumulator frames.'[36] In the absence of ventilation, it seemed, overalls, head coverings and respirators were quite inadequate to deal with the amounts of dust scattered around the works. Adelaide's response on this occasion was to provide a detailed translation of an extensive stringent set of rules recently drawn up by the German government for application in accumulator works. Once more, it seems, factory regulators in Continental Europe were well ahead of their British counterparts and Adelaide was pleased when similar rules were applied in British workshops. Returning the following year, however, to check on progress she was surprised to find that all the girls had been dismissed and replaced with male workers. The women, it seems, had been too troublesome with their repeated attacks of 'lead colic'.[37] Male workers were regarded as much more robust. The vexed question of whether women were more susceptible than men to lead poisoning might have been a burning unresolved question in medical circles, but it had clearly already been settled in the minds of employers. Thus the accumulator works ceased to be a matter of concern for the lady inspectors, although no doubt male replacement workers soon joined the ranks of lead poisoning cases.

In the summer of 1898 Adelaide found she had a new ally in the Home Office to whom she could 'remit the care of cases of lead poisoning.' Professors Oliver and Thorpe, who had caused so much turmoil in Staffordshire, were not government employees. Rather they had been commissioned by the Home Secretary to carry out an investigation and present a report. Their presence and perhaps their inept handling of the situation had, however, underlined the lack of medical expertise within the Factory Department itself, which increasingly was broadening its remit to include health as well as safety. In July, Whitelegge had confirmed his own personal commitment to industrial disease prevention with the appointment of the first officially designated Medical Inspector of Factories, Dr Thomas Legge. Like Whitelegge, Legge had a background in public health having spent his first years as a physician investigating sanitary measures in major cities across the Continent of Europe. His arrival in the Factory Department marked a significant shift in the regulatory focus of the Inspectorate and in the way health policies were to be formulated and implemented. These were now to be informed both by current medical knowledge and by a more sophisticated use of statistical data. Adelaide viewed the appointment with considerable relief. 'Where medical matters are involved I now have the advantage of conferring with Dr Legge,'[38] she observed with characteristic understatement. In fact, with Thomas Legge's arrival, she had gained probably her most important colleague in the Home Office. They had much in common, both administratively and personally. Both were 'peripatetic' and to some extent outwith the normal structure of the organisation. It was something that provided a degree of common ground and understanding. Most importantly, however, Dr Legge's values and his approach corresponded rather closely with her own. Thoughtful, meticulous and painstaking, Legge considered that evidence, not ideology, was the appropriate basis for action. Socially reserved and undemonstrative, some thought him cold to the point of rudeness. But he was also highly principled and deeply committed to the improvement of industrial conditions. These were all qualities that Adelaide both understood and admired. There was, in fact, an uncanny series of similarities in the backgrounds of these two earnest, hard-working individuals. The son of a non-conformist Minister, Legge's family roots were also in Aberdeen. Born in Hong Kong to missionary parents, just three months before Adelaide, he had attended Clackmannanshire's Dollar Academy while his parents pursued their work in China. Like Govie's gymnasium, (attended by one of his first cousins), the Academy placed a strong emphasis on the development of science and mathematics, and the convergence of this education with a strong social conscience had led him into medicine. Like Adelaide he was international in outlook, a legacy of his parents' missionary travels during his early boyhood, and he was proficient in several languages.

There was an instant rapport between the new Medical Inspector and the new Principal Lady Inspector. To Adelaide's obvious approval Legge's first report, presented in 1899, featured a veritable feast of statistics on lead poisoning, exhaustively analysed. Cases were broken down by age, sex, severity, frequency and importantly, job type, providing the basis for a new set of Special Rules in the Potteries which focussed less on the technological processes involved or even on the sex of the workers, but more particularly on the requirement for locally applied exhaust ventilation. The installation of ducts, hoods and fans wherever workers were exposed to lead-laden dust was, he considered, 'the sheet anchor' of protection.[39] Legge's approach epitomised the new enthusiasm for the use of statistical data to inform the prevention and control of industrial disease, and a growing assumption that it was the responsibility of employers to provide a safe environment for their workforce. In conjunction with the new Factory Act of 1901, which removed the employers' right to arbitration, this approach would gradually begin to make inroads into the problem of lead poisoning and numerous other industrial diseases. In 1900 there were 1,058 cases of industrial lead poisoning notified to the Home Office, including thirty-eight deaths. By 1921 these figures had fallen to 230 reported cases with twenty-three deaths, despite a steady increase in the number of people working in lead-related industries.[40] It was, of course, men who were the main victims of the disease, for it was they who formed the majority of the workforce where lead was employed.

Throughout this period cases in women contributed around 20 per cent to the overall total. Ultimately, Legge's data would show that it was the level and frequency of exposure to the dust, not the sex of the worker, which determined the susceptibility to lead poisoning. There was, however, an important caveat to this conclusion for women did have a special reason to fear the effects of the disease. Legge, always careful to base his arguments on scientific data, summarised his attitude to this in his comprehensive textbook *Industrial Maladies*, published in 1934. 'There is no doubt as to the baleful influence of lead on the uterine functions. I personally hold the view that the only restriction which should constitute a bar is employment directly interfering with the function of maternity, and employment in lead is the only one I know.' Keen to maintain a social distance from what he called the 'moral' aspects of the matter, however, he added 'I would prefer to leave it to women to say how far moral dangers should lead to restrictions.'[41] In 1898 Adelaide looked forward greatly to working with the newly appointed Medical Inspector.

Chapter Eight
SORROWFUL TIMES

Adelaide's first few years as Principal Inspector were marked
by a series of family difficulties, sadness and tragedy, of which
Isobel's committal was only the first. Her response appears to
have been a combination of relentless stoicism, punctuated by
periods of complete withdrawal, in many ways similar to her
behaviour at Girton. One sadness was the geographical dispersal
of the family, particularly her brothers, who were progressively
migrating across the world. Max was by now settled in a
flourishing business in Australia, returning home at intervals
to confer with Uncle Jamie (James Skelton) and seemingly
getting on reasonably well with George Yuill. Alex, meanwhile,
had joined the Bombay and Burma Trading Corporation and
was rising up the ranks of its managers. Walter had gone to
Canada, although he was still struggling to make a success of
his fish canning business. He clearly hoped that, ultimately,
Ralf would be able to join him in Vancouver as a partner, but
the various ups and downs of the business during the years up to
1900 meant that this decision was never quite made. Adelaide,
always assiduous in her efforts on Ralf's behalf, tried her best to
engineer the partnership, but it was not to be. Ralf, pessimistic
about his prospects in the shipping industry, was himself
keen on the plan, but as Walter confronted the uncertainties
of several poor salmon seasons and the endless difficulties of

raising sufficient capital he was forced to consider alternatives. 'We need to get the opinion of the mother and Sissy,'[1] Walter wrote to Ralf in July 1898, outlining the latest of a series of setbacks. 'They are both away in Switzerland and I am here quite alone,' wrote back Ralf miserably three weeks later.[2] The need to consult his mother and eldest sister in part reflected the responsibility all the brothers felt for the financial security of the women in the family. 'When one considers how much the mother's future comfort and happiness depend on our doing well and being able to help her one feels the necessity of running as few risks as possible,' he wrote.[3] But it also underlined the value they placed on the advice of Blanche Emily and Adelaide. On this occasion the advice, when they returned, was for Ralf to pursue a course in banking, something that gained for him a distinction in his examinations and a post at the Chartered Bank of India, Australia and China.

Ralf, however, was still unsure about the direction of his life and career, something that aroused maternal feelings of responsibility in his eldest sister. Of all the brothers Ralf was perhaps the most gentle and the least confidently determined, and Adelaide worried about him. By 1900 he was still unhappy and unsettled, a feeling compounded by his rejection, early that year, as a volunteer in the Boer War. The doctor had detected heart trouble. Ralf, fired up by the 'tremendous eagerness to go out there'[4] prevalent among young men at the time, had desperately wanted to join the Imperial Yeomanry with several of his friends. At the end of January that year, however, he was forced to watch them all sail off without him. Observing his bitter disappointment, Adelaide consulted Uncle Jamie who recommended a holiday and found him a passage to Egypt on one of his ships. It would give Ralf time and space to think through his future, he said. Ralf, considerably heartened by the plan, thoroughly enjoyed his trip to the Middle East and returned with a decision. He would go to South Africa anyway as an employee of the bank,[5] from which position he could register as an army reservist. The war was now definitely progressing towards a favourable conclusion from the British point of view. 'The repulse of the Boers at Ladysmith seems to have been a fine piece of work,' Ralf observed in February 1900 just before setting off for the Cape.[6] A month later Blanchie was writing to ask about his initial impressions of Capetown and whether he had arrived in time for the Mafeking rejoicings. 'There were tremendous doings in London and a great deal of rowdy celebrations in the North, and London is now gay with things over the taking of Pretoria,' she wrote.[7]

With the ending of the war, however, Ralf again became restless. He would soon be stood down as a military reservist and he remained uncommitted to banking as a career. The solution, he decided, was to obtain a position in the developing South African Civil Service. A close friend who worked at the Government Offices in Bloemfontein was prepared to lobby on his behalf. Adelaide, by now a thoroughly committed member of the British administration, approved wholeheartedly. 'It would be so good to have the possibility of doing good public work at the beginning of the re-organisation of South Africa,' she told him, and rapidly began organising influential contacts to smooth his way.[8] A letter from Alice's husband, William Macdonnell, to Sir David she was sure would help. The identity of 'Sir David' is unclear but she also had another string to her bow. 'An opportune moment has come,' she informed Ralf enthusiastically 'a dinner invitation the day after tomorrow with Lady Ilbert.'[9] She knew that the Ilberts were close friends of Sir Alfred Milner, the current administrator of the Orange River Colony in South Africa. Before embarking on his current career Sir Alfred had been assistant editor of the controversial newspaper the *Pall Mall Gazette*, contributing to the paper's repeated exposés of appalling working conditions. Adelaide's lobbying, via the Ilbert's, on her brother's behalf was clearly a success, for in the autumn of 1901 Ralf became one of 'Milner's Kindergarten', a team of British lawyers and administrators recruited to oversee reconstruction in this war ravaged territory and establish a system of government based on the British model. Ralf's role in this endeavour was that of Assistant Auditor General for the Orange River Colony, a position he held until 1911, confirming him in his decision to make a permanent home in South Africa. Subsequently, in the years immediately preceding the First World War, he would go into partnership with a friend to establish a sugar producing farm at Empangeni in Zululand, a place that Adelaide herself would come to love.

By the middle of 1901, therefore, all Adelaide's brothers had left the family home to seek their fortunes overseas. Blanchie, writing to Ralf in June that year, expressed the sense of sadness prevailing at Hadley Wood. Even Dennis, the family dog, was pining. 'Poor chappie, he still sits regularly either at the drawing room window or the gate waiting for a 'boy' in the evenings. We all like to hope for such an arrival too. Home is not the same without any of you noisy boys. Don't forget we shall all be waiting for you in the same sort of way when you do come back.'[10] The coming back, however, would only be for short, infrequent visits, and in Ralf's case not for many years. Blanchie, herself, had by this stage left for pastures new, although these pastures were somewhat nearer, allowing for regular holidays with her mother and sisters. She had initially been employed as an assistant headmistress at Bolton School for Girls in Lancashire but in the summer of 1901 she was appointed as headmistress at Birkenhead High School in the small village of Oxton across the River Mersey from Liverpool. It was an appointment that was both exciting and challenging. The school, which had been declining for several years, had recently been purchased and re-opened by the Girls Public Day School Trust with a view to turning around its fortunes. Blanchie's appointment at the age of just thirty-two, suggested that her reputation as a teacher was by now in very good standing. 'Continuous efforts are made to maintain efficiency by the adoption of the best and most modern methods of instruction,' stated the School Prospectus. 'Particular stress is laid upon the formation of character by moral and religious training, and on fitting girls for the practical business and duties of life.'[11] 'Blanchie has no light task ahead of her, practically starting a new school,' remarked Blanche Emily in a letter to Ralf, 'on the other hand she will have the more credit if she succeeds.'[12]

As Blanchie took up her post in Birkenhead, Adelaide and Dr Legge began work on the first of several joint enquiries. Predictably it once more involved lead poisoning. This time the subject was the metal enamelling and tinning industries, largely based in the Midlands with other branches in London and in the Lancashire town of Eccles. Primarily focussed on the textile industry, Eccles was a typical small northern town, exuding a degree of civic pride in the small-scale grandeur of its town hall, but largely characterised by its grime and poverty. Rows of overcrowded terraced houses were, as ever, enveloped in the smoke of nearby chimneys. Adelaide visited the town for the first time in the autumn of 1900. Here she found girls with no overalls or washing facilities taking their meals at the 'powdering benches' of an iron plate enamelling works where the finely ground powder, containing high levels of lead and arsenic, was pressed into a metal base before firing. She observed with despair how the dust from the clothes of one woman was liberally sprinkled into the tea of her companion as the two chatted over a meal break together. She went on to visit fifty-two other workshops that year, everything from watch and clock dial manufacturers to bridle makers, where metal was coated with a mixture of tin and lead.[13]

In the Midlands tinning was carried out in the manufacture of 'hollow-ware', metal containers for the table such as bowls, jugs and teapots. And here, in the towns of Wolverhampton and Bilston upwards of two thousand women were employed in japanning, the painting and decorating of these items with a fashionable black varnish containing both lead and mercury. Once more Adelaide noted the lack of ventilation, the absence of washing facilities and 'the almost universal practice of taking meals in workrooms.' Most of the girls, she observed, had no idea they were working with materials dangerous to their health until, that is, they began to suffer recurring bouts of sickness. Mary Paterson, who accompanied Adelaide on some of these visits, was more than a little annoyed by this state of affairs, and not only with employers. Exasperated by the meek acceptance of the workers she noted them 'looking on illness in general in their patient, if somewhat irritating way, as "what you have to expect."'[14] Mary, an admirer of self-reliance, was frequently baffled by the apparent inaction of the poor. Adelaide, by contrast, tended to view the acquiescence of the maltreated as stoicism, her concern tending to provoke a sense of maternal responsibility rather than criticism.

Adelaide did not, however, deliver her part of the report on the enamelling and tinning industries in 1901 as promised.[15] She cited a number of staffing difficulties, the first of which was the transfer of Lucy to temporary special service in South Africa. In March that year, during the second Boer War, thousands of Boer women and children had been removed from their homes by the British and taken to internment camps. Conditions in the camps were reportedly extremely bad, the inhabitants living in squalor with inadequate food and shelter. One informant was welfare campaigner Emily Hobhouse who had visited the camps in June 1901 and had sent back a series of damning reports. These had been published in national newspapers and, conscious of public outrage, the government determined to send their own official delegation to investigate the situation. Millicent Fawcett was selected to lead the investigation and

Lucy, with her inspection experience, was chosen to accompany her. She set off for South Africa in August that year and did not return until the end of the following February. Her absence prompted the secondment, once more, of a reluctant Mary Paterson to London. Mary was already feeling that resources in Scotland were completely inadequate. Not only could she barely address a fraction of the needs of cities like Glasgow, but other areas of Scotland were almost completely neglected. Now things seemed likely to get worse. In an attempt to ameliorate the situation Adelaide was offered the services of a 'temporary inspector' to help fill the gap. Adelaide was pleased, but emphasised in her report for that year that the need to train the new temporary inspector had produced a further drain on her time. Moreover, having spent time on this training, she said, the person concerned developed a 'serious illness' and had to resign, necessitating further training of the replacement. It was a convincing catalogue of difficulties but all was not quite as it seemed. Two candidates for the post of 'temporary lady inspector' had been interviewed by Edward Troup and Arthur Whitelegge. One was Geraldine Hodgson, a graduate of Newnham College, Cambridge. Geraldine had gained a first in Moral Sciences and had an impressive record in teaching and lecturing. The other candidate, Hilda Martindale, was similarly well-educated. Having spent two years at Royal Holloway College, she had qualified as a sanitary inspector and, at Bedford College, had studied industrial hygiene and public health under the tutelage of Thomas Legge. She was also well-travelled. Adelaide had heard her speak at Toynbee Hall about her work with disadvantaged children in a number of different countries she had visited. Hilda, however, could not match Geraldine's glittering academic qualifications and Troup and Whitelegge offered the post to Miss Hodgson. Adelaide was clearly annoyed. She had been allowed no part in the selection process and, in her opinion, the wrong person had been chosen. Whether she had a special aversion to Miss Hodgson is unclear but there is little doubt that she favoured Miss Martindale. Years later, Hilda, who went on to have a highly successful career in the inspectorate, professed herself to have been somewhat bemused by the subsequent turn of events which she learned about from other inspectors. Immediately after her appointment the unfortunate Miss Hodgson had apparently been subjected to an initiation that bore little or no resemblance to 'training'. Over a period of one week she was sent out alone on a rigorous, unrelenting schedule of factory visits to some of the most challenging textile factories in the North of England. It was an experience that left her bewildered and terrified. At the end of the week she returned home to Sussex and a few days later the Home Office received a letter tendering her resignation. She had, she said, been forced to resign on the advice of her doctor, who considered that her heart would not stand up to the strain of this type of work. Adelaide, clearly well satisfied by this outcome, wrote a most sympathetic and understanding letter to Miss Hodgson and proceeded to suggest to the Home Office that the second candidate be appointed. Thus Hilda, having initially been informed of her rejection, was suddenly surprised to find that she was, after all, to be offered an appointment. Beginning work that summer she described her own gentle, gradual, and highly supervised introduction to the work. And in October her temporary appointment became a permanent one. I never really understood what went on, she wrote later.[16]

The circumstances surrounding the appointment of Miss Martindale underlined once more the steely determination that lurked beneath the mild exterior of the Principal Lady Inspector. In the same year, however, there was evidence of another side to Adelaide, the vulnerability that intermittently expressed itself in a complete withdrawal from the scene whenever distress threatened to overwhelm her. At Girton she had fled to Troutwells when her inability to cope with College life had become too much. Now, in 1901, the demands of her work seem to have brought on another crisis. She was forced, she said, to take a prolonged period of leave because of illness and the need of 'some weeks of absolute rest for my eyesight.'[17] Like her illness at Girton, it was a curious, unexplained ailment, and something that did not, apparently, prevent her making a trip to Germany with her mother and sisters. Early in September, Blanchie wrote to Ralf from an 'air spa'[18] in Baden where the four were holidaying. Everyone was in much better health, including Sissy who 'for once had taken a long holiday, six or seven weeks.'[19] Curiously this 'holiday' had been described as sick leave to the Home Office. And it was a period fortuitously timed to coincide with Blanchie's long summer vacation.

Adelaide had, however, been ill on several occasions during the previous twelve months, with influenza, with colds and sore throats and with toothache that, according to Blanchie, 'swelled her face to an unwanted plumpness.'[20] Typically she now seems to have made a private and determined decision to withdraw from the scene to replenish her physical and psychological reserves. The holiday may also have been prompted by pressure from Blanche Emily who by now seemed to have developed a somewhat exacting matriarchal style. Adelaide's frequent absences from home and her excessive busyness were becoming the subject of comment. It was a criticism that fell less immediately on Blanchie who was no longer living at home and invited less direct comparison with her more conventional and attentive sister Mary. Blanche Emily's most obvious demands, however, centred on the requirement for regular letters, suitably spaced to allow a regular flow of news. (She was disappointed if two letters came on the same day). Inevitably censure was more likely to fall on the boys in this respect. Walter seems to have been the chief offender. 'Still no letter from Walter' was a frequent postscript to many of her communications to his siblings. At one point she forbade the rest of the family to write to Walter until he mended his ways. When he did eventually respond his mother was only partially satisfied. 'Had a letter from Walter at last – the first since 19 October. It is quite short and, I feel, very inadequate. He is apologetic but his only excuse is being very busy – and that his right arm still troubles him in spite of massage and other remedies. However, his handwriting looks firm enough.'[21] Poor Walter was probably experiencing the first symptoms of the multiple sclerosis that would develop a few years later.

The holiday in Germany, however, was clearly a great success for everyone. The weather was perfect and the scenery beautiful. The hotel was a delight, filled with agreeable company and there were walks and drives and visits to concerts. Blanche Emily was looking better than she had done for years. And finally, it seemed, she was willing to draw a line under the fruitless search for better accommodation closer to London. There appeared to be nothing that suited both her aspirations and her pocket and everyone had become tired and dispirited by the endless house hunting. Now an agreeable alternative had presented itself. When Blanchie and Adelaide returned to work in mid September she and Mary would move on to the Hôtel Masson in Montreux by Lake Geneva. They would remain there for several months, abandoning the housekeeping cares of Hadley Wood. No longer were Blanche Emily's letters and conversation to be punctuated by the phrase 'when we move back into town'. And Mary seemed to have settled happily into the role of her mother's companion and was enjoying life. Adelaide would have treasured the memory of this holiday, however it was contrived, for it was the last they would all spend together.

By October 1901 she was back in her office in Victoria Street, ready to resume her work on several important problems that had been occupying her at the beginning of the year. It was a significant time for the factory inspectorate, for this was the year a new Act came into force. In part, the Factory Act of 1901 simply represented a consolidation of previous factory legislation which had accumulated in a piecemeal fashion over the years since the first Act of 1833. However, in addition to various new regulations, it also contained some important new procedural features, notably in terms of the application of factory regulations to small workshops and improved procedures governing the development of Special Rules in the Dangerous Trades. The right to an arbitration process which had delayed the implementation of so many of these Rules was to be removed and, in the event of objections, replaced by a special enquiry conducted by a 'competent person' appointed by the Secretary of State.[22] Adelaide was gratified to find that several of the new regulations appeared to stem directly from the results of enquiries made by herself and her staff, notably their findings in the Lucifer match factories, the flax mills, the white lead works, the Potteries and the metal enamelling industries. Significantly there was a new emphasis on the provision of ventilation, particularly mechanical ventilation, and on matters such as the separation of working and eating areas and the limitation of hours spent working with dangerous substances. All of these were highly relevant to a problem that had occupied her immediately before she went to Baden, that of mercury poisoning.

High exposure to mercury could produce a condition called 'erethism', characterised by weakness of the muscles, involuntary tremors and an uncontrollable nervous irritability. Those particularly at risk were workers employed producing felt from rabbit fur in the hatting industry. The 'rabbit fur girls' as they were called, were employed in a process called 'carrotting', where the fur was scrubbed with a solution of mercury and nitric acid to remove grease and thus increase its felting properties. In the summer of 1898 Adelaide had decided to conduct a thorough investigation into this problem and had

dispatched Rose, Lucy and Mary Paterson to make detailed
enquiries in every workplace in England and Scotland where
the process was carried out. On their return to London they
had described how the work was usually done on a wooden
bench with a hard scrubbing brush in damp ill-ventilated
workrooms. The women were repeatedly splashed as they
dipped the brushes into wooden bowls containing the solution.
'Married women all wrap up their wedding rings to preserve
them from the mercury,' Rose observed.[23] After 'carrotting'
the skins were removed to stoves for drying, exposing those
who filled and emptied the stoves to fumes of nitrate of
mercury. Conditions were clearly very bad and the number of
such workplaces exceeded all expectations. Despite the legal
requirement to register all factories and workshops with the
Factory Department many of those involved in carrotting
were previously unknown. Mary Paterson, for example, found
one such factory in Glasgow which employed three hundred
women. It needed 'considerable structural alterations to
render the occupation tolerably free from injuriousness to the
workers,' she reported.[24] Here the hands of the women were
black and their nails stained a deep yellow. Three quarters of
them showed the secondary effects of mercury poisoning in
the poor condition of their teeth and gums and several talked
of injury to the eyes, both from the fumes or more directly as
a result of the 'mercury liqor [sic]' squirting into their faces.
Others described feelings of giddiness, excessive salivation
and stomach pains. The only ventilation in the factory was a
small opening in the roof. Far from protecting the workers, this
appeared to draw the fumes past their faces. Space was very
restricted, with as many benches as possible crammed together
and, with few exceptions, the women took their breakfast and
dinner at the benches where they worked. Only one man was
employed here, whose job it was to mix the liquor. 'His teeth
were much blackened and decayed,' Mary observed.[25]

As a result of the enquiry the Chief Inspector of Factories had issued a circular to all occupiers engaged in the production of felt hats, emphasising their obligations under the law, and the following year Mary and Rose had set about enforcing these regulations in what they considered to be the worst factories. Adelaide, herself, had focussed her attention on the factory in Glasgow, where she had insisted on the installation of a mechanical ventilation system. Previously ventilation had been provided simply by open windows which, on windy days, had actually increased the spread of dust and fumes. Ignoring the protestations of the employer that the coughing of the workers 'was done on purpose because I was in the room' she enlisted the help of the newly appointed Home Office Engineering Advisor to design and supervise the installation of a suitable system.[26] It had turned out to be an expensive year for this particular employer for Adelaide had also insisted on the installation of washing facilities, the provision of gloves and other protective clothing and a limit on the hours of work of those exposed to poisonous substances.[27] For now, under the new Act of 1901, she had new regulations at her disposal. Of course the existence of regulations would not in itself cure the problem, and its most immediate effect was to increase the workload of the lady inspectors. Mercury would remain on Adelaide's agenda for several years. In 1913, however, before the special circumstances of the war intervened, she was able to report that there had been only one notified case of mercury poisoning that year.[28]

The gulf between the regulations and the situation on the ground became very clear in the case of another problem to which Adelaide returned in the autumn of 1901. Forty years before the appointment of the women inspectors a Parisian physician called Auguste Delpech had described the strange behaviour of workers employed in the rubber industry. They suffered, he said, from mental derangement resembling alcohol intoxication. The culprit was a solvent called bisulphide of carbon[29] used to spread the rubber into thin layers on fabric for the production of mackintoshes and India rubber boots. In 1898 Adelaide had watched many young girls carrying out this process, for by the end of the nineteenth century the rubber industry in Britain employed nearly eighteen thousand people, of which over seven thousand were women and young girls.[30] In 1899 Dr Thomas Oliver had given evidence to the Dangerous Trades Committee about the psychotic effects of bisulphide of carbon. He described episodes in which workers had suffered 'an extremely violent and maniacal condition whereby, in their frenzy, have precipitated themselves from the top rooms of the factory to the ground.'[31] Despite the fact that the injurious effects of the substance had been known for many years, however, the only preventative measure currently in place in these factories was the judicious barring of top floor windows. Later that year, therefore, Special Rules had been instituted which stipulated that the troughs containing bisulphide of carbon should be covered, that spreading should only be done in the presence of a fan which drew fumes away from the workers and that cloth should be conveyed to the drying chamber by means of an automatic machine. No worker could be employed for more than five hours continuously in the presence of bisulphide of carbon and meals should be taken in specially designated rooms. To all intents and purposes appropriate preventative measures were in place. Three years later, however, the women inspectors could find little evidence of these precautions in the factories they visited. In Manchester in 1901 Adelaide found several young girls clearly intoxicated. 'The mother of one girl I saw at home tells me that she sits down in a stupor whenever she comes home, refusing food, and can only be got to bed by being carried there, while, if aroused she gets wild and excited.'[32] And in one workshop, the employer, far from protecting the workers, had in fact spread the hazard to the surrounding population. Electing to achieve adequate ventilation by carrying out the process in an open covered yard at the back of his premises, he seems to have succeeded in intoxicating several local residents. There was much to be done.

Rubber boots and mackintoshes were well-established in the nineteenth century but many other products were relatively new, and the hazards they created for the producers were often unforeseen. One August day in 1900 a young girl called Nelly lost an eye in an accident at work. She was employed at an aerated water factory, carrying away the cases of filled bottles and stacking them onto a trolley. As she waited for the next case one of the bottles burst, flinging shards of glass in all directions. Nelly was only one of many casualties of the bottling factories. During the previous twelve months alone there had been 159 reported accidents in this industry, including one fatality. Ten had involved the loss of sight of one or both eyes, and the remainder resulted in lacerations to the hands, face or upper body.[33] By the end of the nineteenth century sparkling or aerated water had become a fashionable addition to the middle class dinner table. The acquisition of this version of mineral water with its presumed health giving properties no longer required an expensive visit to Cheltenham or Royal Tunbridge Wells. There were now seventeen major water factories situated in London and around the towns of Manchester, Sheffield and Norwich, employing more than five thousand people. In November 1900, Whitelegge asked eminent ophthalmic surgeon, Simeon Snell, to visit the major factories and prepare a report. With the help of Dr Legge, Dr Snell produced some impressive statistics. In just one week in a single factory, for example, 222,520 bottles were filled with sparkling water and either wired or plugged with a marble stopper. Of these, 1,608 had burst, showering those around with glass. In another factory fifty-six out of 82,000 siphons had exploded under pressure. Out of 1,600,000 five and ten ounce bottles filled per day, he calculated, 2,962 would burst.[34] The timing of these events was, it seems, entirely

unpredictable. They could occur at any stage in the production
process. In one factory sixty accidents occurred in bottling,
while thirty six others happened during labelling.

In some factories goggles had been provided but the
employers argued that the workers were reluctant to wear them.
To Adelaide, fresh from her experiences in the Potteries, this
story had a familiar ring. In this case, the employers claimed,
there was a prevailing belief that the goggles themselves
damaged the eyes, something that Dr Snell was quick to
discount. He found no evidence of damage resulting from
the goggles, or indeed that any of the workers refused to wear
them, but he did conclude that the goggles were uncomfortable
and, more importantly, failed to protect the remainder of the
face and the neck.[35] As an alternative he proposed aluminium
gauze masks that covered the whole of the head and included a
leather collar to protect the neck. It was a useful step forward
but enforcement fell once more to the factory inspectors, and
more particularly the lady factory inspectors, for most of the
people employed in this industry were women. Every problem
identified, it seemed, created more work. But the rewards were
equally great and, with the new Act, there was an increasing
sense of progress. Soon, however, Adelaide would find herself
distracted once more by family tragedy and the loss of more
loved ones.

For Blanchie, in Birkenhead, things had been going well.
Pupil numbers were growing and there were plans to expand
the school by the purchase of new premises. In October 1903,
however, a year after the holiday in Germany, Ralf was surprised
to receive a letter from her postmarked London. He already
knew that Adelaide had moved out of the house in Hadley Wood
and acquired a new flat in town. It was ostensibly a matter of
convenience, particularly over matters of early morning railway
journeys, but probably she also needed a degree of freedom from
the pressure of domestic concerns. Chelsea Gardens, situated

in Chelsea Bridge Road provided, as Blanchie described it, 'a nice little flat close to the river'. Blanchie, it seems, had spent only ten days of the new term at Birkenhead before becoming tired and breathless. She had been advised by her doctors to take a term off to get well and was now staying in Chelsea Gardens while Adelaide was away at a conference in Brussels. 'I mean to get my heart in working order by means of mild open air. Mama, Alex and I go to Budleigh Salterton tomorrow.'[36] Alex, Adelaide's youngest brother, was home on leave until December and Christmas was to be spent in Brighton with his sisters. That year had brought sadness in the Anderson family with the death of Douglas in Scotland. It was unsurprising, given his condition, and he had by now spent many years away from home. But the event would have been much on everyone's mind as they made plans to gather together at Christmas, that most emotional of family times. Now, however, there was also growing unease about Blanchie's health.

Medical opinion had apparently decided that Blanchie's 'generally limp condition' was due to an attack of influenza earlier in the year. Uncle John Ford concurred with this view and was apparently quite cheerful about it. Perhaps he had no wish to be discouraging or perhaps he was genuinely unaware of the cause and severity of Blanchie's symptoms. It was in fact a second attack of the 'limp condition'. In 1900 she had been forced to return early from the autumn term at Bolton school, again spending Christmas in Brighton with Adelaide. 'I have five weeks to get strong again and the sea air should do me good,' she reported optimistically on that occasion.[37] Now Blanchie was convinced that once more she would be returning to school after Christmas to begin the spring term. When the time came, however, her condition was worse, not better. She wrote a sad letter to the school governors, explaining that she had been advised by her doctors that she needed a further three months' rest.[38] While Blanchie clung on to the hope of eventual recovery, however, it was becoming increasingly clear to her employers that she was too ill to continue in her post. Miss Baines of Clapham High School, appointed as acting headmistress in her absence, was soon confirmed as a permanent replacement. Blanchie returned to Chelsea Gardens, but the flat, was now effectively a prison, its long flight of steps and her breathless condition preventing any contact with the outdoors. Adelaide, busy with her job, could offer only limited care and support and, as her sister's condition worsened, the decision was made to move her to a nursing home in Surrey. It was there, on the morning of 25 June, that Blanchie died with Adelaide at her bedside. The death certificate citing 'valvular disease of the heart (mitral)' as the cause of death indicated long-standing coronary damage, most probably as a result of rheumatic fever as a child. Once more the family made the miserable journey to Brookwood Cemetery.

Blanchie's death would have been a devastating blow to Adelaide and to her mother. Vibrant, determined and successful Blanchie had been full of life. Her absence seemed inexplicable and left a huge gap in the family. And for Adelaide, in particular, she had been a close and like-minded companion. Now two sisters were effectively gone from her life. Mary was similarly bereft. The previous autumn she had embarked on a secretarial course, sharing the flat at Chelsea Gardens with Blanchie and Adelaide. She had, said Blanchie, at last decided on a career, going each day to Miss Gradwell's secretarial school to learn shorthand, typing and book keeping. Urged on by Blanchie she had begun to enjoy it and to develop ambitions to become a private secretary. With Blanchie gone, however, Mary's aspirations seem to have evaporated. After the funeral she returned to Hadley Wood and to the old life with Blanche Emily. The two were soon on the move again, travelling to Cannes where Aunt Mary [39] (Alexander Gavin's sister) was living. That winter, they stayed at a series of unsatisfactory guest houses where Blanche Emily complained incessantly about the food, the company and the expense. Her own health was deteriorating and the cold brought on another attack of her 'back', although 'the old bronchial trouble was no worse.'[40] They had decided to remain in Cannes until March, she told Ralf in January. They had been advised not to go to North Italy until April because it was so cold, but she worried that Cannes was too expensive. Finance seems to have been a constant preoccupation, a difficulty alleviated by Max who sent money at regular intervals to pay the bills.

Blanche Emily was depressed and unwell, desperately seeking solace in a change of scene, her letters rambling over the minutiae of conditions in the latest accommodation, the recent deaths of elderly relatives and complaints about the behaviour of others. Walter was in trouble again for his failure to write 'I had a letter from Walter at last. He wisely says no more in the way of excuse.'[41] Even Adelaide invited a degree of censure. 'I expect Sissy has been too busy to write and we only get short letters' and 'I am annoyed that she is not sending letters on to people – though I know she is busy.'[42] It was a family custom that letters were circulated around to ensure that everyone was up to date with all the news. Adelaide had, in fact, fled to Alice, now living once more at Bridgefield, the Macdonnell family home outside Aberdeen. Adelaide had arranged a working trip to Glasgow and from there she had travelled to the old house at the Bridge of Balgownie, for it was here that she could most comfortably nurse her grief. It was a desperate time and sadly there was more to come. By July Blanche Emily had returned to England, but not to Hadley Wood. Instead she moved into Whitethorns, a private nursing home in Surrey. She was suffering from pleurisy and was to undergo an operation. Both Max and Alex had sent money 'so I shall be comfortable.'[43] The details of her treatment are unclear but she wrote to Ralf to tell him that it had been a success, 'although it was much more painful than I expected and it needed all my fortitude not to disgrace myself. I am a little disappointed that my prayers towards recovery are so slow.' This was to be her last communication with Ralf. Perhaps she realised this all too well for she concluded her letter with a touching farewell to her much-loved absent son. 'Always remember my dear, dear son that you have been a comfort to me all your life.'[44]

A few weeks later Max arrived in England on business and immediately recognised that Blanche Emily was seriously ill. He elected to prolong his visit to help his sisters who were by now taking turns to sit with their mother for hours at a time throughout the day and night. Adelaide would always remember his support during Blanche Emily's last days. Max was the calm, stable elder brother, the one on whom she could rely, and his presence during this dreadful time was beyond price. 'Can you imagine what a comfort Max has been?' she wrote to Alex later. 'Mary and I dare not think what our desolation would be without him.'[45] Blanche Emily died early in the morning of Sunday the 18 October. 'It was,' said Adelaide 'a very blessed and peaceful passing.' And this time the journey to Brookwood, on a brilliantly sunny day, was a comforting one, surrounded by family and friends. The two sisters immediately wrote long letters to the other brothers, detailing the manner of their mother's death. Blanche Emily was devoted to her faith and these were letters that described prayers, bible readings and hymn singing during her last hours. They also left no doubt about the supreme importance of Christian faith in Adelaide's own life. She urged her brothers not to grieve or regret, dwelling on the 'beautiful and comforting hopes that have come with her death. I long for peace to be in your heart,' she concluded.[46]

Beneath all this, however, Adelaide was mentally and physically exhausted. A family friend wrote to Alex to express her sympathy, and her concern, 'Adelaide and Mary are so brave and strong but I think they are both very tired after the long strain – especially Adelaide.'[47] It was Max who proposed that the three of them should treat his journey back to Australia as a long and much needed holiday. They would accompany him as far as Egypt and then return refreshed to England in the New Year. Early in December, therefore, they set off on their voyage together, enjoying the milder Mediterranean days at sea and the visits to ports along the way. Finally parting company with Max in Port Said, Adelaide and Mary returned to Hadley Wood early in January. Both were now faced with a redefinition of their family roles. Immediately after her mother's death Adelaide had written to Alex and Ralf to tell them that they must be assured that she and Mary would now be living together in the future 'as far as possible in the old home-like conditions.'[48] She seems to have imagined (rightly or wrongly) that 'her dear scattered brothers' craved the knowledge of a secure home base back in England, a base presided over by a matriarchal presence. And it was natural for her to assume that she herself must now take over that role. When the immediate shock of change had subsided, however, the family arrangements took a rather different turn for, whatever her good intentions, Adelaide found she had outgrown 'the old home-like conditions'. She soon returned to her flat in Chelsea Gardens from which she could conduct her increasingly busy working life, and it was Mary who took over Blanche Emily's domestic role. The finances for this seem to have been provided by the brothers who together agreed to transfer their share of Blanche Emily's estate to Mary and a new house was bought in Haslemere, Surrey. Fairhaven, with its lovely surroundings and beautiful garden, became the Anderson home, a place to which everyone could return and, when needed, retreat. Here, over the years, family gatherings would come and go and friends would be entertained. Mary lived at Fairhaven for the rest of her life, adopting the position for which she had essentially been prepared over several years, her unfailing hospitality, (presumably involving particularly

good tea parties), earning her the affectionate family nickname
of 'thé la la'. For Adelaide, the repeated shocks of the last few
years had left an indelible mark and there would continue to be
periods when her vulnerability would break through the mask
of calm control. But a period of family stability now appeared
to lie on the horizon. The next few years would allow her to
concentrate with increasing energy on her work.

Mary and Walter at Fairhaven, circa 1908.

Chapter Nine
CLEAN LINEN AND CLEAN SOULS

In 1852 a Scottish clergyman called George Dickson preached a sermon on the subject of cleanliness. It was, he reminded his flock, 'a personal duty which we owe to ourselves individually, a social duty which we owe to society and a religious duty which we owe to God.'[1] Predictably the link between cleanliness and morality, prevalent during the nineteenth century, soon extended to a similar association between personal hygiene and social status. Thus *Routledge's Manual of Etiquette* in 1860 advised that 'in these days of public baths and universal progress, we trust that it will be unnecessary to do more than hint at the necessity of the most fastidious personal cleanliness . . . a soiled shirt, a dingy pocket handkerchief, or a waistcoat that has been worn once too often are things to be scrupulously avoided by any man who is ambitious of preserving the exterior of a gentleman.'[2] By the 1880s, the urban middle classes were more than ready to embrace the social values that would distinguish them from the lower orders. The maintenance of clean clothes and household linen represented an important element of these aspirations. All this, however, created a problem. The large quantities of dirty washing generated by middle class households frequently exceeded their capacity to maintain the desired standards of respectability. Many houses lacked the space, the equipment, the staff or the water to provide a regular supply of clean linen. Drying was a particular problem since items hung outside in the smoke laden air of large cities rapidly became covered in sooty smuts. And the increased demand for laundry services could no longer be met by local women who had traditionally supplemented their family income by taking in washing. The answer to these difficulties, as ever, was steam power, this time in the form of commercially operated laundries with established water supplies, employing groups of women who operated increasingly sophisticated technical equipment. Not only did laundries provide a service to middle and upper class households but they also found a ready market amongst the thousands of clerks and businessmen living in single rooms, whose rising social status required high standards in terms of personal appearance. By the end of the nineteenth century approximately seventy thousand women in Britain were employed in steam-powered laundries, a figure that would rise to over one hundred thousand by the beginning of the First World War.[3] In London the proliferation of laundries to serve the needs of the wealthy inhabitants of Kensington and St John's Wood earned for the neighbouring district of Kensal Town the title of 'Soapsuds Island'.

Like most forms of 'universal progress' competitive cleanliness came at a price and, unsurprisingly, the price was paid by those with no access at all to any sort of social ladder. The majority of laundries established during this period were small businesses situated in basement rooms or on the ground floors of multi-occupancy dwelling houses. The atmosphere of laundry premises was damp and steamy with fetid odours arising from dirty clothes, for windows were invariably sealed to prevent sooty particles alighting on newly washed linen. Working hours usually exceeded sixty over six days, rarely with any provision for meal breaks and often including night work. The work was not only physically arduous, but also hazardous. A typical power driven laundry now contained a washing machine in which clothes were agitated in a metal drum, a rotating hydroextractor that removed water via centrifugal force and a heated calender[4] which smoothed and dried items at the same time. This equipment was driven by belts and pulleys powered by a small steam engine. There was usually a heated drying closet for starched items or items otherwise unsuited to mangling which would be ironed by hand using gas powered irons. The introduction of technology into this industry had significantly shifted the balance from health issues, associated with long hours, poor air quality and a hot damp environment, to safety issues where there was a real risk of serious injury. Steam power increased the speed at which processes were carried out and workers were often young and inexperienced. To the ever present risk of burns and scalds was now added the possibility of crushed limbs as workers fed items into the rollers of the calenders or scalping as a result of hair or clothing being caught in the belts and pulleys which drove the equipment. The speed with which these changes were adopted resulted in many employers purchasing steam engines without the necessary operational knowledge, adding boiler explosions to an increasing range of potential hazards. Others bought cheap and faulty laundry equipment, purchased, Adelaide noted, second, third or even fourth hand.

Laundries had first come to Adelaide's attention when she was lecturing at Toynbee Hall. In 1889, with New Unionism sweeping the country, a group of London women had formed the highly successful, if short-lived, Amalgamated Society of Laundresses. The demand was for an amendment to the Factory Act that would bring laundries under factory legislation and inspection. The campaign attracted thousands of members. There were rallies in Hyde Park, questions in Parliament by radical MPs and, importantly, the support of male trade unionists. Laundry work was unequivocally a female occupation and these women posed no threat to male employment. The demands of the laundresses, however, like those of the matchmakers, centred not on their physical conditions but on their working hours and pay, and ultimately they were defeated. In 1891 Conservative Home Secretary, Henry Matthews, argued that the laundry industry was too diverse in size to implement universal rules on working hours. His real concern, however, seemed to be that regulation would undermine the economic efficiency of those laundries run by institutions and charitable organisations. They often, he said, depended for their income on laundry work and operated under conditions that made it difficult for them to be compliant with working time legislation. Many such institutions existed in England but no doubt he also had in mind the numerous laundries situated in Irish religious institutions. The current Government relied for its majority on a number of Irish MPs who strongly opposed any such regulation. The motion was thus thrown out, the laundresses retreated and their fledgling union withered and died. By 1895, however, there was a new Liberal Government and a new Factory Act, with laundry regulations based largely on the recommendations of the Labour Commission. Institutional laundries were still exempted from the legislation but commercial laundry owners, at least, were now legally required to install guards on machinery and report any accidents that resulted in three or more day's absence from work.

It was not until 1900 that Adelaide was able to turn her full attention to the enforcement of these regulations. That year, after several years of persistent lobbying, she had secured the establishment of the 'West London Special District', an area of London bursting with small workshops, dressmakers, milliners and laundries. Here women were employed in large numbers and Adelaide had argued successfully that the area should be the domain of the women inspectors alone. It was an arrangement readily acceded to by the male inspectors who probably viewed the loss of their jurisdiction over dressmakers and laundries with a certain amount of relief. Adelaide had long been exercised by 'sanitary matters' in these workshops, bombarding the hard-pressed Sanitary Department with an ever-increasing mountain of issues which lay firmly within their realm of responsibility, but unfortunately not within their capacity to successfully address. In 1900 the Home Office announced its intention of carrying out a special enquiry into ventilation in factories, harnessing the expertise of Professor John Scott Haldane who had previously investigated the air in coal mines, and on the notoriously fume-ridden Metropolitan underground railway. Adelaide was determined that small workshops should form part of this enquiry and secured an assurance that they would, in fact, be included in the first phase of the investigation. Haldane's report, published in 1902, contained precise criteria for air standards in 'ordinary rooms' based on the proportion of carbonic acid (carbon dioxide) in the air, recommendations soon to be incorporated into the new factory regulations under the Act of 1901. Adelaide was well-satisfied with this result, particularly since the validation of a new portable air sampling device, developed during the investigation, had been carried out by her own staff. By 1905 the women inspectors were regularly collecting samples and sending them off for analysis, an activity considerably aided by the appointment that year of a scientifically qualified inspector, Mildred Power. Adelaide was quick to capitalise on Mildred's skills, and to point out to Arthur Whitelegge that Miss Power could carry out the necessary analysis herself, thus saving the department much time and money. In the event, however, the problem of ventilation would prove to be a particularly intractable one. Measurement was one thing but prevention, in closed underground workshops, was quite another. Undoubtedly there were improvements, one of which was a marked reduction in the use of flueless gas stoves, much promoted as the answer to heating problems and, of course, a significant source of poisonous carbon monoxide. Haldane had shown that levels of carbonic acid varied consistently with levels of carbonic oxide (carbon monoxide) and thus the former provided a reliable marker for the latter. At least Adelaide and her staff now had a scientifically based regulatory framework within which to conduct their protracted negotiations with the purveyors of 'sweated' goods.

It was in the area of laundry safety, however, that she was to achieve one of her most notable successes. She began by carrying out a detailed investigation into conditions in the West London District, an area which, she argued, 'presented in a small compass all the characteristic features of the trade.'[5] She intended to determine the specific nature of accidents which occurred, their frequency and their causes. It was essentially a systematic survey of a representative sample designed to identify the primary focus for preventative measures and provide a blueprint for action elsewhere. Informed by the methods of Thomas Legge this was the new approach to industrial health and safety now practised within the Factory Department.

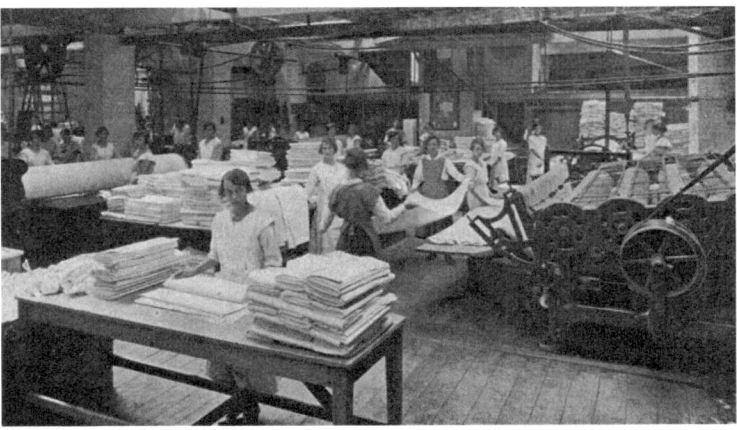

Wolverhampton Steam Laundry in 1924 showing a calender on the right of the picture. (Reproduced with the permission of Wolverhampton City Archives.)

Lucy, dispatched once more to the back streets of London, reported on thirty-seven serious laundry accidents over a twelve-month period, investigating each in detail. Adelaide insisted that all the women inspectors visited these sites as a form of training in hazard awareness. She, meanwhile, examined the data. She concluded that unguarded calenders and wringing machines were responsible for more than half the accidents. Moreover, since accidents of all types increased in July and December in accordance with the high points of 'The Season', safety problems appeared to be exacerbated by long hours and fatigue, as well as by the hiring of inexperienced workers at times of excessive demand. Two fatalities were caused by falls through unguarded trapdoors but most accidents involved machinery. Thus a young boy, suffered partial strangulation and subsequent paralysis when he was dragged by his coat into the overhead shafting, while one woman's arm was severed by the revolving cage of the hydroextractor.[6] Limb amputations were in fact the most frequent type of injury suffered by laundry workers, while burns were also common. Adelaide was constantly concerned about the loose clothing worn by workers. Women in hot rooms, she noted, 'naturally wear the neck of their bodice loose and often finish it with a lightly knotted ribbon or scarf.'[7] She found one girl with a badly burned face whose scarf had been caught in the rollers of the calender. 'Nothing but the presence of mind of the forewoman,' she said, 'saved this girl from a sudden and terrible death.'[8] Twenty-year-old Margaret Williams, a worker at Bristol Steam Laundry in Westbury on Trym, was not so lucky. In 1887 she was killed when the hydroextractor she was using burst, apparently as a result of overloading and excessive speed. The ill-informed use of second-hand steam engines featured in a number of accidents. One worker whose hand had been crushed was clear on this point. 'Since the boss tied the old mangle up to the new engine she has taken to leaping back and forth that alarmin'' and that sudden-like that its a wonder I've not been caught out sooner.'[9]

The findings in West London provided the basis for an extended, wide-ranging project that continued until 1913. It was to prove one of the most effective intervention programmes undertaken by the women inspectors and, as such, represented one of their most significant achievements. In 1902 Adelaide assigned Inspector Anna Tracey to the task of collating national data in order to monitor trends in the number and types of laundry accidents over succeeding years. The results, when viewed from the perspective of 1913, were extremely gratifying. At first glance there appeared to be a slight increase in the total number of serious accidents when one compared earlier with later years. But since the arrival of Thomas Legge in the Factory Department statistics had acquired a new level of sophistication. Accident figures now took account of the number of people employed and were presented not as raw numbers but as rates per thousand workers. Only then could real increases or decreases be accurately assessed. During the period there had been a huge increase in the number of steam-powered laundries such that by 1913 the industry now employed over one hundred thousand workers. Taking this into account the rate of accidents had reduced steadily between 1904 and 1914, a decline arrested only by a sudden rise in 1911, the year of the Coronation of King George V.[10] As the great day approached thousands of visitors had descended on the capital filling up every available hotel and boarding house. It was a particularly hot summer that year and those who had come to cheer the event were considerably exercised by their duty of cleanliness. Hundreds of inexperienced laundry workers were thus recruited to satisfy their needs, and payed the inevitable price. This was a short-lived reversal, however. Overall the progress in laundry safety provided Adelaide with a justifiable degree of satisfaction.

The mainstay of Adelaide's approach was a programme of workplace visiting. Prosecutions were relatively rare, averaging only two or three per year, reflecting a growing ethos within the inspectorate that such actions were both time-consuming and expensive. Twenty inspections could be carried out in the time it took to prepare for a court hearing. The greatest deterrent, Adelaide concluded, was provided by a limited number of highly publicised actions. Thus in 1913 she sanctioned a prosecution by inspector Mabel Vines of a laundry in Edinburgh where a young girl lost the use of her hand as a result of an unfenced calender. The success of this prosecution, she considered, 'materially strengthened administration of fencing requirements in Scotland'[11] for the story was widely covered in the Scottish press. Most effective prevention work, however, was achieved by means of advice and education. Despite her small staff Adelaide presided over an impressive programme of workplace inspections. Inspector Emily Sadler, who took over responsibility for the West London Special District in 1904, visited 571 laundries that year. Adelaide, herself, appears to have combined administrative duties with continuing hands-on inspection and in particular preferred to undertake the training of new staff. One new recruit described the rigours of this process. 'After a long morning of most energetic inspection of laundries in one of the least salubrious of suburbs, and when the inner man called for refreshment as one o'clock came, Miss Anderson said brightly: "Now we can take the opportunity to pay some mealtime visits." It was not until nearly three o'clock that she said, "I think a cup of tea somewhere would be pleasant before we go on to the next place."'[12] The energy of the 'frail little friend' was it seems inexhaustible and she expected nothing less of her staff.

Inspections were also combined with the delivery of circulars to employers advising them of the dangers of laundry machinery and pointing out their obligations under factory law.

The division of responsibility between worker and employer was often a grey area however, and one where the male and female inspectors differed markedly in terms of emphasis. Many male inspectors, for example, would have agreed with Mr Seymour, Inspector for East London, when he remarked that 'so many accidents occur purely through carelessness or inattention on the part of the operatives.' With barely disguised irritation he observed that 'calender hands in laundries are constantly getting one or more fingers drawn in between the roller and the iron, and on enquiry I am generally told that the girl was turning her head to speak to someone else and not watching her work.'[13] The women inspectors had no time for such attitudes. Adelaide viewed it as quite unreasonable to lay the responsibility for safety on the shoulders of the workers, more particularly because of their youth. These were often young, tired girls between the ages of fourteen and eighteen who could be found feeding the rollers of calenders for up to sixteen hours a day. 'For a moment's inattention to their dangerous charge they may have to pay by the loss of the right hand in the most horribly painful manner.'[14] Emily Sadler felt it was particularly important to discourage employers from shirking their responsibilities.

> I have been much struck over and over again by the gratuitous comments of occupiers[15] on their accident reports as to the reason for the accident. Again and again the phrase occurs 'due to her own carelessness,' or 'the girl had no right to be using this machine.' Such phrases should form no part of their report. How can a girl of fifteen who has had an accident after working nearly a five hours' spell in a steam laden factory, vibrating with machinery, be said to be careless?[16]

The need for worker training was something else that Adelaide was keen to lay at the door of the employer. Mary

Paterson was appalled at the practice of 'putting young girls to operate dangerous machines without their having previously learned with an experienced worker.'[17] Emily agreed and knew the real situation on the ground. 'How can a girl refuse to put clothes through the dangerous ingathering feed rollers of an unfenced wringer if she has been ordered to do so by the forewoman.'[18]

A notable improvement during the years preceding the First World War was the development of effective guards for laundry equipment. Initially employers were hostile to the idea, claiming that suitable guards simply did not exist. Anna was scathing about this form of excuse. 'Surely the manufacturers of England cannot be baffled by the production of an efficient guard for the machines if they give the matter their earnest attention.'[19] Adelaide, as ever, was more diplomatic. 'The rapid recent development of machinery of a specialised kind in laundries produces a situation and a class of risks which leaves most Inspectors of any experience almost at the same starting point; knowledge has, in fact, to be acquired by all alike.'[20] She persuaded the Home Office to promote an exhibition of guarding equipment, specifically designed for laundries, to be held at Islington's Agricultural Hall. Here members of the Factory Department, laundry engineers and employers met and reached agreement on the most effective methods of safeguarding laundry machinery, an agreement subsequently embodied in a Home Office memorandum to employers on machinery safety. Now it was most definitely in the economic interests of manufacturers to give the matter their 'earnest attention' and to supply and fit approved safety devices. Adelaide, well-satisfied, heaped enthusiastic encouragement on interested parties. 'The process,' she said, 'had been greatly helped by the many beautiful examples of fencing exhibited in the Hall, which were the outcome of past years of less formal interchange of ideas between inspectors and engineers.'[21] She proceeded to develop a large information base on safety equipment which inspectors in the field could recommend to employers. By 1913 she reported with obvious delight that 'the whole matter is now so well in hand that every variation in operation or construction of machinery, and every variation in method of fencing, is at once brought to my knowledge.'[22]

Adelaide's relentless optimism could often lead her to overstate the extent of progress in industrial health and safety, but here it seems her satisfaction was justified. Not only had her staff made a real difference but they had also demonstrated a growing proficiency in the inspection of machinery. Now they were able to give informed advice to employers in this previously male preserve. And, just as in the Potteries, much additional information was acquired by seeking out the victims of industrial accidents and visiting them in their own homes. The reports of the women inspectors suggested that they had a strong interest in the personal circumstances of individual workers' lives, something that rarely, if ever, seemed to preoccupy male inspectors. Thus Inspector Mabel Vines described the circumstances of two victims of accidents:

> These accidents are terribly pathetic. For not only do they mean pain and suffering, and in many cases, permanent injury, but the worker losing his or her means of livelihood, is very often suddenly plunged into destitution. Such was the case with Mrs M. whose arm was injured in a steam mangle. When visiting her about three weeks after the accident I found her starving and cold. No fire and no food and her arm was worse than it was a week ago, she told me.[23]
>
> Recently I visited the home of a young girl, who fifteen months previously had been injured in a calender accident. Her left hand was entirely gone, but with the sound right hand she had been doing all she could to help with the family needlework.

The family had been nearly starving, the father out of work, there were several little brothers and sisters, and she had been the only one old enough to give substantial help.[24]

Adelaide encouraged such visits and ensured that they received ample coverage in her reports, not least because they often highlighted the longer-term consequences of injuries which certifying surgeons might have described as 'slight' or 'not severe'. Many laundry workers whose arms were drawn into rollers suffered from crush injuries which were not immediately apparent but which might result in amputations weeks or even months later. Lucy had sought the opinion of a London surgeon who had carried out a number of these amputations. 'The combination of crushing and burning of the flesh,' he told her, 'is so destructive that even where the results are at first not apparently severe a form of mortification follows, necessitating amputation.'[25] Similarly, laundresses burnt by rollers and irons or scalded by steam often suffered injuries which penetrated deep into the skin and could result in serious infections at a later stage. Too often these were wrongly classified as 'slight'.[26] The distinction was an important one. For, with the advent of the Workmen's Compensation Act of 1906, many of the follow-up visits carried out by inspectors enabled injured workers to claim compensation payments for injuries which had initially been recorded as minor and non-disabling, but which had essentially deprived them of their livelihood. Payments were invariably small, but in a harsh and unforgiving world they could make the difference between survival and starvation.

There was, however, another side to the laundry industry where the abuse of workers took a less visible but nevertheless equally pernicious form. When the Reverend Dixon informed his congregation of God's interest in cleanliness he was tapping into a strong vein of nineteenth-century religious thought. In the Victorian mind there was a strong association between

dirt and sin, particularly sexual sin. Women and girls were of
course the chief recipients of the public censure that followed
sexual activity outside marriage and many were dispatched to
institutions where they were subjected to a pitiless reformatory
regime. These 'Homes for the Penitent', otherwise known as
the Magdalene Homes,[27] had originally been established in
the late eighteenth century in an attempt to stem the rising
tide of prostitution. By the late nineteenth century, however,
they were primarily the destination of 'fallen' girls and women
as well as numbers of the 'feeble-minded', 'inebriates', and
those whose behaviour was considered by their families to
be either promiscuous or difficult in some other, unspecified
way. The system was highly convenient for the large number
of religious institutions that depended for their income
on the laundry industry, for it provided a ready supply of
cheap labour. Moreover the cleaning of clothes operated as a
kind of sinister metaphor for the cleansing of the soul. The
majority of homes were affiliated to religious organisations,
both Anglican and Roman Catholic, and many were convents
staffed by nuns. The reformatory regime consisted of hard
work, religious instruction and prayer. As a sign of penance
all forms of vanity or pleasurable activity were discouraged
such that hair was shorn, personal clothing and possessions
confiscated and contact with previous friends and family
forbidden. Friendships, particularly 'special friendships' with
other inmates were not allowed and much of the day's activities,
including work and meals were conducted in silence. It was
a brutal regime although for many women, particularly those
who found themselves pregnant and alone, options were so
limited that Magdalene Homes could sometimes seem like a
refuge, marginally preferable to the workhouse where they were
likely to face similar treatment as well as starvation and disease.
Women who arrived with babies in their arms at the door of the
Homes for the Penitent, however, found that their infants were

immediately removed from their care and offered for adoption. It was another useful source of income for the institution concerned. The majority of admissions were of young girls, some as young as eleven years old. Many remained there for the rest of their lives, although others left after a few years, either because they were considered sufficiently reformed to be placed in service or, alternatively, regarded as so disobedient as to be incapable of salvation. Others simply ran away. In January 1908 an extension to the Factory Act of 1895 placed the inspection of institutional laundries under the jurisdiction of the Factory Department and unsurprisingly it was to Adelaide and her staff that the task fell.

By 1906 Adelaide had, in fact, already anticipated the extension to the Act, incorporating its requirements into her programme of work. In 1902 she had undertaken a tour of institutional laundries in France, Belgium and Germany, returning with the conviction that employment in such establishments should, like those on the Continent of Europe, be brought under factory regulations. There had followed three years of 'voluntary inspection' of institutional laundries by Hilda Martindale in England and by Mary Paterson in Scotland. Lucy, meanwhile, had carried out a similar survey as part of her work in Ireland. Hilda had been greatly concerned by what she found in English institutions. It was a repetition of the situation encountered by inspectors in commercial laundries several years earlier. There was no provision for ventilation, no fire escapes, no screening of stoves for heating irons or of steam escaping from the copper. Once more laundries were sited in dirty underground basements, the combination of gas lights and dirty washing producing a stuffy, foul atmosphere that was unrelieved by any form of access to outside air. Here young girls slaved for long hours each day. And Hilda observed obvious apprehension amongst the staff lest she might speak to the workers. Considerable care was taken to ensure that she had no opportunity to do so. Lucy and Mary reported similar findings in Ireland and Scotland.

Adelaide's obvious enthusiasm for this extra burden of work, apparently voluntarily undertaken despite the mountain of other tasks awaiting the attention of the women inspectors, invites some explanation. She was by now, of course, seriously engaged with the problems in commercial laundries and confident of her ability to make a difference. Laundries were a success story that served to enhance the reputation of the women inspectors. In earlier years, however, any proposal to bring institutional laundries under state regulation had been thwarted by Irish MPs concerned about the inclusion in the legislation of religious reformatory organisations.[28] The advent of a stronger Liberal Government in 1905, served to remove this obstacle and provided those concerned about such institutions with an opportunity which had not been available for many years. It is fairly clear, therefore, that the primary purpose of the investigations carried out by Hilda, Mary and Lucy in the years before 1907 was the construction of an unassailable case for bringing institutional laundries under state regulation. The Factory Act of 1907 placed these institutions under the regulatory control of the Factory Department.

Six months before the Act became law, Anna Tracey had been dispatched by Adelaide to carry out a survey of all 'Homes, convents and penitentiaries' in England. She identified 106 such institutions, reporting details of the number and ages of inmates, the nature of the religious institutions in charge, and the working conditions.[29] Anna, by now well acquainted with what could happen in laundries, was nevertheless shocked by what she found. The heat from the ironing stoves, usually lit by the girls at four o'clock in the morning, was unbearable. 'I was told that sometimes in the summer the girls were almost 'melted.'[30] It was an observation backed by a complementary report by Inspector Mildred Power who, armed with the latest wet and dry bulb thermometers, produced a series of readings taken inside and outside laundry premises at different times of the year. The floors and walls of these premises were wet and dirty, the foul air saturated with a steamy fog through which you could barely see across the room. Antiquated and unguarded machinery was an almost universal feature. 'I have had my heart in my mouth more than once when I watched young girls feeding dangerous machinery without the most elementary form of guard,' she observed. 'How these laundries have escaped terrible accidents is beyond me to explain.'[31] Almost certainly, of course, as she well knew, it was a lack of reporting that had produced this particular form of clean sheet. Unregulated establishments were under no obligation to inform the Home Office of accidents. But, she pointed out, the sisters in religious institutions had their own explanation for the absence of injuries. 'They attribute their immunity to the goodness of God,' she observed despairingly.[32] Hours of work was perhaps the only area where there existed something approaching compliance with Factory Law. Most institutions, Anna noted, restricted their working hours to less than the statutory maximum of twelve per day. But there was a sting in this tail. 'Of course,' she said, 'attendance at church or chapel is a great feature and takes up a large part of each day.' Bible study classes were similarly prominent. A complete absence of free time was compounded by holidays that Anna considered to be a 'bad imitation of the real thing.'[33] As she note in a subsequent report, such 'holidays' invariably occurred on religious festival days, notably Christmas Day and St Mary Magdalen Day, and most of the day was spent in church or 'in retreat'.[34]

Adelaide gave considerable prominence to the findings of these voluntary inspections in her Annual Report for 1907 and twelve months later, armed with the requirements of the new Act, she sent Anna out to conduct a detailed inspection of the 389 charitable institutions now registered with the Factory

Department. The total number of inmates in these institutions,
Anna reported, was 9,251, of which 2,510 were under eighteen
years of age. All but eleven were women or girls and in almost
every case the primary source of income was laundry work.
Officially her brief was to inspect arrangements for health and
safety, but she obviously found that certain other aspects of
these institutions were extremely dispiriting.

> After visiting all these Homes I cannot but feel some regret that
> the managers do not see their way to a wider introduction of other
> means of employing the energy and latent talents of the women
> and girls committed to their charge.[35]
>
> The youth of so many of the girls found in homes for penitents
> is a most deplorable feature and the tendency is ever towards their
> being taken younger still. Many times I have met little girls of
> thirteen or fourteen sent there under circumstances which fill
> one's heart with pity.[36]
>
> . . . it is grevous that the sins of others should be so heavily
> visited upon these poor children to whom the simple natural
> joys of home life are now denied. For real home life can never be
> attained in the life of 'a Home'.[37]
>
> I could not help noticing what I can only describe as deadness.
> Factory girls are alive and Home girls are so dead. I do not feel
> anyone on the inside of an institution can realise the deadening
> effect of this ceaseless round of work, this iron bound routine
> which is never broken by easy contact with outside life. It is
> wider development that is needed, quite apart from the moral
> development such as Bible classes and chapel inspire.[38]

Rose Squire and another inspector, Emily Slocock, were
also sent to visit institutional laundries. 'The inmates appear
to an outsider accustomed to ordinary factory life to be too
severely disciplined and to work under unnatural and somewhat
strained conditions,' observed Emily.[39] Rose, meanwhile, found

the inmates 'in a depressed and listless condition, and a state of dress and person that reflects no credit upon those in charge.'[40]

Anna's report also contained references to certain 'innovations' that she occasionally encountered, but in doing so she effectively highlighted the more usual state of affairs.

> In some cases the managers have made bold experiments. They have done away altogether with silences, the girls are trusted to go out; like normal human beings they go to entertainments and the results are more than encouraging.[41]
>
> One or two homes have gone so far as to let them wear the garb of everyday life, discarding the hideous clothes so often adopted. In these cases there is no difference between this and any other small well-managed laundry. The girls are bright and talk to each other quietly and naturally.[42]

There is little doubt that Adelaide was the directing mind behind the collection of these reports. She was, after all, in overall charge of the work undertaken by the women inspectors and the final arbiter of the content of their Annual Reports. She justified this content first by noting that most of the observations made by her inspectors 'fell under the headings covered by Section 5 of the new Act (ventilation, hours of work, safeguarding of machinery).' Second, however, she noted that certain other observations had been made which 'do not fall under those headings, but as they are of the greatest importance they must be understood by anyone engaged in administering the Act if this is to be effected.'[43]

Adelaide's interest in Magdalene laundries was no personal whim but rather a reflection of more general concerns amongst certain feminist groups about the fate of women in these circumstances. Like many in society she undoubtedly shared contemporary anxieties about moral degeneration and clearly espoused traditional views on sexual morality, particularly among women. But there were two conflicting strands of opinion regarding the treatment of those who were considered to have fallen into moral danger. The religiously inspired tended to emphasise solitary prayer and silent contemplation, a search for personal forgiveness and redemption. For many of the sisters in these institutions their success was measured primarily in terms of the number of individuals who chose to remain behind closed doors for the rest of their lives and devote themselves to God. In Roman Catholic institutions such individuals were known as 'consecrated penitents', taking holy vows similar to those of the nuns and held up as a moral example to new inmates. By contrast a rather more utilitarian approach to reform, inspired by the ideas of philosophers like Jeremy Bentham whose writings Adelaide had studied with enthusiasm at Cambridge, emphasised the value of useful, incentivised work to enable individuals to remain and prosper within normal society. Anna, designated as the principal mouthpiece for the women inspectors on this subject, makes it clear where the women inspectors stood on the matter, returning to the subject again and again.

> In two homes, the only two known to me, the girls are paid normal wages, and are treated very much as they would be in any carefully conducted workroom outside. The wages increase as the girls' value increases and they depend of course also on conduct and general behaviour as in any outside place.[44]
>
> It always seems to me that incentive for improvement is sadly lacking; whether they work well or badly, whether they are 'meek and lowly in spirit' or give way to appalling temper their bed and board is still assured and their hope of independence is still about the same.
>
> I still feel that the blot on the employment of girls in a home is the lack of wages, or some other system by which self-interest and self-respect is stimulated.[45]

Despite her obvious religious commitment Adelaide herself had little enthusiasm for the Homes for the Penitent, and none at all when the regime they espoused was accompanied by low standards of care. Her initial impression of many of these institutions is contained in her report for 1905 when the inspectors were carrying out preliminary visits in advance of the 1907 Act.

> The mischief which has resulted from the acquiescence in a low standard in charitable work is incalculable, and it is deplorable that reproach is seldom attached to sheer incompetence, provided it is cloaked under sufficient good-will and charitable intention. The money spent in maintaining women and children in an institution under circumstances of overcrowding, or of uncleanliness, or of bad ventilation, or of depressing and incessant labour, or an insufficient and unsuitable diet, or under the supervision of ill-paid and incompetent matrons, had better be spent in helping them another way.[46]

Her support for her former pupil and lifelong friend Lettice Fisher (neé Ilbert), who worked tirelessly to provide accommodation and financial help for single women and their children, indicate the nature of 'another way', which Adelaide found both morally and economically acceptable. Her response to the findings of the women inspectors, however, has to be seen both in the context of the time and within the constraints of her own position. As ever, she focussed on the possible rather than the ideal and trod a cautious, judicious path. Within her limited sphere of influence, and of course in keeping with her duty as a loyal apolitical civil servant, she concentrated on providing information, carefully averting public censure by placing the comments of the women inspectors within the framework of health and safety assessment. The inspectors, with their legal right of entry into these institutions, were uniquely placed to obtain information that others could not, and Adelaide was determined to protect this right, not only from the criticism of the Home Office but also from the suspicions and resentment emanating from the institutions themselves. She was, therefore, primarily concerned to build bridges into hitherto impenetrable fortresses, to do what she could to improve practical conditions. 'Those who were religiously and charitably disposed to care for such individuals deserved admiration and respect.' Anna was quoted as saying, 'I cannot speak too highly of the kindness shown to the inmates by those in charge of them.'[47] On another occasion she declared, 'It is only the goodness of the Sisters and others in charge, their constant unwearying patience with troublesome cases, and their own bright example of duty, faithfully done, that makes for brightness in these Homes.'[48] To the modern eye it makes for uncomfortable reading. But praise and encouragement invariably tended to diffuse hostility and pave the way for the acceptance of advice. Thus the reports after 1907 paint a cautiously optimistic picture of increasing improvements made by the staff of various institutions in response to guidance from the factory inspectors. Ease of gaining admittance was particularly emphasised. One sister, famously hostile to outside interference, finally conceded that Adelaide had been extremely helpful and that she considered the new Act to be 'a splendid thing'. She had initially assumed that the lady factory inspector had come to 'interfere with the work of reclaiming those who had fallen by the wayside to whom I am giving the whole of my life and thought.'[49] On another occasion, Adelaide reported enthusiastically that 'My ring at the front door was promptly answered in a far shorter time than would generally be the case in an ordinary trade factory.'[50] She had been told it was virtually impossible to gain admission to this particular Home with its high walls and closed doors, and certainly not after 6 p.m. Some of this success was down to her usual tactic of making friends with those who exerted the most influence. 'I was very glad to receive from the Church Penitentiary Association an invitation to join Miss Tracey in attending a central conference of the associated sisters and superintendents of these industrial homes; it is in every way a gain that there should be the fullest understanding between them and us of our mutual responsibilities in their industrial work,' she concluded with relentless positivity.[51] It was difficult for those in charge of these institutions to argue with such sentiments, especially now that inspection was required by law. If the accident figures and other reports are to be believed there was, at least, a marked improvement in the health and safety of the girls employed in the Homes for the Penitent during the Edwardian years. Other aspects of this regime, however, lay well beyond the responsibility of the factory inspectorate, and thus beyond their capacity to engineer any significant change. As ever, they could only provide the information, give vent to their concerns, and hope that others would take up the baton.

Chapter Ten
BEYOND THE FACTORY

Early in 1904, those campaigning for a lady inspector to be resident in the Potteries finally got their way. The role was assigned to Hilda Martindale who arrived in February to establish an office and a semi-permanent residence in the North Staffordshire Hotel. Nothing much had changed in the six towns, except the regulatory position. New Special Rules, agreed after a long period of arbitration, had recently come into effect, but the process of ensuring that these were implemented promised to be a long and difficult one. Despite the fact that employers who had agreed to the use of a leadless glaze were exempted from the new regulations, most opted to continue using lead, and to continue dragging their feet when it came to the requirements of the Special Rules. Male inspectors were generally hostile to Hilda's presence and even the local MP weighed in with an unhelpful question in Parliament. 'At whose instance had a lady inspector been sent to the Potteries?' Mr Douglas Coghill, the Member for Stoke, wanted to know, 'and how long would she be staying?'[1] Hilda, with her usual vigour and determination, began a long programme of workplace visits which, over the next few months, covered every earthenware and china factory in the district. In what had, by now, become a standard approach she also visited local hospitals and called on workers in their own homes. There emerged the usual catalogue of desperate cases where women suffering from lead poisoning were struggling to bring up large families in abject poverty. Often they relied on Parish Relief or the wages of their older children to stave off complete destitution. Occasionally, Hilda was able to assist workers in gaining some compensation from employers for their condition. In 1902 the Potters' Insurance Company had been set up to provide benefits to those who succumbed to lead poisoning. Workers paid a premium of 1 per cent of wages and received compensation payments that were broadly in line with those paid out under the existing Workmen's Compensation Act which, by now, offered some limited compensation payable by employers to victims of industrial accidents. Affiliation to the Potters' Insurance Company was compulsory for employers but by 1903 only a small fraction of firms in the earthenware and china industry had joined the scheme, leaving the majority of sick workers with no recourse to any kind of income.[2] Even those with access to such payments were often unaware of the fact. Women, in particular, assumed that the scheme only applied to male workers. It would not be until the passage of the new Workmen's Compensation Act of 1906 that a universal no fault state scheme would be extended to cover a limited number of industrial diseases, including lead poisoning. Adelaide, as ever, was inclined to put an optimistic gloss on this state of affairs, assuming that the new insurance scheme would soon percolate through to the majority of firms and pointing to an 'unforeseen gain' of its introduction. It provided, she said, 'an enforced increase of knowledge among the manufacturers of the circumstances of individual cases of plumbism', cases which had in the past 'been hidden away in obscurity.' She herself, 'often had occasion to note an incredulousness on the part of employers as to the reality of the suffering caused.'[3] It was perhaps not the employers at whom these remarks were aimed however. This increase in knowledge, officially recorded, would be useful to those who might be able to act in ways that she and her staff could not.

Adelaide had been pleased by Hilda's assignment to the Potteries. It had the ring of a Special Enquiry about it, a mode of operation for which the women inspectors had gained a good reputation and Hilda was beginning to make inroads into the intransigent hostility of the employers. Her thorough approach and moderate success, however, soon resulted in another development that was rather less welcome. Twelve months after her arrival in Stoke she was informed by the Home Office that she was also to become the 'Lady Inspector Resident in Ireland'. Henceforth only four months of her year were to be spent in the Potteries while the remainder would be spent in either Dublin or Belfast. Both Adelaide and Hilda balked at this arrangement. Adelaide, who had not been consulted about the appointment, argued that it imposed a huge strain on a single woman, forced to live alone in an unfamiliar and inhospitable environment. Unlike a man, who would no doubt be accompanied by his wife and family, such a woman would be placed in an intolerably difficult and vulnerable position. Women should therefore be exempt from transfer to locations remote from their home and office base. Hilda, clearly reluctant to move to Ireland, agreed wholeheartedly. However, Adelaide's case seemed unconvincing at best. Women inspectors were, by now, well-used to hazardous journeys and spending nights alone in strange towns, And to argue on the basis of women's vulnerability was hardly in keeping with the pursuit of equality of the sexes in terms of professional opportunities. The arguments continued throughout the summer of 1906, finally culminating in a promotion to Senior Inspector for Hilda which provided her with the services of a personal clerk and a substantial rise in salary. This last benefit allowed her to set up home in Belfast in an agreeable location with an English housekeeper, and the companionship of her much loved pet dog. Hilda was moderately satisfied by this outcome, but Adelaide remained unconvinced.

The women inspectors had long been exercised by the unique complexities of Irish industry and Hilda's appointment was the latest in a long line of attempts to enforce factory regulations in this far flung outpost of the British Isles. Lucy had been the first to confront the situation in Ireland, arriving in Belfast back in the autumn of 1897. Here she had encountered that peculiarly Irish phenomenon, 'the Gombeen man'. In most parts of the United Kingdom, the first Truck Act of 1831 had long ago dealt with the most basic excesses of the Truck system, the failure to pay workers in coin of the realm. In the outer reaches of North West Ireland, however, payment in goods, and usually overpriced and poor quality goods, was manifestly alive and well, particularly if you earned a meagre living as an outworker. In some rural areas, notably in Donegal, a combination of large families and an insufficiency of land meant that by the end of the nineteenth century few families were able to support themselves by traditional farming. The result was that large numbers of women were left alone during the summer months while their menfolk travelled to work on Scottish farms to earn a wage which, hopefully, would sustain the family through the winter. The women, meanwhile, earned small amounts from lacemaking, embroidery and knitting, invariably falling victim to the agents (the Gombeen men) who purchased the raw materials for their endeavours, thus controlling access to work and the sale of their goods. Women would tramp for up to twenty miles to collect a parcel of wool from agents who in turn had been supplied by the large hosiery firms of Belfast and Londonderry. Other agents distributed plain white handkerchiefs for 'sprigging', the addition of a fancy lacework border. When the women returned a few days later with the fruits of their labour they would be paid by the agent 'in kind', and often not the sort of 'kind' that was of any use to them.

'Sure and what should the likes of meself be after with such like
ilegance?' remarked one habitually bare-footed woman who had
been presented with a pair of thin elastic sided boots.[4] Only
marginally more useful were the agents' vouchers distributed
to 'pay' for basic provisions, exchangeable only in the agent's
shop. Goods were often of poor quality and prices fixed by the
agents invariably meant that vouchers were insufficient to pay
for whatever was purchased. The difference, of course, had to
be paid for by more work – and so the cycle of grinding poverty
and perpetual debt continued.

Lucy had set about this problem with enthusiasm during
her first visit to Ireland, arriving in the small country town
of Ardara in September 1897. However, she had discovered
almost insurmountable barriers to the enforcement of the
law. Women in Donegal, fearing exclusion from the only
work available to them, were terrified to speak out about
the situation. And everyone else, it seemed, was involved in
collusion to maintain the status quo. Parish priests, doctors,
landowners and local businessmen all refused to discuss the
matter, while local magistrates were often themselves operating
as agents. Travelling the length and breadth of the county on
her bicycle Lucy attempted to talk confidentially to the women
in their own homes about their experiences. Yet each time she
believed herself to be in possession of information that would
support a prosecution, she found herself thwarted by a lack of
co-operation on all sides. No-one would talk publicly, let alone
present themselves in court. The Irish weather, throughout
these ultimately fruitless journeys, played its own part in
sapping her resolve. Retreating one night, soaked, frozen and
exhausted to her room in the McNellis Hotel, (also, it seemed,
a centre for Gombeen activity), her frustration finally exploded
on to the pages of her diary. 'Am depressed and appalled at
the extraordinary feebleness and terrorism of this country, the
want of truth and independence, the terror of all high and low

of appearing or being unpopular, the utter disregard for law and justice – terrible tales of the corruption of magistrates.'[5]

This uncharacteristic despair, however, was soon replaced by the hatching of an elaborate conspiracy to catch and prosecute a notoriously powerful Gombeen man – or in this case woman – a certain Mrs Boyle. Twenty miles away in Belleek Lucy had found a sympathetic ear in the form of, Mr Lyons, the Methodist Minister, who had a useful suggestion to make. Perhaps she should enlist 'an informer' who would visit Mrs Boyle's shop, listen to the conversations which took place there, and then give evidence in court. The 'informer', Lucy decided, was to be her trusted friend and colleague Mary Paterson who would visit Ireland incognito, masquerading as a lady artist engaged on a leisurely trip to paint the surrounding countryside. It was perhaps an implausible disguise during a typically wild and wet Irish autumn, when all but necessity kept everyone indoors, but Lucy was fired with a new enthusiasm. She seems to have kept Adelaide in the dark about this unorthodox plan. It was undoubtedly unethical and probably illegal and the Principal Lady Inspector would almost certainly have forbidden it. Earlier in the year Lucy had begun to pursue what she considered to be the real source of the Truck problem, the wealthy textile firms of Belfast and Londonderry who sanctioned a system that provided them with an endless supply of skilled cheap labour. Many agents were themselves pawns in this system, making a sparse living in a harsh economic climate, albeit at the expense of their fellow strugglers. Lucy, however, had received a wire from Adelaide advising against any attempt to prosecute the manufacturers. She suspected the intervention of high politics in the form of Unionist MPs, currently propping up the Conservative government. 'This *smells* of the Home Office,' Lucy noted in her diary.[6] Now, therefore, she decided not to seek Adelaide's advice. It was better for her not to know. Instead she contacted the recently retired May Tennant (née Abraham) who, as the daughter of a Dublin barrister, was able to advise on a competent lawyer to present the case when it reached the Magistrates Court. Mary Paterson arrived a few weeks later to begin her furtive investigations. It was all a great success and Mrs Boyle was fined the princely sum of £40, a huge sum by the standards of most fines during this period. Several more prosecutions followed, raising hopes that these well-publicised actions would provide a timely warning to others engaged in the practice of Gombeening. The inspectors would discover, however, that it would take more than a few high profile cases to reform a system which had operated unchecked throughout North West Ireland for many years.

Lucy, herself, paid a high price for her activities in Ireland, for by the time she boarded the steamer back to England she was feeling 'very seedy'. Somewhere during her travels in Donegal she had contracted typhoid, an illness that would keep her away from work for several months. Adelaide, recently confirmed as Principal Lady Inspector, had some difficult decisions to make. She was convinced that Ireland needed her urgent attention but it was clearly a challenging place to work and she had insufficient staff. With May's resignation and Lucy's prolonged absence, the inspectors were currently down to three in number. Early in 1899, however, she elected to make her own visit to Donegal to discover for herself the extent of what appeared to be widespread disregard of factory law. She decided to present herself as a tourist enjoying a fortnight's holiday. Lucy had shipped her bicycle over to Ireland but Adelaide was not a cyclist. Instead she travelled by traditional Irish jaunting car, an open horse-drawn cart in which passengers sat on long outward facing benches and chatted together as they bounced along the rocky roads. The friendliness of the 'peasant women' towards an apparently innocent English visitor made it easy to gather anecdotal evidence. She found a system of payment in kind that was both blatant and deep-rooted in the culture of the area. Not only did it affect rural outworkers but also large groups of other labourers such as masons and roadworkers. She recognised, however, that 'long work of patient skill'[7] would be required to build a case for prosecution in court. The remoteness of many of the townlands meant that agents travelled long distances with small carts, giving out groceries in exchange for knitwear and lace. It was very difficult to find them, still less to be present when a transaction was taking place. None of the workers would even have recognised coins of the realm, she realised, for they had rarely seen any.

Adelaide had returned home convinced, as Lucy had been, that the only way to acquire information was to visit the area as a sympathetic English lady, although it is unlikely that she sanctioned deceit, at least not officially. It was Rose who was the next to venture into this regulatory quagmire. In September 1899 she arrived at the small coastal village of Dungloe, a favourite with visiting trout fishermen. Establishing herself at the single small hotel as a lone lady tourist, she spent three weeks roaming the surrounding rocky heathland known as The Rosses, chatting to local people, camera and sketchbook in hand. She had no aptitude for drawing and confessed later that she never mastered the operation of the camera. But there would have been no need to deny her official status. It would simply not have occurred to anyone to question who she really was. And inside tiny stone cottages she accepted invitations to shelter from the rain and take tea, and walked miles alongside barefoot women as they tramped along stony tracks to visit shops or herded cattle across the bogs. Conversation was natural and easy, and inside shops, where she made a pretence of buying small items, she observed women handing over lace and knitted socks and receiving goods in return.

Rose was careful in the way she described the nature of her encounters with the women of The Rosses, writing ambiguously in her Annual Report that she carried out her investigations 'in such a manner as not to exercise power, but rather as to invite confidence as one woman to another.'[8] It was a form of words that disguised the obvious deceit involved and allowed Adelaide to write about Rose's 'remarkable preliminary success in gaining the confidence of the peasant women'.[9] When the deceit came to an end, however, and Rose was revealed as a factory inspector preparing to conduct a prosecution, a tide of fury was unleashed. Local people refused to speak to her or to provide her with transport and the atmosphere in the hotel, where the owner was himself an agent, became distinctly frosty. Such was the hostility that she required the protection of officers of the Royal Irish Constabulary to travel to and from the courthouse. People of every walk of life had been shown to be complicit in the Truck system. And it was not only fear of the powerful Gombeen men that provoked this ostracism and resentment. For Rose had turned out to be a representative of the British Government and, as such, an automatic enemy of large sections of the population. Whatever their reservations about corruption amongst their own people, Rose's behaviour could only have served to confirm their suspicions about the perfidious ways of the English. She, meanwhile, clung resolutely to the belief that ultimately her actions were for the good of the rural workers of Donegal. The end, she considered, more than fully justified the means.

Throughout all this turmoil Rose's irrepressible sense of fun was never far away. One wet and windy day she accompanied Mr Sharkey, a court official, in a hopeless attempt to serve a summons on a witness who had failed to appear in court. A long journey by jaunting car was followed by 'a walk of a mile across a trackless bog, in a wind against which, without Sharkey's hand, I could not stand.' They arrived at 'a lonely cabin on a slab of rock' and, having nailed the summons to the door, the inhabitants as usual being either absent or in hiding, they began to retrace their steps. As Rose attempted to cross 'a turbulent stream by the rocking stones', she missed her footing and fell heavily. 'Lying on my back, the shallow water flowing round me, I saw Sharkey bending over me with such a look of consternation in his face that the absurdity of the whole situation overwhelmed me, and to his still further discomfiture I laughed so much that it was some moments before I could grasp his hand, outstretched to pull me up.'[10] 'Humour', Rose reported with obvious delight, was 'never far to seek in Ireland', particularly in the courthouse where it 'illuminated the whole proceedings from start to finish.' The series of prosecutions instituted by Rose in 1899 produced mixed results but few were enacted without significant drama. During one case, heard in February 1900, Rose described a scene of 'indescribable tumult'. The defending solicitor fiercely attacked the stipendiary magistrate and demanded his withdrawal from the Bench, calling him a liar. Following this 'the utmost confusion prevailed, several persons talking at once and each raising his voice louder to drown out the other.' The defendant, it seems, 'insisted on so frequently interrupting his own solicitor that at last the exasperated lawyer sat upon his client, not metaphorically but physically, using his elbows alternately to push back the protesting head that appeared first on one side and then on the other of the eloquent advocate.'[11] This particular drama finally terminated at the High Court of Appeal in Dublin, conducted in a 'beautiful building' and 'an atmosphere more dignified but scarcely less humorous.'[12]

The conclusion of this last case, Squire v Sweeney, in fact had serious consequences for the whole prosecution of Truck in Ireland. A Dungloe shopkeeper who was also a local councillor mounted a spirited appeal on the grounds that the outworkers were not actually employees. The High Court of the Queen's Bench finally ruled that in every case it must be proved that there was a contract of service with the worker and that he or she should have personally executed the work. It was a ruling,

Rose said, that effectively placed Irish homeworkers outside the protection of the Truck Acts. It also nullified the results of all previous convictions achieved by both Lucy and Rose since 1897. It was a huge disappointment for the inspectors and a serious obstacle to their efforts to defeat the practice of Truck in Ireland. Like Adelaide, however, Rose was always inclined to grasp at straws of optimism. The system had at least received 'a serious check'[13] from the publicity that had ensued from their activities. Workers were perhaps rather more emboldened than before, she felt. And there was perhaps another way forward. What was needed, she suggested somewhat paradoxically, was more agents. Competition would drive some to pay in cash to retain their workers, and in this way the system might die a natural death. Adelaide was happy to include this suggestion in her report but also added her own thoughts on the matter. What was also needed was a prohibition on the payment of wages in shops. (She could not resist adding that this was already illegal in Germany). It was also important to have fixed paydays and the explicit provision for the occasional (and presumably unannounced) presence of inspectors or constabulary when wages were paid. Her final comment on the matter, however, was aimed at the more general situation prevailing in parts of Ireland, and the difficulties it had created for her staff. 'Much will be achieved when local magistrates have learned that convictions and penalties must follow on every case proved in court of infringement of the law.'[14] For the discovery of the Truck system in Donegal had opened up a much wider, far reaching issue than the enforcement of factory regulations. It had exposed, throughout one county of Ireland, and perhaps throughout the country as a whole, a pervasive absence of respect for the law of the land. This, Adelaide concluded, was a matter that went well beyond the responsibility of the Factory Department. It required action at a much higher level of government. The problems in Ireland, she was keen to emphasise, had occupied most of her senior staff for the greater part of the previous year, and it was unlikely that she could ever commit similar resources to such a venture again.

When Mary Paterson had visited Ireland for the first time she had unexpectedly encountered another industry that would become the focus of the inspectors' attention for several years. On Christmas Eve 1898 she had arrived on the island of Innishmore in Galway Bay. She was hoping for a brief seasonal respite from her attempts to ensnare the elusive Gombeen men and was looking forward to a peaceful Christmas Day. On the island, however, she found scores of fisher lassies hard at work, the majority of whom were Scottish. Their job was to gut, salt and pack the herrings, which had just been landed from the fishing boats, a process Adelaide would have remembered from her childhood days in Aberdeen. In a strange sort of reversal of the trek of Irish labourers across to Scotland, these women, who had been working since April, had travelled progressively from Peterhead in Aberdeenshire, to Stornoway in the Outer Hebrides and from thence to the west coast of Ireland. In the months that followed Mary also pursued this industry up and down the east coast of England and Scotland as itinerant women followed the progress of the herring fleet. Many of those she found in Stornoway in May and June appeared in Shetland and Fraserburgh in July and August. By September they were in Scarborough and Grimsby, moving on to Yarmouth and Lowestoft in October and November. Sometimes they worked in Hull on fish packed in ice brought in by Norwegian steamers. In every port she found the same insanitary conditions, inadequate food and damp, dirty sleeping accommodation. Most women lived in the sheds that, during the rest of the year, were used to house the fish barrels. Wooden boards were nailed together to form rough bedsteads, usually two beds on top of one another 'in the manner of berths on board ship' with three women in each berth.[15] Existing factory regulations which stipulated the number of cubic feet of space required for each worker were subverted by the same device the inspectors had found in many other workplace, the raising of the roof. Here Mary found parts of the ceiling cut away so that the space under the rafters could form part of the calculation. Meals were cooked and eaten in these sheds. Sanitary accommodation was 'of the most insufficient and primitive kind' and the ground in both the working and living areas was impregnated with the

Fisher lassies at Peterhead, Scotland, early twentieth century

decaying remains of fish. Outbreaks of fever, Mary observed, 'periodically thrust these conditions upon the notice of local authorities' but in each town the season and therefore their concern was a short-lived affair. As the fleet moved on, then so did the workers.[16]

These women were highly skilled. An experienced lassie, it was said, could gut fifty herrings in a minute. But the herrings arrived in millions. The amount of pay a woman might expect was posted up on the wall, but gave no indication as to the amount of work required to earn this wage. The women, she observed, 'meekly accepted their conditions as inseparable from the fish' and signed agreements that precluded any chance of prosecuting their employers, the traders who purchased the fish on its arrival in port.[17] And at some stage these men had negotiated an exemption from working hours legislation in respect of the gutting, salting and packing operations. The perishable nature of the product they argued, required immediate processing. No similar exemption existed for work in the smokehouse where kippers were produced, but the result was that women tended to work in both areas during a twenty-four hour period. Thus a girl of fourteen who had spent twelve hours in the smoke house informed Mary that she had only worked six hours at gutting and was therefore within the regulations.

The plight of the fisher lassies received a great deal of attention from the lady inspectors during the years that followed this report. Adelaide herself made further visits to Ireland, including one in 1906 when she interrupted her inspection schedule to make a short trip to Dublin to collect her degree from Trinity College. Back in England she made repeated visits to east coast ports, often accompanied by junior staff, to catalogue the list of abuses visited on the herring girls and to see what could be done. The focus of the women inspectors, as ever, was on the regulations that could be applied, the improvements in sanitary conditions, the introduction of contracts of employment and the limits on working hours. The main effect of their attention, however, was not the grudging compliance of employers with a new level of enforcement, but something much more surprising and heartening. The fisher lassies, with a new awareness of the injustice of their employment conditions, began to protest. And for once, it seemed, Adelaide was happy to include examples of industrial unrest in the text of her Annual Report. 'For the first time in our experience', she reported, 'a revolt has been

attempted by women in the fish curing industry.'[18] Initially
these revolts were unsuccessful. In 1910, for example, three
women at Lowestoft were dismissed for refusing to work
beyond the statutory twelve hours and the following year in
Grimsby a larger group of workers from South Shields refused
to continue working after twenty-four hours of continuous
labour. They had broken their contract of employment, their
employer claimed, and would pay them neither wages nor
return fares. By 1912, however, the balance of power seemed to
have shifted. There was a record catch that year, with millions
of fish awaiting processing, an abundant harvest that coincided
with a wave of strikes which were sweeping across the country.
Adelaide's response was perhaps the nearest she ever came to
publicly expressed support for industrial action. Grasping the
opportunity, she used the growing panic of the employers to
bring them to a discussion with representatives of the Factory
Department, including the senior women inspectors. Over
several days of meetings, convened at the major centres of the
fish curing industry, the participants negotiated voluntary
agreements designed to reduce the working hours and improve
conditions in the ports.[19] Despite their voluntary nature, the
results of these agreements were encouraging. In 1913, after a
series of unannounced inspections, Adelaide reported that there
was general adherence to the limits on working hours and some
significant improvements in the standard of accommodation.

Adelaide was frank in attributing many of these
improvements to the 'movement' of the women themselves and
was not afraid to say so in her Annual Report. Moreover, she
noted that improvements in the conditions of male workers
in the industry had also come about primarily as a result of a
strike, for it lead to an agreement between their hastily formed
union, The Fish Curers' Association, and their employers.
She reported these events in a series of carefully worded
statements, designed to be descriptive rather than approving.

'For the first time I heard of a case of revolt against late hours, a number of girls at Lowestoft having refused to work late. In consequence the employer refused to allow them to begin work the next day without a promise not to do it again.' 'A group of women [in Grimsby] struck against the hours which usually reached sixteen out of twenty-four.' 'The workers have always acquiesced readily in the late hours but they are feeling now that the hours have lengthened unnecessarily.' 'Not only from the women so largely employed in the herring curing, but also from the men . . . has come the movement towards more reasonable hours of work.' [20] The inclusion in an official report of statements such as these was a significant diversion for Adelaide. She was, of course, rarely willing to pin her colours to a trade union mast, but this did not prevent others from doing it for her. When, in 1912, thousands of women employed in small workshops in London came out on strike, the July edition of *The Standard* was fulsome in its praise. 'Miss Anderson is to be heartily congratulated on the work that has been done during the year by herself and her very competent and energetic staff. She has succeeded in calling our attention to this very important development in industrial history: the rise of woman towards some knowledge of her trade value.' [21]

The events in Ireland and those on the quaysides of Eastern England had, in their different ways, demonstrated the limits of the state's ability to influence and control the conditions of work. Adelaide was defeated by the system in Ireland but was evidently encouraged by what, the *Women's Trade Union Review* called 'the new spirit of self-reliance of working women', [22] which she had encountered amongst the herring girls. And she was probably secretly gratified by the perception that she had contributed to this. Although she would ultimately favour the development of Workers' Councils based in individual workplaces, rather than large trade unions, she saw no inherent contradiction between negotiated settlements and regulatory control. Indeed she looked forward to the advent of a time when factory inspectors would assume the role of 'mainly technical and expert advisors and counsellors in factories.' [23] It was perhaps somewhat ironic, therefore, that during this period her ability to control her own personal working conditions was increasingly becoming a source of irritation and unease. When Hilda was informed about her relocation to Ireland, there had been no consultation with Adelaide and senior figures in the department seemed surprised, not only by the nature of her objections to the proposal, but by the very fact that she had presumed to make them at all. It was a portent of other even less agreeable things to come. In 1907 the Department convened a Staffing Committee to conduct its decennial review. Again the Principal Lady Inspector was not invited to play any part in these proceedings. The committee consisted of Whitelegge and two senior Home Office officials. Their recommendations for the future organisation of the women's branch dealt a blow that sent Adelaide into one of her periodic withdrawals, this time two months leave, advocated by a concerned Arthur Whitelegge who considered she was becoming 'ill and overdone'. [24]

The Committee considered that the present arrangements governing the women's work were increasingly wasteful in terms of time and money. Now that so many women inspectors were based in London the travel and accommodation bill was enormous and it was noticeable that the women carried out fewer inspections than the men. Too much time was spent in travelling. It would be better, they decided, if the women's inspectorate was organised on similar lines to the men's, with resident senior inspectors based in Divisions across the country who organised the work of their area and supervised their own junior staff. The seeds of this decentralisation had, unwittingly, been sown by Adelaide herself several years earlier when she had argued forcefully for the Special West London District to be placed under the control of the women's branch. Two years later, again in response to the concerns of the women inspectors and their supporters, Hilda Martindale had taken up residence in the Potteries. And now she had been moved for part of the year to Ireland. Hilda had begun to operate with a degree of autonomy, partly by virtue of her geographical isolation, but also because she was by now an extremely capable inspector and keen to take on more responsibility.

Adelaide was deeply upset by the Committee's proposal, and wrote immediately to Herbert Gladstone, the current Home Secretary, to express her dismay. The reorganisation would 'most injuriously affect our work'. It was 'contrary to the whole spirit of all my past evidence' and would produce 'a narrowing of responsibility and scope of work of the experienced inspectors. My own powers to arrange and guide the work of individual members of my staff on the lines best fitted to their nature, capacity and experience would be seriously limited.' [25] It was a letter which seemed to reveal the real source of her disquiet, the loss of personal authority and control over her staff. In particular, she argued, she regretted the loss of her regular meetings where she gathered her senior inspectors together in her London office. During the weeks that followed Adelaide seems to have become increasingly distraught as she fought ineffectually against the implementation of the reorganisation. By the autumn of 1908, however, Mary Paterson had been transferred to London as Deputy Principal Lady Inspector and Senior Inspector in charge of the South Eastern and South Western District, and Rose and Emily Sadler had been designated Senior Inspectors in charge of the Manchester and Birmingham Districts respectively. Lucy, struggling increasingly with uncertain health, had finally taken the decision to retire in September that year and Hilda therefore remained in Ireland. It was proposed that senior inspectors would be allocated juniors to work under their supervision and three new recruits were appointed accordingly and distributed around the country. More senior inspectors and more juniors were proposed to cover the other Divisions. Viewed from an organisational perspective this arrangement appeared eminently sensible. It also represented a significant endorsement of the work of the lady inspectors, an indication that they were now viewed as a fully operational part of the Factory Department with prospects for considerable expansion. The senior women inspectors showed no sign that they were anything other than pleased with the new arrangements. Enthused by the challenge, they rapidly began to establish their Divisional offices, often putting up cheerfully with wholly inadequate facilities in the interests of getting the new system rapidly underway. With amusement and no hint of resentment Rose described how she was moved into a single office in Manchester with her three junior staff and a clerk, no furniture or typewriter and piles of paper all over the floor. She later described the four years she spent as Senior Inspector in the North West as 'the happiest and most useful in my official experience'. She seemed to have loved the 'atmospherically gloomy but socially bright and attractive city' of Manchester and have enjoyed good relationships with male inspectors, employers and trade unions alike.[26] And all the senior inspectors relished the prospect of training and supervising younger colleagues. 'I enjoyed passing on any knowledge I happen to have acquired,' remarked Hilda later, 'and so I welcomed the arrival of newly appointed inspectors.'[27]

Adelaide, meanwhile, was allocated spacious rooms in the palatial Home Office in Whitehall, an arrangement she hated, feeling isolated from her staff and from the day-to-day business of factory inspection. It was now most unlikely that any worker would brave the grandiose entrance to this fortress of government power to come to see her. It was all so unlike her modest basement offices in Victoria Street. In November that year she wrote to Whitelegge that 'an immediate modification' was necessary to prevent (a) a breakdown in the health of the Principal Lady Inspector and the Deputy Principal Lady Inspector and Senior Lady Inspector Miss Squire or (b) complete congestion in dealing with the sudden multiplication of work, correspondence and reports.' [23] It is unclear why she felt that the redistribution of part of her work to other staff should have increased rather than reduced her own workload and there is no indication that either Hilda or Rose shared her concerns. The remainder of her letter tended to reinforce the view that it was her own loss of control that lay at the root of her anxiety. 'The care and trouble caused by this imposition on me of excessive work, with decreased control of its rate and amount, and decreased opportunities of conferring with my staff,' she said, 'have been accompanied by insomnia, and as soon as it is possible to arrange matters I must ask for a few weeks rest.' [29] Whitelegge responded by suggesting that she immediately take some leave. 'None of the staff were called on to do more than a reasonable day's work, except in emergencies,' he told her.[30] No doubt he had formed the opinion that the reorganisation would proceed rather more smoothly without the relentless grumbling of the Principal Lady Inspector.

Adelaide accepted Whitelegge's suggestion and retreated for two months to lick her wounds, returning the following February in a calmer frame of mind. The re-organisation, however, had exposed in her a degree of rigidity and need for control which, when denied, threatened to destabilise her mental well-being. Significant cracks had appeared in her normally calm façade. Her over-arching sense of duty would always trump any feelings of personal slight and she possessed a strong capacity to accept, at least overtly, unwelcome circumstances when they became inevitable and simply get on with the job. But this was tempered by a strong belief in her own judgement which could often feed a compulsion to demonstrate that she had, in fact, been right all along. There is more than a hint of 'I told you so' in parts of her subsequent reports. After 1908, a year described by her as one of 'unforeseen stress and strain', she was always careful to include a catalogue of rather gloomy statistics that appeared to indicate that decentralisation had not resulted in the efficiency savings so confidently expected by the Home Office. The number of miles travelled by the women inspectors, she observed, had not reduced but had increased year by year. It was, she presumed, the result of the number of short journeys undertaken 'to and fro'.[31] Moreover, in the Midlands Division, she added pointedly, there are 'specially long railway journeys *across* the country', her italics emphasising the fact that fast and efficient transport links generally ran northwards from London.[32] Thus the reorganisation had not been matched by any increase in the number of inspections undertaken, which had actually fallen. She further observed that the presence of regional offices, and the posting of their addresses on factory walls, had not produced any corresponding increase of visits to these offices by workers. 'Complaints from women and girls must always continue to direct the work,' she asserted. In 1909, as in all previous years, the overwhelming majority of complaints and enquiries, more than half, continued to emanate from the London area. Similarly, approximately one quarter of interviews with persons of all types took place in the West London Special District as 'distinct from the Divisional offices.'[33] In 1911 she once more reported a decrease in the overall number of inspections and pointed again to the efficiency of the West London District, the only place where inspections had increased. If it had not been for this, she noted, the decrease in the Kingdom as a whole would have been even more pronounced. The increase in clerical assistance provided to the Divisions was, she conceded, 'a relief to them' but 'the field of activity being so far wider and vaguer it is not possible to state the result in any definite form.'[34] In truth the insurmountable volume of work was no worse than before but

Adelaide seemed determined to underline that reorganisation had done nothing to alleviate the situation.

In 1913 another event took place that would have further fuelled her sense of marginalisation in the control her own staff. That year the Home Office decided to appoint a senior inspector to replace Mary Paterson who had recently resigned to become National Insurance Commissioner for Scotland.[35] It seemed that none of the existing inspectors were of sufficient seniority to fill Mary's post. The answer, they decided, was the appointment of a woman called Constance Smith. Constance was the daughter of a Gloucestershire clergyman and a writer of moderately popular Victorian novels. A devout Christian, she was a member of the Christian Social Union and sat on a number of committees which lobbied for improvements in employment conditions. She was concerned, well-educated and keen to become involved in the field of industrial reform. However she had no practical experience of factory inspection or indeed of industrial workplaces. Clearly in earlier years this would not have represented a significant obstacle but by now training, relevant qualifications and experience were essential prerequisites for such a senior post and new posts required the completion of a mandatory two-year probationary period. The unusual means by which Constance was appointed provoked a question in the House of Commons from a Dr Chapple, the Member for Stirlingshire, who was no doubt familiar with Mary Paterson's work in Scotland. 'What were the exceptional circumstances under which Miss Smith had been appointed?' he wanted to know. Was her appointment the result of qualifying examinations, was it permanent, did it carry a pension and what were her special qualifications, as distinct from or superior to those possessed by inspectors already on the staff of the department?[36] In reply Home Secretary, Reginald McKenna MP, admitted that Miss Smith's appointment was indeed permanent, was exempt from the normal probationary period, had been made without examination and at the same salary as existing senior inspectors. It did not, however, carry a pension. The Prime Minister had, it seemed, employed a device called an Order in Council to engage the services of Miss Smith, a means whereby he could make a political appointment to the Civil Service without recourse to the usual routes of entry. Miss Smith had been appointed on the grounds of 'her special knowledge and special experience of industrial conditions.'[37] Chapple, of course, had smelt a nepotistic rat, for Constance was an intimate friend of Gertrude Tuckwell, who, as niece and successor of the now deceased Emilia Dilke, was currently President of the WTUL. The Liberals had returned to power in 1905 and in 1908 Asquith had become Prime Minister. Constance's membership of influential Liberal networks, through her attachment to Gertrude, seems to have been a significant determinant of her sudden elevation to the post of Senior Lady Factory Inspector.

Probably a few eyebrows were raised in the Home Office over this development but there was unlikely to have been much concern. Social connections continued to play an important role in Civil Service appointments. Moreover, the view that women inspectors were primarily philanthropic amateurs rather than well-qualified professionals still persisted in many parts of government. A few years later, during the war, Adelaide would be offered the services of two temporary, unpaid inspectors, considered suitable to tackle the ever-increasing mountain of work on the grounds that they were both the daughters of Earls. No comment by Adelaide on Constance's appointment has survived, but a year earlier she had expressed criticism of the promotion to Senior Inspector of one of her existing staff, Mabel Vines, whom she considered to be lacking in sufficient experience for the post. It is difficult to imagine, therefore, that she approved of the offer of a senior appointment to someone who possessed neither experience nor qualifications. Soon, however, any anxiety about re-organisation, promotion and patronage would fade into insignificance as the cataclysmic events of 1914 eclipsed all other concerns. It would be in the immediate aftermath of war that Adelaide would confront the longer-term legacy of Constance's appointment.

Chapter Eleven
ADELAIDE'S WAR

'Suddenly as a thief in the night came the Great War' declared
Rose in her memoir of 1927.[1] There was, she described, 'a
spectacle of bewildered employers and workers, not knowing
whether to carry on or cease work. Knots of women and girls
stood outside their factories and workshops uncertain whether
to go in or not – some employers, foremen and managers had
at once been called up.'[2] Adelaide also described the 'sudden
alarm and shock of war'[3] and the phase of unemployment which
followed on immediately after the declaration of 4 August.
Everyone, it seemed, from tool manufacturers to theatrical
costumiers were out of work, for all over the country orders
were cancelled and the supply of raw materials dried up. The
north of England was hit particularly hard with most textile
factories having closed down by October. 'The work of years
seemed in danger of being swept away in a few days,' said Anna
Tracey.[4] 'We are done, killed dead,'[5] said one industrialist who
was considering using his factory kitchen to bake bread for his
displaced and hungry workforce. In Grimsby, so recently the
focus of the best catch in living memory, the fishing industry
was brought to a complete standstill. Five trawlers had been hit
by mines and most of the rest had been requisitioned by the
government.

Almost as suddenly as it had begun, however, this period of

uncertainty came to an end as firms adapted their production to wartime needs. By the end of 1914 most textile factories had re-opened, turning over their production to flannel blankets and khaki cloth. Tailors in Leeds and London had moved to the mass production of army uniforms and canvas knapsacks. Similarly leather workers began supplying army boots. In Birmingham a pen maker began to manufacture surgical instruments and jewellers applied their skills to the production of military buttons. Up and down the east coast the herring girls, who only months earlier had begun to benefit from better conditions at the dockside, now abandoned their traditional itinerant lifestyle and moved into the jute works of Dundee. Here they helped to provide the millions of sandbags that would be sent to the trenches over the next four years. Their particular situation in some ways echoed the immediate effect of the war on the work of the women inspectors, for suddenly so much of what they had achieved in previous years now seemed less relevant as priorities shifted. The workforce began to change as thousands of women were recruited to take over jobs left vacant by men, a process that was fraught with health and safety risks. In the North Western area alone, for example, thirty-three female crane operators were later reported to have suffered 'serious injuries involving bone fractures, lacerations or crushing of parts of the body.'[6] And unexpected hazards emerged as new processes were developed to meet wartime needs. In aircraft factories scores of women were recruited to carry out the 'doping' of aeroplane wings, varnishing the wings with a lacquer to make them waterproof. The powdered 'dope' was dissolved in a solvent called tetrachloroethane, a substance subsequently found to be associated with an increased risk of a liver disease known as 'toxic jaundice'. Use of tetrachloroethane was discontinued in 1916 but only after seventy cases, including twelve fatalities, had come to light.

One of the biggest employers, of course, was the armaments

industry. Popularly known as 'the canary girls', munition workers filled shells with amatol, a mixture of trinitrotoluene (TNT) and ammonium nitrate, the yellow powder staining their faces and hands a lurid yellow. Soon TNT would also be identified as a significant hazard. In July 1914 only eleven women had been employed in the existing Royal Ordinance factories but two years later this had risen to eighteen thousand, with a further seventy-six thousand employed in the new factories constructed during 1915. The conduct

Women 'doping' aeroplane wings during the First World War. (Reproduced with the permission of Smethwick Heritage Centre. Originally published in *From the Factories to the Front Line*, Mary Lee and Chris Sutton, 2015.)

of the war, however, did not just depend on the number of shells and guns the country could produce. The troops needed provisions and army vehicles, the wounded needed stretchers and medical supplies, and the horses needed nose bags. In short the country needed everything, barring luxury goods, and it needed them on a massive scale. Most items were manufactured under government contract in factories and small workshops classified as 'government-controlled'. By 1916 there were about three thousand such establishments, employing approximately

1.25 million people, of which about one fifth were women.[7] The rest were largely unskilled men considered too old or unfit for military service or young boys below conscription age. As the demand for military recruits increased only a skeleton staff of skilled men was retained in the workplace.

Initially the entry of large numbers of women into the workforce seems to have had an energising effect on Adelaide, engendering a burst of patriotism and pride at the way women had responded 'in a spirit of goodwill and unselfish service' to the needs of the nation.[8] As female workers poured into unfamiliar jobs she talked of their selfless absorption with their work on behalf of the soldiers and sailors. They were all, she said, determined to apply their best efforts to help their men at the front. Employers too came in for large helpings of enthusiastic praise. 'The introduction of women into the workforce,' Adelaide observed, 'has been accompanied by a striking degree of solicitude on the part of the managers for their welfare and comfort.' There was 'a sudden blossoming of innumerable cases where the foremost thought was to stand by the weakest of the workers.'[9] She had not heard of a single case where a woman had been dismissed. She also, of course, took the opportunity to underline the remarkable adaptability of the women and the undreamt of skill they had brought to jobs hitherto reserved for men. The words of one managing foreman of 'a great shell factory' were reported with judiciously applied italics. *'There is more in this than people think, women have been too much held back.'*[10]

Despite her habitual optimism, however, Adelaide would have known that the rapid recruitment of thousands of inexperienced workers and the imperative for enormous levels of production would almost certainly lead to large increases in industrial accidents and occupational disease. The situation was further compounded by a drastic reduction in the number of male inspectors, for by the end of 1914 more than a third had either joined the army or had been seconded to other departments on war related work. By 1914 there were twenty women inspectors, four of whom had Divisional responsibilities, but this was hardly sufficient for the task that now faced them. Not unreasonably, therefore, Adelaide confidently expected a significant increase in her staff. In this, however, she was to be disappointed. Writing to Arthur Whitelegge in 1915 she pointed out that 'it has been impossible to overtake more than a fraction of the work necessary for the health and safety of women.'[11]

Emphasising the need to appoint more female inspectors she added that men above and below military age would be 'useless' as factory inspectors while plenty of women of the right age and qualifications were readily available. She only succeeded, however, in obtaining three extra inspectors in January 1916 and an additional six in August of 1917. Four of these appointments were voluntary and unpaid. Moreover Treasury officials made sure that every new appointment letter contained the word 'temporary' heavily underlined in black ink. Like their contemporaries in the factories, these new recruits should not expect to retain their jobs when men returned from the front. Accepting this with reluctance, Adelaide decided to put down a marker for the future. It would, she argued, be extremely advantageous when the war came to an end to have such a pool of experienced women from which to select new inspectors.[12] By 1915, however, the focus of government priorities seems to have shifted away from traditional industrial health and safety as it had been practised during the pre-war years. In part, this represented a downgrading of industrial concerns. Set against the spectacle of unprecedented slaughter on the battlefields injuries in the factories and workshops seemed trivial by comparison. But it also signified a new preoccupation with other aspects of the workplace derived from a resurgence of old fears associated with mass female employment. When young women were drawn into factories in large numbers, often away from home and with money to spend, it was argued, a lack of parental guidance and a lack of mature responsibility placed them in serious moral danger. Such risks were considered to be exacerbated in times of war when fatalistic attitudes fostered carefree and careless behaviour. The moral fibre of the nation was thus under serious threat, and the answer to this problem was 'welfare'.

The change in emphasis seems to have crept up on Adelaide almost unawares, for it came, initially, in the form of a response to TNT exposure and toxic jaundice. In February 1915 Home Office pathologist, Dr Bernard Spilsbury, conducted a post-mortem on a man who had been poisoned while employed in the production of explosives. Like the victims of tetrachloroethane the man had died from toxic jaundice but in his case, Dr Spilsbury concluded, the cause was exposure to TNT. Thomas Legge, already embroiled in the problems surrounding aircraft doping, realised with some alarm that the vast majority of those exposed to TNT, and therefore at risk of poisoning, were women employed in the shell filling factories. By the summer of that year his fears were confirmed. He had identified forty-six cases, of which two were fatal. Over the course of the war there would be a further 430 cases including 111 deaths.[13] Toxic jaundice was thus designated a notifiable disease in January 1915, attracting a raft measures in the munitions factories that would help to stem the rise in cases during the next three years. Building on the lessons of the lead works and the Potteries there was to be improved ventilation to reduce dust, protective clothing, washing facilities and the separation of working and eating areas. Significantly, however, the women factory inspectors, with their long experience of industrial workplaces, were to play very little part in the implementation and enforcement of these measures. Instead the task was placed in the hands of specially appointed female welfare supervisors who would be part of a new welfare system, rapidly to be enshrined in law and rolled out across all government controlled workplaces. 'Welfare' was to be a central part of an integrated wartime health and safety system.

Adelaide had initially been delighted by the government's new enthusiasm for industrial welfare. It was something for which she had lobbied, largely unsuccessfully, for many years. To Adelaide, welfare meant the introduction of practical comforts in the workplace, canteens, cloakrooms, seats, supplies

Adelaide Anderson's official pass, authorising her entry into factories during the First World War.

of clean water and of course respectable lavatories. Moreover, she had long advocated the presence of female supervisors who, she considered, would ensure that the concerns of ordinary women workers were addressed. With typical recourse to the biblical, therefore, she noted in her Annual Report for 1915, that 'a question arises like the riddle of Samson, why has the manufacture of war on a terrible scale led at last to the systematic introduction of hygienic safeguards that Factory Inspectors have advocated for many years.'[14] She was, of course, well aware

of the answer to this question. Essentially the government
needed to attract more young women into the workforce and
thus needed to convince them, and more particularly their
parents, that factories were suitable places for young women
to work. To this end the newly formed Ministry of Munitions
designated one of its multifarious committees specifically to the
consideration of issues related to women's work. The Women's
Employment Committee, one of the numerous sub-committees
which comprised the Health of Munition Workers' Committee,
was set up in 1916. The same year, much to Adelaide's initial
satisfaction, the Police, Factories (Miscellaneous Provisions)
Act, popularly known as the 'Little Police Act', enshrined in
law the requirement for 'special provision to be made at the
factory or workshop for securing the welfare of workers'.[15]
The content of this provision, obviously targeted at women
workers, included arrangements for the preparation or heating
and taking of meals, the supply of drinking water, of protective
clothing and seats in workrooms, the provision of lavatories,
cloakrooms and facilities for washing and the availability of
ambulance and first aid arrangements. Finally, there was a
requirement for the 'supervision of workers'[16] and it was here
that Adelaide's aspirations began to part company with those
of other organisations concerned with working conditions,
notably with women's trade unions. The members of the Health
of Munition Workers' Committee knew that there remained a
strong antipathy towards female employment amongst sections
of the influential middle classes, and that much of this disquiet
centred on moral rather than strictly practical concerns.
Thus, they argued, the 'supervision of housing would prevent
women and lads from lodging with disreputable people'[17] and
'supervision outside the factory might be necessary to ensure
that girls and boys living away from home were not demoralised[18]
during their free time.'[19] Specially appointed supervisors were
advised, alongside the provision of practical facilities, to

develop recreational activities for the workers, presumably to divert their minds from other, less wholesome activities. Adverts placed in local newspapers sought applications from mature responsible women who were experienced in the running of a household. The relationship between worker and welfare supervisor, it seemed, was to be based on that between mistress and servant. Meanwhile the appointment of the paternalistic employer, Seebohm Rowntree, as the first Director of Welfare Services confirmed the nature of the model the government had in mind. What was proposed, it seemed, was a series of well-ordered, well-controlled industrial communities.

It was not long before complaints about welfare supervisors began to filter through to Adelaide and her staff. Largely untrained and with no experience of industrial conditions or industrial workers, many supervisors began to extend their gaze beyond the practical concerns of the workplace to include the private lives of the workers, censuring their behaviour, their personal appearance and other aspects of their general lifestyle. 'It is no uncommon thing to hear of some stupid act of petty tyranny quoted as an example of "welfare",' observed Inspector Isabel Taylor.[20] Even Adelaide, resolutely determined to present a positive picture of welfare services, was forced to admit that there had 'in certain cases been unsuitable or futile and mistaken appointments.'[21] Most concerning was the unsympathetic and often incompetent approach of supervisors to matters of health and safety. 'They were asked to design protective clothing for jobs they knew nothing about and had never done,' said one worker.[22] Unsurprisingly, this 'protection' often turned out to be both useless and uncomfortable. Another described how the breathing difficulties of a young girl, exposed to gas escaping from a furnace, were dismissed as 'purely psychological'.[23] Some supervisors were well aware of the resentment their presence provoked. 'We appeared to the workers in the light of spies who were going to watch and report to management . . . or as goody goody people who were going to poke their noses into the workers' private affairs,' remarked one supervisor employed by Armstrong-Whitworth's Munitions Factory in Newcastle upon Tyne.[24] Rose considered the guidance that supervisors received from the Ministry of Munitions was in part to blame. Charged with caring for workers' well-being they were also told to consider themselves as part of management and not as workers' representatives. It was an instruction intended to ensure that they steered clear of trade union activity, another source of governmental anxiety. Unnerved by the widespread industrial unrest of the pre-war years the government was keen to discourage the development of unions, particularly within government-controlled establishments. Welfare seemed to offer a useful alternative in terms of addressing workers' concerns about employment conditions. For welfare supervisors, however, the awkward boundary between employer and workers was a difficult one to negotiate. It placed them in an uncomfortable and somewhat untenable position. And the fact that, unlike women inspectors, they had no legal backing for their activities made things even more difficult. It was very hard for them to stand up against autocratic employers, Rose observed.[25]

Not all welfare supervisors were resented, however. As Isabel Taylor remarked, 'Unfortunately the good work put in by some supervisors tended to be overshadowed by the ineffectiveness and unwise actions of others.'[26] Some were, indeed, remarkably successful and popular. On a bleak morning in February 1917 Adelaide had occasion to visit the Howe Bridge Spinning Company in Atherton, near Manchester, one of the largest mills in Lancashire. Here she encountered a young lady called Margaret Dibben, recently appointed as welfare supervisor. Margaret was the daughter of a Warwickshire vicar and had enjoyed a happy and comfortable upbringing in a small country village. Before the war she had attended Manchester's Victoria University, obtaining a Master of Arts in History in 1915. She was a cheerful, energetic young woman who was determined to make a success of her new job. In common with many daughters of the clergy, Margaret had planned to work in some form of social work when she left university, but the advent of the war had caused her to rethink her immediate ambitions. Keen to contribute to the war effort, she had opted to work in a factory that made shell fuses rather than applying for one of the more genteel occupations considered more appropriate to her social class. It was, she considered, a unique opportunity to gain experience of life on the factory floor from the standpoint

Margaret Dibben (centre) and workers at Howe Bridge in 1917.

of the workers. Thus her application, eighteen months later, for the post of welfare supervisor at Howe Bridge had been based on this working knowledge rather than any experience of running a houseful of servants. Adelaide was immediately impressed by Margaret who clearly enjoyed good relations with both her employer and the girls under her charge. In fulfilment of her obligation to encourage recreational activities she had introduced gym classes, a singing club and, rather incongruously, a hockey league at the factory, all of which turned out to be hugely popular.

When she left Howe Bridge in 1918 Margaret treasured the ever-growing bundle of letters she continued to receive from the girls. 'We still keep on with hockey but we never win, although we are not downhearted, we shall win sometime,' she was informed by Martha Peacock.[27] 'We hope you like your new work but that you would rather be at Howebridge [sic] so that we could have you back again,' wrote Mary Birchall, adding 'we are going on fine with the gymnasium class', and 'in the singing class I am likely to be picked out for the competition for the Shield in Manchester.[28] 'I only wish you was with us. We shall feel lonely without you,' complained Lizzie Barker, attaching a touching little poem accompanied by a shower of kisses. 'Flowers may wither, Blossoms may die, Friends may forget you, But never will I,'[29] while Ethel Jenkins mused over the possibility of coming to visit. 'Some of us would like to come to London but we think we might get lost. Have you learned how to say "who dost tha think has got wed" yet. If not I will learn you when I come.'[30] Many years later, when Margaret was the mother of two young children and living in South Africa, she was still exchanging letters with some of the women who had worked at Howe Bridge, swapping news and photographs of homes and families. In 1917, Adelaide made a mental note of this somewhat unusual welfare supervisor. It was someone she would like to have on her own staff, she decided.

Meanwhile, Adelaide was finding that the women inspectors were becoming overwhelmed by the demands of the war. In addition to the need 'to overcome the belief that had suddenly spread that the Factory Acts were "in abeyance"' there was also the 'breathless endeavour to watch over the application of the incessantly flowing Emergency Orders.'[31] These Orders allowed the suspension of certain aspects of the factory regulations, notably the limits on overtime and the prohibition of night work for women. The Factory Act of 1901 had incorporated the facility for the government to introduce such measures during times of national emergency. Now the need for twenty-four hour production to meet the relentless demand for military supplies had resulted in the issue of thousands of Emergency Orders. At the start of the war these had been issued to individual firms on a temporary basis, but later, as the situation became more critical, they were granted to whole industries for an indefinite period. The policing of these orders fell to the women inspectors, for when it came to their terms and conditions, it was moral issues that were once more to the fore. Women could only work at night if there was a 'responsible woman' on the premises to ensure that they were not left alone with male workers. Both Adelaide, herself, and her senior staff, seem to have shared governmental anxieties about these nocturnal perils. Their reports suggest that they devoted an extraordinary amount of time and effort to the enforcement of such requirements, often at the expense of more traditional health and safety concerns. Thus, in the early hours of 9 February 1915, Hilda Martindale visited the premises of Joseph and Jesse Siddons Ltd, a Staffordshire foundry engaged in the production of soldiers' mess tins. To her apparent consternation she found three young women under the age of twenty, 'none of whom could be considered a responsible woman working alongside four men.'[32] When Mr Siddons arrived the following day he found he was required to remove the women from the nightshift and replace them with young boys. His protestations that the men were long-serving employees, married men and 'entirely trustworthy' were to no avail.[33] Almost as a footnote Hilda noted that the manufacturing process involved no use of lead and therefore did not constitute a danger to health. Curiously, she made no mention of the more general risks associated with foundry work, despite the fact that official accident figures for 1914 had shown seven thousand reported accidents in this industry with twenty-seven fatalities.[34] A components company in Bournville, Birmingham, who were making cartridge clips for shells, ran into similar trouble with the lady inspector. If they wished to continue employing young women at night, said Hilda, they were required to appoint either 'a matron or a nurse' to provide protection.[35]

Like so many others during the war Adelaide found herself confronting new and difficult problems at work against a background of severe personal anxiety. Max and Walter were both abroad in 1914 and were, in any case, well past the age of military service. Ralf, at thirty-seven, was also above the current age range, but the years since the Boer War had done nothing to dampen his sense of patriotic duty and he was determined to do his bit. As soon as war was declared, therefore, he had immediately returned from South Africa and offered his services to the army. In September 1914 he was assigned to the Army Service Corps (ASC), a series of units established to provide logistical support to the troops in France. With his recent experience of farming it seems he was considered suitable to command a Horse Remounts Company, responsible for the provision of horses to the British Expeditionary Force. And it was probably his experience of colonial living and working that determined his specific allocation to the First Indian Cavalry Division. He arrived in France early in 1915 after a brief period of training and was assigned the rank of second lieutenant. Although he was officially behind the front line, Adelaide would have had little doubt that his situation was neither safe nor comfortable. Fellow recruits to the Remounts Companies described constant hazardous movements across country, the shelling of railway stations as horses arrived and the frequent stampedes of terrified animals. Members of the Company were frequently required to take horses up to the front line, gaining first hand experience of the bombardment of the German guns. Driver James Mackenzie, a member of Ralf's company, wrote to his wife describing the terrible living conditions. Everything he possessed was 'wet to the skin' and the men slept huddled

together for warmth in freezing conditions. 'My hair fairly
freezes,' he reported, and 'when the morning came we looked
like a lot of half-drowned cats.'[36] Food rations were meagre
and often shared with the streams of wounded returning
from the trenches and the equally long columns of refugees
fleeing the German advance. Ralf's only surviving letter seems
to confirm this bleak picture. Writing to his sister Mary in
1918 when he was eagerly looking forward to the Armistice,
he greatly hoped for 'better accommodation' in the future,
'instead of the improvised shelters against banks in sunken
roads. As the weather gets worse the prospect of a decent roof
over one's head is not to be sneezed at.'[37] How much of his
daily wartime experiences Ralf shared with his sisters at the
time is unknown, but the knowledge that her brother was in
France would have been enough to produce a nagging worry
at the back of Adelaide's mind. Increasingly black bands were
appearing on the arms of the women she met in the workplace
and news of tragedies amongst the families of her friends was
never far away. At the beginning of June 1917 she heard that
May Tennants's eldest son, nineteen-year-old Henry, was dead.
Henry, with his passion for aeroplanes, had joined the Royal
Flying Corps and was carrying out an observation flight over
France when the engine of his aircraft failed. He and his co-
pilot, Sydney Coates, had been killed when the plane plunged
to earth and burst into flames.

Alex's situation was a particular source of anxiety. In 1899 he
had taken up an appointment with the Bombay Burma Trading
Company and by 1914 had risen to a senior managerial position,
based in Rangoon. This highly successful company, founded in
the late nineteenth century by the six Scottish Wallace brothers,
was by now the leading producer of teak in Burma, as well as
having other interests in cotton, tea, oil and shipping. When war
broke out, however, Alex also felt the call of duty and offered his
services to the Indian army, enlisting with the Sixth Division

under Major-General Charles Townshend. He too began his military career as a Second Lieutenant. In October 1914 Turkey had entered the war and there was a need to protect British oil interests in the Ottoman province of Mesopotamia.[38] Like most people in Britain Adelaide initially heard nothing but good things about this distant campaign. During 1915 the British Indian forces had progressed steadily and seemingly effortless up the River Tigris towards Baghdad, brushing aside ineffectual resistance from Turkish forces who seemed disinclined to fight. Compared to the horrors of France, there seemed little to worry about. In July 1916, however, she was shocked to receive a letter from Wallace Brothers, sent via George Yuill's office, informing her that Alex had been taken prisoner by the Turks. Retreating to the comforting routine of Civil Service procedure she immediately jotted on the top of this letter '3.7.16, ackd & gave out informn'[39] but she would have been far from comforted by the information it contained. Seven months previously, on Christmas Eve, Alex's company had been involved in an unexpected and bloody battle with Turkish forces. Hundreds of British soldiers had been killed and Alex himself had been wounded in the shoulder when a shell exploded nearby. In the first months of 1916, weak from his wound, he had suffered first from influenza and then from jaundice, becoming one of those forced to endure a gruelling retreat to a place called Kut-al-Amara. Devoid of medical facilities or adequate transport and miles from reinforcements the survivors were soon surrounded by the Turks. The Siege of Kut that followed lasted for a total of 147 days, the company finally surrendering at the end of April when food rations began to run out. Adelaide would learn later that Alex was lucky to survive the freezing conditions and near starvation of that winter. The following September he wrote to her from Castamoni where he was held prisoner 'I hope I shall never know anything as bad. Bitter rain, flooded trenches, hard frost, soaked through.'[40] From July 1916 until

the company's liberation by British forces in the middle of
1918, Adelaide, Mary and the other brothers strove to maintain
communications with Alex, sending letters which occasionally
got through and even more occasionally received replies, often
many weeks or even months later. These were letters of cheerful
fortitude and determined optimism on both sides, talking of
commonplace things, news of relatives and enquiries about the
arrival of small home comforts lovingly packed and sent via the
Red Cross by Adelaide and Mary. 'Dearest Sissy, Would you
please send me a sponge. Mary perhaps remembers the size I
like – goes into one of those camphor tins about 4 ins square.'[41]
'Have fleas but prefer these to bugs and lice.'[42] 'Two cases of
frostbite, led them to give up cold baths in the morning.'[43] As
they were moved from one camp to another there were reports
of harrowing journeys, sometimes in burning heat but more
often in ice and snow over mountain passes. On arrival in
late December 1917 at new quarters in Chungry, a deserted
farmhouse, Alex wrote of the conditions with weary sarcasm.
'One of the comforts of this place is fresh air – no windows.
All the arrangements are so excellent we have been trying to
telegraph lots of people congratulating them on their choice
of abode for us.'[44] He knew nothing of the fate of his men but
was clearly uneasy. Early in his captivity he received an enquiry
from a Mrs Smith about her son Edwin. 'Dearest Sissy, please
could you say I am very sorry but I can gather no information.
There are only officers here. I wish I could hear about my own
men, I gather I am lucky to be here – their place seems less
attractive – not saying much.'[45] As time went on Adelaide and
Alex embarked on an exchange of coded messages to evade the
Turkish censorship. It began with requests for Adelaide to write
to the American Embassy, to 'enliven Cousin Jonathan',[46] an
attempt to obtain some monetary support which would enable
the prisoners to buy extra rations. The request was ultimately
unsuccessful but it established a form of communication that

enabled Adelaide to answer some of Alex's questions about the progress of the war. 'I have been very pleased to see that JB, Cousin J and Froggy are all so cheery and determined to carry on their business,' wrote Alex early in January 1918. 'They are a good stout firm and I hear JB is opening out a new plot of ground in his east garden. I wonder if there is any likelihood of Jock selling out to him.'[47] Later that month, he continued, 'Is it a fact that Maudie and Allen are making a match of it? There seems to be some talk of it. If so what a pity Bruno has not stayed on to be best man.'[48] The subterfuge no doubt provided both with a diversion and a renewed sense of hope, as well as a small sense of victory over Alex's captors. Despite his frequent attempts to make light of his situation, however, it was clear that conditions in the camp were gradually worsening. From two injured officers, freed in an exchange deal with the Turks, she heard that there was malaria, cholera and typhoid fever in the camp. For Adelaide, increasingly fearful about the final outcome as she awaited each letter, this would have been a long drawn out strain, adding to the anxiety she already felt for the safety of Ralf, and the ongoing frustrations of her own work.

Back in the Factory Department her enthusiasm for 'welfare' was rapidly diminishing. All these moral patrols took time away from the proper business of health and safety inspection and she herself seemed to be spending an inordinate amount of time negotiating with Trade Union officials, on behalf of the Home Office, the terms and conditions under which women could be substituted for men. And then there was the seemingly endless stream of special enquiries required to feed an apparently insatiable government appetite for information. There was the Employment Substitution Committee (Shops and Industrial), the Board of Control of Liquor Traffic, The Board of Trade Commercial Intelligence Branch and Labour Exchanges and the War Office Contracts Department. Most insistent were the demands of the Health of Munition Workers' Committee seemingly intent on exploring every aspect of work in the armaments factories. While the health and safety of the canary girls appeared to be the main focus of their attention, however, all over the country other working women were falling victim to industrial accidents and occupational disease. The operation of unfamiliar machinery by inexperienced operators was a particular problem. The Chief Inspector would later describe how there had been a resumption of unsafe practices during the war and a failure to use machinery guarding. And diseases which had previously been confined largely to male workers were now becoming more common in women. Anthrax, for example, had been known as woolsorter's disease before the war, reflecting the fact that most cases occurred in the men who unpacked and sorted through the dirty fleeces that arrived from the Middle East for use in the textile industries. This was a notifiable disease and statistics collected during the war showed a marked rise in female cases. For many women the chance to demonstrate their working capabilities came at a considerable price. By 1918 Adelaide was prepared to be surprisingly frank about welfare. It could not, she said, be 'merely a superimposed factor on unreformed factory life. The workers knew very well where the shoe pinched and that welfare cannot be either a graft or a veneer on poor or bad conditions.'[49]

There was another reason for Adelaide's growing antipathy towards the welfare system, for the Ministry of Munitions, not content with encroaching on the territory of the Factory Department, now seemed intent on purloining its hard-pressed staff. Although this represented a gratifying recognition of the professional competence of the inspectors it was also an acknowledgement that the administration of the welfare system was in serious difficulties. The first to be transferred was Dr Edgar Collis, now working with Thomas Legge as one of only two Medical Inspectors of Factories. In 1916 Dr Collis was selected to replace Seebohm Rowntree who retired as Director of the Welfare Department that year. Shortly afterwards, Winston Churchill, the current Home Secretary, also requested the services of Irene Drury, one of the more experienced women inspectors whom he wished to act as a 'special advisor' to the Welfare Department. This appointment, however, was not a success, Miss Drury's secondment serving only to illuminate the serious conflicts developing between the Factory Inspectorate and the Welfare Department. She returned to the inspectorate within weeks 'Her position among many female welfare officers was too indefinite for her experience and gifts of organisation to take effect,' reported Rose diplomatically, if rather tortuously.[50] It was clear that all was not well in the Welfare Department and May Tennant, from her position on the Women's Employment Committee, began lobbying Churchill and a reluctant Arthur Whitelegge for the deployment of Rose to help sort things out. In March 1918, Rose was finally asked to join Dr Collis as Co-Director. Adelaide, powerless to resist, was nevertheless extremely unhappy about this turn of events. Rose was by now her own Deputy and her trusted friend, the last person she wanted to lose. Rose, too, was unenthusiastic. 'I knew very well the troubles that beset the Welfare Department,' she lamented. It was only after a long interview with Churchill that she was persuaded to accept the appointment. 'I fell victim to his importunity,' she said. On arrival in the department, however, she described the staff of over one hundred as an 'inharmonious crowd . . . occupying all the houses down one side of Northumberland Street.' She observed 'jealousies and gossip' 'disintegrating forces' and 'difficulties of mushroom growth'.[51] Rose did her best with this unpromising material but the war had only months to run. And she was, in any case, strongly of the opinion that the administration of welfare should have been the preserve of the Factory Department, and specifically of the women's branch. It was, she said, unnecessary to set up a new organisation that lacked the experience of industry and the 'traditions and status appertaining to the officers of an old department.'[52] Adelaide was less direct and more diplomatic but her own resentment was clear. 'While new departments set up large staffs for the new kinds of duties,' she said, 'the Factory Department remained simply expert advisors as regards conditions in factories without any increase in staff.'[53] With her unerring sense of duty she found herself severely conflicted by the establishment of the Welfare Department, agreeing with its objectives but thoroughly disapproving of its methods. She was undoubtedly a strong advocate of the view that young girls needed moral protection during the war, something which led her to be an enthusiastic member of the 'Archbishop's Committee for the Spiritual Welfare of Munition Workers', established to provide facilities for the moral and spiritual guidance of those employed in the armaments factories. But she recognised that many welfare supervisors were both arrogant and patronising in their approach. And of course she shared Rose's view that what was needed was a much more central role for the women inspectors.

In March 1917 her departmental loyalty was unexpectedly tested again, this time at the behest of Millicent Fawcett, currently President of the National Union of Women's Suffrage Societies, (NUWSS). Millicent wanted her to join a Women's Suffrage Deputation, due to meet with the Prime Minister, Lloyd George at the end of the month. Adelaide had joined the NUWSS, the non-militant wing of the suffrage campaign, many years earlier but had always avoided direct involvement with the cause, pleading, as ever, her need for Civil Service neutrality. In this she had been supported by Aunt Elizabeth Garrett who had similarly tended towards a rather lukewarm public stance. Aunt Elizabeth knew she needed to maintain the support of wealthy donors to her hospital and could not afford to alienate those who would keep things financially afloat. It was a difficult call but Millicent understood her sister's conflicting loyalties.

Adelaide would have liked to consult Aunt Elizabeth about her own position, but by now the famous woman physician, the first to be qualified in Britain, was a frail and confused old lady, confined to her house in Aldeburgh. In December that year she would pass quietly away almost unnoticed in the heat of the war. Adelaide, meanwhile, agonised over whether she should take part in the deputation. She delayed so long and wrote so many letters to Home Office officials, requesting to know whether it was permissible for her to attend, that Millicent must have despaired. Perhaps Adelaide, with her fear of public speaking and her dislike of public demonstration, secretly hoped that she would be forbidden to go, but every reply seemed to indicate the contrary. Thus she finally agreed to join an august body of campaigners which included Mary MacArthur of the National Federation of Women Workers, Charlotte Despard of the Women's Freedom League and Emmeline Pankhurst of the Women's Social and Political Union, an organisation that had agreed to suspend its militant activity for the duration of the war. There were also representatives of various women workers' groups which included munition workers, engine cleaners, lorry drivers, textile workers, cooks, nurses, doctors and teachers. In the event Adelaide confined her participation to a short, lack-lustre speech which outlined the contribution that women had made to the war effort. She hurried back home as soon as she decently could, no doubt with a certain amount of relief. Perhaps, however, she had been right to question the propriety of her appearance at the deputation for newspaper reporters were quick to seize on her attendance in their coverage of the event. The Principal Lady Factory Inspector was not one of the 'usual suspects' and her appearance at any form of demonstration was bound to excite comment. The next week Herbert Samuel, MP for Cleveland, asked the Prime Minister in the House whether the Principal Lady Factory Inspector was one of those who had taken part in the deputation and, if so, whether this was in

accord with the principles which had hitherto regulated the
conduct of officers of the Civil Service. Was this participation
in a political movement to be regarded as a precedent, he
wanted to know. The Prime Minister told him that under the
'exceptional circumstances' of the deputation special permission
had been granted to Miss Anderson to attend.[54] Samuel, a
Liberal supporter of female suffrage, felt sufficiently guilty to
write to Adelaide in advance of his Parliamentary question to
apologise and explain. It was not, he said, anything personal.
He was just interested in confirming that the usual rules had
not changed.[55] The episode would, however, be quite sufficient
to deter Adelaide from taking part in any 'political' activity
ever again, even long after she had left the Civil Service.

Meanwhile, a welcome application form had arrived on
Adelaide's desk. Margaret Dibben had suffered her own
personal tragedy during the war with the death of her older
brother Harry in January 1918. Harry's death was not a direct
consequence of the fighting, and yet it is difficult to avoid the
conclusion that he was indeed one more casualty of the war.
Like his father, Harry had become a clergyman and, having
studied theology at Trinity College Oxford he was at the
beginning of his career in 1914, serving as a curate and a school
teacher. In May 1915, however, he had volunteered to go to the
front as an army chaplain. Less than twelve months later he
was invalided home after a medical board found that he was
suffering from 'neurasthenia as a result of the continued strain
of active service.'[56] Essentially, like so many others, he had
suffered a mental breakdown in response to the horrors he had
experienced at the front. Like his sister, however, Harry had a
strong inclination towards participating in some kind of social
work and, after returning from France, he had spent much of
his time helping at boys' clubs run by the Birmingham Street
Children's Union. It was work he loved and by December 1917
it seemed he had recovered sufficiently to take up a post as

Vicar in the Leicestershire mining village of Overseal. Early in the morning of New Years Day 1918, however, his body was found on a railway line. Officially his death was recorded by the Coroner as an accident. He had been hit by a train while supposedly visiting the signalman at nearby Ashby Woulds. On hearing the news of Harry's death Margaret immediately left Howe Bridge and returned to her family, only to confront a further tragedy at the end of May when her devastated father collapsed and died. It is hard to imagine her state of mind during this period but the crisis seems to have precipitated a decision to do something she had been considering for some time. In February that year she gathered herself together and submitted her application to the Factory Inspectorate. Perhaps it reflected a desire to make a complete break from the circumstances surrounding Harry's death, and to embark on something that would preoccupy her thoughts. And perhaps it also represented a feeling of immediacy generated by the war and its consequences, that ambitions must be pursued at once, not put off until circumstances appeared more propitious. To the great regret of her employer, therefore, she never returned to Howe Bridge. In June she successfully completed her Civil Service examinations and by the beginning of October Adelaide had welcomed her into the department.

Margaret's career as a factory inspector, however, was to be a short one and the reason, strangely, was engineered by Adelaide herself. By the end of 1918 both of her younger brothers were home, safe, if not particularly well. Alex was looking gaunt and weak, but he was now able to enjoy a period of recuperation. He would spend several weeks at Fairhaven, ministered to by an attentive Mary, before returning to Rangoon. Ralf, however, had unexpectedly experienced a longer term of service than most. In official terms he had had what might be termed a 'good' war for, like Alex, he had risen to the rank of Major and had been mentioned in dispatches. But just as he was settling down to enjoy his own period of rehabilitation he had received a letter to say that his demobilisation had been cancelled. He was to report back for duty immediately. It was his farming experience that had provoked this new and presumably somewhat unwelcome recall, for he was now required to command a company of British soldiers who would help and advise in the restoration of large swathes of France's devastated farmland. It was several more months of hard work for which he would receive yet another mention in dispatches and also the award of one of France's highest honours, the Mérite du Agricole (Chevalier).[57]

By April 1919, however, Ralf was back in England once again and temporarily staying at Adelaide's current London flat in Buckingham Gate, just round the corner from Buckingham Palace. He was in good spirits and planning his return to Empangeni. But Adelaide apparently had other ideas. What he needed most for his rehabilitation, she decided, was a new romantic interest, and she already had someone in mind. Margaret, she considered, was the ideal candidate. It was a interesting move, even for the inherently controlling and frankly manipulative Adelaide, but perhaps by now she saw herself very much as the directress of family affairs, particularly when they concerned her younger brothers. That spring, therefore, she instituted a serious matchmaking campaign, inviting Margaret to lunches at Buckingham Gate and then to afternoon teas at Fairhaven. Even Adelaide must have been surprised at the immediacy with which her efforts bore fruit. The couple met for the first time at a lunch in Adelaide's flat on 6 May 1919. Three weeks later they announced their engagement and three weeks after that they were married in a hastily arranged ceremony at St Michael and All Angels Church in Bedford Park, London. 'There will be no reception but friends are welcome at the church,' said the announcement in *The Times*.[58] The wedding, on 11 June, was just one week after Margaret's last day as a

The family at Fairhaven shortly after Margaret and Ralf's engagement. Left to right: Max, Adelaide, Margaret, Ralf and Alex (seated).

factory inspector. Adelaide was delighted at the prospect of welcoming her new sister-in-law into the family. She may, of course, have harboured hopes that falling in love with Margaret might keep her favourite brother at home in England. If so, however, these were to be rapidly dashed, for Ralf was taking his new bride back to the farm in Zululand and Adelaide was to lose her new inspector after only twelve months of service. Exchanging London for Empangeni represented a considerable leap of faith for Margaret. Not only was she leaving a widowed mother to whom she was very close, but she had no experience of living abroad and certainly no knowledge of farming. Moreover, she was about to give up a career that had been the focus of her ambitions for a considerable time. As Adelaide well knew, however, Margaret was a decisive and determined individual and once her mind was made up there was to be no dithering or delay. After three days at Fairhaven followed by a ten-day honeymoon in Bude, Cornwall, the couple embarked on a whirlwind tour of friends and relatives before sailing for South Africa on 18 July. Adelaide, happy and sad at the same time, joined Alex and Mary at Waterloo Station to wave them off, and turned her attention back to the Factory Inspectorate. Now the long war was over there were significant challenges ahead, and there was to be no return to business as usual.

Chapter Twelve
A BUILDER OF RUINS

At the beginning of 1923 Adelaide copied some lines of poetry onto the flyleaf of her diary. 'Builders of Ruins' by contemporary poet and devout Catholic, Alice Meynell, talked of an individual's worldly achievement, 'We build with strength the deep tower-wall', and the crushing of pride by apparent failure, 'That shall be shattered thus and thus'. The poem concludes with subsequent rescue through God's grace, 'the years interpret everything aright/And break our pavements through with flowers.'[1] Adelaide, the equally devout Anglican, was no doubt reflecting on her own prolonged struggle to come to terms with dramatic and unwelcome changes in her life which, in the years since 1918, had threatened to overwhelm her self-confidence and destroy her sense of mission. The verses underlined not only her steadfast belief in a higher force that determined the direction of her life, but her equally strong conviction that 'all things worked together for good'.[2]

The period immediately after the war had begun well enough, for at the end of 1918 both Adelaide and Thomas Legge found themselves the proud recipients of the award of Commander of the Most Excellent Order of the British Empire (CBE). Both had been honoured for their service to the Factory Department during the war and congratulations flowed into Adelaide's office from two directions. Colleagues in the Factory Inspectorate were delighted that the Department itself had at last received some recognition, while professional women saw the award as one more feminist chink in the masculine armour of the Civil Service. Not everyone offered fulsome praise, however. The women's branch of the Factory Inspectorate had been inescapably associated with the welfare system during the war and women trade unionists regarded Adelaide's connection with this much-derided system as the real determinant of the award, a case of the establishment rewarding its faithful servants. Lillian Barker, the welfare superintendent at the largest munitions factory, the Woolwich Arsenal, had been similarly honoured. With some justification trade unionists felt that state delivered welfare had contributed to the neutralisation of union activity, keeping it out of factories and thus preventing workers from negotiating their own working conditions. It was a disagreement that highlighted the uneasy relationship that always existed between Adelaide, as a state employed Civil Servant, and those who campaigned for industrial reform. Rose received the lesser award of Member of the Order of the British Empire (MBE) in 1919, also in recognition of her services both to the Factory Department and the Welfare Department. She returned only briefly to the Inspectorate after the war, initially moving on to the Women's Training Branch of the Department of Demobilisation and Resettlement, charged with the redeployment of female workers. In post-war Britain this somewhat thankless task was focussed on the removal of females from the industrial workforce and their transfer into work considered more suitable for women. Wartime promises that men would find their jobs waiting for them when they returned now had to be honoured, or at least acknowledged. In the first fortnight after the Armistice, therefore, 113,000 women were discharged from their employment and this rate of dismissals continued all over the country for several months.[3] The thousands of women who wished to remain employed were directed instead towards domestic service as the middle and upper classes struggled unsuccessfully to recreate the old order. They had found it impossible to find good servants during the war and now hoped for better things. Many, however, would be disappointed, for domestic service, as Rose pointed out, was now 'distasteful to the large majority of women.'[4] She herself moved back to the Factory Inspectorate briefly in 1920 but soon returned to the Home Office as a Principal Administrative Officer involved in the development of factory regulations. In the Factory Inspectorate she was missed tremendously, not least because of her ability to lighten the atmosphere of grave decorum that tended to surround the office of the Principal Lady Inspector. Adelaide remained either unwilling or unable to relax into anything approaching an informal style with her close colleagues. On the plus side, however, Rose's departure created the opportunity for the promotion of Adelaide's own favourite protégée, Hilda Martindale, to the position of Deputy Principal. Hilda seems to have been quite unfazed by the rather quaint Victorian protocol of Adelaide's working relationships. 'Some of my colleagues considered I was worthy of sympathy,' she remarked on being allocated a desk in Adelaide's room. 'She was regarded as very serious-minded and a little aloof, but I had no regrets. I realized there was much to learn and that she was an excellent teacher.'[5] Hilda was a staunch ally and a good friend.

Notwithstanding the post-war rash of honours, there was little doubt that industrial health and safety had declined considerably during the war. The Chief Inspector's Report for 1919 made for sobering reading. Like its immediate predecessors this report was a slim volume, bearing little resemblance to the large tomes bursting with statistics that had been the norm before 1914. However, as new Chief Inspector R. E. Graves pointed out, some facts and figures had by now found their

way back into its pages and these painted a bleak picture of
the current state of affairs. The number of fatal accidents was
1,385 in 1919 as compared with 1,287 in 1914, despite a post-
war reduction in the workforce.[6] Strangely the number of non-
fatal accidents appeared to have decreased but this, Graves
concluded, was almost certainly a reflection of 'a great laxity
in reporting', another effect of the war.[7] Reporting systems, so
carefully designed and enforced in the years before 1914, had
now fallen into disuse, not least because the army of clerks
employed in the Home Office to disseminate information had
largely disappeared on the Western Front. Fatal accidents, on
the other hand, were more difficult to ignore and thus a much
better guide to the general state of things.

Another guide was the type of comments that appeared in the
reports of inspectors on the ground. There had, for example, been
a general neglect of fire precautions, and the routine inspection
regimes for equipment such as steam boilers, grinding wheels,
cranes and hoists had all fallen by the wayside. The inevitable
result was a catalogue of fatalities and injuries as fires broke
out, boilers exploded, spinning grindstones shattered and chain
links broke. In the textile factories there was a resurgence of 'the
old evil of cleaning machinery whilst in motion', something
that accounted for 225 serious accidents in the woollen and
worsted industries.[8] Locking mechanisms on machinery guards
were frequently tampered with, the studs of one lock having
been found in the coat pocket of a seriously injured man. Mr
Bremner-Davis, the Inspector for Kent expressed his general
disillusionment with the attitudes towards safety that now
prevailed throughout industry. 'Many had hoped that large
numbers of men returning from the forces would bring with
them a sense of discipline and order which would tend to make
them use guards and observe precautions. Unfortunately this
effect is much less marked than might have been expected,'
he observed gloomily.[9] Inspector Bennett of Stockton agreed.

Accidents, he noticed, were much more common amongst men returning from the colours. 'They seem to have forgotten the precautions necessary to avoid industrial accidents.'[10] Twelve men died in Cardiff docks when the 'empty' oil tank of a ship exploded. A naked light had been used for illumination while carrying out repairs, igniting the vapour inside. Elsewhere in the shipyards 'the practice of placing young inexperienced boys in great danger' had resumed. 'Young boys were set to work on staging up to 40 feet from the ground.' In the Clyde shipyards alone forty-six boys ranging from fourteen to sixteen years of age fell from heights during 1919. Four of these died and the remainder were seriously injured. 'Investigation failed to elicit any evidence that these lads were properly instructed and warned of the risks,' the inspector noted.[11] Rather the employer was keen to attribute the cause of the accident to carelessness or wilful neglect on the part of the boys themselves. It was all too reminiscent of Adelaide's observations in steam laundries before the war when she noted the heavy price paid by young tired girls 'for a moment's inattention'.

Perhaps the most unexpected feature of the 1919 report, however, was not its content but its organisation. Essentially this had changed from a model based on geographical area to one based on topic. No longer, therefore, did each District Superintendent describe the situation in his own patch with all its varied industries and problems. Now such reports were amalgamated into more general sections with titles such as 'Use of Electricity in Factories', 'Dangerous Trades' and 'Industrial Diseases'. For Adelaide this meant the demise of her own special section 'Report of the Lady Inspectors'. Her information on women's conditions was now to be subsumed under new headings, which included both male and female workers. It was a change that had been mooted immediately before the war by Arthur Whitelegge and was now taken up by his successor, R. E. Graves. Whether Adelaide recognised the long-term implications of the new approach is difficult to know, but implications there certainly were. The amalgamation of information on male and female workers within a single section of the report was, in fact, the precursor to a much more substantial change, the amalgamation of the male and female branches of the inspectorate itself which would take place two years later. Somewhat paradoxically the employment of unprecedented numbers of women during the war had led, not to a new appreciation of the special nature of the work of the women inspectors, but rather a feeling that the work of male and female inspectors was essentially the same. An equally important factor in the argument for amalgamation, however, was the increasing extent to which women inspectors had become identified with the enforcement of the Little Police Act during the war. For some more traditional elements in the Home Office it had seemed entirely appropriate that women inspectors should occupy themselves with the requirements for canteens, cloakrooms, respectable lavatories and separate living quarters for males and females. For others, however, the proper business of factory inspection was the investigation and prevention of industrial accidents and disease and, in this respect, many of those who favoured amalgamation were concerned to prevent the women's branch from becoming a channel for industrial social work. Whether by preference or direction from above, the preoccupation of Adelaide and her staff with the enforcement of welfare regulations and allied matters had carried over into the immediate post-war period. Thus in 1919, when the new format of the Annual Report appeared, welfare related sections were allocated to the women inspectors. 'Welfare in Factories and Workshops', was compiled by Adelaide herself, 'Sanitation' was co-authored by Inspector Emily Slocock and 'Hours of Work' by Hilda. Women inspectors also contributed extensively to two other sections written by male inspectors, 'Night Employment of Young Persons' and a short chapter on 'Ambulance and First

Aid' which, somewhat optimistically, attempted to catalogue the number of workplaces now offering ambulance rooms, first aid boxes and trained nursing staff. With the exception of a fleeting reference to Inspector Anne Smith who had 'been paying special attention to Potteries in which women are employed',[12] the names of women inspectors were completely absent from sectional reports on more traditional aspects of health and safety.

Adelaide seemed more than happy to collude with this somewhat unbalanced state of affairs, remaining extremely enthusiastic about the amount of space now allocated to welfare related subjects. She remained convinced that she had solved her 'riddle of Samson'. This terrible war, she concluded, had provided a heaven-sent opportunity for the development of industrial welfare. She was thus determined to preserve the momentum that had been created in 1914, and to take back what she considered to be the rightful place of the women inspectors in the system. 'A very large part of the time of the Inspectors throughout 1919 has been absorbed into bringing into operation Welfare Orders already made,' she reported, adding with obvious satisfaction, 'The women inspectors have also gladly given a good deal of time to newly appointed women welfare supervisors who seek their counsel and help.'[13] Disillusionment with the welfare system had led many to question whether such matters had any place at all in the state regulation of industrial conditions, but for Adelaide this was never an issue. All that remained to be decided, she considered, was the identification of the responsible state agency, and this of course was to be the women's inspectorate.

In 1919 she was appointed to chair the Women's Employment Committee, convened by the government to consider the future of industrial welfare. It was clear from the start that several members of this committee had serious misgivings about the whole subject. They noted that the concept had become tarnished during the war. It had acquired 'an unpleasant significance' in labour circles because it had involved 'excursions into the field of private home life normally outside factory administration.'[14] Mary MacArthur, the Secretary of the National Federation of Women Workers (NFWW), was vociferous in her condemnation. At a Federation conference in 1918 she had declared that among women workers, there was 'no word in the English language more hated than welfare.'[15] Adelaide, however, clung resolutely to her conviction that welfare was essential to the health and well-being of the workforce and, ably supported by a contingent of women inspectors, she secured a majority recommendation that such provision should continue as a State requirement. There should be a return to original notions of practical comfort and well-being as an integral part of a wider health and safety system, proper training and qualifications for welfare supervisors, and, importantly, a special role for women factory inspectors as workplace advisors with legal powers of enforcement.

Quite apart from a general unease with the moral underpinning of welfare measures during the war, however, there was plenty of evidence in 1919 that the system instituted in the munitions factories had failed to deliver on its promise of better working conditions for all. It had not, as intended by the government, been successfully 'pressed upon the attention' of other employers.[16] Working hours represented perhaps the only area where there had been significant improvements. Few people now worked more than forty-eight hours per week and, for most workers, the week now consisted of five days. Some of the experiments carried out in the armaments factories had demonstrated beyond reasonable doubt that such reductions not only reduced fatigue and improved the health of the workforce but also, counter intuitively, increased production. The reports on welfare and sanitation, however, painted a much less agreeable picture. The so-called improvements catalogued during the war seem to have been confined largely to the munitions factories where the reach of government had been easier to maintain. Elsewhere there seemed to be a general lack of enthusiasm amongst both workers and employers. In 1919 Inspector Miss Coombes surveyed 154 workshops employing 3,800 women in the City of London. She found canteens provided in only two, a kitchen in eight and a gas cooker in the corner of the workroom in thirty. There were no arrangements at all in the remainder.[17] In the Midlands 'no general progress could be reported in the various metal industries.' In the tin plate works, where the work was described as 'very rough and heavy', attempts were made to provide 'suitable clogs and aprons' but 'the results as regards the appreciation of the workers' were 'somewhat disappointing'.[18] In Swansea, similarly, the provision of new equipment and buildings for canteens had been ignored by the workers and in some cases 'the appliances had been roughly handled'. In the textile factories the movement towards welfare was also 'generally backward,' she noted.[19]

> In the tenement weaving factories of Lancashire and Yorkshire the only attempt at welfare is a steam kettle which is found in each shed and of which the occupiers are inordinately proud, although the District Inspector had difficulty getting them installed. The occupiers of these weaving sheds do not believe in pampering the workpeople. They tell one that the workplace is not a place for comfort but for work.[20]

Facilities for washing were noticeably absent in many places. In a fruit preserving factory the employer, when asked about such facilities, pointed out the tank where dirty jars were washed. Other employers were keen to point out impressive rows of new basins that were 'strangely lacking in soap and towels.'[21] In a large clothing factory where delicate decorative trimmings were made the washbasins had 'an

unused appearance'. 'I have been mystified at the apparent
lack of connection between washed hands and dainty work,'
remarked a bewildered Miss Coombes.[22] Attempts to enforce
Orders for the provision of drinking water in factories were
thwarted by another, very practical problem. In rural districts,
houses and workshops alike were often supplied by single
pumps or wells, many of which were contaminated. Typhoid
was still a frequent visitor to many towns and cities around
the country. And in Yarmouth and Lowestoft the migratory
herring girls were once more at work, seemingly without any
of the better facilities so successfully negotiated in 1914. Hilda,
encountering these workers for the first time since 1914, was
horrified at their conditions. Lack of accommodation in the
town meant that most walked several miles to work each day
and there were no mess rooms, no lavatories and no cloakrooms
to dry their soaking clothes when they arrived at the dockside.
They stood for many hours in sheds of which three sides were
open to the weather. Many women suffered from sores on their
hands where the salt had penetrated open wounds caused by
the gutting knives. Ambulance rooms, first aid boxes and the
presence of trained nursing staff were all, of course, beyond
the wildest dreams of the herring girls. Welfare provisions 'are
more urgently needed here than in any other trade,' Hilda
concluded desperately.[23]

Elsewhere the twin problems of cleanliness and decency
were once more on the agenda. 'Reports from all the Divisions
show a general falling off of standards,' remarked Emily
Slocock. Constance Smith, inspecting the situation in North
Western textile towns, found a typical situation where there
was no sewerage system and that the 'old fashioned pail closet
with all its attendant objectionable features' was still the
most usual facility available. 'Offensive effluvia', no separate
accommodation for the sexes, no doors, and lavatories opening
directly onto the workrooms were common findings. Pails were

usually emptied into a cesspool adjacent to the mill. Managers, it seemed, were surprised when the inspectors expressed dissatisfaction with these arrangements. 'The requirement for separate doors is often considered an unreasonable fad,'[24] she noted. This situation was repeated in towns and villages across the country, the worst conditions being found in South Wales, Devonshire and Cornwall where arrangements were 'still incredibly and almost ludicrously antiquated.'[25] Here lavatories were not even divided into cubicles and were simply earth floors, the excrement falling into a ditch below the bar which formed the seat. These pits were emptied at 'uncertain intervals'. In one large creamery in a small town in Devon the 'conveniences' were considered by one inspector to be 'in a state too disgusting for print.'[26]

When these features of the working environment are considered, Adelaide's preoccupation with welfare is perhaps easier to understand. Those remote from the situation on the ground may have believed that the welfare system had, by 1919, raised standards across the industrial landscape, but it was clear to the women inspectors that conditions in many workplaces were frankly appalling. It was only in the larger factories, and particularly in the much vaunted munitions works, that workers benefited from the facilities proclaimed so optimistically and unrealistically by the regulatory requirements of the Act. The fundamental question remained however. Who should be responsible for bringing about improvements? It was here that Adelaide diverged significantly from her friends in the NFWW, for women trade union leaders were united in the view that employment conditions, including welfare measures, were a matter for negotiation between employers and organised labour. The unfortunate direction in which state regulated welfare had moved during the war had only served to reinforce this view. Adelaide, as noted earlier, was by no means averse to the idea of negotiation, but wartime neglect had led her to reaffirm her commitment to state regulation. The reports her inspectors brought back to her in 1919 suggested that a road which relied exclusively on negotiation would be a very long one indeed.

It was not only women's trade unions that were out of step with Adelaide's ideas on welfare, however. The report of the Women's Employment Committee had represented something of a personal triumph, incorporating as it did all her aspirations for welfare provision, but her satisfaction was to be short-lived. Official attitudes, now freed from the imperative to encourage and accommodate female employment, were already moving in an entirely different direction. The Health of Munition Workers' Committee was soon to transmute into the Industrial Health Research Board, developing a program of research to investigate the effects on performance of factors such as repetitive work, lighting, noise, temperature and various other physical and ergonomic aspects of the working environment. In 1921 an organization with similar scientific interests, the National Institute of Industrial Psychology,[27] would be formed with support from industrial sponsors. The recommendations that flowed from these two institutions, directed at the workforce as a whole and unashamedly aimed at production maximization, were largely uncontaminated by the moral tone which had undermined much of the wartime system. This new form of welfare held considerably more appeal for employers who were increasingly inclined to initiate and adopt measures on a voluntary basis.

The State's retreat from welfare provision, which effectively negated the recommendations of the Women's Employment Committee, coincided, early in 1920, with another major shift in governmental thinking. It was announced by Home Secretary, Edward Shortt, that the women's branch was to be 'fused' with the men's factory inspectorate to produce a single organisation. Adelaide, vehemently opposed to such a development, began a fierce correspondence with Shortt and with Permanent Secretary Edward Troup, arguing that such a move would undermine all the improvements already made in women's industrial conditions and inhibit all the work still to be done. Women's needs, she was convinced, would be sidelined within a 'fused' organisation. It was an argument predicated on her twin assumptions that women had special needs in the workplace and also required special protection under the law. In 1920, however, this was an argument she was bound to lose. Not only had women's 'special needs' become synonymous with welfare measures during the war years but it was also increasingly difficult to argue that the work of male and female inspectors differed in any substantial way. They investigated the same types of risk and enforced the same regulations. Importantly they now had similar qualifications (although not of course the same salary) and in the years leading up to the war they had been organised in a similar type of hierarchy, with female Superintending Inspectors operating out of Districts distributed around the country. Moreover 'fusion' was in tune with the times, at least in terms of the aspirations of well-educated middle class women. Professional equality and universal suffrage were both now on the political agenda.

Adelaide lost her battle with Edward Shortt, if indeed it was ever a genuine battle, and on 10 August 1920 she received a memorandum from Mr Graves describing the details of the re-organisation. This, she was informed, had now been approved by the Treasury and was due to come into operation on 1 January 1921, or as soon as practicable thereafter. The Inspectorate was to operate with ten divisions containing a total of eighty-five districts. Some divisions and districts would be under the charge of women inspectors but, where the divisional inspector was a man, a woman deputy would be appointed. The number of women inspectors was accordingly to be increased. For Adelaide this represented a further erosion of her own authority and control, a development against which she had fought unsuccessfully in 1907. However, the greatest blow was contained in one stark sentence. 'The post of Principal Lady Inspector will be abolished.'[28] It was mitigated slightly by the following statement, that two deputy chief inspectors were to be appointed, one of which was to be a woman. Having lost the battle, as she saw it, Adelaide determined, as ever, to bow to the requirements of her Civil Service masters and accept the inevitable. She began to make plans for the implementation of the reorganisation. It never seems to have occurred to her, however, that the woman's post of deputy chief inspector would go to anyone but herself.

On the morning of Thursday 12 May 1921 she arrived in her office to be handed a letter from Number 10 Downing Street. It informed her that 'at the request of the Prime Minister, the King had been pleased to approve that she be appointed as Dame Commander of the Order of the British Empire' (DBE). As she wrote to Alex later, she was 'greatly surprised and wondered why.'[29] She imagined, however, that it signalled her definite appointment as deputy chief inspector, a position not yet officially finalised. That afternoon, however, she received other, much less welcome news from Home Secretary Edward Shortt. After careful consideration, apparently, he had come to the conclusion that the new post should be entrusted to new hands and he had decided therefore to appoint Miss Constance Smith. Adelaide, accordingly, should retire from the Civil Service on 20 June. The shock was overwhelming. 'It seemed almost like dying,' she wrote to Alex, 'to face sudden goodbye to my work and all my colleagues.' That afternoon she wrote 'I went home to bed with a temperature!' By the following morning, some elements of her habitual determination had returned and she decided at least to challenge the retirement date, pointing out that 'except in cases of misconduct a month's notice was the minimum.' While she had been prepared for a change in her work, she noted, she had not been prepared for a sudden total severance from the Civil Service. She asked for the usual three months. Before the end of the same afternoon, she received a curt reply 'offering me August 1st.'[30] There were, however, other considerations. Adelaide had just passed her fifty-eighth birthday, two years short of the normal Civil Service retirement age and thus two years short of a full pension. Again she entered into correspondence, this time with Permanent Secretary Edward Troup. Adelaide asked that her two years working for the Labour Commission, prior to her appointment as an inspector, should be taken into account. This would bring her period of service up to thirty years. The request, however, was refused as not reckonable service and her pension was correspondingly reduced. Moreover it later emerged that the intention had been to inform her of the award of DBE after she had received news of her compulsory retirement. The unfortunate order of events, the result, apparently, of administrative bungling, created the impression for Adelaide that the award represented a pacificatory sop rather than a reward for long service. The whole episode was hurtful and humiliating.

The role of Constance Smith in this chain of events is not entirely clear although there is little doubt that influential social networks played some part. Constance had first been appointed as a senior inspector in 1911, under the Liberal administration of Herbert Asquith. Now, in the early 1920s, the Liberals were once more in ascendance, the coalition government having been under the premiership of Lloyd George since 1916. For many years Constance had been part of the coterie of radical liberals surrounding Charles and Emilia Dilke and, despite the death of both these powerful characters by 1911, the influential circle they had created in and around Sloane Street remained intact. Emilia's niece, Gertrude Tuckwell, had been Emilia's successor as President of the WTUL and although she had

retired from official trade union work in 1918 she had remained
extremely active in public life, serving on a range of committees
such as the Central Committee on Women's Training and
Employment, the Royal Commission on National Health
Insurance and, with May Tennant, the Maternal Mortality
Committee. Originally a prime mover in the formation of
the women's branch of the inspectorate Gertrude was now an
equally strong supporter of amalgamation as the way forward,
both in terms of advancing industrial reform and securing
professional equality for women. Almost certainly she would
have viewed Adelaide's presence as something of a stumbling
block in terms of the successful achievement of 'fusion'. Like
many reformists she was probably also irritated by Adelaide's
steadfastly neutral stance, particularly when it came to support
for trade unions. Meanwhile Constance's relationship with
Gertrude was manifestly close. The two had shared their
domestic arrangements ever since May had left the flat in Tite
Street to marry Jack Tennant and it is clear that Gertrude was
inordinately fond of Constance. In Gertrude's 'short memoir'
following Constance's death in 1931, we hear about the 'humility
of Constance's great nature', how she had 'great knowledge and
was marvellously well-educated' and how the flat they shared
together was 'made delightful by her pretty things.' During the
war she 'helped us to keep the British section of the International
Association of Labour Legislation alive.' 'Ask Constance,' we
are told 'was the unfailing resource when large questions of
policy had to be decided, or small points of accuracy were to
seek.' Perhaps more galling from Adelaide's point of view was
Gertrude's description of Constance's steadfast contribution
to the wartime spirit. 'All through those gloomy war days,'
apparently, 'it cheered one to see her arrive always fresh and
exquisite at the HO. Great occasions found her "more than
usual calm" when many showed the effects of the nervous strain
under which they were working.'[31] And struggling temporary

inspectors would, it seems, always turn to Constance to discover where they had gone wrong in their understanding of the regulations. More significantly, however, in October 1919, Constance and Thomas Legge had been appointed as British government delegates to the first conference of the International Labour Organisation (ILO) held in Washington, USA. In previous years Adelaide had always been the obvious choice to represent Britain at international gatherings where women's working conditions were on the agenda. The decision to send Constance instead seemed to signal a significant shift in Home Office preferences, notably those of the new Permanent Under Secretary, Malcolm Delevingne, a strong supporter of amalgamation. Constance's choice of companions on the journey to America is also of interest, for she elected to travel in the company of trade union delegates Margaret Bondfield and Mary MacArthur. It was a rather public alliance that Adelaide would no doubt have studiously avoided. Shortly after the conference Constance was awarded an OBE in the New Year Honours list, a rather curious decision since her record as a factory inspector contained nothing that would mark her out above others of her rank. Moreover her performance at the ILO had not been particularly successful and she had failed to gain British ratification of the Maternity Convention dealing with women's employment before and after childbirth. However, observed Gertrude, she presented her report with 'disarming demureness' and 'great approval was expressed to me afterwards on the complete appropriateness and harmonious colouring of her clothes.'[32]

It is easy to see Constance as a conspirator in a plot to oust Adelaide and this was certainly the opinion of many of Adelaide's friends, one of whom referred to Constance in an angry and hastily scrawled note as 'that snake Constance Smith'.[33] Adelaide herself must have had such misgivings and the fact that, unusually, she kept this defamatory missive, is

perhaps indicative of such. Whether Constance was also a
pawn in the affair, however, is difficult to determine. She seems
to have been desperate to reassure Adelaide that she had no
inkling she was to be made Deputy Chief Inspector. On 19
May she wrote to Adelaide pleading her complete amazement
at the turn of events and denying all knowledge that Adelaide
'had any intention of retiring'. 'It is all very bewildering and
for the moment I am too startled to take in all this involves
for myself. I can only see a tremendous opportunity and
responsibility with which I never dreamt of being called to
grapple with.' Signing herself 'with love, yours ever' she added a
tentative postscript. 'It would be a comfort if I might hear from
you.'[34] Adelaide's reply was typically gracious, congratulating
Constance on her appointment, outlining the circumstances
of her own 'retirement' and adding that she was doing all she
could, in the short time left to her, to ensure that Constance
'shared with the Chief Inspector the direction of a steadfast
set of women.'[35] On the twenty-fourth Constance wrote again,
apparently greatly distressed.

> My dear Adelaide. I am completely overwhelmed by your note. It
> seems perfectly incredible that you should have been so treated and
> I don't know how to put into words what I feel about it. I do know
> what every member of the branch must feel! And whatever is in
> their minds of pain and indignation must necessarily as you will
> understand be intensified in mine by the special circumstances of
> my appointment. Any pleasure I could have felt in that is quite
> poisoned by this staggering news.
>
> For the generosity of your good wishes and your effort so to
> influence the course of things that there may be smooth working
> in the difficult future I thank you from my heart. Not just because
> I am grateful I am the more unhappy. I wish I could make you
> understand how deeply the whole situation troubles me.[36]

Constance, however, was a strong a supporter of the amalgamation and highly critical of Adelaide's leadership of the women's branch. The present arrangement, she considered, had grown up under pressure of circumstances rather than as a result of deliberate planning and now consisted of an uncoordinated system fraught with conflicts and overlapping responsibilities. In January 1920, immediately prior to the first meeting of the official Committee to discuss the reorganisation of the Factory Inspectorate, she wrote to committee member Violet Markham. 'It would be a thousand times better to pull down the old crazy patched-up house and build new on a modern foundation.'[37] A week earlier she had sent a confidential memo to Violet setting out her position. She had, she said, heard people refer to the women's branch as a 'back number, sadly out of date'. In the new world of the 1920s, she considered that professional women expected to compete equally with men. If the Department continued to 'wrap women in silver paper and provide them with a chaperone in the person of the Principal Lady Inspector' it would become increasingly difficult to recruit them. Relationships with male inspectors, she considered, depended so much on diplomacy that 'a huge amount of time was wasted on exercising tact.'[38] Interestingly she explicitly requested that Violet should show this correspondence to no-one, except Gertrude Tuckwell. Some of the language of this memo, however, is reproduced in the final report of the Committee, suggesting that Constance did indeed influence its recommendations. Moreover some of her other letters to Violet indicate that she considered her views to be representative of the majority of the women inspectors, and that Adelaide was tending to obscure this by insisting on complete unity from her staff in opposing the move. Writing to Violet again, in March, Constance described her own resistance to Adelaide's request for support and the consequences she anticipated as a result. 'I have been *very* careful and *very* courteous and have not lost my temper at all, but I expect nonetheless to be treated as an outcast henceforward!'[39]

However, many of the other women inspectors were, in fact, extremely doubtful about the amalgamation, as Inspector Isabel Taylor discovered when she conducted an impromptu straw poll on the subject. Most, including Hilda, were equivocal and uneasy, wanting to know exactly what form 'fusion' would take, whether they would lose their existing autonomy, whether they would be subservient to the men and, importantly, how the salary structure would be arranged. Senior Inspector Henrietta Escreet referred to 'a kind of modern fictitious equality, where women would be less, not more free.'[40] At least some of these fears were to be realised, notably those relating to the salary structure. Across the salary scales, women of equal rank to men were to be paid at a lower rate. It was a decision that infuriated many contemporary feminists who, in the aftermath of the first steps towards universal female suffrage, had begun to feel they were making real progress. May Tennant, who had watched the negotiations carefully, lost no time in telling Malcolm Delevingne exactly what she thought of such injustice. An opportunity to underline the Civil Service commitment to equality as described in the recent Sex Disqualification (Removal) Act[41] had, she informed him, been lost, along with the support and goodwill of many interested in labour reform. For his part Delevingne responded rather weakly with the hope that the department could avoid any 'unsettling controversy' over the matter and that 'the salary question would take care of itself over time.'[42] When the amalgamation eventually took place both Hilda and Rose had hoped for the post of Deputy Chief Inspector but now, it seems, Constance, despite her limited experience, had become the 'safe pair of hands' who could carry the policy through. In the longer term, however, she was perhaps as much a victim of the manoeuvrings of the Home Office as was Adelaide herself. Notwithstanding Edward

Shortt's declaration that he was entrusting the amalgamation to 'new hands' Constance was already sixty-six years old in 1921 and inevitably her tenure was to be a short one. She too seems to have become dispensable once the process was complete, occupying the position of Deputy Chief Inspector for only four years. She retired in 1925, to be replaced by the long serving and highly experienced Hilda, who would remain in post until her own retirement, on a full pension, in 1937. Sadly for Constance, the terms of her original appointment meant that she received no Civil Service pension at all.

Adelaide, meanwhile, was deluged with letters of sympathy and support. Old workmates like Mary Paterson, Lucy, May, and Arthur Whitelegge wrote to express their shock and indignation. Current inspectors and other colleagues, both male and female, wrote of their bewilderment. 'Your treatment has been abominable', 'we cannot imagine the department without you.' And relatives and friends were unequivocal in their outrage. 'We boiled together,' wrote Adelaide's cousins, Margaret Stevenson and Mona Geddes. 'Did this leave Miss Constance Smith in one of the most important posts and justify her position?' Margaret wanted to know. 'If so it was clever if very unscrupulous.'[43] Rose, in particular, was distraught at the news.

> My dearest Adelaide,
>
> In the first few days of these happenings which have turned our world upside down and stunned us, I felt unable to write to you but now I feel impelled to try and write (speech is impossible one breaks down!) I am at a loss to express the love, gratitude admiration and honour which I have for you and in which I hold you. I want to thank you from my heart for your help, guidance and inspiration – for your love and sympathy . . . during the years of stress and strain, yet years of absorbing interest and service, that we both have hoped and prayed and furthered, to some extent at least, the Kingdom of God.[44]

'Miss Squire seems a little lonely,' observed Hilda, 'she has looked in on me a good deal . . . I feel I am living in a state of artificiality and that reality has disappeared.'[45] Hilda herself was finding it difficult to adjust to her new role as a Superintending Inspector, a post that placed her in charge of several newly appointed young men. '. . . we have to do things we have never asked or wanted to . . . I can see the men are going to tax my maternal instincts fearfully! They are so helpless and stupid.'[46]

Amongst this ever growing file of letters was one from Lady Rhondda, prominent suffragist and campaigner for industrial reform, who was writing 'on behalf of a large number of men and women who include many of your personal friends and fellow workers.'[47] She wanted to invite Adelaide to a dinner, which they proposed to organise in her honour. Thus on 21 October 1921 over three hundred people arrived at the fashionable Princes Restaurant in Piccadilly, the cavalcade of cars and carriages apparently putting a temporary stop to traffic in central London. The list of those who consumed Consomé Souveraine, Selle de Bhéhague à la Moderne, Bombe Renaissance and various other delights that evening resembled a directory of early twentieth-century movers and shakers in the field of industrial reform. Presided over by Lady Rhondda, the event was an extraordinary display of loyalty from individuals across the political spectrum and the seating arrangements, no doubt, provided the organising committee with ample opportunities for point scoring. Alongside an array of titled aristocrats, the current chief inspector of factories, R. E. Graves, as well as Mary Paterson and Rose, occupied seats near Adelaide at the top table, while other long serving women inspectors such as Hilda and Lucy were situated close by. (May was similarly placed but was unable to attend because her younger son, Archie, had just undergone surgery). Constance, meanwhile, the new Deputy Chief Inspector, was allocated a seat far removed from this elevated position, while

Edward Shortt, who was judiciously, or perhaps mischievously, allocated the seat next to Adelaide, sent his excuses and a replacement official. Louisa Garrett Anderson, daughter of Aunt Elizabeth Garrett, wrote to tell Alex all about the event. 'Mr Shortt funked the dinner at the eleventh hour, as we expected he would. He pleaded a chill and wrote an oily letter and sent Sir John Baird to represent him and sprinkle a little more oil.'[48] In contrast to Mr Shortt, however, 'The Clan was splendid', arriving in force from Aberdeen, Manchester, Cambridge, Edinburgh, Eastbourne and sundry other places around the British Isles where members of the extended Anderson family were now based. Adelaide, meanwhile, had resurrected the long white dress that in 1892 had graced the Queen's Drawing Room. She 'looked very nice in her court gown,[49] trimmed up to bring it into fashion,' enthused Louisa, 'and Lady Rhondda and Mrs Fawcett received the company which numbered 312. I think Adelaide was pleased by it all and her speech was very charming and touching under most difficult circumstances.'[50] Adelaide had delivered a mixture of reminiscences, philosophical musings and optimistic thoughts about her own possible future. The greatest tribute was paid to 'the working woman of our land who stands at the back of all our work . . . the burden of her toil, striving and suffering . . . and the exceptional freedom (of the women inspectors) from any illusion as to the hardness, the gradgrind character of the old factory system . . . and their good fortune to come in on the eve of a great awakening.' About herself she observed that '. . . with the tension of daily routine relaxed, the mind is relaxed, and lightly springs to ways before the greatest pressure of working life began, to dreams and visions in early morning hours and for a new search for the pattern in the web on the loom, designed by the brighter command behind our human plans.'[51] Adelaide, a devotee of the contemporary Arts and Crafts movement, had recently taken up a new hobby which had clearly inspired this analogy. She had bought herself a spinning wheel and a small table loom and was busily engaged in learning the skills of traditional textile production. Involvement in creative manual work, it was argued, not only preserved Britain's heritage and traditions but also improved the quality of life for the individual concerned.

Adelaide at her spinning wheel in 1921

Adelaide's resilience and determination were obviously starting to re-emerge, along with a desire for a new outlet to absorb her energies. 'I thought a few months ago I was heartbroken at the parting from dear familiar colleagues', she said in her speech on 21 October, 'Alas for human consistency – I am *not*! – for I am nearer all my colleagues by a lighter more ethereal tie – and may even be able to help the aims of the department by work outside on converging lines.'[52] She moved, with her housekeeper and much loved cat, into a new home, a little white cottage in Coulson Street, a short walk from Holy Trinity in Sloane Square where she was a regular attender. She found time for visiting exhibitions and art galleries and for spending time with relatives and old friends. And, encouraged by colleagues and publisher John Murray, she began to write *Women in the Factory* a memoir of her time in the Factory Department. The first draft of the book would be finished by the following March. However her 'dreams and visions in the early morning hours' were increasingly focussed on the wider world and particularly on South Africa. She had written to Alex earlier in the year. 'I am alright and beginning to see that being fairly poor and out of a job sooner than I thought and at the same time perfectly free may be full of compensations. As soon as I have settled up everything and got a clear idea of what is my income I will make plans if possible for a time of travel.'[53] She was clearly concerned about money, exploring various sources and seeking Alex's approval for her decision to ask Mary for some outstanding rent relating to time spent in her flat. It would cover the cost of redecoration obligations, she said. Uppermost in her mind, however, was a desire to visit Ralf and Margaret. The couple's obvious happiness had been clouded during the last two years by the early deaths of two babies. Now Margaret was pregnant again and the baby was expected in January. 'Of course I can't go to SA in the next few months,' Adelaide told Alex, 'but it may prove possible in the autumn.'[54] Alex had

taken careful note of these remarks. When it was proposed that
Adelaide's friends and colleagues at the dinner should be asked
to contribute to a fund for Adelaide he anonymously donated
£100 to bring the final sum up to £1000. Adelaide, touched
by the generosity of so many, began to make plans to visit
Ralf's farm in Zululand. On 29 January 1922, Margaret gave
birth to a healthy baby girl. The child, named Barbara, (for
Margaret's mother Eliza Barbara) was also given the middle
name of Blanche in honour of her Anderson grandmother. Her
delighted Aunt Sissy was invited to be godmother. She would
have liked to leave for South Africa immediately but this had to
be delayed for Max had written to say that he was planning to
come to England for a prolonged visit in the spring. Her older
brother had suffered a personal tragedy two years earlier when
his wife Charlotte had died after contracting liver fluke from a
family pet. In 1920 he had remarried and was now bringing his
new wife Winifred and one-year-old twins, Peter and Pamela,
to introduce them to the family. Adelaide, torn between seeing
Max and his family and meeting her new godchild, booked
her passage to South Africa for 21 April, providing her with a
fortnight to spend with Max and his family. Their prolonged
stay at Fairhaven was to prove quite a challenge for poor Mary
who was quite unused to small children and by all accounts
singularly intolerant of their behaviour. For their Aunt Sissy,
however, the opportunity to meet her new niece and nephew
was a complete delight and only served to heighten her happy
anticipation of meeting Barbara Blanche.

Ever on the lookout for a means of continuing her work, she
also had another reason for visiting South Africa. In August
1920 she had been spending her annual holiday at Bridgefield
with Alice Macdonnell when a letter had been forwarded to
her from Mr Hugh Fowler, Deputy Chief Factory Inspector
based in Pretoria. Mr Fowler had been speaking to Margaret in
Empangeni and sought Adelaide's advice on the appointment

of women factory inspectors in South Africa. He had noticed an article in *The Times* which referred to the proposed amalgamation in Britain. Adelaide was keen to advise but, of course, equally keen to persuade Mr Fowler that his best course lay in the establishment of a separate women's branch, 'the organisation on which we have hitherto relied rather than our new and yet untried modification.'[55] There had ensued a lengthy correspondence which ranged across factory regulations, the role of women inspectors and, in particular, the development of industrial welfare. Adelaide's undoubted enthusiasm to participate in the reform of South African industry, however, was tempered by a degree of colonial naivety. 'South Africa is still in swaddling clothes as an industrial country,' wrote Mr Fowler hesitantly, and 'welfare is almost unknown – perhaps with tact and perseverance we can accomplish something . . . a certain class of manufacturer not only fails to recognise his responsibilities but regards welfare work as ridiculous when applied to Europeans and raving madness when connected with natives.'[56] Nevertheless he still hoped to 'thank her in person for her advice in the future.' When Adelaide found herself 'retired' that time appeared to have come. It was an opportunity for maintaining her 'ethereal tie' with her former colleagues. Moreover she had written to the emergent League of Nations Union and the Industrial Law Bureau of the Young Women's Christian Association (YWCA) to tell them of her proposed visit and in each case had received an enthusiastic response. Miriam Caxton of the League of Nations had sent her a lengthy list of people she might like to visit, while Mary Piercy of the YWCA was sure it would interest Adelaide to 'see the splendid work of our association in South Africa . . . to study legislative proposals concerning women which seem most in accordance with the teaching of Christ.'[57] Adelaide was pleased at the prospect of visiting both these organisations, for the objectives of each were much in tune with her own.

There were, however, other organisations keen to capitalise on her visit and these were firmly rebuffed. When she heard from Margaret that South Africa newspapers had been reporting that she would be 'addressing women's enfranchisement meetings' she immediately drew a firm line. 'I am sorry to hear it. My whole object in coming, while having a real holiday, is to learn all I can about the country, its industry and its people, not to express any views, political or otherwise.'[58] For Adelaide there was no question of retirement offering freedom from the shackles of civil service impartiality. Rather she clung on resolutely to such principles. Thus, with her political neutrality and no doubt her latest hat, firmly in place, she travelled from Waterloo Station to Southampton on the morning of Thursday 21 April 1922, waved off by Max and a large party of other family and friends. She was booked on the maiden voyage of the RMS *Arundel Castle* the latest and smartest addition to the Union Castle fleet which, like all Union Castle liners bound for the Cape of Good Hope, left promptly at 4.00 pm. By late afternoon, therefore, Adelaide was installed comfortably in her First Class cabin and heading happily down Southampton Water.

Chapter Thirteen
THE TRAVELLING SPINSTER

Adelaide was good sailor and a relaxed one. She loved sea voyages describing the 'myriad rainbows on the spray of the waves'[1] and the 'glorious and exquisite sunsets, from the first golden rays in the sea to the last crimson glow and shell pink reflections.'[2] Sometimes there were storms, forked lightning and torrential rain that she found exhilarating. At worst the rough sea was 'uncomfortable' and 'easily soothed by a tablet of aspirin.'[3] One morning she awoke to find many of her fellow passengers had been awake all night in various states of seasickness and terror. 'Many of the barman's bottles had been smashed' and the barbers shop had been 'thrown into confusion.'[4] Adelaide, however, had slept peacefully through it all. There were endless on board entertainments in which she participated fully. She played quoits, took part in quizzes and made herself a costume for the fancy dress party, 'a seventeenth-century spinster', complete, no doubt, with the spinning wheel which had accompanied her on the voyage. She watched with delight as children played in an improvised swimming pool on deck, enjoyed concerts from the band and good conversations at the captain's table. Sunday morning religious services were carefully segregated affairs, with saloon passengers looking over a gallery from above at the steerage passengers below. Observing that the large congregation was mainly steerage she described 'a striking scene and a beautiful service, with little children gently moving about, playing quietly or sitting on their mothers' knees.'[5] Most of these people were part of the surge in emigration to the colonies that took place after the war. Adelaide invited one of the mothers to tea in her cabin in the afternoon having first, as was the required protocol, obtained the captain's permission. 'We had a good talk,' she said.[6] In Capetown she transferred to the SS *Kenilworth Castle* for the on-going journey to Durban where she disembarked to spend a night in the Marine Hotel. A warm and welcoming Ralf arrived the next day to drive her to the farm in Empangeni.

Adelaide with Barbara at Empangeni in 1922

Adelaide spent a month in South Africa during this first visit. She was fascinated by the life that Ralf and Margaret had made for themselves, thoroughly enjoying the trips they arranged for her to see the surrounding countryside. And she was captivated by her small goddaughter. The baby seems to have reawakened the maternal feelings that had formed part of Adelaide's own childhood as the eldest sister of a large family. Photographs of Barbara Blanche show her held aloft in her godmother's arms and happily seated on Adelaide's knee looking at picture books. These were duly dispatched around the world to other members of the family. Max's young children had been a source of considerable pleasure and now Barbara and her sister June, born three years later, were to be a further source of pride. They were, after all, the fruit of her own project to bring her parents together.

There was of course another important side to her visit for she also travelled widely with Mr Fowler of the Factory Inspectorate and with contacts arranged through the ILO and the YWCA. Slipping comfortably back into her factory inspecting role she systematically observed and advised on machinery guarding, the prevention of industrial disease and most particularly on the need for welfare measures. Her advice to Mr Fowler was heavily weighted towards the introduction of facilities such dining rooms, cloakrooms, sanitary arrangements, recreational activities and the establishment of Industrial Councils whereby workers and employers could agree upon the form these facilities should take. If no-one would listen in England she was determined to return to her theme in South Africa with its newly emerging factory regulations. Mr Fowler appeared a willing recruit to the welfare agenda. But the time was not fortuitous for this type of development. The South African Factory Department was already in danger of contraction, the victim of government spending cuts and Adelaide found herself enlisted as an advocate for the preservation of the status quo, rather than as a lobbyist for significant expansion. Once aware of this, however, she was more than happy to provide Mr Fowler with as much help as she could. She was, after all, well acquainted with the practice of fighting ones corner in the struggle for depleted resources. And she also knew the energising effect of praise. She wrote a lengthy private letter to Mr Malan, the Minister for Mines and Factories, in which she enthused about the way his inspectorate operated in South Africa and described how pleased and surprised she had been at the great progress that had been made in health, safety and welfare. Making no mention of the cloud that hung over the Factory Department she offered him her good wishes for 'the whole of this great work of social development in industry.'[7] The effect seems to have been remarkable. Mr Malan had apparently been about to capitulate to the forces ranged against him but now, suddenly, he was prepared 'to enter the fight to the last ditch'. 'Common sense has prevailed,' Mr Fowler wrote later to Adelaide. 'Our Factory Division is not to be swept away in a cavalier manner. The fight was successful due to Mr Malan keeping a stiff heart and we are extremely grateful for your help. Your notes came at just the right psychological moment and tipped the beam of justice in the right direction.'[8] It was all very gratifying for Adelaide herself, helping to restore her self-confidence and fostering a growing belief that, perhaps, she still had something to offer the industrial world.

All too soon the visit was over but Adelaide's enthusiasm for travel, which had previously been constrained by the demands of her work, now enveloped her ambitions. When she returned to England in October 1922 she immediately began making plans for another, longer trip to visit her 'dear scattered brothers'. A visit to Australia to see her birthplace could, she decided, also include another meeting with Max and Winifred, and of course the twins. The young children in her family were always a considerable draw. Moreover she could also see Walter who was currently working in New Zealand. This would be followed by a sentimental journey to see the place where her parents had met and married and finally, she decided, she would like to visit China, Japan and India. She spent a few months back in London planning this trip in extraordinary detail, writing to various contacts, acquiring letters of introduction, visiting Dickens and Jones to buy suitable clothes and studying the life and culture of the places she was to visit. Selected well-travelled friends such as Lucy, Margaret Bondfield and Thomas Legge were invited to dinner with the express purpose of providing her with information about Australia, New Zealand, India and the Far East.

Adelaide's enjoyment of this time was considerably enhanced by the presence of Alex, at Fairhaven on a month's furlough from Burma. Later he wrote to Ralf noting how good it had been to spend a few weeks with Sissy. And, like her, he had been captivated by Max's twins. 'I've no complaints at all about having nieces and nephews, they are full of interest'. Now he was hoping he would soon be able to get to know Barbara. 'Sissy of course is tremendously full of her praises. She obviously enjoyed every moment of her time in South Africa and seems to be thinking seriously about going back there.'[9] By Christmas 1922, however, Alex had returned to Burma and Max and his family were back in Australia. The following February Adelaide spent two days at the cottage that Louisa Garrett Anderson shared with fellow doctor Flora Murray. The cottage, called Paul End, was at Penn, next door to Troutwells, home of the Ilberts, and Adelaide no doubt took the opportunity to renew her acquaintance with Sir Courtney and his family. Her reaction to Paul End, however, was curiously muted in tone. Another visitor to the cottage had described it as 'a gem . . . overlooking green fields', the garden 'covered with the sweetest borders in which were masses of forget-me-nots, wall flowers, white stocks, tulips perfectly coloured'. Inside there was central heating, hot water, excellent food, wonderful curios and ancient pottery . . . and 'the most comfortable beds I have ever been in – soft downy mattresses, linen sheets and lavender scented.'[10] This particular visitor, who had been a fellow doctor at Endell Street Military Hospital during the war,[11] was delighted at the range of books 'on liberty, freedom, etc. as regards women's rights' and described her joy as 'we tramped the country thro' the village into the woods . . . and talked until our tongues ached.'[12] Adelaide, by contrast, reported tersely that her visit to Paul End consisted of 'wet walks with LGA, needlework and reading'. Apparently unimpressed by the range of feminist literature on hand, and presumably the absence of books on moral philosophy, she spent most of her time reading 'EGA's letters of 1860 to ED'[13] and writing various letters of her own. Admittedly, after the joys of South Africa, she might have found the English countryside in February rather disappointing, and she rarely showed much interest in the interiors of peoples' houses, but perhaps she was also out of sympathy with the views of Louisa and Flora. Despite the falling out between Alexander Gavin and James Skelton there seems to have been no general antagonism between other members of the two families. Indeed Adelaide had continued to be a frequent visitor to Elizabeth Garrett Anderson's London house in Upper Berkeley Street and often stayed at the Garrett family home in Aldeburgh. But Louisa and Adelaide were not natural companions. Louisa had originally belonged to the militant arm of the suffrage campaign, spending a brief period in Holloway prison in 1912 for throwing bricks through windows. It was something that would undoubtedly have earned Adelaide's intense disapproval. Following her visit to Paul End she returned to London early on Monday morning, recording prosaically that she 'caught the 9.15 train to Marylebone via Beaconsfield' but making no mention of luxurious food, lavender scented beds or ancient pottery.[14] Back at Coulson Street the final draft of *Women in the Factory* was completed and handed over to John Murray for publication. She was now more than ready to return to Empangeni and the morning of 28 March 1923 found her once more at the station, this time at St Pancras, to board the boat train to Tilbury and the Aberdeen line SS *Euripedes*. This was to be a much longer trip and she was waved off by an even larger party which included her sister Mary and a whole crowd of Anderson cousins, as well as Beatrice Webb and Hilda Martindale. 'A cheery parting' with roses from Hilda and 'much hugging' from everyone else, she noted happily in her diary.[15]

On April 23 she was reunited with Ralf and Margaret and of course with Barbara, now an energetic toddler, 'excessively vigorous in walking' and 'growing in vitality with lovely riotous movements.'[16] Unlike Mary, Adelaide was captivated rather than troubled by the exuberance of young children. Her diary is filled with fond little anecdotes about her adored niece. On being given a new frock one day, Barbara 'made a fascinated and fascinating study of herself' in two long mirrors. 'The dress matched her blue eyes', noted Aunt Sissy approvingly.[17] And Barbara 'had discovered the use of a mouth organ and played softly on it by herself.'[18] Adelaide clearly spent a great deal of time with her goddaughter. The two fed the farm's chickens together, went for long walks to the river that bounded Ralf's land and, with Margaret, undertook excursions to places like Richard's Bay where they drove past cane fields, through swamps and prairies, saw huge freshwater lakes and finally enjoyed the sandy shore by the sea. At the end of each day Aunt Sissy took over Barbara's evening bath when the young child was tired but 'sweet and charming'.[19] Meanwhile, when Barbara was asleep, letters home were written, books were read and Adelaide's blue brocade hat was newly trimmed. Much spinning and weaving was accomplished, for the wheel and loom had been unpacked and set up on the second day. Altogether it was a wonderful holiday.

A few days before she left Empangeni Adelaide recorded in her diary a conversation with Margaret when the two 'talked sympathetically much of the afternoon.' Margaret asked how Adelaide would feel about such a rural farm life. Would she miss her public work? 'I explained,' said Adelaide, 'I had not chosen public work and adaptation to rural life depends on friendship, books, peace and something worth doing.'[20] It was an enigmatic reply, which perhaps pointed once more to her own

Adelaide with Barbara at Empangeni in 1923

sense of mission, given not chosen, but there is little doubt that Adelaide was indeed missing her public life, and was already making plans to resume it. She spent 'nine absorbing days' in Capetown[21] before embarking on the next leg of her journey and met a numbers of MPs, trade unionists, factory inspectors and government officials as well as visiting a range of workplaces. She was also taken to see 'a good little home for friendless girls' and finally the Marion Institute, which she described as 'an admirable club for coloured industrial girl workers'.[22] Her advice and endorsement of labour activities in South Africa were much sought after and she was more than happy to oblige.

Throughout this time, however, her mind was already turning to another emerging opportunity, the seeds of which had been sown early in March, just before she left London. She had received a letter addressed to her at her club, the University Women's Club, from Harold Butler,[23] a founding member of the ILO secretariat. Having heard that she was to visit China and Japan he asked for her assistance in compiling confidential reports on labour conditions in each of those countries. He suggested that she might write an article that could be published in the organisation's journal the *International Labour Review*. This, he suggested, would 'necessarily be somewhat less outspoken' than her confidential reports, 'that is to say supposing that you find the conditions leave much to be desired, as I expect you will.'[24] If she had the time, Butler continued, he would also appreciate any information she could provide on labour conditions in any other countries she might visit. He offered every assistance in providing contacts and letters of introduction, not only in China and Japan but also in South Africa, Australia and New Zealand. Adelaide's reply, agreeing enthusiastically to his request, reveals the extent to which her round the world 'holiday' had already been mentally reformulated. Thanking Mr Butler she told him that she was already fully in touch with South African officials, manufacturers and labour leaders, and the Foreign Office had

provided introductory letters to the British Consul in Peking
and to officials at the Embassy in Tokyo. Her network of friends
in high places still seemed to be largely intact. She was also, by
now, in regular contact with the YWCA in China, including,
in particular, a correspondence with their industrial secretary, a
British welfare worker called Agatha Harrison.[25] In 1920, Agatha
had been asked by the YWCA to go to Shanghai to study
working conditions for women and children and advise on a
course of action. Her first visit to a cotton mill had, she said,
'been burnt on my memory.'

> The workroom was crowded with people ranging from a few
> months to seventy years of age. Some of the women at the
> machines had bound feet that measured about five inches. And
> everywhere children. In odd corners babies lay in baskets asleep,
> or women sat feeding them, and you could scarcely walk for
> tiny tots that swarmed the rooms. Some were working hard on
> unguarded machines, others seemed to be running around. The
> dust was appalling.[26]

Here women and children worked twelve-hour shifts,
seven days a week. There was a complete absence of any
form of industrial legislation in China. Agatha's primary
recommendation, therefore, was that the focus of the YWCA
should be on the development and subsequent enforcement
of factory regulations. Filled with outrage at the plight of the
workers she had immediately offered her own services for the
job, but she had soon realised that she possessed neither the
relevant knowledge nor the necessary skills and experience. The
proposed visit to China of a former Principal Factory Inspector
thus presented itself to her as a heaven sent opportunity. When
Adelaide arrived in Capetown at the end of May a letter from
Agatha was waiting for her.

I want to prepare you for something that I think will happen in the near future and that is you will be asked to come and help us instead of making a passing visit. The Christian forces here are the only group that have made any serious attempt to attack the industrial problem. In Shanghai as a result of much agitation a commission is to be appointed to go into the question and to make recommendations. But we are in a terrible predicament because there is literally no-one in China who has any expert knowledge on this question. I fully expect that long before you get this letter a cable will have reached you asking you to come and help us. I frankly do not know how to make the urgency of the matter clear to you. If I could have five minutes talk with you I know that at the end of it you would say you would come. There is no one who can do what you can do at this juncture.[27]

The plea was irresistible to Adelaide who was already half persuaded that her future work lay in China. On the same day she had received a cablegram from Bishop Logan Roots, an Episcopal clergyman now working at the American missionary centre in Shanghai. He similarly hoped she would extend her stay in China to investigate working conditions there. She discussed the matter with the Archbishop of Capetown who strongly encouraged her to respond positively to the invitation. Her own sense of mission, now fully rekindled, was further fuelled when, a week later, she was introduced to the Prime Minister of the Union of South Africa, General Smuts. On discovering her intention to visit China, he talked enthusiastically about Bertrand Russell's recent book *The Problem of China*,[28] presenting her with his own copy to take away and read. The book, based on Russell's visit to China a year earlier, contained an interesting section on the Treaty Ports[29] to which Adelaide would be heading later that year. Here, Russell noted, the Europeans and Americans lived in their own quarters with well-paved streets and lighted houses, the shops full of American and English goods. This was, however, in stark contrast to the 'cheerful disordered beauty' of the old Chinese part of the town 'with narrow streets, gaily decorated shops and the rich mixture of smells characteristic of China.' In the European town, he said, there was 'safety, spaciousness and hygiene, ugly cleanliness and Sunday-go-to-meeting decency,' while in the Chinese town there was 'romance, overcrowding and disease.'[30] Adelaide may well have made an analogy between this state of affairs and that existing in her own city, London, where such wide disparities of income and lifestyle existed within short distances of each other. She considered that the book 'sparkled' with important insights on Chinese life which, Russell thought, 'brought much more happiness to the Chinese than English life brought to the English', for he considered that China was still overwhelmingly a rural country primarily involved in agriculture and maintaining its strong culture and traditions. He did not, however, feel this happiness to be 'true for the women'.[31] 'There is the magnet for me!' wrote Adelaide in an enthusiastic letter to her sister Mary.[32] She did not comment further on Russell's work which also abounded with references to the evils of imperialism, the destructive effect of industrialisation and the new path of socialism, inspired and supported by the Russian communist party which, he considered, China was now following. However, before she left South Africa for Australia she left a message to be forwarded to Logan Roots. She advised him that she expected to arrive in Shanghai in October and that she was now 'considering his request'.[33]

On board the *Diogenes* bound for Melbourne she found plenty more time for reading, enclosed in her cabin as 'the roaring wind arose and great waves whitened like snow with spindrift broke over the decks.'[34] The voyage from Capetown had begun deceptively peacefully. Adelaide had recorded how she had glimpsed 'in the slight swell, the softened outline of

South Africa in the morning mist, aglow at its peaks near the sea edge.'[35] On this voyage, however, there was to be no opportunity for quoits, walks or social activities. She did manage to 'make friends with a nice Irish mother from Tipperary and her five children', having 'slipped down into third class regions after morning service on Sunday.'[36] But on the upper decks the full force of the unrelenting storms was highly visible. 'I never saw such waves before,' she said. With characteristic focus on the beauty rather than the fear she described the 'vivid blue edge between the grey rising mass and the foam'. However, even the normally unflappable Adelaide, who considered the ship to be 'stout and steady', confessed to sleeping 'half-dressed' as during the night large seas 'came with force against the cabins on the promenade deck.'[37] She must have realised for the first time what her parents had endured on that journey to England through the roaring forties sixty years earlier. 'I thought the next sea would break all the windows,' she told Mary.[38] On 3 July, however, after a final, particularly rough night, the ship eased thankfully into its berth in Melbourne harbour and Adelaide was able to behold the city that she had last seen as a small baby. It had of course changed dramatically in the intervening years but since she had no memory of the place this hardly mattered. She could simply admire its present state. Forty years of the gold rush had seen the city grow into one of the largest and wealthiest in the world. Known as 'marvellous Melbourne' it had spread in all conceivable directions with buildings of every type, luxurious villas, small cottages, offices and factories, sprawling over an ever increasing swathe of the surrounding plain. Its growing population, around seven hundred thousand by 1923, was served by modern efficient public services and a plethora of schools, churches, learned societies, libraries and art galleries. Already the indisputable capital of the State of Victoria, it had, in 1901, become the seat of government for the newly formed Commonwealth of Australia. The gold rush had eventually petered out and Melbourne had suffered a number of recessions during the early years of the twentieth century, but when Adelaide arrived it was once more experiencing a period of moderate prosperity. It was still the capital city and, as such, was home to the most prestigious university in the country. It was here that Adelaide was to stay with old family friends, Sir David Masson, the Professor of Chemistry and his wife, Mary, who, she discovered, had named their house The Chanonry, with fond remembrances of that other Chanonry in far off Aberdeen. Adelaide was impressed by Lady Masson, if a little unsure of her somewhat blunt manner. In a long circular letter to friends and family Adelaide wrote hesitantly, 'I can't pretend to tell you what she is really like,' adding however, 'like ourselves she has sympathies with "underdogs" as well as with hard workers and thinkers. I never met anyone who – with the salt of humour – better combines daily maternal anxiety that her friends shall be properly cared for – and that they shall give their best in the world.'[39] Of Melbourne itself she was somewhat equivocal. It was, she decided, 'a stately city' and she 'supposed in the spring and summer it might be lovely, as the poet says "O sweet queen city of the golden south, piercing the evening with thy starlit skies."'[40]

Adelaide's time in Melbourne began with a Mayoral Reception, immediately on the afternoon of her arrival, and continued in this vein for the next month. Her visit was to prove a whirlwind of factory tours, newspaper interviews and photographic sessions, meetings with trade unionists and factory inspectors and talks delivered at lunches, dinners and conferences. She was undoubtedly something of a celebrity in Melbourne and it was not long before she assumed her habitual role of commenting on the conditions she found in the factories of the city, noting systematically the presence, or more often the absence, of lavatories and messrooms, canteens and cloakrooms, machinery guarding and protection from fumes. She had no official authorisation for these visits but the overriding importance of her obvious governmental and social connections meant that no-one questioned her right to inspect the factories of Melbourne. In fact she seems to have been seriously overworked, so keen was everyone to claim her attention. 'I was as free to come and go with factory inspectors as I was in South Africa and that is saying much,' she told everyone.[41]

Meanwhile she received increasingly passionate letters from Agatha underlining the urgent need of her presence in Shanghai. 'You mention getting to China at the end of the year, but we want you *now* that is by Sept at the latest. Cannot you cut short your time in Australia? And please do not fix a time to limit your stay in China.' Agatha could never quite grasp that others might not share her own particular set of priorities. 'The Government needs your help,' she continued, 'the local centres need your help; the universities who are beginning to consider training workers for factory inspection need your help; the Shanghai Municipal Council too and above all the Church in China that is struggling to lead the way, not only for all those in China who are aiming at the best industrial standards but for all the churches the world over that are trying to find a fine expression of Christianity. . . . I *believe* you will come,' she concluded fervently. 'You are needed here so terribly and will find a *very* warm welcome waiting for you here.'[42] To underline her case Agatha often included news clippings from the North China Daily News, the leading British newspaper in Shanghai. Invariably these were of horror stories. One such, reported under the casually ill-conceived heading of 'Notes for the Day' ran as follows:

An inquest was held yesterday by magistrate Li and Mr Jacobs on a child employed in the Anglo-Chinese Cotton Mill who met her death in tragic circumstances. A verdict was returned that she was

drawn into the machinery from underneath a handrail by her feet
while asleep at four o'clock in the morning.[43]

'When I was in a factory the other day at 3.30 a.m.,'
commented Agatha, 'I saw several children asleep on the floor
between the machines and can well understand how the above
happened. It occurs to one that it is the *right* of a child to be
asleep at 4.00 a.m.'[44]

The combination of this barrage of pressure from afar and
the demands on her immediate doorstep seem to have taken
its toll on Adelaide. Halfway through her visit to Melbourne
she retreated to bed with 'a cold and a high temperature'. It
was probably a relief when, on 25 July, after a final visit to a
factory, lunch with Miss Dow, the local lady factory inspector
and one last meeting with three other colleagues, she finally
collected her luggage from The Chanonry and boarded the late
afternoon sleeper train for her namesake city of Adelaide. 'Take
care of yourself,' advised Mary Masson, as she waved her off,
'but not too much care.'[45]

Arriving at ten o'clock the following morning, no doubt
after an indifferent night's sleep, Adelaide was warmly
welcomed by Max and Winifred and two excited children.
There followed the inevitable and unavoidable press interviews,
but it was clear, at least to her family, that she was looking
tired and anxious and they determined to make sure she had
some rest and recuperation. The evening was 'quiet and restful
with Max and Winifred, family talk and my plans discussed,'
she noted.[46] The next morning she was presented with a rare
treat, breakfast in bed! There followed peaceful days of walks
with Winifred, reading and letter writing, drives to beautiful
gardens and parklands and a visit to the zoo with the children
where she shared their delight at the kangaroos and the 'jumbo
hippo'. Adelaide was much less frenetic and demanding than
Melbourne and Max and Winifred were determined to look

after her. The city, she thought, was 'one of the loveliest in the world, well-planned with delightful "townlands" or parks ringed round the city dividing it from the suburbs, and the Mount Lofty range behind.'[47] The visit gave her the time and space she needed to clear her thoughts and come to terms with what she now considered was her mission and her duty. On the second Sunday she attended Choral Eucharist at the cathedral and afterwards wrote a letter to Logan Roots saying she would be glad to extend her stay in China to assist in his investigations. She also sent a cable to Agatha 'I am ready to make all the response in my power to the invitation given me.'[48]

How far Adelaide was aware of the developments that had influenced the direction of the YWCA's work in China during this period is uncertain. Agatha had hinted at it in her letter when she talked of the establishment of the Labour Commission in response to 'much agitation'. There were echoes here of Britain's New Unionism in the 1880s, although the political background in China was quite different. The previous few years had seen the rise of the New Culture movement which sought to promote Western ideology as a route to emancipation. The movement represented a challenge to the dominant Confucian code with its strict rules governing social organisation, individual behaviour and, in particular, the hierarchy of relationships between family members. New Culture was underpinned by a nationalist desire to strengthen China through modernisation and thus free the country from both internal conflicts and the ambitions of imperialist powers. The movement, which centred on demands for individual freedom and equality of opportunity, also extended into the area of employment rights and industrial reform. It was strongest in the Treaty Ports of China's Eastern seaboard, established in the mid-nineteenth century following the Opium Wars. Here, where foreigners were exempted from local laws, trading conventions, taxes and various other obligations, a number of countries had set up their own 'concessionary areas' where inhabitants enjoyed many of the pleasures and facilities they might expect at home. In Shanghai the British and American inhabitants had joined forces to form what was known as the International Settlement, where private clubs, a racecourse, luxury shopping, dances and tea gardens, offered the 'Shanghailanders'[49] a colonial life with a Chinese flavour. Behind the glossy façade of 'The Bund',[50] however, large numbers of Chinese were employed in dangerous, insanitary factories, with no protection provided by any form of factory legislation.

Within the International Settlement British and American missionaries had established their own institutions, notably churches, medical centres and of course schools which provided, at minimum cost, western-inspired education for the local population. Thus many local Chinese, including large numbers of women, began to absorb, not only the English language and the Christian religion, but also American and European values. Women were prominent in the New Culture movement with female industrial workers joining with middle class intellectuals to demand educational opportunities, labour reform and freedom from traditional customs such as arranged marriages and foot binding. During the early 1920s women factory workers in Shanghai were repeatedly involved in the 'agitation' alluded to by Agatha, taking part in disruptive strikes and demonstrations which were often several thousand strong. Hence the YWCA, with its educational programmes, had inadvertently become a prominent player in the development of New Culture, ably assisted, following the First World War, by the ILO. With an agenda focussed on the reform of industrial conditions the objectives of these two organisations fortuitously came together. Just as in England, therefore, Adelaide was about to step into a politically charged environment. Characteristically, however, she seemed disposed to ignore the ideological underpinnings of the situation and focus on the task in hand, the improvement of industrial conditions. This time, of course, there would be no Civil Service structure to provide a justification and protection for her political neutrality. On the positive side, however, she could now openly enjoy the company of like-minded workers who drew on religion for their inspiration and motivation.

In the event Adelaide did not reach China until the end of November. After leaving Max and Winifred at the beginning of August she pursued an unrelenting itinerary, part work, part holiday. It took her briefly back to Melbourne and then to Sydney where she lectured at the Women's College of the University and stayed in the flat of an old friend 'high up with a marvellous view of the harbour'. One 'glorious day' she was driven through the National Park and Kurungai Chase 'with a shimmer of blue irises in all the open glades' and then on across the Hawkesbury River to the Blue Mountains. 'I wonder if you know, as I did not,' she wrote to Mary, 'how unique and interesting the avifauna of Australia is, the darting brightness of rosellas, the flight of the yellow crested parrots, the charming notes of the bellbirds and the sounds of that delightful creature, the cookaburra.'[51] After Sydney she went to New Zealand where she took a round trip, encompassing Auckland and Wellington in North Island, across to Christchurch in South Island, and from there back to Auckland via Napier, Rotorua and Hamilton. Auckland claimed the lion's share of her time for this was where Walter was based and she had not seen her brother for several years. Walter was unwell, suffering increasingly from the muscular weakness that had now been diagnosed as multiple sclerosis. He was struggling to walk even with the aid of sticks. But he was delighted to entertain Adelaide, hiring a driver to take them around to view the local sights. The two had trips out together, lunches and dinners and meetings with friends. These were happy, precious weeks, the memory of which Adelaide would treasure, for it was the last time she would have the company of this particular brother.

Adelaide with Walter in 1923

In Christchurch she visited the pretty timber church of St
Michael's and All Angels which now stood on the spot where
her parents had been married in the little wooden shed all those
years ago. It was the 'mother church' she wrote in her diary
ambiguously, 'decorated with lovely arum lilies, just like an
Italian picture.'[52] She noted with pleasure that the little bell
tower her parents had seen was still there, now complete with
its bell. Then it was a brief return to Sydney followed by a trip

to Brisbane where 'the lovely lavender-purple Jacaranda trees were in full bloom when I came up the river on the coastal steamer right into the town.'[53] Finally, however, it was time to say good-bye to Australia and board the SS *Tango Maru* for Hong Kong.

By now it was early November. Adelaide's timetable had slipped considerably, despite her reluctant abandonment of a trip to Japan. The areas around Tokyo had suffered a major earthquake at the beginning of September causing mass destruction and thousands of deaths and a visit there now seemed out of the question. However, she had agreed with an increasingly impatient Agatha that it would be useful to pay a short visit to Hong Kong and the adjacent province of Canton to see a little of industrial conditions there before going on to Shanghai. She had a letter of introduction to the Governor tucked in her bag as well as contacts within the influential mercantile company of Butterfield & Swire arranged by Walter. She was sure these would help her gain entrance to important manufacturers in the colony. Agatha, meanwhile, continued to pursue her with increasingly pressing letters. 'Everyone is agog that you are coming.' 'I just cannot tell you how eagerly I am waiting for you. When I see you stepping on land a great burden will fall off my shoulders.' 'Your coming is going to make history in China.'[54] Mary Dingman, an American worker with the YWCA, was also on her way to China. She had met Adelaide in Auckland and the two had established an instant rapport. Now they made common cause. 'I look forward to meeting you again in Shanghai' wrote Mary Dingman, adding with apparent amusement, 'I have had several letters from Miss Harrison. I think she is pining for you.'[55]

On board the *Tango Maru*, however, Adelaide was calm, relaxed and seemingly unconcerned by the pressure waves emanating from China. Two days into the voyage she began the letter addressed to 'Friends' where she gave lyrical expression to many of her experiences in Australia and New Zealand, as well as to the obvious joy she experienced during the current voyage. Busy with her reports for the ILO she described how she was working comfortably in her cabin at a writing bureau with the windows wide open. Here she could watch the passing islands in the Great Barrier Reef Channel which grew 'lovelier and lovelier' as she took in the 'pinky purple isles with faint blue shadows as they melted away in the distance' and 'the noble mountainous Hitchinbrook standing out with deeper blue.' 'I suppose some day all this exquisite loveliness will become widely known to civilised people,' she mused, 'and be praised by poets in fitting words.' There followed a delightful view of the Spice Islands[56] as the ship sailed close enough to Ceram to see the 'houses, roads and forests clothing the mountains, coming down close to the sea with a fringe of cocoa-nut [sic] palms at the water's edge.' 'White and pink-sailed ships, boats, shoals of fish and flights of birds make it all gay and alive,' she enthused, 'And tomorrow we cross the line at one o'clock.' During a brief stop at Zamboanga in the South Philippines, 'a picturesque place with beautiful coconut palm groves and paddy fields', she was able to go ashore for a few hours and see the Filipino houses, 'slight wooden thatched . . . very picturesque under the palms'. Thinking of her own recent efforts with the wheel and loom she particularly admired the skills of the local people. 'Their weaving of cotton and fibre and their basketry have the grace of an ancient craft,' she said. A few days later the ship docked in Manila and she encountered the old walled town, 'the meeting of East and West in an extraordinary way . . . Spanish in original construction, with its winding streets, churches and public buildings, Filipino in its people but also Chinamen in every street, carrying things in the Chinese manner, suspended in a basket between poles, Eastern shops, Eastern bullock carts and Chinese-looking boats on the canals.' [57]

The intrinsic Adelaide, self-contained and determined to do

things her own way and in her own time, was fully restored. And she was supremely happy. 'It is all so fresh and vivid and I am so strong and renewed in life,' she wrote.

> I have a surging up of pictures and thoughts and feelings whenever I turn on the lamp of memory. I have proved the truth of those words "we cannot lose ourselves where all is home" the beautiful way in which apprehensiveness about the immense travel ahead of one grows quiescent and apparently disappears as week after week, and month after month, comes serenely on. And regrets over the interesting experiences that are cut short by the pressure of time in getting to China fade away gently in the pinky opal haze that is characteristic of the Australian distance. Travel is less and less the passing from one place to another. It is the taking up in a fresh way into one's own consciousness of our inheritance in this splendid world of humanity and Nature.[58]

Adelaide had lost nothing of her old firmness, however. Serene she might be, but she had already written to Agatha making it clear that she had no wish to spend much time in official receptions, formal dinners or giving lectures to large audiences. 'Avoid any plans for public addresses,' she instructed her. If some lectures at the universities were necessary she would try to meet the need 'provided they were to small gatherings and simply for the purpose of conveying essential information to people who can, in turn, act on it.'[59] Her focus was to be on the very practical matter of investigating conditions in industrial premises. Her experiences in Australia had reminded her that much time and energy could be wasted on non-productive official engagements. And she also had an intense dislike of large audiences. 'I am not endowed physically for public speaking,' she told Agatha.[60] Her emphasis on her physical stature was not entirely a cover for social anxiety, for she was tiny and softly spoken and in the 1920s the microphone had barely arrived on the scene. Adelaide had grown up in a world where women with large personalities and voices to match had shouted and raged at noisy crowds, demanding universal suffrage and workers' rights. She could only watch with horror and terror as these women faced down the abuse hurled at them as they held their ground on precarious platforms. Even in the more sedate surroundings of the lecture hall, however, Adelaide was not a success. Her serious and reserved nature meant that she was rarely able to combine the need to inform with the facility to entertain. A year later, in England, the author Winifred Holtby would attend one of Adelaide's lectures on the subject of industrial conditions in China. Despite Winifred's strong interest in the topic she was dismayed by the monotony of Adelaide's delivery. 'So slow I almost slept,' she wrote to her friend and fellow writer Vera Brittain.[61] Agatha, by no means a shrinking violet herself, was surprisingly sympathetic towards Adelaide's worried misgivings. 'I shall guard you like a dragon,' she assured her. 'I am making no engagements until you arrive and I have the opportunity of knowing what you wish to do.'[62]

Agatha's impatience for Adelaide's arrival was in some ways understandable for she herself was due to leave China at the end of February and was anxious for someone to continue the work she had started. Moreover the first meeting of a Child Labour Commission for which she had worked long and hard, was scheduled for 23 November. By the time Adelaide arrived in Hong Kong, Agatha had already crossed swords with the Chairman of the Commission.

> They are trying to say that nothing can be done unless the Chinese Government acts. What is happening in this settlement is a disgrace to every man and woman in it. It is a terrible thing to think that in 1923 with a knowledge of our tragic history at the back of us a group of mainly foreign men and women can sit splitting hairs over the legal possibility of regulating work for

children under twelve. I am afraid I lost my temper yesterday. I asked him if he would answer as a man not as an official! I badly needed you yesterday.[63]

Agatha was also dubious about Adelaide's proposed visit to Hong Kong and keen to warn her about the obvious tensions between the missionaries and the other British inhabitants there.

I do not know what touch you have had with missionary work but you will soon sense a rather delicate situation for between the community people and the missionaries a great gulf is fixed. HK is an extraordinary cliquey place and you will be meeting some of the government people who have very little to do with Chinese church leaders. We have been told for instance that it is not of the least interest to the Peak ladies (as the women folk of the government and business circles living on the Peak are referred to) that your help has been asked for by the National Christian Council (they are only interested in you!). They are quite indifferent to its existence and quite unaware of its possibilities. Our General Secretary in HK would very much have liked you to stay in the association house during your time in HK but it may be more politic to allow the Peak ladies to have their way in the matter of your entertainment.[64]

Adelaide may well have smiled to herself on receiving this letter. China might be a completely alien land but this kind of thing, at least, was familiar territory. She had considerable experience in negotiating a difficult path between opposing vested interests. And she, of course, was completely at home amongst the wealthy and powerful. In Hong Kong she visited several factories and then had a long meeting with the Governor. He told her that 243 factories were officially registered, of which about eighty employed women and young persons. In Hong Kong as a whole, however, he estimated that around ten thousand women and girls were employed. The Child Labour Law, Adelaide considered, was 'meagre' but its administration, under the good offices of a 'pleasant young British Sanitary Inspector', was about as good as it could be. And not all working conditions in the area were poor. Before she left Canton she found herself extremely impressed by the conditions experienced by thousands of outworkers engaged in 'beautiful work . . . embroidery on silk muslin.' The opportunity to meet with some of these skilled and well-paid women was, she said, a valuable addition to her own outlook on work in China. It was however 'regrettable' to see nothing provided for the health and safety protection of factory workers over the age of fifteen. 'Fencing of transmission machinery and exhaust ventilation for injurious dust is mostly lacking,' she observed. All this was recorded in a long confidential report which she dispatched to Harold Butler in Geneva.[65] Having extracted a promise from the governor that he would give certain matters his attention she moved on to a meeting with the Chinese leader Dr Sun Yat-Sen in Canton. Here, however, she drew a blank. 'He frankly said he could not give attention to conditions of labour until the Civil War was nearer settlement,' she told Butler. Even Adelaide, with her seeming ability for tunnel vision where labour matters were concerned, had been forced to agree. Recently appointed as President of the Southern Government of Hong Kong and Canton, Sun Yat-Sen was desperately trying to consolidate his rule in the face of violent opposition from various warlords and republican revolutionaries. The conflict had reached a crucial stage. With fighting raging just outside the town, Adelaide had been rushed away by Hong Kong officials concerned for her safety. Meanwhile Agatha's desperate pleas were becoming ever more insistent.

When the cable came from HK that you were delayed a week it was almost as though I were hearing that you had been delayed a year so terribly do we need you. The last word we have is that you will arrive on the 'Russia' This boat has been delayed four days on account of storm. We fervently hope this does not mean that you will get here any later than the first. I am sorry to be so insistent but everyday counts just now.[66]

Poor Agatha's sigh of relief must have been audible to all when, on the evening of 1 December 1923, the *Empress of Russia* finally anchored at the mouth of the Whangpoo River and its passengers boarded the tender to take them into Shanghai.

Chapter Fourteen
CHINA

Adelaide's first view of the Shanghai waterfront, The Bund, with its 'gaiety and surging human life', impressed and amazed her. Its grand buildings, vibrant colours, exotic smells and 'the brilliant mingling of all races of East and West' bombarded her senses from every direction.[1] As the tender progressed along the fifteen miles of muddy river towards the customs jetty it was joined by an incredible variety of water-craft converging on the city from every port in China, and beyond. Stepping ashore she found her luggage had already been collected, tied together and slung on to a bamboo pole across the shoulders of two 'coolies', whereupon it was 'somehow safely conveyed to my destination.'[2] Her destination was the British section of the International Settlement in Shanghai, and more specifically Quinsan Gardens, a Western style terrace of tall redbrick villas with large shady porches. Its front windows overlooked a park on the opposite side of the road, a green space with lawns, trees and flowerbeds where foreigners could walk and their children could play in safety. The area, described by writer Paul French as a centre of 'serious do-gooding', was filled with Christian missions and educational centres.[3] Number five, where Adelaide was allocated a study/bedroom, was next door to the Christian Bookshop and Reading Room and home to various workers attached to the National Christian Council in China (NCCC) and the YWCA. Arriving on a cold evening in December she was touched to find a newly lit fire in her room and an assortment of 'attractive properties lent by fellow inmates of the house' to help her feel at home.[4] Quinsan Gardens thus offered an island of peace and tranquillity, a retreat from the seething bustle of Chinese Shanghai where upwards of one and a half million people lived and worked.

As ever, however, there was little immediate opportunity for her to benefit from the charms of her surroundings. In spite of Agatha's well-intentioned promises, she had been unable to curb completely the Chinese enthusiasm for welcoming an honoured guest. Barely had Adelaide unpacked and settled into her room than she was required to host an 'At Home' at the YWCA hospitality centre. Here she met a bewildering array of Chinese dignitaries, as well as the British and American Consuls with their assorted retinues of officials. Shortly afterwards she found herself the subject of a welcome dinner hosted by the Ningpo[5] Chamber of Commerce, admittedly a rather more useful affair in terms of her general objectives. This was followed by a similar event where she met a group of 'Chinese gentlemen wishing to promote friendship with foreigners'.[6] These included representatives of the Asiatic Petroleum Company, the Bank of China, the Ningpo Commercial Bank and the Ningpo-Shaoxing Steamship Company. Here she was introduced by the Chief Mandarin of the District as 'the superintendent of a very large factory in England.'[7] She wisely decided against any attempt to correct this misnomer. The concept of a woman factory inspector would have been beyond the lexicon of most Chinese businessmen. Then it was on to Tientsin[8] Province to stay for a few days with William Ker, the British Consul, and his wife Lucy. The British were always delighted to entertain one of their own and social events abounded as expatriates vied to meet this Dame of the British Empire. Escaping back to Shanghai, Adelaide received a letter from Lucy Ker at the beginning of March. 'It was so delightful to have you and we miss you very much. We look forward to your return and please don't forget the two women's clubs are giving you a reception on the 29th. We are anxious to send out invitations – I saw a notice in the Peking paper that you were lecturing in Peking on 31st – no doubt that is false.' 'I think you should have the rest of the steamer and not come by train my dear,' Lucy continued. 'You have only one life to live, so don't let people kill you with overwork.'⁹ It was clearly going to be difficult to get any work done at all.

Adelaide soon realised, however, that much of her job in China would involve, not so much the gathering of information but rather the winning of hearts and minds. Agatha's own work, collecting reports on labour conditions and 'invoking and guiding public opinion on child labour, night work, excessive hours and health and safety' had, Adelaide wrote to Harold Butler, been quite remarkable, not least because she had brought together the various Christian bodies in the area with women's social action groups, including those of foreigners, to form a united movement pressing for reform.¹⁰ She had also attracted the interest of the governing body in Shanghai, the British dominated Shanghai Municipal Council, whose support would be needed if any progress was to be made. Adelaide was moved to write to Malcolm Delevingne at the Home Office to ask for some formal recognition of Agatha's work, a request he seems to have neatly deflected by suggesting that, regretfully, she had petitioned the wrong department. He forwarded her letter to the Foreign Office where it was carefully filed and forgotten. Meanwhile in Shanghai the most tangible outcome of Agatha's efforts was the establishment of the Child Labour Commission which proposed to make a number of recommendations on the development and enforcement of factory regulations. Whatever the content of these recommendations, however, there remained the need to convince employers and, particularly Chinese employers, of their importance. Agatha had perceived, quite rightly, that the credibility attaching to a former British factory inspector would be invaluable in this respect. 'The Peking regulations, slight and vague as they are,' Adelaide told Butler, 'are of course promulgated, but here the matter rests and they make no provision for sanctions or for inspectors.'[11] Shaking free of as many social engagements as possible and the effects of a heavy cold (against which she reported she had now been 'innoculated'), Adelaide, accompanied by Agatha, embarked on a tour of the surrounding area to meet all the major manufacturers. Here over numerous cups of tea she emphasised the great commercial benefits that, she told them, would inevitably flow from good working conditions. She emphasised 'the great past loss in England through the ignorant neglect of the human agent in industry and the modern discovery that even in the most highly developed mechanical work the economic fundamental is labour.' It was a lesson that Britain had been forced to learn, she said. 'I informed them about the enormous importance to their nation of not taking over the factory system without also applying modern ideas of health, safety and welfare of the worker. I spoke to them of the appeals made to me and to Miss Harrison by Chinese workers as being on the same lines as those made one hundred years ago by the early factory workers of Great Britain, against treatment as mere appendages to machines and against ill-treatment of their children while earning their daily bread.'[12] Adelaide's habitual optimism, her belief in the human propensity to do the right thing, was once more much in evidence as she warmed to these themes. 'They listened most attentively to us and our interpreter and pressed us to visit all their factories,' she noted.[13]

Visiting the factories was, of course, a much less uplifting experience. Whilst in Tientsin she had taken a trip to Peking and visited a Lucifer match factory which employed over a thousand workers. White phosphorus was in full use and she had personally removed one eleven-year-old boy with a suppurating wound of the upper jaw to the Peking Medical College Hospital. Back in Shanghai she found numerous other cases of phossy jaw at the St Luke's and St Elisabeth's hospitals and various factories and cotton mills with 'the most dreadful and dangerous conditions.'[14] The lack of fire precautions was a particular concern with fire escapes and staircases frequently blocked with materials and doors and windows barred. Soon after her arrival a Chinese silk mill was burned to the ground with the loss of over a hundred lives. And at almost every factory she encountered excessively long hours, no mealbreaks, no rest days and a complete lack of fencing for machinery. The plight of the children, in particular, filled her with horror. Most factories, she noted, were more like nurseries than factories, 'at least as far as the age of the children went.'[15] In the numerous silk filatures[16] the working day was twelve or thirteen hours long, sometimes even longer with overtime. Here she found children as young as five working in heat and steam which, she considered, was unacceptable even for adult workers. The job of the youngest children was to brush the cocoons and prepare them for the reelers by removing waste and exposing the silk thread. It was an operation carried out over basins of nearly boiling water with the inevitable scalds to small fingers. Older children of seven or eight, meanwhile, worked at the spinning machines rarely with any form of protective guarding. 'It is grievous to see the drooping little figures at the close of the day urged on by Chinese overseers walking up and down with canes in their hands,' Adelaide noted sadly.[17] 'The silk filature workers tell me that a large proportion of the young children die in a short time. Many of these children look so ill that in Britain a factory inspector would immediately suspend them under section 67 of 1901 for examination by the certifying surgeon,' she added, with typical recourse to her familiar regulatory ground.[18] Her response to what she saw, however,

moved her to other statements that she would probably have
viewed as unnecessary and unhelpful back in Britain.

> I plainly told the employers that the children in Shanghai mills
> are suffering and probably dying as they did in the early years in
> British mills. But bad as things were in the latter when I began
> work in 1894, I had never seen or imagined anything so terrible as
> I have seen here. I warned them of the ruinous waste of national
> life that continuance and extension of such employment of child
> life would mean and pushed aside the difficulty of legislating and
> administering laws. I urged them to shoulder the responsibility as
> enlightened manufacturers themselves.[19]

Agatha was by now well acquainted with the working
conditions in Chinese factories but Adelaide was encountering
them for the first time and the experience provoked unpleasant
memories of her early days in the British Inspectorate.
Observing 'the pressing intensity of expression and attitude in
the workers'[20] as young children made their way home after a
long shift, she felt herself back in a Lancashire cotton town.
And at least in Blackburn, Bolton and Burnley the children
had been 'half-timers', spending part of their day in school.
Here in China these children had just completed twelve hours
work with no fixed time for meals and the prospect of six
identical days ahead. She watched sadly as 'all coming out had
to dodge or buffet their way through the incoming stream of
those who would take their places at the whirring machines
until the dawn of a new December morning.'[21] Returning to
Quinsan Gardens she talked over the best way forward with
Agatha. The most immediate need, she agreed, was to tackle
the worst excesses of child labour. Regulation and inspection
of industry in general was a laudable longer-term aim but, in
the meantime, the voluntary compliance of employers with
basic rules governing the employment of children might save at

least some from disease, injury and early death. In Shanghai an important factor, she considered was the influence that might be exerted by one or two of the larger British firms operating within the International Settlement. 'If only the British employers are regularly informed as to the disease and suffering caused they will not be able to stand it without moving on,' she declared firmly.[22]

Together with Agatha she formulated a series of proposals and called a meeting with prominent members of the Shanghai Employers Association. It was not, Adelaide made clear, an alternative to the current Child Labour Commission on which she was now a co-opted member. It was simply an addition, a response to her recent factory visits. Thus, with Mr Mackay, a senior manager at Butterfield & Swire, in the Chair, Adelaide and Agatha presented the details of their immediate first proposals. Firms should cease to employ any more children under the age of ten, rising by steps to fourteen years by the end of 1928 at the latest. And each firm should immediately employ an experienced British welfare advisor who would work with a Chinese assistant to address conditions in the factories. Finally a conference should be convened to address the problems of night work, excessive working hours and the maintenance of health, safety and first aid in factories. As Adelaide outlined these proposals she must have had a sense of beginning her working life all over again. However the response was encouraging, particularly as Mr Brooke-Smith, a representative of the large and highly influential company Jardine-Matheson, came along to offer his support. Jardine-Matheson had already raised the age of entry into its factories and had appointed welfare supervisors, he told the meeting. No commitments were entered into by other employers at this stage, Adelaide informed Harold Butler in a subsequent letter, but it seemed a promising start and she was also in discussion with the Chinese Educational Association, the principal body involved in the training of teachers, about the possibility of schooling for young children. Compulsory primary education, she considered, was central to the curtailment of children's employment, despite the resistance that would inevitably ensue from both employers and families. In 1833 a similar move[23] had been extremely unpopular with British parents keen to capitalise on their children's ability to contribute to the family income, and now Chinese parents were similarly reluctant to forego their children's meagre wages. 'They press to get their children into the mills and Chinese employers speak of it as a "charity" to let them in,' she told Butler.[24]

At the end of February Agatha returned to England for a period of rest and relaxation with her mother at the family home in Bristol, for she had been working tirelessly in China for three years. In many ways she was reluctant to leave but she was now confident that matters were in competent hands. Adelaide immediately turned her attention to the provinces adjoining the Shanghai District. Here, of course, employers were uniformly Chinese and she began a round of meetings with Provincial Governors, Members of the Provincial Assemblies and representatives of Employers' Federations. Many of these meetings were facilitated by Mary Dingman who had access to a large network of colleagues working for the American Church Missionary Society. Adelaide and Mary travelled together to towns across Chekiang, Kiangsu and Nanking where they encountered similar conditions to those prevailing in Shanghai. There were occasional longer trips to Peking where Adelaide gave a series of lectures to doctors at the university on the subject of industrial disease. And Dr Yen, Chinese Minister of Commerce and Industry, was persuaded to make his first visit to the Peking match factory to witness conditions there for himself. Most of Adelaide's activities, however, were focused on attempts to broker voluntary agreements for some basic improvements with local employers and to secure support from

Provincial Governors for the forthcoming recommendations of the Shanghai Child Labour Commission. Uniformity of regulation across the region was of paramount importance if all employers were to agree. The cotton mill owners in Shanghai, she told Butler at the end of April, would welcome regulations limiting employment of all children below a reasonable age provided these regulations were applicable to and rigidly enforced in the adjoining provinces of Chekiang, Kiangsu and Nanking. The argument was, it seemed, that the effect of prohibitions solely inside the 'water-tight' compartment of the International Settlement would be to drive the children out into worse conditions outside.

By the beginning of June she was able to write to Agatha with obvious satisfaction. 'Well dear Agatha Harrison you will surely soon get a copy of the report for we hope the Council[25] will publish it without delay.'[26] After much wrangling the members of the Shanghai Child Labour Commission had finally and unanimously signed up to an agreement. The report, she noted, contained three sections. Part I described, in unflinching detail, the employment conditions in Shanghai and surrounding districts, while Part II looked ahead to the future implementation of the International Labour Convention, agreed at the Washington, USA, conference of the ILO in 1919. The content of this Convention, however, was considered unrealistic in the present circumstances of China and it was the final section of the report that constituted the basis for immediate improvements in the current state of affairs. 'In Part III we come down from a hill-top view over a promised land,' reported Adelaide. Biblical analogies, like factory regulations, were never far from her mind and, as ever, the approach was pragmatic and realistic. 'We come down to a workaday scrutiny of ways of making a very small beginning in safeguarding child employment.'[27] With the exception of a weekly rest day (fortnightly only, was agreed) Adelaide, ably supported by Mary

Dingman, had got virtually everything she wanted. Age of employment was to begin at ten, rising to twelve within a period of four years. Children under fourteen were to be prohibited from working longer than twelve hours out of twenty-four, including a compulsory rest for one hour in the day and were also to be prohibited from working at dangerous unguarded machinery, at work likely to injure their health, or in dangerous places. This last item meant that precautions against fire risks would become effectual wherever children were employed. 'I hope you will approve of what is practically your child!' she told Agatha. 'I know you will rejoice over the way things are moving in China.' Governor Han of Nanking, whom Adelaide considered to be 'in the Confucian sense a Princely man' had already signed up to the proposals and, provided the provinces of Chekiang and Kiangsu were also willing to agree, the recommendations of the Commission 'modified into practical workableness' would take effect as the new Peking regulations, applicable across China. 'Isn't the recognition by the leading Chinese of our caring for the children of China a gracious, quick thing?' she concluded with typical optimism. 'I never knew British officials act so promptly as Governor Han!'[28]

Agatha replied in characteristic fashion, always wanting just a little more. The final recommendation of Part III had specified the appointment of trained factory inspectors to enforce the regulations. 'Can't you get the Municipal Council to appoint a Factory Inspector before you go and couldn't it be either Miss Martindale or Miss Escreet? Please don't leave China without leaving a Factory Inspector to work for the Council and as so many women are workers it can be a woman.'[29] Agatha was restless and far from enjoying her period of 'relaxation'. Instead she was racing about the country mustering support for Chinese labour reform and cultivating useful contacts. She longed to be back in Shanghai. 'Do you miss me a little?' she wanted to know.[30] At the end of June Adelaide took a holiday in the mountains at Kulung which boasted a 'healthful climate and beautiful scenery', as well as the Fairy Glen Hotel, which advertised itself proudly as 'British owned and managed'. Here she retreated briefly into the familiarity of an English middle-class atmosphere. 'I did nothing but write and adore the flowers,' she reported to Agatha. 'I like June weather here far better than in the winter and feel so much better in every way since the fruit of the work of so many people began to show itself.'[31] But she sensed her friend's frustration. She wished Agatha could have seen the new beginnings with her own eyes. 'Perhaps you will return when the fruit begins to ripen?' she added.[32] Meanwhile she had already written to former colleague Henrietta Escreet to introduce her to the idea of factory inspection in China. Henrietta was, in Adelaide's opinion 'a very fine woman and an admirable inspector.'[33] She said as much to Bishop Logan Roots, with whom she stayed briefly at the end of August[34] and to whom she was attempting to hand on a number of batons before she left China. As well as the question of establishing a Factory Inspectorate in the country she also hoped that he would specifically pursue the question of phosphorus poisoning in the Lucifer match factories. White phosphorus had been banned in the British Empire since before the war and she wondered whether, as a first step, this ban ought also to apply to foreign factories in the International Settlement. She had also conducted several promising exploratory meetings with the Employers' Federation in Shanghai about the question of children's education. And, finally, she had continued her charm offensive in areas beyond those immediately bordering Shanghai. The Labour Commission Report was widely read in China, she reported, prompting the Tuchun of Hupeh Province to visit factories in Wuchang, Hankou and Hanyang. He had 'shown great interest in the matter and declared his intention of acting along the lines initiated by Governor Han of Kiangsu.'

By August, with the drafting of new child labour

regulations well underway, Adelaide's mind was turning back to her original schedule. She had already stayed in China much longer than she had intended and she still hoped to visit Japan. She was also looking forward very much to a planned visit to India before returning to England. She eventually left Shanghai during the second week of September but managed only three weeks in Japan, again staying at the YWCA. The country was still in the process of recovering from the earthquake and instead of visiting operating factories, which were in short supply, Adelaide found herself reluctantly 'over-pressed with demands for teaching.'[37] However, those labour conditions she observed were, she reported to Butler, 'interesting and encouraging.'[38] They had, she told him, improved following the recent attendance of Japanese trade union officials at the Annual ILO Conference. Perhaps, she thought, this was an example that might be followed by the Chinese. According to Butler, repeated criticism of Japanese labour conditions at the conference had 'piqued the pride of the Japanese.' She wondered if this apparent growth of 'nationalistic spirit' might be harnessed to produce similar results in China.[39]

Leaving Japan, she diverted to Burma for five weeks to visit Alex. It was important to take the opportunity to see the country before her brother retired and returned to England the following March. In Burma she found fewer women employed than in either Japan or China with most working in shops or as clerks. She had little to report other than to comment that 'labour conditions still needed attention.'[40] Sadly, her much anticipated visit to India, so carefully organised via a long series of letters to and fro, had to be abandoned, for in October she received an unexpected invitation from the Foreign Office to serve on a government committee, the Boxer Indemnity Advisory Committee. Should she agree, she was required to be back in England by the end of the year. Thus Christmas Day

1924 found her off the coast of Marseilles on board the new
P&O liner *Maloja*, busily completing her various reports on
labour conditions and preparing them for dispatch to Butler at
the ILO headquarters in Geneva. Such was her enjoyment of
long voyages she had decided to make the whole return trip to
England by sea. Butler's request for information about labour
conditions in the Far East had considerably enhanced her
enjoyment of what she often referred to as her 'long holiday',
and the long slow progress home provided ample time to
complete the task he had set her. Regretfully, India would have
to be postponed, she decided, for despite her disappointment
it would not have occurred to her to refuse the Foreign Office
invitation. She still considered herself to be a public servant and
it was, therefore, both a duty and an honour to serve. Buoyed
up by her recent success in China, she had now fully regained
her confidence and composure, and she eagerly relished the
prospect of moving once more in the old familiar government
circles.

The establishment of the Boxer Indemnity Advisory
Committee had first been proposed early in 1923. Its purpose
was to consider the suspension, cancellation or diversion to other
purposes of the indemnity payments remitted by the Chinese to
the British government following the Boxer Rebellions of 1899
and 1900. The rebellions, aimed primarily at foreign imperialism
and missionary activity across northern China, had finally been
suppressed by an alliance of eight foreign powers, including
Britain, and had resulted in the requirement for the Chinese to
make annual payments to these governments as compensation
for the damage sustained, (including the murder of several
missionaries), and the military expenditure incurred. Originally
intended to continue for forty years these remittances had, by
1923, become the subject of contention, for the political sands
had shifted considerably over the previous quarter of a century.
The Manchu Government, under which the Boxer atrocities

had been committed, had by now been overthrown. Moreover, China had been an ally against Germany (an original member of the alliance) during the First World War. Other members of the alliance had progressively suspended the payments due to them or had diverted the money towards development projects in China. The continuation of the British indemnities in their present form now seemed unsustainable.

The process of establishing a commission, however, had proved to be far from straightforward. Returning to England at the beginning of 1925, Adelaide found that, unbeknown to herself, she had for many months been at the centre of a controversy over the composition of the committee. The British government had let it be known that they favoured a similar option to that adopted by the Americans in the matter of indemnities, the diversion of funds towards the development of Chinese education. Child education was traditionally female territory and its inclusion on the agenda had provoked considerable pressure to include a woman on the Commission. Adelaide, a former high-ranking civil servant who also had recent experience of working in China, seemed the obvious choice, but not everyone agreed. Objections were raised on the grounds that she had no specialist knowledge or experience in the field of education. In reality, however, opposition to her appointment stemmed rather more from a general objection to the conservative make-up of the committee. In the context of a minority Labour government, heavily dependent on the support of Liberal MPs, the composition of the Indemnity Committee was a sensitive issue. Adelaide, it seems, had now become associated both with 'the establishment' and with an imperialist agenda, neither of which was attractive to many of those currently in positions of influence. Many MPs favoured the appointment instead of the eminent socialist, and anti-imperialist philosopher, Bertrand Russell. After his year long lecture tour in China, Russell was now considered to be one of the foremost experts on the country and its affairs. Adelaide had admired *The Problem of China* when she had read it on her way to Shanghai, but disagreed with his view that unfettered industrialisation, promoted by Western imperialist powers, threatened to destroy all that was best in traditional Chinese culture. She could not accept that industrialisation *per se* was a bad thing. As in Britain, it was the manner of the process, the exploitation, the child labour and destruction of health and well-being that preoccupied her attention. And she, of course, had seen much that he had not seen. The industrialisation he feared, far from being on a near horizon, was by now well underway in many parts of China. It was almost certainly beyond the point of no return. As Adelaide had written to Beatrice Webb all those years ago, it was important to consider the way things were, not how they might be. There was, however, a more fundamental issue over which there could be no meeting of minds with the atheist Russell. Adelaide could not abandon her often-expressed opinion that China, above all things, needed Christianity. It was perhaps this that most unified those who opposed her appointment in favour of Russell. They feared the insidious effect on Chinese culture of Western inspired education, particularly if, as in Britain, the church played a prominent role in its organisation. The committee already contained one Christian missionary in the form of Oxford Professor William Soothill who had spent twenty-nine years in China founding, it was said, numerous schools as well as '150 congregations'.[41] The arguments over this issue had continued throughout much of 1924, finally being resolved by the fall of the minority government after only ten months in office. In the General Election of October that year the Conservatives gained a landslide victory and, thus in January 1925, when Adelaide arrived back in England it was she and not Russell who took up the remaining place on the committee.

Official business can move very slowly, however. The first

part of the year was spent in reaching the point where, in June, the Chinese Indemnity (Application) Act finally reached the Statute Book, allowing the Committee to begin its work of advising 'from time to time' on the allocation of funds to 'such educational and other purposes beneficial to His Majesty and the Republic of China.'[42] Adelaide must have wondered why she had foregone her much hoped for trip to India. After her busy schedule in China she found it extremely difficult to be idle. She decided, therefore, to channel her energies and her frustration into writing an account of her experiences in the Far East and in the spring she began *Humanity and Labour in China, An Industrial Visit and its Sequel*. Much of this book was written at Grove Cottage, part of Troutwells House in Penn and close to Paul End where she had spent a weekend with Louisa and Flora early in 1923. It was perhaps a rather curious choice of venue for, although Penn provided peace and solitude, it would also have provoked many poignant memories. Just before she left for China she had received a letter from Sir Courtney Ilbert expressing 'a thousand thanks' for sending a copy of her previous book *Women in the Factory* and wishing her 'Bon Voyage.' The book, he said, was a delightful gift that both he and Lady Ilbert would read with great interest. The Ilberts were tremendously fond of Adelaide. They remembered the shy, awkward young woman they had first met in the 1880s and, ever afterwards, had rejoiced in her various achievements. 'Its wonderful to think of your flight all over the world and blessed to know how much you will enjoy it, renewing your growth like an eagle's after your years of stiff work. I wish I could have seen more of you but you know how tightly stuck I am.'[43] Sir Courtney was indeed 'tightly stuck', by the trials of very poor health. When Adelaide arrived to write her second book both he and Lady Ilbert had very recently died, within months of one another, and Troutwells was no longer the happy family home she remembered. And Louisa was also grieving.

Soon after Adelaide's visit to Paul End early in 1923 Flora had developed a cancer that had killed her within a few months. Adelaide, opening an Australian newspaper in July that year, had been shocked to see the notice of her death. Flora had been buried in the churchyard at Penn, her headstone eventually bearing the exuberant inscription 'We have been gloriously happy', added when Louisa died some twenty years later.

The book Adelaide wrote in these rather subdued surroundings, however, turned out to be a rather good one, a highly informative and entertaining description of her experiences in China. It was rather disappointing therefore that, ultimately, John Murray, to whom she submitted the proposal, declined to publish it. Sales of *Women in the Factory* had been poor, a victim it seems of limited interest in industrial conditions, particularly after the First World War when much of the nation was gripped by the dual miseries of personal anguish and economic depression. When it came to the publication of *Humanity and Labour in China* Adelaide seems to have had somewhat unrealistic expectations about its likely appeal and she and John Murray became embroiled in an increasingly acrimonious correspondence over the company's sales projections and the scale of royalties they were prepared to offer. Murray also became somewhat irritated by Adelaide's seemingly rather cavalier attitude to deadlines when it came to the submission of the final manuscript. When, in January 1926, she found herself travelling back to China she sent back, at intervals, a series of incomplete versions, which had been somewhat inadequately proof read by the ship's purser. Eventually negotiations between Murray and Adelaide broke down and the book was eventually published by the Student Christian Movement, a respectable enough Press but one with rather limited reach in terms of general readership. Sales of *Humanity and Labour in China*, like those of its predecessor, were destined to be modest.

In the autumn the Boxer Indemnity Advisory Committee finally convened its first meeting under the Chairmanship of Lord Noel Buxton, Minister for Agriculture and Fisheries. The committee consisted of a small group of accountants and finance experts, supplemented by Adelaide, Professor Soothill and two high-ranking officials from the Chinese Embassy in London. In terms of allocating funds, however, the meeting proved to be fruitless, for China it seemed was in turmoil. Sun Yat-Sen, whom Adelaide had met in Hong Kong, had died in March and into the vacuum had stepped an unlikely alliance of poor workers and well-educated university students, united in an anti-imperialist and anti-Western agenda. In Shanghai, where the alliance was strongly supported by the emergent Chinese Communist Party, there was growing labour unrest, much of it centred on trade union organised labour disputes over lack of employment rights. Elsewhere in the city, amongst the poor and powerless, there was a now a groundswell of opposition to the Child Employment Bill, so laboriously crafted by Adelaide and her successors. The Bill was unpopular amongst the poor for it would prevent young children working in factories and hence reduce already minimal family incomes. Butler had received a letter from Mary Dingman saying that nothing could be done about child labour at the moment. Nationalist passions were running high, she said. 'The Chinese will not hear of protection of child labour because it is a foreign idea.'[44] The political ramifications of Adelaide's work in Shanghai had, it seems, caught up with her in a somewhat alarming way. During the following three months there had followed a series of violent incidents and arrests which notoriously came to a head on 30 May when several demonstrators were shot dead and many more were injured. Hundreds of Chinese had gathered outside the Louzha police station in Shanghai, where a group of arrested students were being held. A panicky station commander, left unsupported by the police commissioner who, it was reported, had not seen fit to interrupt his visit to the racecourse to deal with the matter, had given the order to fire. There had followed a period of strikes and violent demonstrations across China and the stability and economic prosperity of the country seemed to be under serious threat.

In London, Lord Buxton was becoming increasingly uneasy about handing over indemnity money to a clearly precarious Chinese Government. Eventually, in November, he decided that a diplomatic delegation should visit the country in order to discuss the situation with local Chinese officials. More recently there had been encouraging reports of a calmer atmosphere, particularly in Shanghai, and it was important, not only to assess the wisdom of making payments at all, but also to ensure that no decisions on their utilisation should be allowed to reignite the embers of a highly inflammable situation. The man chosen to lead the delegation was Lord Willingdon, a Liberal Peer and career diplomat who had formerly been Governor of Bombay and Madras. Accompanying him was to be Professor Soothill and Adelaide. There is no hint of uncertainty in Adelaide's response to this proposal, rather she seems to have relished the prospect. In January she had a letter from Manchester businessman and long-term friend Sir Christopher Needham who expressed the view that it was very public spirited of her to go for he was sure she would find many difficulties to be overcome in the chaotic state of China. Adelaide, however, was calmly confident. She was, she said, very glad to go. 'My work before brought me close to some of the greatest needs in China. I found people of all kinds very lovable and have a strong hope that the prevailing aims for which we go out will win the co-operation of the people of China.'[45] She also secretly hoped that she could reawaken the apparently dormant matter of child labour, notably through the good offices of the ILO. She wrote confidentially to contacts at the Ministry of Labour and the Foreign Office seeking financial support for a visit to China by

an ILO Labour specialist, Pierre Henry, whom she hoped might
be able to visit China in the coming months. Having secured
tentative agreement from both departments she promised to let
them know if the situation in China seemed 'a favourable field
for carrying the matter further.'[46] She had also, apparently,
written an encouraging letter to Mary Dingman, which in
November provoked the following touching reply, 'I cannot tell
you how I treasure the dear ending to your little note – how
true it is that understanding clears away all difficulties.'[47] Thus
Adelaide set out for China with the Willingdon Mission on 29
January 1926. It was almost exactly a year since she had arrived
home from Shanghai and she was soon enjoying the delights
of a long sea voyage once more, this time on the rather older
but equally comfortable SS *Morea*. Just before leaving she had
received a letter from Lily Hass, the new Industrial Secretary
of the NCCC. The Industrial Committee was due to meet on
19 February and child labour regulation was on the agenda,
she said. 'We shall be so glad to see you. We hope you will be
able to discuss the situation even though your days will be very
full. We are counting on your visit and looking forward eagerly
to your arrival.'[48] It was not Agatha, but it almost might have
been.

Adelaide's days were indeed very full and on this visit
she was staying, not with her Christian colleagues in
Quinsan Gardens, but with the British Consul in Shanghai.
Throughout the following six months she and other members
of the delegation toured China to meet numerous advocates
of institutions and causes who wished to press their case for
a share of indemnity funds. Adelaide herself tended to be the
first port of call for those wishing to acquire money either for
industrial welfare or for educational programmes of various
sorts. Two such communications, in particular, caught her eye
and found their way into her personal report. Professor Taylor
of Yencheng University in Peking approached her in his capacity

as Chairman of the Committee on Rural Co-operation, to press
for the development of a 'strong school of economics'[49] which
would offer professional training courses for industrial welfare
workers. Rather differently, a representative of 'the Chinese
women of Tientsin', a Mrs Mei Ting, presented her with a two-
page letter in which she urged the establishment of schools for
young boys and girls with a view to improving their education
and particularly their 'vocational and healthful education.'[50]
The essence of this letter was subsequently incorporated
into the submission provided by the Chinese YWCA which
Adelaide attached to her own report, at their request. The
women of the YWCA sought funding, first for universal basic
education, second for investment in forestry and farming and
third for improved infrastructure in the form of roads and
railways. Ultimately, however, the first two of these, the ones
closest to Adelaide's heart, were to become casualties of the on-
going political situation. Chinese provincial governors, largely
military in nature, were unanimous in their opinion that the
British should now take a back seat in any discussions regarding
the use of the money. At best the delegation should act in an
advisory capacity, and only at the request of the Chinese. The
British Government's refusal to compromise over this matter,
even in terms of more moderate proposals for a majority Chinese
Committee, turned out to be a severe stumbling block in the
negotiations. It fuelled Chinese suspicions of Western-based
imperialistic ambitions, rendering the issue of education, in
particular, a highly sensitive one. The YWCA made this point
very clear in its own report. Failure of the British to concede
control would, they concluded, engender the feeling that 'the
fundamental purpose in returning the money is not for the
best interests of China.' It would, they added darkly 'make it
extremely difficult to maintain the friendly relations between
the two nations.'[51]

    In the end, therefore, the delegation returned to Britain with the least controversial of all its potential recommendations. The British would use the money to do what they did best. They would build railways. Adelaide was disappointed but, by this stage, unsurprised. Her reconnection with her Christian colleagues in Shanghai had made her realise the gravity of the events that had taken place since her previous visit to China, and she knew that in any matters associated with child labour she must tread very carefully. Lily Hass had proved to be a wise counsel in this respect. Writing to Butler in May, Lily had advised against a visit by Pierre Henry, pointing out the sensitivity of Chinese people to the feeling of being 'singled out by the ILO'. They resented international criticism and interference in their industrial organisation. 'We have not seen our way to push Child Labour Law at this time,' she told him. 'It was,' she said, too much tangled up with international problems. It would be unfortunate to have industrial reform that in any way ran counter to the growing feeling of nationalism.' Lily, however, was keen to emphasise that while the immediate prospects for legislation were not good, a great deal of work was proceeding quietly but steadily behind the scenes. 'Good educational work is being done and more employers are interested in taking forward steps.'[52] Pierre Henry was extremely disappointed by this advice but Adelaide, close to the situation on the ground, was happy enough to comply. In June she also wrote to the officials at the Trade Union Congress (TUC) in London warning them against plans to make contact with labour leaders in Shanghai. They had asked Adelaide for names and addresses but she thought such correspondence inadvisable. 'At present, under military rulers, any labour officials are liable to be put in prison,' she told them. 'The situation needs study on the spot with much discretion.'[53] Adelaide had indeed studied the problem on the spot and had found the Chinese employers themselves happy to discuss employment conditions. She was personally 'happy to press the matter on them as one they are duty bound to face'⁵⁴ but, she pointed out, more fundamental issues had to be settled first, the formation of a stable government and the establishment of security in the country. She had also discussed the matter with military leaders in various provinces and had reluctantly come to the conclusion that the matter must be deferred, at least for the moment.

Members of the Willingdon Mission in China, 1926. Adelaide and Lord Willingdon seated front row, centre. William Soothill, back row, second from left. (Reproduced with the permission of the Women's Library, LSE. Originally published in *Women of Courage*, Susan Yeandle, 1993.)

At the end of June the Willingdon Mission came to an end and the participants left behind the turmoil of China and went their separate ways. Professor Soothill, disappointed at the final recommendations, returned to his academic post in Oxford, while both Lord Willingdon and Adelaide went to Canada. For the former this was to take up a new appointment as Governor General, a position he would hold until 1931. For Adelaide, however, the trip was a sad one. A month before she

had left for China she had received news of the death of her
brother Walter in New Zealand. She had originally toyed with
the idea of returning home via the United States for she had
never visited America but now, she decided, she would return
home via Vancouver where he also had a home and business
interests. The execution of his will was proving to be particularly
complicated, involving two sets of solicitors operating under
different jurisdictions, and she needed to discuss the winding up
of his affairs with his friends and colleagues. She finally arrived
back in England at the end of July where a rather plaintive
letter from Agatha awaited her. Agatha was now working in the
United States, but China was still very much in her thoughts
and she had hoped to discuss the Boxer Indemnity money with
Adelaide. 'I wanted to know your feelings about it – especially
the statements about welfare,' she wrote, 'and then I heard you
were sailing to Canada.'[55]

Adelaide did not reply to this letter until January. Possibly
this was an evasion of the relentless pressure Agatha tended
to exert when focused on a particular goal. She would almost
certainly have disapproved of the turn things had taken.
Alternatively, however, Agatha's letter may simply have gone
astray for, immediately on her return, Adelaide had left her
little house in Coulson Street and moved to a mansion flat, in
a block called Allen House just off Kensington High Street.
From there she wrote a long letter to Pierre Henry, explaining
why she had not supported his proposed visit to China, and
another to Agatha, maintaining firmly that she was personally
pleased with the eventual decision of the Committee and that
the infrastructure projects might indirectly help the cause for
which they had both been working. The idea that building
railways might materially assist in the development of schools
and factory welfare facilities required an imaginative leap of
faith, but Adelaide's old unswerving loyalty to the State and
its machinations was once more to the fore. There was much

support, she added, from the other members of the Commission on the matter of child labour and it was still on the agenda. And, she concluded 'The people's fears that imperialistic attitudes will prevail are based on false propaganda about the way the British government operates.'[56] Finally she wrote to Lord Buxton to express her support for the eventual decision of the Committee over which he had presided. The tone of his reply suggested a certain amount of relief at the warmth of her letter. 'My Dear Dame Adelaide, I very much appreciate your writing to me and the terms of your letter gave me much pleasure. I am extremely glad to hear that you agree with the line I took.'[57] He was by now facing a barrage of criticism from those who had been strongly committed to educational programmes in China and he was grateful for her unexpected support. Not only had Adelaide endorsed the decision to build railways but she had also approved the even more controversial addendum that the materials for these railways should be sourced entirely from Britain. It was completely justified, she reassured Lord Buxton, 'since the main cause of the higher costs of production in this country lies in the special care here for the health, safety and standard of living of the workers.' This, she considered, 'held up a principle that China probably needs, more than any other great nation, to press for a condition of true civilisation.'[58] Whatever her admiration for the Chinese people, it seemed there remained in Adelaide a strong underlying conviction that Britain constituted an advanced society and, as such, had a duty to set an example for the rest of the world to follow. Moreover, her remarkable facility to accept and vigorously defend any government decision, however questionable, once it had been made, was apparently undiminished. She had not, however, given up on China. The matter had, like her trip to India, simply been postponed.

Chapter Fifteen
A SENSIBLE OLD LADY

At the beginning of 1929, Adelaide received a letter from a
man called William McKnight. Long since retired and with
an interest in archaeology, Mr McKnight had recently been
on a trip to Egypt to view the antiquities and watch the
archaeological digs currently being undertaken by teams from
Britain and the United States. What had most impressed him
at these sites, however, was not the artefacts emerging from the
ground, but the cruel treatment visited on children employed by
the archaeological teams. Young boys, alongside older stronger
men, scurried back and forth carrying sacks of sand and debris
unearthed in the process of the dig. They worked, he noted,
from sunrise to sunset and were 'subject to being whipped to
make them work speedily.'[1] In some ways, he added, the work
was preferable for the younger children because it released them
from the alternative, 'the foul air of the ginning factories'[2] but
he was afraid that this was 'counterbalanced through the strain
on their weakened bodies during the hot hours of the summer
days.'[3] McKnight followed up his correspondence to Adelaide
with a lengthy report he had prepared on the subject. He had
also sent copies of this to the London office of the ILO.
    Adelaide's interest was immediately aroused. The months
since the dissolution of the Boxer Indemnity Committee had
seen an uncharacteristic gap in her activities, at least as far as

labour conditions were concerned. The situation in China was still unsettled and uncertain and there seemed no immediate prospect of progress in the matter of labour legislation. In October she had been contacted by a member of the Chinese Department of Industry, Commerce and Labour, Mr Thomas Tchou, asking if she might be willing to return to China to advise on the development of a Chinese Factory Inspectorate. She had been enthusiastic about this, replying that she would be very happy to come as an unpaid advisor, provided her expenses were paid. However there had followed a protracted correspondence over the timing and funding of the proposed visit and by the beginning of 1930 no firm arrangements had been made. In Britain, her contacts within the Factory Department were steadily diminishing. Things had radically changed since 1921 and many of her old colleagues had now joined the ranks of the retired or had moved on to other things. Even Thomas Legge, who in 1925 had been knighted for his long service and his major contribution to industrial health, had resigned at the end of 1926. In his case the departure had been on a point of principle, something that must have given Adelaide pause for thought. In 1921 Dr Legge had attended the Annual Conference of the ILO in Geneva and, in accord with his brief from the British Government, had been a key player in securing an International Convention banning the use of lead in indoor house paints. Although the number of notified cases of lead poisoning had gradually fallen over the years, the disease had remained a prominent cause of industrial ill health and, while case numbers might be falling, fatalities were actually rising. In 1926 there had been twenty-eight fatalities in the United Kingdom.[4] That year, however, the British government reneged on the agreement Legge had worked so hard to achieve, bowing to pressure from the manufacturers and refusing to ratify the ILO Convention. Legge, who had spent much of his career attempting to rid British industry of the scourge of lead poisoning, resigned in protest. He spent the remaining few years of his working life acting as an advisor to the TUC. Typically Adelaide made no public comment on the actions of her long-time friend and colleague but it is hard to imagine her taking a similar line. Her response to decisions with which she disagreed was always to protest, and then adapt and carry on. Unlike her highly principled grandfather, and now Thomas Legge, she judged that, ultimately, more could be achieved by continued presence than by an abrupt and dramatic exit.

Meanwhile, several months of 1928 had been spent once more in Empangeni with Ralf and Margaret. She informed John Murray, at the time still chasing the final draft of her book about China, that this was due to 'prolonged illness during the sunless year of 1927.'⁵ She was, it seems, less and less enamoured of the London smog and drizzle and regularly felt the need to recuperate in the warmth of the South African climate. She also wanted to discuss the question of Barbara's schooling. Her position as godmother was one she took very seriously and she considered it both her duty and her right to be involved in this type of decision. She was aware that Ralf and Margaret were already considering a boarding school. This was, of course, a common solution to schooling problems amongst expatriates, although in this case the decision was driven more by the ever present threat of malaria, than by dissatisfaction with local schools. Barbara had suffered recurring attacks of the disease for over a year and two of Margaret's friends who had already lost children had subsequently elected to send their siblings away to school in England. Adelaide had assumed, therefore, that 'boarding' meant 'boarding in England' and when she arrived in Empangeni she already had a suitable one in mind. On her return home she planned to take Barbara with her. This, however, turned out to be a step too far for Margaret. She could not contemplate a geographical separation of this magnitude from her elder child and she had seen the disruptive effect

on children and their families of this kind of arrangement. A
school would have to be found in a malaria free area of South
Africa she decided. She was, however, willing to delegate to
Adelaide the job of visiting, vetting and finally selecting a
suitable South African establishment. Her choice was a girl's
boarding school just south of the beautiful mountainous area
known as Drakensburg.

Back in England in 1929, the prospect of investigating the
situation in Egypt was appealing to Adelaide in a number
of ways. First and foremost it involved an issue close to her
heart, the problem of child labour. And, like conditions in
China, it took Adelaide back to the fundamental business of
worker protection that had formed the basis of her years in the
Factory Department. Importantly, however, it also held out the
prospect of working once more in conjunction with the ILO. It
was this organisation that seemed to fit most readily with her
aspirations to contribute to the cause of international labour
conditions. Towards the end of 1929 she needed little persuasion
to accede to Mr McKnight's suggestion that she visit Egypt
during the coming winter months. She hoped to be on her way
by November, but she had reckoned without the complicated
array of politics surrounding such a visit. When she had sailed
into Port Said with Mary and Max after Blanche Emily's
death in 1905, the country had been a British Protectorate,
essentially a colony of the Empire. But Egypt had experienced
a revolution in 1919 and was now an independent Kingdom.
Britain had conceded this independence in 1922 but had never
fully recognised Egyptian sovereignty over the southern region
of Sudan. Moreover it had retained complete control over the
economically important Suez Canal. Relations between the two
countries thus remained fragile and uneasy. Adelaide, on this
occasion careful to do her political and historical homework, was
aware of this and contacted the Foreign Office to seek official
approval for her visit. The reply was predictably ambiguous.

They would raise no objections to her going but could not officially sanction it, and of course could not offer any funding. McKnight's report had been widely circulated in Egypt and had done little to improve frosty diplomatic relations. The opinion of the British Embassy in Cairo was that Mr McKnight was 'a most poisonous creature with no manners.'[6] The official who had interviewed Adelaide at the Foreign Office subsequently wrote to Sir Percy Loraine, Egyptian High Commissioner, to warn him of her arrival. 'Her visit is a sort of by product of the McKnight reports,' he reported, 'but she strikes me as a sensible old lady who is unlikely to go off the deep end.'[7]

There were, however, other difficulties. The ILO could not endorse her going under their banner either. Egypt was currently considering whether or not to join the League of Nations. Negotiations were at a delicate stage and any criticism of labour conditions might rock an already precarious boat. Added to this Adelaide seems to have become caught up in an acrimonious turf war between two Christian missionary associations, the YWCA and the Church Missionary Society. Constance Padwick a central figure in the Missionary Society had spent many years in the Middle East, building strong ties with the Muslim population. She sent a lengthy, strongly worded letter to Mary Dingman, warning her off any interference by foreign visitors. The Church Missionary Society, said Constance, was doing all kinds of important useful work in Egypt and would not be helped by the arrival of other organisations. She could not see what role the YWCA could possibly play. It members did not speak Arabic, she reminded Mary, and they had no knowledge or understanding of the country. British investigators were, she considered, particularly unwelcome. 'Swiss or Swedish might not be so irritating,' she conceded, 'since there is not much to fear from *little* countries.'[8]Constance particularly objected to any enquiry about the boys used in the archaeological digs. 'A little pressure at the *American end* would surely make each

digging camp put right anything that had been going wrong
– if there were anything,' she concluded.[9] Conscious of British-
American relations Harold Butler was similarly uneasy at the
prospect of raising the question of conditions at the digs.
Personally, he told Adelaide, he was far more concerned about
the ginning factories.

By Christmas Adelaide had accumulated a voluminous and
dispiriting correspondence with Constance Padwick and she
was no nearer acquiring some official credentials that would
gain her access to Egyptian industry. In the New Year, however,
Butler suddenly found another possible sponsor for her visit
in the form of the recently developed Association for Social
Progress, an arm of the League of Nations. Its Secretary was
delighted to step into the breach and arrange for the President
of the British Section, the Earl of Lytton, to dispatch a
diplomatic letter, drafted by Butler, to His Excellency Abd al-
Rahman, at the Ministry of Justice in Cairo. The letter referred
to 'allegations' that had been made about the conditions of
child labour in Egypt but emphasised that in no way did this
imply the need for an official enquiry, which was in any case,
he stressed, a matter for the Egyptian authorities. It was noted,
however, that a distinguished and experienced member of
the Association just happened to be on the brink of visiting
Egypt and it was thought that His Excellency might share the
view that this offered 'an admirable opportunity for a purely
unofficial and very friendly survey of the situation.'[10] Abd al-
Rahman's response was unexpectedly positive. He extended a
warm welcome to Dame Adelaide. By mid January, therefore,
she was on her way, despite a last desperate plea from Constance
that the project should be abandoned or at least delayed. Mary
Dingman replied sweetly that, although she knew Constance
still questioned the wisdom of Adelaide's visit, she was sure that
she [Constance] would 'do all in her power to help.' Adelaide,
she said, was 'a very dear and delightful person and because of

her long experience works with great tact.' 'She sails on the 17th and will be in Cairo six days later,' she added firmly.[11]

Adelaide spent two months in Egypt and produced an extensive report for Butler at the ILO. Running to more than sixty pages it was later condensed into an article for the *International Labour Review*.[12] The bulk of her report focussed on Egyptian industry making only passing reference to the archaeological digs, with which she had no direct contact. The excavations, she argued, were the responsibility of foreign organisations and hence change was more likely to result from 'the force of outside observation and the exercise of public opinion.'[13] Industrial conditions, by contrast, lay within the jurisdiction of the authorities in Egypt who had sanctioned her visit. It was perhaps a dubious justification for ignoring the digs, a concession, no doubt, to the concerns of both Constance and the ILO. However it also reflected her own continual preference for working within an administrative framework that offered a degree of legitimacy. In reality, she was now entirely free from official constraints but the civil service code remained firmly in her head and continued to exercise a tight control over her behaviour. The Foreign Office was entirely correct in their assessment that she was unlikely to 'go off the deep end.' They did, however, endeavour to keep track of her movements expressing some concern in the early days of her visit that she seemed to have disappeared off the diplomatic radar. 'This lady arrived ten days ago – has any more been heard of her?' the High Commissioner wanted to know. 'She has not applied to us at all.'[14] They were reassured to find that Adelaide had 'merely been to tea with His Excellency',[15] although it seemed she was already on her way to inspect ginning factories in Upper Egypt. They would invite her to luncheon on her return, they decided. The mere meeting for afternoon tea had, however, opened up a large number of industrial doors to Adelaide as well as providing access to employers' associations, local authorities, universities and a variety of educational and training establishments. She and Abd al-Rahman had got on extremely well, no doubt in part because they shared a strong belief in the central importance of universal elementary education. It was, they agreed, an essential prerequisite for the development of a civilised industrial society. In later years, Abd al-Rahman would, as Minister of Education, focus much of his energy on the expansion of educational provision in Egypt. For the moment, however, he was happy to discuss with Adelaide the question of Egyptian factory legislation and eager to receive what she could tell him about contemporary initiatives in other newly industrialised countries. Adelaide, well-satisfied, had set off immediately after this meeting to begin her investigations. Making good use of Egypt's rapidly developing railway system she embarked on a journey of biblical proportions, travelling from Sohag and Asyut in Upper Egypt to Tanta in the heart of the Delta, and then from Zagazig in the southeast to Damanhur in the northwest. Most of her attention was focussed on the large number of ginning factories but she also visited factories engaged in oil pressing, leather tanning, sugar refining and flour milling, and in the manufacture of soap, cigarettes, tiles, cement, copper utensils, mineral water and cardboard boxes. While small-scale handicrafts were still much in evidence it was clear that industrialisation was well underway in Egypt, with all its attendant hazards. The report she produced on her return to England was a model of its type, detailing in systematic fashion, the factors leading up to her visit, her meetings and contacts, her level of access to workplaces, the nature of existing Egyptian legislation and finally her findings and recommendations.

As in China, Adelaide's attention was drawn most often to the plight of the children who worked primarily in the ginning and other textile related trades. An average sized ginning factory employed about three hundred people, of which a considerable proportion were 'quite young and adolescent boys and girls feeding the ginning machines.'[16] She estimated that about half of these workers were under fifteen years of age and many were under nine. Meanwhile very small children knelt or sat on stone slabs for hours at a time, picking off spots, stains and extraneous matter from the ginned cotton as it emerged from the machines. The children she considered to be 'generally fragile, undersized, overstrained and anxious.' 'The sinister figure of the Egyptian task master stands whip in hand,' she reported. In several factories she described the 'almost automatic hitting of the children with canes and whips to spur them on with their work.' The factories ran from 5 a.m. to 8 or 9 p.m. but no-one, she observed 'seemed to feel it necessary to see that young workers have any regular pause for a meal.' And she agreed with Mr McKnight that there was an urgent need of protection from 'injurious dust and machinery in motion.' She, herself, often found it impossible to stay long in the vicinity of the ginning machines. 'The irritation caused to the respiratory passages was overpowering,' she reported. And everywhere she saw workers in loose flowing garments working in close proximity to 'low shafting of the most dangerous kind.' The only answer to this all too familiar situation was, she considered, the establishment of regulations and a competent and judicially minded inspectorate to enforce them. First, however, there was a need to begin the gradual process of eliminating child labour. When sufficient elementary schools were provided, she argued, the number of children employed would necessarily decrease. 'The safety, health and welfare of the child,' she concluded 'is an absolute and over-riding interest of the nation, as well as the natural right of the child. Other rights in industry can only be profitably discussed when that matter is properly settled.'[17] It was a succinct statement of her most deeply held beliefs.

Adelaide returned to England at the end of March and began the process of writing her report. She took considerable time

Little silk weavers in Damietta, Egypt, 1930, a picture taken by Adelaide.

over this, asking Mr Burge, Director of the London Branch of
the ILO, to bear in mind that she was attempting to produce
a document that would 'sufficiently inform Abd al-Rahman of
the irregularities and abuses without antagonising him' [18] and
at the same time supply both the ILO and the Association with
details of the conditions she saw. The next few months proved
to be a busy and exhausting period, for the ILO also wanted
her article for the next edition of the *International Labour
Review*, and the YWCA, apparently undeterred by Constance
Padwick, wanted an abridged version of her findings to inform

their forthcoming international meeting. They planned to discuss the organisation's future work in Egypt. There were also numerous speaking engagements which always tended to raise Adelaide's level of anxiety, and she was beginning to feel increasingly harassed by Mr McKnight who wrote to her incessantly enclosing, for her comments, various papers, letters and meeting reports, all of which he insisted she return to him for fear they should fall into 'the wrong hands.' She must have heaved a sigh of relief when he professed himself to be leaving 'the damp and cold of the English climate' for a period of recuperation in the South of France. The recent death of his brother, he said, had left him 'unfit to take any more active steps on behalf of Egyptian children' and he was suffering from 'rheumatism in his head.'[19]

In the midst of all this activity, Adelaide found herself reluctantly moving house again. She had discovered when she returned from Egypt that the rent at Allen Court, like that of most apartments in the area, was due to rise steeply in June. It seemed she could no longer afford to live in Central London, a place where she had been happy for many years. Most of her life she had been a city dweller, comfortably at home in a busy urban environment, surrounded by stimulating company and with access to theatres, concerts and galleries. It was with a rather heavy heart, therefore, that she set about exploring the outer suburbs. However by the summer she had found a flat in a modern block called Gloucester Court in the pretty village of Kew, just round the corner from a convenient railway line into London. To her surprise she found she rather liked 'the peaceful and beautiful surroundings'[20] and she loved the nearby Botanical Gardens.

By the time she had moved her belongings into her new home copies of her report had been distributed to the Foreign Office, the ILO, the Association for Social Progress and of course the Egyptian Ministry of Justice. It was a tactfully

written document, containing a typical mix of concern and
encouragement that was the hallmark of her approach. It
seemed to have been well-received in Egypt and the situation
looked promising. The British Consul in Cairo, Richard Turner,
wrote to tell her as much, noting that the legislative committee
were now 'paying some attention to labour legislation, with
particular reference to conditions in the ginneries.'[21] A Labour
Bureau had been established to oversee the development of
regulations and to safeguard the interests of the workers and
some initial drafts of factory legislation had been produced.
These prohibited employment of children under the age of
nine in the ginning factories and provided for the regulation
of conditions and hours of work for those between the ages
of nine and thirteen. There was to be inspection of factories
and punishment of offenders against the law. Discussions had
been initiated with 'Labour Syndicates' representing different
employment groups. This encouraging progress, however, was
about to be interrupted by events largely unconnected with
labour reform. Like China, Egypt was experiencing a period
of political uncertainty and was hovering precariously on the
brink of social unrest. Increasingly there was conflict between
warring factions and riots on the streets. Attention began to
shift away from the conditions of employment. Adelaide was
saddened, but unsurprised. She was, by now, all too well aware
that industrial reform could not proceed in a vacuum, indifferent
to its political and social context. It required both a degree of
national stability and public support if it was to progress. Her
report was now with the ILO and she was sure that, in the
future, its recommendations would be implemented. She herself
was beginning to feel tired and drained. The schedule in Egypt
had been punishing and there had been little time for rest since
her return home. Now, she informed William McKnight, she
also felt the need to 'retire for a well-directed medical overhaul,'
a course of action with which, fortunately, he agreed.[22] In

October, therefore, she boarded a train for Scotland to seek out the comforts of Alice's hearthside at Bridgefield.

After Christmas she returned to Kew, refreshed and ready to engage once more with the prospect of a visit to China. Butler at the ILO was now corresponding directly with the Minister of Industries in Nanking, Dr Kung, and it had been agreed that Adelaide should visit China in an advisory capacity accompanied by an official from the ILO, Monsieur Camille Pône. In advance of the visit she prepared a memorandum for Dr Kung containing a series of principles which, she considered, underpinned the development of an effective factory inspectorate and the selection and training of inspectors. Meanwhile the news from Egypt was suddenly much better. At the end of May 1931 a letter from Mr Burge at the ILO in London arrived enclosing a draft of the new extension to Egyptian Labour Law. Now the regulations which applied to the ginning factories were to be extended to a whole range of other industries that Adelaide had included in her report. These further regulations were currently in draft form and he invited her comments which he would convey to 'the proper quarter.'[23] Adelaide was delighted. She had previously been in touch with the firm of Platt Brothers in Oldham, major manufacturers of textile machinery, and now, in anticipation of the regulations, they were engaged in fitting exhaust apparatus for the extraction of dust in several ginning factories. More recently she had acquired from the same firm a set of photographs of the most recent machinery guarding which, she considered, should be enclosed when the draft regulations were returned, with her comments, to Egypt.

The visit to China, however, was still proving problematical. The Chinese had set an arrival date of mid July. Adelaide was adamant that this was completely out of the question. It would, she said, be impossible for Europeans to work in the heat of a Chinese summer. It would be a direct threat to her health. She could not think of arriving before September. And the ILO had proposed a cheaper route to China via the Trans-Siberian railway. Again she stubbornly refused. She would go by ship via Canada, or not at all. A lengthy three-way correspondence ensued between Dr Kung, Butler in Geneva and Adelaide in Kew. She was not, however, in any great hurry for she had just embarked on a personal project, the result of an extremely important decision. She had decided to make her permanent home in Kew and, for the first time in her life, she would purchase her own house. She appears to have had some savings to finance this venture, possibly part of the legacy she received from Walter, for it was to be a new house, a cottage built on a piece of land previously belonging to an adjoining mansion called Courtlands. It fronted on to Broomfield Road, a quiet leafy street just round the corner from Gloucester Court and close to Kew Gardens. Built in her favourite Arts and Crafts style, the cottage, which she named Arbour, had a nice old walled garden that she planned to fill with trees and flowers. It was also equipped, she told her good friend Edith Lyttelton, with every modern labour saving device. Whether this project played any part in her determination to delay her trip to China is uncertain but, as she told Edith later, by August building work was well underway and she was thus quite able to leave things to progress in her absence. 'And by November when my homeward voyage began,' she added, 'the cottage was well begun, the roof tiles were on and the interior work was finished.'[24] She did, of course, get her way over the timing and manner of her trip to the Far East. She boarded the Canadian Pacific Steamship *Duchess of Bedford* for Canada on 14 August and crossed to Vancouver by First Class Rail where she boarded the *Empress of Asia* for Shanghai. She finally arrived in China in mid September. Monsieur Pône, meanwhile, arrived a month earlier via the Trans-Siberian railway.

The atmosphere that greeted Adelaide when she disembarked in Shanghai was very different to the one she remembered during her previous visit. There was a general air of menace with armed squads of Japanese patrolling the streets and standing at the entrances to factories. During the previous months there had been intermittent fighting in the country between Japanese militants and the local Chinese inhabitants, for it was becoming increasingly clear that Japan was determined to expand its military and political power beyond its Concessionary area in Shanghai. In this tense atmosphere Adelaide and Monsieur Pône began to hold meetings with employers' associations, government officials and labour representatives. Factory Law, based on Adelaide's recommendations in 1924, had finally come into being two months earlier, and now the objective was to draw up an agreement for the establishment of a Factory Inspectorate. Within the International Settlement the atmosphere was relatively calm. The British gun boats which still patrolled just outside the harbour provided a sense of security and the British and American inhabitants regarded themselves merely as onlookers in the conflict between China and Japan. They considered it unlikely that they themselves would become targets of aggression. In the various provinces adjacent to Shanghai, however, the situation was unstable and threatening. Adelaide, apparently undeterred, continued to travel around, often alone. 'Nothing can be certain in a country so situated,' she wrote to Max later, 'but whatever the risks, known and unknown, I have been shielded and guided through them all.'[25] She considered, she said, that no-one would feel inclined to attack an apparently harmless old lady. And she continued to have faith in the gentleness and courtesy of the ordinary Chinese people. In the course of two months she drew up a document detailing the necessary elements of effective factory inspection and set about obtaining agreement from interested parties. Her work was thus largely administrative and diplomatic but hands-on inspection was never far from her mind. General MacNaughton, Chairman of the International

Settlement Authority, discovered as much one day when he invited this apparently genteel old lady for a Sunday morning drive to the park. Adelaide had just toured eight factories in Shanghai with the Chief Officer of the Fire Brigade and, in response to the General's invitation, she suggested that he conduct a similar tour. It was important, she said, 'to acquaint the employers with the shocking dangers over which they presided.' The rickety wooden factories, huddled close together in narrow back streets, were crowded with workers on the upper floors, the only exits being via wooden staircases, largely blocked with materials. And often these were flammable materials such as solvents stored in open cans. 'I cannot rest while I think of these workers,' she told the General, providing him with a list of the names and addresses of the employers in question. 'In the case of fire, hardly any workers could escape.'[26] He wrote her a hurried note the next day. He would visit the factories, he promised. 'Rest assured anything that can be done will be done,' he said, adding hopefully, 'I look forward to seeing you on Sunday morning?'[27]

Despite apparently satisfactory progress, the gulf between Chinese and Foreign factory owners in Shanghai and their mistrust of one another proved to be the major stumbling block in the brokering of an agreement to establish a factory inspectorate. The owners of factories in the International Settlement objected strongly to the inspection of their premises by Chinese Inspectors and their general intransigence on this point threatened to derail the whole process. Moreover, Shanghai, as one of the most industrialised and economically successful areas of the country, was likely to be hugely influential in terms of persuading employers elsewhere to agree to the enforcement of factory regulations. Much of Adelaide and Monsieur Pône's efforts were directed at this problem during their final weeks in China. An agreement was finally reached that inspection in the Settlement would be carried out in conjunction with special 'Deputies' appointed by the Settlement Authorities. Any enforcement matters arising would then be jointly discussed between the Deputies and the Shanghai Municipal Council which, although dominated by the British, did include Chinese representatives. The Deputies, meanwhile, would be 'granted the special privilege' of attending the Chinese Government Institute for the Training of Factory Inspectors, in order to acquaint themselves fully with Factory Law. This face-saving form of words seems to have been acceptable to both sides. It was not a perfect solution but it offered the best chance of progress and by mid November the first inspectors were beginning their training. On the 18th she wrote to Mr Burge enclosing a 'Proposed Agreement Concerning Factory Inspection in Shanghai', on which she noted that this had been 'discussed on November 6th 1931 and in the main accepted.'[28]

Adelaide and Monsieur Pône were feeling moderately satisfied as they prepared for their respective journeys home. Adelaide, in particular, seemed to be experiencing a new surge of optimism, perhaps over-optimism, writing enthusiastically to Monsieur Pône from the SS *Parocles* which she boarded at the end of November. Describing an 'At Home' she held at the YWCA for British and Chinese officials just before her departure she noted a willingness on all sides to work together for the improvement of factory conditions. There was no doubt, she said, that General MacNaughton, in particular, 'would do much for our cause.'[29] She also wrote to Dr Kung, Minister of Industries, expressing her hope for the future of industrial reform in China and her high regard for Mr Kenneth Fu who had been appointed Director of the recently established Training Institute for Factory Inspectors. Following a frenetic round of meetings with the various Local Authorities during the last days in November she had been impressed by their desire to co-operate with the enforcement of the regulations. She was, she said 'full of hope for the coming united endeavour' and 'looked forward to the steady advance by China of the art and science of factory regulation towards the health, safety and welfare of factory workers.'[30] She would, she told him, keep in regular contact with Mr Fu and make available to him any information and advice she could offer. As she boarded her ship Mr Fu had handed her a small package. It contained a photograph of her taken with his family, and a little ivory carving, an example, he told her, of Chinese art and craftsmanship. He hoped it might occupy 'a small corner of her desk in England.' Thanking her for all her work he added that, although China faced great problems, with 'the good advice she left and future prudence' they hoped to accomplish something before long. He would, he said, always treasure the memory of the busy but happy days they had worked together during her sojourn in China. And he was sure they would be able to continue their friendship through correspondence.[31] Adelaide would similarly treasure her memories of this period and of all her visits to China, for the country and its people had gained a strong hold over her affections. The little carving was placed on a ribbon and frequently worn around her neck. It seemed to represent for her a token of her steadfast faith that ultimately things would turn out well for the people of China.

For a short time, it seemed, there were indeed grounds for cautious optimism. In December she received a letter from Eleanor Hinder, an Australian proponent of industrial welfare, whom she had met in China. Eleanor, who was currently working with the YWCA in Shanghai, wrote to say that, although there had been further disagreements over factory inspection between Chinese employers and those representing the International Settlement, it had now been agreed that the latter were willing to allow some Chinese inspectors to be drafted into the service of the Settlement to conduct inspections. The proviso was that they remained responsible to the Municipal Council rather than the Chinese Authorities.

The French Concessionary Authorities had also agreed to this. It was not quite the same agreement that Adelaide had negotiated but Eleanor was pragmatic. The main thing, she said, was to get some regulation and inspection in place. 'You and I will rejoice that your mission definitely moved things forward,' she continued. 'You made possible discussions between the Chinese and the foreign authorities, which is always difficult to get. You made possible the acceptance of Chinese inspectors in the Settlement, even though not under Chinese control, and thus made admission inevitable that factories in the Settlement must be inspected.'[32] Adelaide, similarly a pragmatist, would have been content with this. Increasingly, however, her memories of the country would become bitter-sweet for, if the situation in Egypt had proved difficult, that in China would rapidly became disastrous. Within weeks of her return to England the tense relationship between the Chinese and the residents of the Japanese Concession erupted into violence. The trigger was reputed to be a violent attack by Chinese workers on five Japanese Buddhist monks, one of whom was killed, although it seems to have been generally agreed that Japan was already spoiling for a fight, arguing that it needed to protect its citizens from Chinese aggression. Thus, by the last week in January 1932, there were around thirty Japanese ships, forty aeroplanes and nearly seven thousand troops stationed close to the shoreline of Shanghai. On the night of the 28th the city was subject to a prolonged bombardment by Japanese aircraft and artillery. Numerous Chinese factories were destroyed, many people were killed and in the fierce fighting that followed several residential areas of the city were set on fire. Efforts by the British and Americans to negotiate a peace agreement came to nothing and by the end of February the Chinese leader, Chiang Kai Shek, had moved the government of China to the western city of Luoyang. The Shanghai Municipal Council, with which Adelaide had worked so long and hard, no longer, it seemed, controlled Shanghai, and the subject of factory legislation had virtually disappeared from everyone's agenda. The fate of Mr Fu was unknown, for she was never to hear from him again.

By the end of March the League of Nations had managed to broker an uneasy peace between the Chinese and the Japanese, but it was not to last. Rather it marked the beginning of a long period of sporadic fighting which, in 1937, would finally erupt into what became known as the Second Sino-Japanese War. And Adelaide herself now seemed to be under attack from those who variously considered her work overseas to be either anti-feminist or unacceptable examples of imperialism and colonial interference. A particular opponent was lawyer and feminist activist Chrystal Macmillan. In October Adelaide had been asked to propose the vote of thanks following a lecture given by Eleanor Hinder at a luncheon of the British Commonwealth League, an organisation which promoted links between women working in the Dominions. Eleanor, on a brief visit from China, had described attempts by the YWCA in Shanghai to reduce working hours for women and children and, in addition, to abolish female night work. Following the lecture Chrystal engaged Adelaide in a vigorous correspondence over the matter. She considered these measures, and the prohibition of night work in particular, to be undermining of women's rights. It was a re-run of the old pragmatism versus ideology debates which had raged in England in the 1890s. Chrystal, a strong advocate of 'equality feminism', had noted how English women's exclusion from night work had effectively prevented them working in any industry that involved continuous processes. Subsequently no amount of feminist pressure had managed to overturn this ruling. Thus she considered it to be completely unacceptable to include such a prohibition at the very start of the introduction of factory legislation in a developing country, particularly when such a ban was promulgated under the banner of the ILO. The rights of women in China should be the same as everywhere else, and should be the concern of all women, she argued. 'No-one, least of all one who goes on a mission on the recommendations of the ILO, can say that the welfare of the women of one country is not the business of the women of another.' Thus, Chrystal concluded, the inclusion in a mission connected with factory legislation of one who approved of forbidding women to work at night was 'dangerous to the status of the woman worker in China.'[33] It must have seemed an ill-informed and misconceived accusation to Adelaide, newly returned from a mission to improve the dreadful labour conditions she had encountered in Shanghai, conditions that were entirely beyond the experience of campaigners such as Chrystal. And elsewhere, it seems, she had also provoked the fury of the Anti-Imperialism League who considered that British industrial interests in China were largely responsible for the prevailing factory conditions in the country. They viewed Adelaide's efforts to institute reforms as paltry and largely cosmetic, since real improvements would always be blocked by British and American interests on the Shanghai Municipal Council. Adelaide, they argued, was an apologist for the British industrialists in Shanghai or, worse, actually complicit in their activities.

Adelaide began by replying politely to these communications, keen to justify her work and convince others of her point of view. She had experienced a similar round of combative correspondence on this subject through the letter page of *The Times* a few years earlier. But she soon grew tired of the arguments which did nothing to lift her spirits, miserable as she was over the state of things in China. And once more she was feeling unwell. In February she wrote to Monsieur Pône to apologise for the delay in sending him her part of their joint report. She had 'been sent to bed with catarrh from the severe weather.'[34] However, noting 'the violent and cruel destruction that has followed so closely on our peaceful work', she was, she said, finding it very difficult to draft anything about health and safety for factories that had largely been destroyed and for a government that had been fundamentally changed. The removal of the Chinese government to Luoyang was, she considered, hardly a favourable environment in which to send out reports that needed sustained attention and action. She would like his advice on 'how we should report, or refrain from reporting' during this 'uncertain and formless period.'[35]

Added to this China was now beset by a natural disaster of unimaginable proportions. In August 1931, as a result of unprecedented rainfall, the Yangtze River had flooded a five hundred mile area of agricultural land. The rising waters had initially driven about half a million people from their homes but the full impact of the disaster was still to come. Most of the population were poor farmers dependent on rice cultivation for their survival and the rice fields had been completely swept away. It was estimated that, in the months that followed the floods, a further three and a half million Chinese died of starvation, either in the countryside or in the towns of Wuhan and Nanjing. Others died from disease as outbreaks of typhoid and dysentery swept the area. Adelaide found it impossible to stand idly by in the face of such a disaster. Instead of concentrating on her report, therefore, she set about trying to raise funds for the reconstruction of the Yangtze dykes to prevent further flooding the following year. With MPs Michael Sadler and Sir John Hope-Simpson, she formed the Chinese Flood Relief Committee and began liaising with the Society of Friends, the charity Save the Children and the Conference of Missionary Societies in Great Britain and Northern Ireland. Bishops around the country found themselves in receipt of letters urging them to instruct their clergy to introduce the matter into their Sunday sermons and to install collecting boxes at church doors. Just a few pennies from each parishioner would make all the difference she told them. On the strength of her various connections she also acquired substantial donations from a number of prominent organisations such as the Women's Co-operative Guild, the Women's Industrial League and, through the good offices of Thomas Legge, the TUC. Past and present students of Girton College were similarly petitioned and wealthy patrons with a particular interest in China were contacted. One day in June, for example, Mr George Eumorfopoulos, an eminent collector of Oriental Art, opened up his house with its attached private museum to the general public to view his rare Chinese treasures. Not everyone was enthusiastic however and many people were simply uninterested. A request for the support of the Women's Institute to its chairman, Lady Denman, unexpectedly fell on stony ground. 'Lady Denman refuses – nothing can be done through the WI – evidently not even the moral support of a friendly gesture towards the Chinese,' wrote a somewhat affronted Adelaide to a fellow committee member.[36] By the end of June, however, over ten thousand pounds had been raised and reconstruction of at least some of the dykes had begun.

Adelaide also acquired two new appointments during this period. The first was that of special advisor to the ILO Committee on Women's Work. She was pleased but, as she pointed out to Monsieur Pône who wrote to congratulate her, it was simply the formalisation of work she was already doing for the organisation. In addition she had been appointed to the Executive Council of the Universities' China Committee, an educational charity which, among other things, funded scholarships for students from China. In recent years the administrators of the Boxer Indemnity Fund had been allowed to broaden their remit beyond that of railway construction towards other aspects of Chinese development, notably education. The Universities' China Committee had received £200,000 for this purpose. It was a cause that chimed well with Adelaide's aspirations for the country, but she also hoped that membership of the committee might give her access to some wider contacts within China. Meanwhile she continued her correspondence with Eleanor Hinder. Her natural optimism was beginning to return and for a time things looked more promising. An uneasy peace had returned and in October 1932 Monsieur Pône sent her 'a cheering little file'[37] of some newspaper cuttings which reported the proposed introduction of factory inspection in Shanghai. Amazingly the proposal was for a single inspectorate that operated across the boundaries between the Chinese territory and the Concessionary areas. Eleanor had been to Geneva on her way back to China to seek the help of the ILO in supporting and progressing this move and their followed a flurry of communication between Adelaide and Monsieur Pône as they resumed the preparation of their long delayed report. By December it was complete and dispatched to Shanghai but it soon became clear that the old antagonism between the Foreign Settlements and the Chinese territory had resurfaced once more. There was no longer any co-operation between the Chinese inspectors and those in the Concessionary areas. The patient negotiations of 1931 were now, it seems, a distant memory.

Adelaide had entertained the fanciful hope that the establishment of an effective factory inspectorate, operating throughout China, would come to pass in 1933, exactly one hundred years since the appointment of the first factory inspectors in Great Britain. But instead the year was marked by two major fires in the rubber shoe factories that she had brought to the attention of General MacNaughton in 1931. Over eighty women workers were burned to death, trapped on upper floors. Chinese factory inspectors were still required to confine their activities to Chinese territory and thus had been refused admittance to inspect these factories which lay within the International Settlement. Throughout 1933 the situation dragged on with no sign of an agreement between the parties. At the beginning of 1934 Adelaide received a letter from Eleanor describing how small children were still being employed in foreign operated factories for twelve hours a day, seven days a week. Eleanor considered, however, that it was the Japanese employers, based in the Japanese Concession that were the main hindrance to any agreement between the Foreign Settlements and the Chinese Authorities. Adelaide decided that she would go to the International Labour Conference to be held that year in Geneva. There she might be able to talk to both Chinese and Japanese delegates about the matter. It was perhaps a sign of changing times however that, on this occasion, she travelled, not as an important first class passenger clutching letters of introduction to high ranking officials, but with a party of delegates from the League of Nations Union,[38] availing herself of their all-inclusive package of train, boat and budget hotel. Once there she pursued the Chinese and Japanese delegates with her usual vigour and her usual arguments, emphasising to them the importance of securing good working conditions for industrial efficiency, and the impossibility of obtaining such working conditions without good inspection. 'I also urged them to rely on the powers and good will in this matter of the ILO,' she told Monsieur Pône afterwards.[39] There was, she concluded, a generous response from Mr Cheng, Chief of the Chinese Central Office of Labour Inspection. He considered that Chinese officials were close to an agreement with those in the International Settlement. However, Mr Yoshaka, a senior Japanese delegate, while listening attentively to what she had to say was polite but vague, agreeing only that the Japanese would 'work to that end.'[40] Adelaide concluded, as Eleanor had done, that the real impediment to progress lay with the Japanese. An agreement, she now considered, was an absolute imperative and required definite direction from the ILO. She told Butler as much in a subsequent letter, adding that, in her opinion, this should proceed 'with ultimate appeal on a stated case to the International Court of Justice if necessary.'[41]

Monsieur Pône, meanwhile, who had recently been promoted to Head of the Diplomatic Division of the ILO, was cautious, and dubious about the prospects for immediate progress. 'I am afraid the mission will have to follow a long and devious path before any positive results ensue,' he told her. 'So we must arm ourselves with great patience.'[42] He was right to be circumspect about the situation. In 1933 Japan had withdrawn from the League of Nations in the midst of international condemnation of its aggressive policies in China. By 1938 it would also have suspended its membership of the ILO.

Sadly, Adelaide was unlikely to see any lasting fruits of her labours in China.

Chapter Sixteen
TAKING LEAVE OF ADELAIDE

Adelaide's ability to achieve her objectives in China and Egypt
had, of course, always been limited in the face of international
politics, something that she was perhaps never quite willing
to recognise. Setbacks were invariably met with characteristic
optimism and her steadfast faith that ultimately things would
work out the way they were supposed to. As the 1930s progressed,
however, she was forced to confront some discomfiting
realities about the limitations of her own standing not only
internationally but also at home, in British government circles.
Although still valued for her expertise within the portals of
the ILO, this organisation was itself moving from the heady
idealism of the post-war years to a more realistic recognition
of the complexities of international co-operation. The
complexities surrounding labour regulation were no exception
to this general rule. And beyond the ILO Adelaide's views no
longer seemed to be of any relevance to the civil servants who
now inhabited the British corridors of power. This was made
eminently clear to her when, in July 1934, she wrote to Sir John
Simon, now Secretary of State at the Foreign Office to inform
him of her discussions at Geneva. Seemingly unaware of the
nature or scale of her work in China, or perhaps anxious to
distance himself from the activities of overseas missionaries, he
thanked her politely for her 'interesting suggestions regarding

factory inspection in Shanghai.' He added that she might like
to know that Mr Li Ping-Heng, Chief Chinese delegate to the
ILO conference, had had a long interview with Lord Stanhope
at the Foreign Office a few days previously. Lord Stanhope had
assured Mr Ping-Heng that 'His Majesty's Government took
a great and sympathetic interest in the question and would
use such influence as they possessed with a view to securing
a satisfactory outcome of the discussions between the local
administrations concerned.' 'I have already been supplied with
all the relevant details of these discussions,' he added, 'but if
any different or obscure point arises the help you so kindly offer
would be greatly appreciated.' [1] It was essentially a diplomatic
dismissal of the whole issue, and of Adelaide herself, a point
underlined when she wrote again in October enclosing a copy
of her book, her article on China for the *International Labour
Review*, and a description, for emphasis, of the rubber shoe
factory fire in Shanghai. In reply she received a short note from
an assistant at the Foreign Office. 'Sir John is much obliged
for calling attention to your book and has read your article
with interest.' [2] Also enclosed was a copy of the same letter she
had received in July. It was clear that she was not expected to
contact him again.

In many ways, however, Adelaide chose to ignore these
pointers to a changing world and continued to behave as though
she maintained a position of influence in the higher echelons
of the Civil Service. As the situation in China deteriorated
she wrote letters to prominent officials in the Foreign Office
and the League of Nations to complain about the arms trade
which resulted in British weapons being exported to Japan. Her
habitual neutrality towards the actions of other nations had
finally broken down in the face of aggressive attacks on her
beloved China. It was, she told them, 'a nightmare situation'
and she had 'a growing sense of horror of individual enterprise
for profit in the production and distribution of War material.' [3]

In June 1932 she read in the *Manchester Guardian* that forty-eight ships were scheduled to leave British ports carrying arms to Japan. What was the League of Nations doing about this, she wanted to know. 'Is it possible,' she said, 'that Armament Firms of this country could have received any authority whatever to carry any Munitions of War to that country during or after the weeks of carnage in the industrious region of Chapei, lying alongside the International Settlement?'[4] Like so many people Adelaide had entertained high hopes of world disarmament following the end of the 'war to end all wars' and was now experiencing a growing sense of dread and disillusionment as the League of Nations appeared helpless in the face of this new conflict.

As a member of the Council of Save the Children Adelaide was also exercised about what was currently happening elsewhere in Europe. The organisation had been founded in 1919 to address the plight of starving children during the continuing blockade of Germany after the war. Now, in the early 1930s, attention was turning towards Jewish exiles who had begun to arrive from Germany following the rise of National Socialism under Chancellor Adolf Hitler. As always it was the children that were at the forefront of her mind. She wrote a long letter to her old friend Lord Buxton of the Boxer Indemnity Committee, expressing her concern at Britain's equivocation in terms of taking in German Jewish children whose families, she said, had been 'deprived of their livelihoods and the ability to provide for their offspring through no fault of their own.' 'If we can have a positive *Postal Union* all over the world, that can work and continue without disintegration even in the face of mechanised warfare,' she wrote, 'we can certainly save these innocent child victims from the dire consequences of their sudden deprivation of stable *Family, National* and *State* environment.'[5] Lord Buxton, now retired from active public office and comfortably seated in the House of Lords was probably more realistic than Adelaide about the likely response to an emotive letter from an outraged old lady. He wrote back saying that he had read her letter with 'much interest' but added rather vaguely that he was 'doubtful who was the best person to send it to.'[6] Adelaide telephoned him immediately reminding him forcefully of the decision of the last Save the Children Council meeting to which he had been party. He, himself, she told him, had agreed to send the letter, composed by her, to his contacts at the Foreign Office. Lord Buxton, suitably reminded of what he had forgotten, agreed to send it at once. Her letter, of course, like so many others, received a polite, non-committal reply.

Adelaide had always spread her attention around a number of worthy causes, sitting on various committees and contributing to numerous meetings and conferences. Now largely bereft of any major outlet for her energies she began to introduce even more of these activities into her life, offering her support to organisations and initiatives commensurate with her attitudes and beliefs. With her title of Dame and her long years of experience she was always much in demand within the voluntary sphere. Most of these activities were outwith the governmental arena but an exception was her membership of the Central Committee on Women's Training and Employment which had been established in 1920 to develop training opportunities for unemployed women after the war. Despite its original brief to set up a scheme for training in professional and non-industrial occupations the committee soon seemed to have shifted its focus towards one particular element of the training on offer, the Homecraft Training Scheme. By the time Adelaide was a regular contributor to meetings in the 1930s much of the emphasis was on training women for domestic service. Most of the £70,000 grant allocated by the Ministry of Labour in 1933 was spent on the development of 'homecraft' courses delivered to young girls in highly supervised residential centres around the country, particularly those designated 'distressed areas'.

However, Rose Squire's observation in 1918 that domestic service was 'now distasteful to the large majority'[7] was proving correct, particularly by the early 1930s. Committee meetings reported difficulties in filling all the places in available centres, except perhaps in parts of Wales where unemployment and poverty were particularly acute.

Adelaide's membership of this committee, and by implication her endorsement of its work, was in some ways rather curious. Yet despite her professed commitment to equal employment opportunities for women this had never been the central focus of her motivation. Essentially she concerned herself primarily with the conditions of employment, ensuring that the working environment, whatever that happened to be, was a suitable place for women to inhabit. And, in terms of the training of young girls in particular, she remained essentially Victorian in her approach, focussing on the protection of their moral well-being alongside their physical health and safety. These were the attitudes which had informed many of her opinions about the nature and objectives of industrial welfare during the war, and perhaps had also played a part in her failure to find a place in the new 'fused' factory inspectorate. Now they came to the fore again in another area of activity, her continuing presence on the Board for the Promotion of Religious Training of Social Workers. As the Board's literature stated 'the most valuable social work must be fundamentally personal, and this makes demands on workers which, it is believed, can only be met by a definite religious outlook.'[8] The objectives of the Board were to inject some religious elements into several university based training courses on the subject. Adelaide's own definition of social work was rather broad for it included, not only the more conventional elements of assistance to those with social difficulties, but also her own work in the field of industrial health and safety. Thus she delivered an address at the opening of the 'Health

and Labour Exhibition' in 1935 entitled 'The Spiritual Basis
of Social Work', where she described the development of
factory law as the 'spiritual road which we have begun to
walk on.' Continuing the religious theme, she went on to give
full expression to the commitment that had underpinned her
work. 'Nothing appears to me likely to work out aright,' she
continued, 'which does not allow for the essential significance
of all the help the nations and peoples can derive from true
religious belief. Only on this foundation can science and the
arts exert their full sway in leading us out of the ills, the
conflicts, the disease, the accidents in our present world, into
a nobler, more co-operative, more loving and more loveable
world.'[9]

It was not only women's employment that concerned
Adelaide during the impoverished years of the 1930s. Her
awareness of the plight of workless young men led her to
involve herself with an unusual alternative educational
movement called Grith Fyrd.[10] Its founders were the Order
of Woodcraft Chivalry who based their ideas on those of an
American organisation called the Woodcraft Indians. Grith
Fyrd espoused a mixture of socialism, co-operativism and
anti-urbanisation which, in practical terms, translated into
the development of self-sufficient rural communities based
on self-reliance, communal living and mutual service. In the
1930s two such camps were established with some limited
support from the Ministry of Labour to provide training for
unemployed young men. Adelaide's enthusiasm for Grith
Fyrd seemed to draw on a somewhat contradictory side of
her nature which admired the Arts and Crafts movement of
the late nineteenth century, a movement that eschewed mass
production in favour of individual craft skills. It was an
enthusiasm that had led her to invest considerable time and
energy in developing her own skills in spinning and weaving.
She also, of course, admired the personal qualities which

Grith Fyrd sought to promote. She visited the sites on several occasions and made significant monetary contributions to their maintenance.

Adelaide was not particularly wealthy but she was reasonably comfortable and she was a regular contributor of both her time and money to numerous charities that she seems to have collected along the way during the various stages of her life. There was Lettice Ilbert's National Council for the Unmarried Mother and Child, the Shipwrecked Mariners' Society, and the building of an extension for Girton College. A particular initiative that attracted her attention was a scheme by the British Institute of Adult Education which aimed to improve the access of the general public to the contents of the major London art galleries. Always a well-informed admirer of fine art and a strong supporter of universal education, she considered that everyone should be able to see what, hitherto, had been the preserve of a London-based elite. Moreover, she argued, the National Collections were owned by the people themselves and they had a right to see them. She knew there were many fine works of art languishing unseen in the basements of national establishments, a fact that had come to light during a recent Thames flood when water had got into several such basements. The plan was to put together a number of travelling exhibitions to be displayed in schools and church halls up and down the country. Adelaide set about gathering supporters among her friends and family who would petition the Prime Minister to register his approval and thus make it difficult for reluctant gallery owners to refuse to participate in the venture. The scheme got off the ground with three exhibitions held in Barnsley, Swindon and a little known place in Essex called Silver End. This last was a recently established model village constructed by an idealistic local industrialist on the lines of the early Cadbury and Rowntree communities and perhaps, therefore, a good place to pilot an art education project.

Adelaide was delighted by the response to the exhibitions with ten thousand people, including five thousand children, going to see the pictures, many travelling considerable distances for the purpose. There were also good attendances at the programme of accompanying lectures. She was particularly pleased by the responses of some of the children. One small boy 'very dirty but determined' made no less than sixteen visits to the exhibition each time bringing with him a different group of 'even grubbier friends' to whom he wished to show certain pictures that had particularly pleased him. Adelaide noted with approval that his choice (Matthew Smith's *Apples in a Blue Dish*, Sickert's *Crucifixion*,[11] Stanley Spencer's *Swan Upping* and Ben Nicholson's surrealist *Guitar*) was 'as singular as it was underived' and 'his preference had a consistency which comes from Heaven knows what sources.' Meanwhile a small girl surveying a Matisse nude commented that she 'didn't know people looked so nice without their clothes on.'[12] Ultimately, however, the project was doomed to failure after its first three exhibitions, foundering on the rocks of security concerns and mounting insurance premiums. Anxious gallery managers feared they might never see their pictures again. Unfortunately this was no longer a world where influential people could just make things happen, simply by mustering the forces of their close-knit social networks. But it was an interesting reflection on Adelaide's own passionate belief in the value of universal education, a belief which seemed to have its origins in her first encounters with the women of the Co-operative Guild in the 1880s. Education, she considered, was urgent for both social and economic reasons, 'a great need for our people at the present time', that would 'lighten many difficulties, economically or otherwise and advantage the whole community.'[13] By the 1930s she was convinced that it was 'an urgent matter that the school leaving age should be raised to at least fifteen years.'[14]

Adelaide might no longer be a major player on the national

stage but her energy was undiminished, and she was also enjoying life in Kew, involving herself in the local community and entertaining friends and family at her cottage. Her sister Mary was a frequent visitor, as was her brother Alex and his wife Vera, who had married in 1925 and were now living in Central London. Visitors were invariably taken to nearby Kew Gardens to admire the exotic plants. And her own garden was soon filled with trees and flowers which flourished under her care, even following a particularly hot, dry summer when she had been delighted to discover a garden tap left by the previous owners of the land, from which she could draw water directly from the river. Apart from the usual coughs and colds in winter she was feeling well. In the summer of 1935 she had a letter from Muriel Wilde, Director of the International Press, who wondered if she would consider writing her memoirs. It was a gratifying request and she now seemed to have the time, but she was once more thinking that she might like to travel. The idea of a long sea voyage was irresistible, as was the prospect of another visit to Empangeni. The memoirs could be put off, she decided. By December, therefore, she had lent her cottage to a family friend and had packed away her personal belongings. She booked a return passage on the Ellerman line *City of Exeter* and set off from London just before Christmas. Either during the voyage or on arrival she would have learnt of the death of her sister Isobel, still confined in the Coppice Hospital in Nottingham. Isobel, who had spent nearly forty years in a mental institution, died from pneumonia the day after Adelaide sailed for South Africa and was buried a few days later at Brookwood in the grave of Blanchie and her parents. There was a certain irony in the fact that Adelaide, the one who had visited Isobel so faithfully for all those years, could not be at her funeral, but it was perhaps fortunate that she had the company of Ralf and Margaret soon after hearing the news.

Adelaide with Ralf on her last visit to Empangeni in 1936

She had decided, that this visit was primarily to be a holiday.
The ILO had requested once more that she gather information
for them on factory conditions in South Africa as she had done
in the past, but she was disinclined to do this. Her contacts there
seem to have retired, she told them, and her opportunities for
visiting factories were likely to be limited. Her only concession
to 'work' seems to have been an address to the pupils and staff
at Barbara and June's secondary school in Peitermaritzburg.

Barbara was now in her teens and thus of an age when adult relatives were invariably considered a source of embarrassment rather than pride. She did not enjoy the occasion, nor was she particularly receptive to Adelaide's entreaties that she study her Bible more frequently. Neither Ralf nor Margaret maintained a strong adherence to traditional religious practice and the children had not, therefore, experienced what Adelaide would have considered to be a proper Christian upbringing. It was a disappointment but, with Adelaide's irrepressible optimism, she would not have viewed this as a permanent state of affairs. And it does not seem to have clouded her obvious enjoyment of the visit. She stayed at Empangeni until the middle of April and during her journey home exchanged happy and affectionate letters with Ralf and Margaret. The 'positive Postal Union' was still working well as the ship called in at various ports along the way and she was in good spirits as she disembarked at Plymouth and took the train to London.

It would have been a welcoming homecoming early in May, the garden full of blossom and spring flowers and a pile of post and social invitations awaiting her. There were numerous requests to visit her, many involving children. One was from the local mothers and babies group who wished to organise a tea party in her garden, and another came from the Vicar of Holy Trinity in Sloane Square. Could he bring the choirboys for a picnic at her cottage and a visit to Kew Gardens? Dates were immediately set for these events but soon she was sending out postponements. She had a bout of 'the gastric flu which had been going around,' she said. By the end of June she was telling people that she was 'supposed to be writing my memoirs' but she was 'confined to bed with feverish symptoms.'[15] She was not allowed to sit up she said. After several weeks her condition had shown no signs of improvement and she was growing thinner and weaker. It was decided that she should go to a nursing home for a while and Mary arrived to book

her into an establishment in Royal Avenue, just off the Kings
Road in Chelsea. Her neighbour, Maud White, waved her off,
reporting later that Adelaide was convinced she would be back
in about ten days time. Mary, meanwhile, took up residence in
nearby Cadogen Square so she could look after her sister. Sadly,
however, there was to be no recovery for Adelaide and the ten
days gradually turned into weeks. She had a severe kidney
infection and, in the pre-antibiotic days of the 1930s, there was
little effective treatment. The end came very suddenly on 28
August with Mary at her side. As Alex's telegram to Ralf and
Margaret the following day explained, 'Sissy died peacefully
yesterday. Pneumonia intervened.'[16]

The world Adelaide left in 1936 was very different to the one
she had entered in 1863. Her career had begun in the Victorian era
and had almost extended to the beginning of the Second World
War. It was a period of enormous change in the employment
opportunities available to women, but also in the conditions in
which people worked. She entered the Factory Department on
the cusp of this change when new developments in scientific and
medical knowledge were beginning to influence the practice of
health and safety and new methods of investigation were being
introduced. Adelaide, the moral philosopher and significantly
short on relevant knowledge, elected to embrace these changes
fully, increasingly engaging her staff in scientific research,
technical measurement and statistical analyses of accident and
disease trends to inform policy development. In the process she
helped to improve the employment conditions of thousands of
working women. She did not, of course, achieve this alone, for
the very essence of civil service is its requirement to work with
others within a structured organisation, promoting change by
means of its existing framework of rules, regulations, enquiries
and committees. This story has focussed on the work of the
women factory inspectors but the Factory Department in which
Adelaide worked was largely composed of male inspectors,

many of whom were similarly committed to the contemporary innovative approaches to industrial health and safety. While some might have been obstructive, many others were co-operative, frequently collaborating with the women to address new and difficult problems. The work Adelaide undertook with the help of Thomas Legge and under the direction of Arthur Whitelegge was of particular significance in this respect. However, the essentially male-focussed department Adelaide joined in 1894 was one where women workers were, at best, undifferentiated from men in terms of their needs and problems and, at worst, entirely ignored. Adelaide's special focus, therefore, was to raise the profile of the thousands of women employed in industry and to draw attention to the dreadful conditions in which many of them worked. Her approach was predicated on the assumption that women's needs were different from those of men, and that other women, (women inspectors) were needed to identify and address those needs. At the same time, therefore, one of her most significant achievements was to establish the presence of women in the factory inspectorate and to progressively raise the status of women inspectors to that of equal partners with their male colleagues. By the time she left her post the Factory Department contained a body of well-qualified, well-trained and competent women working on equal terms with men.

Adelaide was, it seems, the right woman at the right time. Notwithstanding the attacks from those who espoused a slightly earlier and purer vision of gender equality, her views on the special needs of women chimed well with the prevailing mood of the period, and presented less of a threat to those who held the reins of power. Calm, courteous and ostensibly demure she was also conspicuously lacking in the shrill radical zeal that would have militated against success in the Home Office. As a result, she quietly succeeded where many more vehement and vociferous women of the period would probably have failed. In many ways, however, she remained a stereotypical middle-class Victorian lady. Her prim manner, intense religiosity and her preoccupation with the protection of female morals all bore testimony to a world that was fast disappearing and by the early 1920s, it seems, she was no longer the right woman for the job. The very equality she had achieved for the lady inspectors had led to the creation of an organisation where special protection for women by women was no longer considered necessary or appropriate.

Victorian and Edwardian women who involved themselves in social reform needed to be determined, focussed and supremely confident of the rightness of their cause. Adelaide, it seems, was all of these, but it was perhaps another characteristic of such women that contributed most to her years of achievement in the Home Office. Above all, she possessed remarkable courage. It is something that is often underestimated in historical analyses of the time, obscured, as it tends to be, by bland official reports and the contemporary habit of stoical understatement. Yet courage was an essential prerequisite for those who ventured into places ridden with extreme poverty, disease and violence, environments that were invariably far outside their own family experiences. In Adelaide's case, autocratic industrialists, patronising magistrates, the hostility of frightened workers and sometimes of male colleagues in the Factory Department all brought their own special additional terrors for a woman who had spent her childhood chaperoned and protected at every turn. Even Constance Smith, arguably one of the strongest critics of Adelaide's style of leadership, conceded with admiration that the iron control exerted by the Principal Lady Inspector was understandable, for she had spent 'a quarter of a century at the Home Office struggling for room to live.'[17] Throughout this period Adelaide needed to draw on other forms of courage too, coping simultaneously with serious family illness, both mental and physical, the loss in different ways of two beloved sisters, and an intense anxiety for the safety of her youngest brothers during the war. In 1921, her own rejection by the department that had become central to her working life was a crushing blow, both to her aspirations and her sense of personal self worth. And once more it was courage that enabled her to shake off the disappointment and, at the age of nearly sixty, to travel alone to the other side of the world. Her involvement in the industrial conditions of China and Egypt was no doubt motivated, in part, by her own need to be useful and occupied, and perhaps also to re-enter a world where her assumptions about women workers and their different requirements still held true. But it should also be remembered that, in addition to her concern for women, she retained throughout her life a passionate interest in the treatment of children. And it was in child labour conditions overseas that she found most to distress her, and to motivate her. Unlike her time in the British Factory Department there is no obvious legacy from these aspects of her work, overtaken as they were by international conflict and natural disaster. But she remained convinced that, ultimately, her own work and that of her friends in the YWCA would bear the fruit that she so much desired, for it was in her response to children that she most often revealed a much softer, less formal aspect to her nature. Whether they be the children in her own family or the small émigrés she encountered on the *Arundel Castle*, the grubby little observers of fine art in Barnsley or the abused and overworked weavers in Egypt and China, all provoked in her a sense of love and an intense desire to protect.

Adelaide's funeral, once more at Brookwood, was held on the morning of the 2 September followed by a memorial service on the twentieth at Holy Trinity, Sloane Square. Between those two dates Alex and Mary were deluged with letters of condolence, for Adelaide's life had been very full, of people, events, organisations and causes. These letters, personal, official and everything in between, were of course from those who had variously liked, loved or at the very least admired her. As such they can only provide a partial view of her character, but there is much that chimes with the personality that emerges from her correspondence and from her work. She was, according to her friends and colleagues, 'determined' 'optimistic' 'good-humoured', 'kind', 'sympathetic' and 'loyal-hearted' and of course 'courageous'. She had 'a vital interest in life' and 'a love of humanity'. She was 'one of the biggest souled people I knew.' All these words and phrases, however, are thrown into sharp relief by some other words, which reveal, to those who encountered her along the way, the incredible personal journey she had travelled. For to fellow student Adela, at Girton, she had been simply 'my frail little friend'.

Adelaide in Durban, South Africa, 1936

NOTES

Abbreviations

BL: British Library

IWM: Imperial War Museum

LSE: London School of Economics Library

MRC: Warwick. Modern Records Centre, University of Warwick

TNA: The National Archives

WL: Women's Library at the London School of Economics

Chapter One

1. Obituary of Dame Adelaide Anderson in *The Times*, 29 August 1936.

2. See chapter twelve.

3. See chapter sixteen.

4. The suffragist song, 'March of the Women', composed by Ethel Smyth, contains the line 'wide blows our banner and hope is waking'. At the suffragist shop in London various goods decorated in suffragist colours of purple, white and green were sold. Many women surreptitiously showed their support for the cause by purchasing these goods without revealing the significance of the colours to other family members.

5. Women working in the munitions industry during the First World War were nicknamed 'canaries' because their skin was often stained yellow as a result of working with TNT powder.

6. Girton College Archives GCAS 2/6//2/1/1. Address by Rt. Hon. Margaret G. Bondfield, at the Memorial Service in Girton Chapel, for Dame Adelaide Anderson, 1 August 1937.

7. Report of the Chief Inspector of Factories and Workshops to HM Principal Secretary of State for the Home Office for the year ending 32 October 1879. C.2489 (London: HMSO, 1880) 100.

8. A. M. Anderson, *Women in the Factory; an Administrative Adventure, 1893–1921* (London: John Murray, 1922).

9. *Women in the Factory*, 286.

10. A. M. Anderson, *Humanity and Labour in China; An Industrial Visit and its Sequel, 1923–1926* (London: Student Christian Movement, 1928).

Chapter Two

1. Letter from Alexander Gavin Anderson to Mary Gavin Anderson, 25 April 1864. Anderson family papers.

2. A. C. Geddes, *The Forging of a Family* (London: Faber & Faber, 1952) 86.

3. The role of lice in the transmission of the disease was unknown during the early nineteenth century.

4. H. J. C. Grierson (former pupil and poet) quoted by A. Shewan in *Spirat Adhuc Amor. The Record of the Gym. (Chanonry House School) Old Aberdeen* (Aberdeen: The Rosemount Press, 1923) 14.

5. Francis Campbell (1823–1911) had a long career in New Zealand, serving as clerk to the House of Representatives for a record thirty-five years.

6. W. D. MacIntyre, ed., *The Journal of Henry Sewell 1853–57*, vol. 1 (Christchurch: Whitcoulls Publishers, 1980) 125ff.

7. H. C. Jacobson, *Tales of Banks Peninsula*, 'No. 9, Early Reminiscences' (Akaroa: H. C. Jacobson, Mail Office, 1893) 121, https://archive.org/details/talesofbankspeni00jacoiala (accessed 28 July 2015).

8. Letter from Alexander Gavin Anderson to Alexander 'Govie' Anderson, 26 June 1864. Anderson family papers.

9. Letter, 26 June 1864.

10. Letter from Blanche Emily Anderson to Mary Gavin Anderson, 23 September 1864. Anderson family papers.

11. Letter, 26 June 1864.

12. Letter, 23 September 1864.

13. Letter, 23 September 1864.

14. The Bible; Psalm 121. In the King James Version, used in the nineteenth century and presented to Blanche Emily, the Psalm begins, 'I will lift up mine eyes unto the hills, from whence cometh my help. My help cometh from the Lord which made heaven and earth.'

15. Letter from Alice MacDonnell to Alexander James Anderson, 28 August 1936. Anderson family papers.

16. This term for Scottish was common during the period and always used by Adelaide.

17. Elizabeth Garrett Anderson was the first woman to qualify as a doctor in Great Britain.

18. Letter from Elizabeth Garrett to Charlotte Anderson, 16 January 1871. Anderson family papers.

19. Letter from Andrew Anderson to Marion Anderson (second wife of Alexander 'Govie' Anderson), 4 February 1871. Anderson family papers.

20. Letter from Blanche Emily Anderson to Mary Marshall, 10 February 1871. Anderson family papers.

21. Letter, 10 February 1871.

22. Letter from Alexander 'Govie' Anderson to Marion Anderson, 9 February 1871, Anderson family papers.

23. Letter, 10 February 1871.

24. Letter, 10 February 1871.

25. Letter, 10 February 1871

26. Letter, 10 February 1871.

27. The Langham Place Set were an influential group of feminists who came together during the second half of the nineteenth century to promote the cause of female emancipation. They established their headquarters at 19 Langham Place, London, from where they campaigned for equal educational and employment opportunities for women and for female suffrage.

28. Letter, 4 February 1871.

Chapter Three

1. E. Kaye, *A History of Queen's College, London, 1848–1972* (London: Chatto & Windus, 1972) 112.

2. R. G. Grylls, *Queen's College 1848–1948* (London: Routledge, 1948) 17.

3. T. F. T. Baker, D. K. Bolton and P. E. C. Croot, 'Hampstead: Frognal and the Central Demesne' in *A History of the County of Middlesex: vol. 9, Hampstead, Paddington* ed. C. R. Erlington (London: Victoria County History, 1989) 33–42. http://www.british-history.ac.uk/vch/middx/vol9/pp33-42 (accessed 27 July 2015).

4. 'Erit nulli propius; sed cedet in usum nunc mihi, nunc alii.' From *Sermona Liber Alta, Sermo II*, by Quintus Horatius Flaccus (Horace). http://www.uah.edu/student_life/organizations/SAL/texts/latin/classical/horace/sermones202fram.html (accessed 28 July 2015).

5. See for example, G. S. Thompson, *Mrs Arthur Strong. A Memoir* (London: Cohen & West Ltd, 1949); E. Sharp *Hertha Ayrton: A Memoir* (London: Edward Arnold & Co, 1926); H. M. Swanwick, *I Have Been Young* (London: Victor Gollancz Ltd, 1935); E. E. R. Mumford, *Through Rose-coloured Spectacles: The Story of a Life* (Leicester: Edgar Backus, 1952).

6. Swanwick, *I Have Been Young*, 117.

7. Girton College Archives. GCAS 2/6/2/1/1. Letter from Adela Kensington to the organizing committee of Adelaide Anderson's memorial service at Girton College, Cambridge to be held on 1 August 1937, expressing a wish to make an address at the ceremony.

8. WL 7AMA/A/03. Lecture notes and essays of Adelaide Anderson during her time as a student at Girton College, Cambridge, 1885–87.

9. WL 7AMA/A/03. Lecture notes and essays.

10. A. Marshall, *Principles of Economics* (London: Macmillan, 1890). Marshall wrote this book during the 1880s. It ran to several editions and remained the standard text for students of economics for many years.

11. P. Groenewegen, *A Soaring Eagle: Alfred Marshall: 1842–1924* (Cheltenham: Edward Elgar Publishing, 1995) 322–23.

12. Mumford, *Through Rose-coloured Spectacles*, 51.

13. Sharp, *Hertha Ayrton: A Memoir*, 61-62.

14. Mumford. *Through Rose-coloured Spectacles*, 51.

15. Swanwick. *I Have Been Young*, 116.

16. Swanwick, *I Have Been Young*, 271.

17. WL 7AMA/A/03. Moral Sciences Tripos examination papers. Girton College, 1887.

18. Girton College Archives. GCAS 2/6//2/1/1. Proposed address by Adela Kensington at the memorial ceremony for Adelaide Anderson, 1 August 1937.

19. Girton College Archives. GCCB 2/1/9/1885–86. F. H. Durham, 'Dame Adelaide Anderson, DBE' *Girton Review*, February 1937.

20. WL 7AMA/A/02.Letter from ME Johnson, Lecturer in Moral Sciences, Cambridge, to Adelaide Anderson, 1 October 1887.

21. Cambridge did not award women full degrees until 1936.

22. *ad eundem*, literally 'of the same rank'. A courtesy degree offered by one university to alumni of another who were resident in the city.

23. WL 7AMA/A/02. Letter from Maud Daniel to Adelaide Anderson, 9 June 1887.

24. Proposed memorial address by Adela Kensington.

25. WL 7AMA/A/02. References from Lecturers in Moral Sciences, Cambridge: J. N. Keynes, 3 September 1887; M E Johnson, 1 October 1887.

26. WL 7AMA/A/02. Reference from James Ward, Lecturer in Psychology, Cambridge, 12 September 1887.

27. Proposed memorial address by Adela Kensington.

28. Proposed memorial address by Adela Kensington.

29. *Shipping Gazette*, 7 December 1887, 12.

30. Proposed memorial address by Adela Kensington.

31. Caird Library 347.792 Orient. C 8204. Orient Australian Annals. Prepared by Various Associates of the Company, 1946.

32. WL 7EGA/02. Papers relating to the marriage settlement of Elizabeth Garrett Anderson.

33. WL 7AMA/A/05. Letter from Rosalind Shore Smith to Adelaide Anderson, 1 August 1889.

34. Toynbee Hall was established by the Barnetts in 1884, in memory of their friend, Oxford academic Arnold Toynbee. Many of those who worked there had previously been students at Oxford University.

35. WL 7AMA/A/05. Letter from Rosalind Shore Smith to Adelaide Anderson, 20 September 1889.

36. WL 7AMA/A/05. Letter from Rosalind Shore Smith to Adelaide Anderson 26 September 1889.

37. Extract from a letter from Ernest Bevin to surviving dock strikers, 1940. Quoted in L. Raw, *Striking a Light. The Bryant and May Matchwomen and their Place in History* (London: Continuum Books, 2009) 171.

38. Govie died in 1884.

39. Dropsy: former term for oedema, the accumulation of fluid in body tissues causing swelling, most commonly occurring in the feet and legs.

Chapter Four

1. Emma Paterson trained as a bookbinder and worked with Emily Faithful, the founder of the women's Victoria Press which employed women as compositors in the face of strong opposition from the male-only compositors union, the London Typographical Society. Paterson founded the Union of Bookbinders and Upholsterers in 1874 and, as their representative, became the first woman to be admitted to a meeting of the TUC. She believed strongly in the establishment of women's trade unions as the means of promoting equality of opportunity for women workers and the improvement of their working conditions.

2. The Amalgamated Society of Laundresses was formed in 1889 to fight for a reduction in working hours that would bring laundry workers into line with textile workers. The Society attracted huge support culminating in June 1891 when a rally in Hyde Park attracted 30,000 supporters including male unionists. Less than a week later, however, a proposed amendment to the new Factory Act of 1891, which would have established a statutory ten-hour day for laundresses, was defeated in the House of Commons by a collaboration of Conservative and Irish Unionist MPs, the latter fearing that the amendment would threaten the operation and therefore the income of laundries run by the church and charities as corrective institutions. Following this defeat the Society rapidly lost members and by 1895 the organization had disappeared altogether.

3. Report of the Chief Inspector for the Year ending 1879, 100.

4. *The Times*, 21 July 1892.

5. H. H. Asquith, *Memories and Reflections, 1852–1927*, vol. 1. Little Brown: Boston; 1928, 229.

6. 'Factory and Workshop Inspection,' *The Times*, 25 January 1893.

7. 'Death in the Workshop', *Daily Chronicle*, 15 December 1892; 'White Cemeteries: Massacre of the Innocents,' *Daily Chronicle*, 21 December 1892.

8. 'Paralysis, Convulsions and Death,' *Daily Chronicle*, 28 December 1892.

9. TNA HO45/9856/B12393AC. Letter from William Tudor of W. Tudor & Co. Hull, to the Home Secretary, May 1896.

10. B. Drake, *Women in Trade Unions* (London: Virago, 1920 republished 1984) 16–20.

11. R. Strachey, *The Cause* (London: Virgo, 1928, republished 1978) 238.

12. 'Factory and Workshop Inspection,' *The Times*, 1893.

13. MRC Warwick. MSS.69/1/2. Diary of Lucy Deane, December 1893–January 1894.

14. WL 7AMA/C/01. Testimonial from Mr Dwyer enclosed with an application letter of Adelaide Anderson. 31 January 1893.

15. WL 7AMA/C/01. Letter from Professor Henry Sidgwick to Adelaide Anderson, 24 February 1893.

16. MRC Warwick. MSS. 69/1/2. Diary of Lucy Deane.

17. MRC Warwick. MSS. 69/1/2. Diary of Lucy Deane.

18. MRC Warwick. MSS. 69/1/3 Diary of Lucy Deane, February–March 1894.

19. MRC Warwick. MSS. 69/1/1. Diary of Lucy Deane, September–December 1893.

20. Eliza Orme qualified as a lawyer in 1888, gaining her degree at the University of

London. She was a member of the moderate National Society for Women's Suffrage and the Society for Promoting the Employment of Women. She was a strong supporter of equal employment rights and opposed protective legislation for women workers. She was often pragmatic in approach and critical of 'strong-minded women who went in for stridency', preferring 'sound-minded women', features which may account for her selection as Senior Lady Assistant Commissioner of the Women's Employment Commission.

21. MRC Warwick. MSS. 69/1/4. Diary of Lucy Deane, March - May 1894.

22. WL 7AMA/C/01. Letter from Adelaide Anderson to Home Secretary, 16 April 1894.

23. WL 7AMA/C/01. Letter from James Bryce to Adelaide Anderson, 3 July 1894.

24. Nottinghamshire Archives. Case Books and Reports of Medical Superintendent, 1880–1966. PL/70/3/15-2119.

25. Letter from Mr W. Lund to Ralf Anderson, 20 November 1894. Anderson family papers.

Chapter Five

1. MRC Warwick. MSS.69/1/5. Diary of Lucy Deane, May–July 1894.

2. MRC Warwick. MSS.69/1/4. Diary of Lucy Deane, March–May 1894.

3. MRC Warwick. MSS.69/1/4. Diary of Lucy Deane.

4. MRC Warwick. MSS.69/1/4. Diary of Lucy Deane.

5. MRC Warwick. MSS.69/1/4. Diary of Lucy Deane.

6. MRC Warwick. MSS.69/1/4. Diary of Lucy Deane.

7. MRC Warwick. MSS.69/1/4. Diary of Lucy Deane.

8. MRC Warwick. MSS.69/1/4. Diary of Lucy Deane.

9. MRC Warwick. MSS.69/1/4. Diary of Lucy Deane.

10. Sweatshops: a term for workplaces in which people were employed in the so-called 'sweated trades', characterised by long hours with low pay in poor conditions.

11. MRC Warwick. MSS.69/1/4. Diary of Lucy Deane.

12. Report of the Chief Inspector of Factories and Workshops to HM Principal Secretary of State for the Home Department, for the Year 1894. C. 7745 (London: HMSO, 1895) 28.

13. MRC Warwick. MSS.69/1/6. Diary of Lucy Deane, July–September 1894.

14. Report of the Chief Inspector of Factories and Workshops to HM Principal Secretary of State for the Home Department, for the Year 1895. C.8067 (London: HMSO, 1896) vol. II, 102.

15. Charges Against a Lady Factory Inspector. *Leeds Mercury*, 2 December 1896. MRC Warwick. MSS.69/1/16. Diary of Lucy Deane, August–December 1896.

16. MRC Warwick. MSS.69/1/17. Diary of Lucy Deane, December 1896–February 1897.

17. Factory Act Offences. *Leeds Weekly Express*, 12 December 1896.

18. Report of the Chief Inspector for the Year 1895, 112.

19. Report of the Chief Inspector for the Year 1895, 98.

20. Report of the Chief Inspector of Factories and Workshops, for the Year 1901. Cd. 1112 (London: HMSO, 1902) 170.

21. Annual Report of the Chief Inspector of Factories and Workshops, for the Year 1896. C. 8561 (London: HMSO, 1897) 340.

22. Hansard, 7 May 1891. Response to a Parliamentary question from Mr Summers, MP for Huddersfield. It was reported that the number of half-timers under the Factory Acts was 98,818.

23. Overlooker: the conventional name for the foreman in textile mills and some other places of work.

24. Annual Report of the Chief Inspector of Factories and Workshops, for the Year 1899. Cd. 223 (London: HMSO, 1900) 274.

25. Report of the Chief Inspector for the Year 1899, 274.

26. Report of the Chief Inspector for the Year 1894, 12.

27. Report of the Chief Inspector for the Year 1894, 12.

28. Report of the Chief Inspector for the Year 1895, vol. I, 99; vol. II, 9.

29. MRC Warwick. MSS.69/1/6. Diary of Lucy Deane.

30. MRC Warwick. MSS.69/1/4. Diary of Lucy Deane.

31. R. H. Sherard, *The White Slaves of England, Being True Pictures of Certain Social Conditions in the Kingdom of England in the Year 1897* (London: AC Fifield, 1910).

32. R. E. Squire, *Thirty Years in Public Service: An Industrial Retrospect* (London: Nisbet & Co Ltd, 1927) 68–69.

33. Anderson. *Women in the Factory*, 285.

34. Report of the Chief Inspector for the Year 1894, 28.

35. Report of the Chief Inspector for the Year 1894, 29.

36. Report of the Chief Inspector for the Year 1894, 35.

37. A. M. Anderson, 'Historical Sketch of the Development of Legislation for Injurious and Dangerous Industries in England' In T. Oliver (ed.) *Dangerous Trades: The Historical, Social, and Legal Aspects of Industrial Occupations as Affecting Health, by a Number of Experts* (Bristol: Continuum, 1902, republished in 2004) 24–43.

38. A. M. Anderson, 'Labour Legislation' In the *Encyclopaedia Britannica, a Dictionary of Arts, Science, Literature and General Information* (Cambridge: Cambridge University Press, 1911, 11th edition) 35–45. https://en.wikisource.org/wiki/1911_Encycopaedia_Britannica/Labour_Legislation (accessed 26 July 2015).

39. Report of the Chief Inspector for the Year 1894, 6.

40. Report of the Chief Inspector for the Year 1894, 60.

41. Report of the Chief Inspector for the Year 1895, 136–186.

42. Report of the Chief Inspector for the Year 1894, 25.

43. Report of the Chief Inspector for the Year 1895, 119.

44. Ankylostomiasis: otherwise known as hookworm. It occurred primarily in Cornish tin mines.

Chapter Six

1. Annual Report of the Chief Inspector of Factories and Workshops, for the Year 1898. Cd. 27. (London: HMSO, 1899) 171.

2. Report of the Chief Inspector for the Year 1898, 172.

3. Annual Report of the Chief Inspector of Factories and Workshops, for the Year 1906. Cd. 3586 (London: HMSO, 1907) 219.

4. Report of the Chief Inspector for the Year 1906, 220.

5. Report of the Chief Inspector for the Year 1895, 38–39.

6. Annual Report of the Chief Inspector of Factories and Workshops, for the Year 1897. C. 8965 (London: HMSO, 1898) 49.

7. Report of the Chief Inspector for the Year 1897, 49.

8. The Humanitarian League was formed in 1891 by Henry Salt, a writer and campaigner for social reform. The League aimed to apply rational principles to oppose all forms of cruelty in society. Its members used tracts, lectures and letters to newspapers to address a wide range of issues including hazardous industries and sweated trades.

9. Mallett C. Dangerous Trades for Women. Humanitarian League, Pamphlet No 9. London: William Reeves; 1893, 8.

10. 'Death in the Workshop', *Daily Chronicle*, 15 December 1892. 'White Cemeteries: Massacre of the Innocents', *Daily Chronicle*, 21 December 1892. 'Paralysis, Convulsions and Death', *Daily Chronicle*, 28. December 1892.

11. TNA HO45/9848/B12393A. Report of an enquiry into the death of Annie Case a white lead worker in the employment of Millwall White Lead Company, Abraham MA. 1893.

12. Blue line: otherwise known as 'Burton's line' is caused by lead sulphide resulting from the reaction of lead with sulpher produced by oral bacteria. It is regarded as a marker of exposure to lead. Inquest into the death of Annie Case, Stratford Express, 12 August 1893.

13. TNA HO45/9848/B12393A. Letter from Reverend Newland to the East London Coroner, 1893.

14. Gone hoppin: annual hop picking.

15. Diachylon pills contained lead oxide and glycerine and were commonly used by women to end unwanted pregnancies. See W. B. Ransom, 'On Lead Encephalopathy and the Use of Diachylon as an Abortifacient', *British Medical Journal* (1900) 1590–91.

16. TNA HO45/9848/B12393A. Report on the results of an enquiry into the employment of women in the white lead trade in Newcastle. Abraham MA. 1895,

17. TNA HO45/9856/B12393AC. Letter from S. Tudor & Co of Hull to the Home Secretary, May 1896,

18. TNA HO45.9856/B12393AC. Petition to the Home Secretary from the female lead workers of Newcastle upon Tyne, June 1896,

19. The Women's Emancipation Union was formed in 1892 with the objective of securing the political, social and economic independence of women. Its members supported total equality between men and women in all aspects of life.

20. J. M. E. Brownlow, *Women and Factory Legislation*, (London: Women's Emancipation Union, 1896) 6.

21. Letter from Adelaide Anderson to Beatrice Webb, 15 January 1896. Anderson family papers.

22. Overpopulation and rural poverty in southern Italy during this period led to a wave of emigration, mostly to the United States but also to England, where the majority of migrants settled in London and took up unskilled work.

23. TNA HO45/9848/B12393A. Report of Arthur Henderson, Superintending Inspector for Scotland and Northern England to Sprague Oram, 29 December 1892.

24. Anderson, *Women in the Factory*, 1.

25. White phosphorus: also known as yellow phosphorus.

26. This toxic effect is now considered to be related to the formation of compounds known as bisphosphonates, produced when phosphorus enters the body via the respiratory tract. These disrupt the action of cells which normally resorb damaged bone. The amount of damaged bone increases and, deprived of a blood supply, this becomes vulnerable to infection.

27. C. Dickens, 'One of the Evils of Match-making', *Household Words*, 5, 110 (May 1852) 152–155.

28. Report of the Chief Inspector for the Year 1895, 115.

29. TNA HO45 9850 B12393D memorandum of Henry Cunynghame 1898.

30. Fifty pence plus costs of £2.32½p in decimal coinage.

31. *Daily Telegraph*, 3 June 1898.

32. *Westminster Gazette*, 2 June 1898.

33. *The Times*, 22 July 1898.

34. Letter from Millicent Fawcett to the editor of *The Standard* 23 July 1898. Letter from Millicent Fawcett to the Editor of *The Times*, 27 July 1898.

35. Report of the Chief Inspector for the Year 1894, 95.

36. Report of the Chief Inspector for the Year 1895, 112–13.

37. Report of the Chief Inspector for the Year 1895, 112–13.

38. Report of the Chief Inspector for the Year 1894, 97–98.

39. Appeal to the High Court, Fuller v Squire, 1901 2 KB 209. Reported in Squire, *Thirty Years in Public Service*, 72-73.

40. In 1903 Adelaide expressed her disappointment that after nearly 10 years as an inspector, (eight as Principal Lady Inspector) her salary was finally raised to £400 per annum, the starting salary of a male inspector. Recounted in a letter from Blanchie Anderson to Ralf Anderson, 2 October 1903. Anderson family papers.

Chapter Seven

1. V. R. Markham, *May Tennant: A Portrait* (London: Falcon Press, 1949) 25.

2. MRC Warwick. MSS. 69/1/15. Diary of Lucy Deane, March-July 1896.

3. MRC Warwick. MSS. 69/1/15. Diary of Lucy Deane, March-July 1896.

4. MRC Warwick. MSS69/1/6. Diary of Lucy Deane, July-September 1894.

5. MRC Warwick. MSS69/1/18. Diary of Lucy Deane, May-August 1897.

6. M. E. Tennant, 'The Women's Factory Department', *The Fortnightly Review*, July–December 1898, 150–51.

7. M. E. Tennant, 'The Women's Factory Department'.

8. Contrary to the portrayal in the novels of Arnold Bennett, notably *Anna of the Five Towns*, the Potteries comprised six towns: Longton, Fenton, Stoke, Hanley, Burslem and Tunstall.

9. Hansard, 63. 29 July 1898, 475.

10. *Daily Chronicle*, 22 January 1898.

11. R. Whipp, *Patterns of Labour, Work and Social Change in the Pottery Industry* (London: Routledge, 1990) 18.

12. Fritting: the process of fusing materials in the furnace which rendered them dustless and less harmful.

13. TNA HO45/9983/B26610. Edward Troup. Lead Poisoning. 19 May 1898.

14. Term used by the Chairman of the Joint Committee of Pottery Manufacturers in Stoke-on-Trent on 21 December 1903. Reported in *The Times*, 22 December 1903.

15. A. Bennett, *The Old Wives' Tale* (first published 1908, reprint by Loki Publishing, 2011) 5.

16. Report of the Chief Inspector for the Year 1897, C.8965 (London: HMSO, 1898) 52.

17. Majolica: earthenware pottery with a colourful clear lead glaze, first developed by Minton's in the mid nineteenth century to mimic the sixteenth-century French Pallissy ware. It was subsequently adopted by a number of other established British firms.

18. Colour dusting: the application of a glaze by applying a dry mixture over the surface of the clay body.

19. Report of the Chief Inspector for the Year 1897, 53.

20. Report of the Chief Inspector for the Year 1898, Cd. 27 (London: HMSO, 1899) 163.

21. Wrist drop: a form of muscular atrophy affecting the hand and wrist following exposure to organic lead. The wrist hangs down flaccidly and the sufferer is unable to lift or extend it.

22. Report of the Chief Inspector for the Year 1897, 53–54.

23. Report of the Chief Inspector for the Year 1897, 101.

24. Report of the Chief Inspector for the Year 1897, 102.

25. Report of the Chief Inspector for the Year 1897, 102.

26. Report of the Chief Inspector for the Year 1897, 102.

27. Professor T. E. Thorpe and Professor Thomas Oliver, *Report on the Employment of Compounds of Lead in the Manufacture of Pottery, their Influence upon the Health of the Workpeople, with Suggestions as to the Means which might be Adopted to Counteract their Evil Effects* (London: HMSO, 1899).

28. Report of the Chief Inspector for the Year 1899, 300.

29. Annual Report of the Chief Inspector of Factories and Workshops, for the Year 1900. Cd. 668 (London: HMSO, 1901) 369.

30. Certifying surgeons were appointed by the Factory Department, originally to certify the age of children working in factories. Under the Factory Act of 1878 they were further required to receive reports of industrial accidents causing death or injury, and to carry out investigations. Under the Factory Act of 1891 their duties were extended still further to include medical reports of industrial diseases and the medical examination of workers suspected of suffering from such diseases.

31. Report of the Chief Inspector for the Year 1900, 368.

32. Report of the Chief Inspector for the Year 1897, 250–251.

33. Grandrille: A ply yarn spun of strands of different colours.

34. 'Sanitary drinks' consisting of lemonade containing sodium citrate were believed to offer workers some protection against the health effects of lead exposure.

35. Report of the Chief Inspector for the Year 1898, 165.

36. Report of the Chief Inspector for the Year 1898, 169.

37. Report of the Chief Inspector for the Year 1899, 260.

38. Report of the Chief Inspector for the Year 1898, 147.

39. Annual Report of the Chief Inspector of Factories and Workshops, for the Year 1919. Cmd. 941 (London: HMSO, 1920) 61.

40. Anderson, *Women in the Factory*, appendix II, 20–21.

41. T. M. Legge, *Industrial Maladies* (Oxford: Oxford University Press, 1934) 64.

Chapter Eight

1. Letter from Walter Anderson to Ralf Anderson, 21 July 1898. Anderson family papers.

2. Letter from Ralf Anderson to Walter Anderson, 12 August 1898. Anderson family papers.

3. Letter, 12 August 1898.

4. Letter from Ralf Anderson to Walter Anderson, 9 January 1900. Anderson family papers.

5. The Chartered Bank of India, Australia and China took over banking interests in South Africa around this time to form the Chartered Standard Bank, based in Johannesburg.

6. Letter, 9 January 1900.

7. Letter from Blanchie Anderson to Ralf Anderson, 7 June 1900. Anderson family papers.

8. Letter from Adelaide Anderson to Ralf Anderson, 3 March 1901. Anderson family papers.

9. Letter, 3 March 1901.

10. Letter, 7 June 1900.

11. School prospectus in Elizabeth Davey, Angela Bolton, and Marilyn Hogan, *Birkenhead High School: A History* (Birkenhead High School, 2002).

12. Letter from Blanche Emily Anderson to Ralf Anderson, 9 August 1901. Anderson family papers.

13. Report of the Chief Inspector for the Year 1900, 370.

14. Report of the Chief Inspector for the Year 1901, 172.

15. This report was eventually published in 1907. A. M. Anderson, and T. M. Legge, *Tinning of Metals: A Special Report on Dangerous or Injurious Processes in the Coating of Metal with Lead or a Mixture of Lead and Tin* (London: HMSO, 1907).

16. H. Martindale, *Some Victorian Portraits and Others* (London: George Allen & Unwin Ltd, 1948) 46.

17. Report of the Chief Inspector for the Year 1901, 171.

18. Air spa: a type of resort common in Germany. The high quality of the air was thought to have health giving properties.

19. Letter from Blanchie Anderson to Ralf Anderson, 4 September 1902. Anderson family papers.

20. Letter, 7 June 1900.

21. Letters from Blanche Emily Anderson to Ralf Anderson. 8 February 1905; 18 June 1905; 25 June 1905. Anderson family papers.

22. Factory and Workshops Act, 1901 (1 Edw. 7 c.22).

23. Report of the Chief Inspector for the Year 1898, 167.

24. Report of the Chief Inspector for the Year 1898, 166.

25. Report of the Chief Inspector for the Year 1898, 168.

26. Report of the Chief Inspector for the Year 1899, 265.

27. Report of the Chief Inspector for the Year 1899, 265.

28. Annual Report of the Chief Inspector of Factories and Workshops, for the Year 1913. Cd. 7491 (London: HMSO, 1914) 171.

29. Bisulphide of carbon: Now usually referred to as carbon disulphide, (CS_2).

30. Report of the Chief Inspector for the Year 1897, 218.

31. T. Oliver, 'Indiarubber: Danger Incidental to the Use of Bisulphide of Carbon and Naptha', in Thomas Oliver (ed), *Dangerous Trades* (London: John Murray, 1902) 472.

32. Report of the Chief Inspector for the Year 1895, 37.

33. Report of the Chief Inspector for the Year 1901, 80.

34. Report of the Chief Inspector for the Year 1901, 72-80.

35. Report of the Chief Inspector for the Year 1901, 72-80.

36. Letter from Blanchie Anderson to Ralf Anderson, 2 October 1903. Anderson family papers.

37. Letter from Blanchie Anderson to Ralf Anderson, 14 December 1900. Anderson family papers.

38 *Birkenhead High School: A History.*

39. Mary Adamson Anderson had qualified as a doctor in France in 1879, subsequently practising in Cannes at a time when the medical profession remained largely closed to women in England.

40. Letter from Blanche Emily Anderson to Ralf Anderson, 18 June 1905. Anderson family papers.

41. Letter from Blanche Emily Anderson to Ralf Anderson, 25 January 1905. Anderson family papers.

42. Letters from Blanche Emily Anderson to Ralf Anderson, 23 May 1905, 18 June 1905. Anderson family papers.

43. Letter from Blanche Emily Anderson to Ralf Anderson, 26 July 1905. Anderson family papers.

44. Letter, 26 July 1905.

45. Letter from Adelaide Anderson to Alexander Anderson, 19 October 1905. Anderson family papers.

46. Letter, 19 October 1905.

47. Letter from Nestie Sanders to Alexander Anderson, (undated). Anderson family papers.

48. Letter, 19 October 1905.

Chapter Nine

1. G. B. Dickson, *On Cleanliness* (Edinburgh, 1852). Quoted in A. P. Mohun, *Steam Laundries, Gender, Technology and Work in the United States and Great Britain, 1880–1940* (Baltimore: John Hopkins University Press, 1999) 35.

2. *Routledge's Manual of Etiquette* (London: Routledge, 1860) 49.

3. Annual Report of the Chief Inspector of Factories and Workshops, for the Year 1912. Cd. 6852 (London: HMSO, 1913) 142–44.

4. Calender: a form of large mangle with heated rollers driven by a steam engine.

5. Report of the Chief Inspector for the Year 1900, 378.

6. Report of the Chief Inspector for the Year 1901, 167.

7. Report of the Chief Inspector for the Year 1900, 379. See also Repasseues, Edgar Degas,1884, reproduced in, McKiernan M, Art and Occupation, Occupational Medicine. 2015; 65: 268–69.

8. Report of the Chief Inspector for the Year 1900, 379.

9. Report of the Chief Inspector for the Year 1900, 379.

10. Data derived from the special reports of Anna Tracey in the Annual Reports of the Chief Inspector of Factories and Workshops for the Years 1900–1913.

11. Report of the Chief Inspector for the Year 1913, 110.

12. Martindale. *Some Victorian Portraits*, 48–49.

13. Report of the Chief Inspector for the Year 1900, 164.

14. Annual Report of the Chief Inspector of Factories and Workshops, for the Year 1902. Cd. 1610 (London: HMSO, 1903) 167.

15. The 'occupiers' of factory or workshop premises: A term usually synonymous with employers or managers.

16. Annual Report of the Chief Inspector of Factories and Workshops, for the Year 1904. Cd. 2569 (London: HMSO, 1905) 251.

17. Report of the Chief Inspector for the Year 1901, 169.

18. Report of the Chief Inspector for the Year 1904, 251.

19. Report of the Chief Inspector for the year 1899, 266.

20. Report of the Chief Inspector for the Year 1900, 377–78.

21. Annual Report of the Chief Inspector of Factories and Workshops, for the Year 1910, Cd. 5693 (London: HMSO, 1911) 120.

22. Report of the Chief Inspector, for the Year 1913, 81.

23. Report of the Chief Inspector for the Year 1902, 167.

24. Report of the Chief Inspector for the Year 1902, 167.

25. This reflected a condition whereby the internal tissue of a crushed limb was virtually destroyed while the external tissue appeared to have suffered only minor bruising. Detailed understanding of this condition only fully emerged during the treatment of soldiers during the First World War.

26. Classification of the depth of burns and the prognostic implications of this, as well as an understanding of the problems of fluid loss and infection, also awaited advances in medical knowledge acquired during the First World War.

27. The name derived from Mary Magdalene, considered to have been converted by Christ and saved from the sin of prostitution.

28. Both Irish Nationalist MPs and Irish Unionist MPs were unsupportive of laundry regulation which might include Irish institutional laundries.

29. Annual Report of the Chief Inspector of Factories and Workshops, for the Year 1907. Cd. 4166 (London: HMSO, 1908) 203–10.

30. Report of the Chief Inspector for the Year 1907, 203.

31. Report of the Chief Inspector for the Year 1907, 203.

32. Report of the Chief Inspector for the Year 1907, 204.

33. Report of the Chief Inspector for the Year 1907, 204.

34. Annual Report of the Chief Inspector of Factories and Workshops, for the Year 1909. Cd. 5191. (London: HMSO, 1910) 151.

35. Report of the Chief Inspector for the Year 1909, 203.

36. Annual Report of the Chief Inspector of Factories and Workshops, for the Year 1908. Cd. 4664 (London: HMSO, 1909) 123.

37. Report of the Chief Inspector for the Year 1906, 186.

38. Report of Chief Inspector, for the year 1909, 151

39. Report of the Chief Inspector for the Year 1908, 123.

40. Report of Chief Inspector for the Year 1909, 152.

41. Report of the Chief Inspector for the Year 1907, 203.

42. Report of the Chief Inspector for the Year 1907, 203.

43. Report of the Chief Inspector for the Year 1908, 123.

44. Report of the Chief Inspector for the Year 1908, 123.

45. Report of the Chief Inspector for the Year 1908, 123.

46. Annual Report of the Chief Inspector of Factories and Workshops, for the Year 1905. Cd. 3036 (London: HMSO, 1906) 263.

47. Report of the Chief Inspector for the Year 1907, 204
48. Report of the Chief Inspector for the Year 1907, 203.
49. Report of the Chief Inspector for the Year 1909, 150.
50. Report of the Chief Inspector for the Year 1909, 152.
51. Report of the Chief Inspector for the Year 1908, 124.

Chapter Ten

1. Hansard, 16 February 1904.
2. The scheme was also known as the 'Potters' Lead Fund'. After a year of operation it had only considered four claims.
3. Report of the Chief Inspector for the Year 1904, 258–59.
4. Report of the Chief Inspector for the Year 1897, 109.
5. MRC Warwick. MSS69/1/21. Diary of Lucy Deane, October–November 1897.
6. MRC Warwick. MSS69/1/21. Diary of Lucy Deane.
7. Report of the Chief Inspector for the Year 1899, 276.
8. Report of the Chief Inspector for the Year 1899, 275.
9. Report of the Chief Inspector for the Year 1899, 248.
10. Squire. Thirty Years in the Public Service, 90–91.
11. Squire. Thirty Years in the Public Service, 95.
12. Squire. Thirty Years in the Public Service, 96.
13. Squire. Thirty Years in the Public Service, 97.
14. Squire. Thirty Years in the Public Service, 277.
15. Report of the Chief Inspector for the Year 1900, 388.
16. Report of the Chief Inspector for the Year 1900, 388.
17. Report of the Chief Inspector for the Year 1899, 270.
18. Report of the Chief Inspector for the Year 1910, 133.
19. TNA LAB15/92. Report on Conferences Between Employers, Operatives, and Inspectors concerning the Employment of Women and Young Persons in the Curing of Herring by Miss R. E. Squire and W. Williams. September 1913.
20 Report of the Chief Inspector for the Year 1910, 133. Annual Report of the Chief Inspector of Factories and Workshops for the Year 1911. Cd. 6239 (London: HMSO, 1912) 154.
21. The Standard, 6 July 1912.
22. Women's Trade Union Review, October 1911, 3–4.
23. Anderson, Women in the Factory, 21.
24. TNA HO45/10553/164207. Memo from Arthur Whitelegge to Edward Troup, 25 November 1908.
25. BL 46065. Letters to Lord Gladstone, December 1907–June 1908.
26. Squire, Thirty Years in Public Service, 133.

27. H. Martindale, *From One Generation to Another, 1839–1944* (London: George Allen & Unwin, 1944) 149.

28. TNA HO/45/10553/164207. Memorandum from Adelaide Anderson to Arthur Whitelegge. 12 November 1908.

29. TNA HO/45/10553/164207. Anderson to Whitelegge, 12 November 1908.

30. TNA HO45/10553/164207. Whitelegge to Troup, 25 November 1908.

31. Report of the Chief Inspector for 1909, 121.

32. Report of the Chief Inspector for the Year 1911, 27.

33. Report of the Chief Inspector for the Year 1911, 27.

34. Report of the Chief Inspector for the Year 1911, 27.

35. The National Insurance Act of 1911 gave workers the right to sick pay of nine shillings per week and free medical treatment for up to twenty-six weeks, in return for a weekly payment of four pennies. The Act also gave workers the right to employment pay of seven shillings and sixpence a week for up to fifteen weeks, in return for a weekly payment of two and a half pence. Mary Paterson was appointed as a Commissioner to administer this system in Scotland.

36. Hansard, 14 August 1913.

37. Hansard, 14 August 1913.

Chapter Eleven

1. Squire, *Thirty Years in the Public Service*, 169.

2. Squire, *Thirty Years in the Public Service*, 170.

3. Annual Report of the Chief Inspector for Factories and Workshops, for the Year 1914. Cd. 8051 (London: HMSO, 1915) 32.

4. Report of the Chief Inspector for the Year 1914, 34.

5. Report of the Chief Inspector for the Year 1914, 34.

6. Report of the Chief Inspector for the Year 1919, 20.

7. TNA MUN5/70/324/17. Report on the Increased Employment of Women During the War with Statistics Relating to July 1916.

8. Report of the Chief Inspector for the Year 1914, 34.

9. Report of the Chief Inspector for the Year 1914, 37.

10. Annual Report of the Chief Inspector for Factories and Workshops, for the Year 1915. Cd. 8276 (London: HMSO, 1916) 15.

11. TNA HO45/10790 300791. Letter from Adelaide Anderson to Arthur Whitelegge, 28 June 1915.

12. TNA HO45/10790 300791. Letter from Adelaide Anderson to Arthur Whitelegge, October 1915.

13. Anderson. *Women in the Factory*, appendix II.

14. Report of the Chief Inspector for the Year 1915, 15.

15. Police, Factories (Miscellaneous Provisions) Act 1916. (6 & 7 Geo V c.31). Part II, Factories and Workshops.

16. Police, Factories Act 1916.

17. TNA MUN/5/93/346/131. Munitions Council: Ministry of Munitions. Reports on Hostels for Munition Workers. May 1917–January 1918.

18. 'Demoralised' in the original sense of 'corrupted'.

19. TNA MUN/5/93/346/118. Munitions Council: Ministry of Munitions. Quarterly Report on Hostels for Munition Workers. August 1917.

20. Annual Report of the Chief Inspector of Factories and Workshops, for the Year 1918. Cmd. 941 (London: HMSO, 1919) 43.

21. Annual Report of the Chief Inspector of Factories and Workshops, for the Year 1916. Cd. 8570 (London: HMSO, 1917) 9.

22. P. Hamilton, *Three Years or the Duration: The Memoirs of a Munition Worker, 1914–1918* (London: Peter Owen, 1978) 75.

23. Hamilton. *Three Years or the Duration.*

24. IWM Mun 24/15. Jayne EB (undated) A Résumé of Women's Welfare Work at Sir W. G. Armstrong-Whitworth & Co. Ltd. 1916–1919, 1–5.

25. Squire, *Thirty Years in Public Service*, 181.

26. Report of the Chief Inspector for the Year 1918, 43.

27. Letter from Martha Peacock to Margaret Dibben, 12 November 1918. Anderson family papers.

28. Letter from Mary Birchall to Margaret Dibben, 1 December (undated, but probably 1918. Mary also 'hopes Margaret enjoyed the 'Victory Ball'). Anderson family papers.

29. Letter from Lizzie Barker to Margaret Dibben, 16 October (undated). Anderson family papers.

30. Letter from Ethel Jenkins to Margaret Dibben, (undated). Anderson family papers.

31. Report of the Chief Inspector for the Year 1914, 39.

32. TNA HO45/10790 300791. Report of Inspector Hilda Martindale, 10 February 1915.

33. TNA HO45/10790 300791. Report of Martindale, 10 February 1915.

34. Report of the Chief Inspector, for the Year 1914, 129.

35. TNA HO45/10790 300791 Report of Inspector Hilda Martindale, 9 February 1915.

36. Letter from driver James Mackenzie to his wife, March 1915. 'The Great War Forum', Tony Lund, 8 November 2006. http://1914-1918.invisionzone.com. (Accessed 19 June 2015).

37. Letter from Ralf Anderson to Mary Anderson, 2 November 1918. Anderson family papers.

38. In 1920 this area became 'the State of Iraq'.

39. Letter from Yuills Ltd to Adelaide Anderson, 3 July 1916. Anderson family papers.

40. Letter from Alexander Anderson to Adelaide Anderson 16 September 1916. Anderson family papers and IWM AJA/3/5.

41. Letter from Alexander Anderson to Adelaide Anderson, 16 September 1916.

42. Letter from Alexander Anderson to Adelaide Anderson. 7 October 1917. Anderson family papers and IWM AJA/3/6.

43. Letter from Alexander Anderson to Mary Anderson. 12 January 1918. Anderson

family papers and IWM AJA/3/9.

44. Letter from Alexander Anderson to Adelaide Anderson, 23 October 1916. Anderson family papers and IWM AJA/3/7.

45. Letter from Alexander Anderson to Adelaide Anderson 23 October 1916. Anderson family papers and IWM AJA/3/4. Private Edwin Smith had, in fact, died the previous April during an unsuccessful attempt by the Black Watch to relieve the siege.

46. Cousin Jonathan: a popular name for the United States of America.

47. JB: John Bull (England). Cousin J: America. Froggie: France. Jock: The 9th (Scottish) Division of the Army. Letter from Alexander Anderson to Adelaide Anderson. 12 January 1918. Anderson family papers and IWM AJA/3/9.

48. Maude: General Maude. Allen: General Allenby. Bruno: Russia. Letter from Alexander Anderson to Mary Anderson, 27 January 1918. Anderson family papers and IWM AJA/3/10.

49. Report of the Chief Inspector for the Year 1918, 43.

50. Squire, *Thirty Years in Public Service*, 178.

51. Squire, *Thirty Years in Public Service*, 179–80.

52. Squire, *Thirty Years in Public Service*, 179.

53. Report of the Chief Inspector for the Year 1918, 31.

54. Hansard. 3 April 1917.

55. Letter from Herbert Samuel MP to Adelaide Anderson, 1 April 1917. WL 7AMA F 01.

56. Conclusions of the Medical Board held at the Royal Victoria Hospital, Netley, on the 5th of March 1916. www.hambo.org/kingscanterbury (Accessed 22 June 2015).

57. Award for outstanding contribution to agriculture (Knight). There are three levels (Commander, General and Knight)

58. *The Times*, 5 June 1919.

Chapter Twelve

1. A. Meynell, 'Builders of Ruins' in A. H. Miles (ed.) *Women Poets of the Nineteenth Century* (London: Routledge, 1907). http://www.bartleby.com/293/index1.html (accessed 31 July 2015).

2. The Bible; St Paul's Epistle to the Romans, 8:28.

3. Squire, *Thirty Years in Public Service*, 190–91.

4. Squire, *Thirty Years in Public Service*, 192.

5. Martindale, *Some Victorian Portraits and Others*, 47.

6. Report of the Chief Inspector for the Year 1919, 3.

7. Report of the Chief Inspector for the Year 1919, 3

8. Report of the Chief Inspector for the Year 1919, 14

9. Report of the Chief Inspector for the Year 1919, 15

10. Report of the Chief Inspector for the Year 1919, 15

11. Report of the Chief Inspector for the Year 1919, 15

12. Report of the Chief Inspector for the Year 1919, 39.

13. Report of the Chief Inspector for the Year 1919, 74.

14. Report of the Women's Employment Committee. Cmd. 9239 (London: HMSO, 1919) 39.

15. Cited in D. Thom, *Nice Girls and Rude Girls: Women Workers in World War 1* (London: I B Taurus & Co. Ltd, 1998) 132.

16. Squire, *Thirty Years in Public Service*, 180.

17. Report of the Chief Inspector for the Year 1919, 76.

18. Report of the Chief Inspector for the Year 1919, 76.

19. Report of the Chief Inspector for the Year 1919, 74.

20. Report of the Chief Inspector, for the Year 1919, 74

21. Report of the Chief Inspector, for the Year 1919, 49.

22. Report of the Chief Inspector for the Year 1919, 49.

23. Report of the Chief Inspector for the Year 1919, 79–80.

24. Report of the Chief Inspector for the Year 1919, 50–51.

25. Report of the Chief Inspector for the Year 1919, 52.

26. Report of the Chief Inspector for the Year 1919, 52.

27. The National Institute of Industrial Psychology was founded in 1921 by Cambridge psychologist C. S. Myers, in collaboration with business man H. J. Welch, as a scientific association to investigate and advise on the improvement of working conditions and human performance. The impetus for its development came from the work of the 'Industrial Fatigue Board' established during the First World War with the objective of maximising production, particular in the armaments industry.

28. Staff Reorganisation. Memorandum from the Chief Inspector of Factories, 9 August 1920. Anderson family papers.

29. Letter from Adelaide Anderson to Alexander James Anderson, 14 May 1921. Anderson family papers.

30. Letter 14 May 1921.

31. G. Tuckwell, *Constance Smith: A Short Memoir* (London: Duckworth, 1931) 31.

32. Tuckwell, *Constance Smith*, 37.

33. The note, which begins 'Dearest Adelaide,' is undated and the signature is undecipherable. Anderson family papers.

34. WL 7AMA/C/03. Letter from Constance Smith to Adelaide Anderson, 19 May 1921.

35. Letter, 19 May 1921.

36. WL 7AMA/C/03. Letter from Constance Smith to Adelaide Anderson, 24 May 1921.

37. LSE PA 787 5/1. Letter from Constance Smith to Violet Markham 30 January 1920.

38. LSE PA 787 5/1. Factory Department: Notes on position in future of the Women's Branch. Confidential memorandum from Constance Smith to Violet Markham 16 January 1920.

39. LSE PA 787 5/1. Letter from Constance Smith to Violet Markham 21 March 1920.

40. LSE PA 787 5/2. Committee on Re-organisation of the Factory Inspectorate.

Memorandum of Evidence. Escreet HC. 22 January 1920.

41. The Sex Disqualification (Removal) Act (9 &10 Geo. 5 c. 71) was passed in December 1919. It stated that 'A person shall not be disqualified by sex or marriage from the exercise of any public function, or from being appointed to or holding any civil or judicial office or post, or from entering or assuming or carrying on any civil profession or vocation'.

42. LSE PA 787 5/1. Letter from Malcolm Delevingne to Violet Markham, 15 August 1920.

43. WL 7AMA/C/03. Letters to Adelaide Anderson from friends, relatives and colleagues,

44. WL 7AMA/C/03. Letter from Rose Squire to Adelaide Anderson, 18 May 1921.

45. WL 7AMA/C/03. Letter from Hilda Martindale to Adelaide Anderson, 15 August 1921.

46. Letter from Hilda Martindale to Adelaide Anderson, 3 September 1921.

47. WL 7AMA CO4. Letter from Lady Rhondda to Adelaide Anderson, 12 July 1921.

48. Letter from Louisa Garrett Anderson to Alexander James Anderson, 24 October 1921. Anderson family papers.

49. Court gown: The dress Adelaide had worn when she was presented at court in 1892.

50. Letter, 24 October 1921.

51. WL 7AMA C04. Speech given by Adelaide Anderson at her retirement dinner 21 October 1921.

52. Speech by Adelaide Anderson.

53. Letter from Adelaide Anderson to Alexander James Anderson, 14 May 1921.

54. Letter, 14 May 1921.

55. WL 7AMA/E/01. Letter from Adelaide Anderson to Hugh Fowler, 18 September 1920.

56. WL 7AMA/E/01. Letter from Hugh Fowler to Adelaide Anderson, 16 October 1920.

57. WL 7AMA/E/01. Letter from Mary Piercy, of British YWCA to Adelaide Anderson, 16 February 1922.

58. WL 7AMA/E/01. Letter from Adelaide Anderson to Margaret Dibben, 8 March 1922.

Chapter Thirteen

1. Diary of Adelaide Anderson 14 April 1923. Anderson family papers.

2. Diary of Adelaide Anderson, 6 April 1923.

3. Diary of Adelaide Anderson, 15 June 1923.

4. Letter from Adelaide Anderson to Mary Anderson, 17 June 1923. Anderson family papers.

5. Diary of Adelaide Anderson, 8 April 1923.

6. Diary of Adelaide Anderson, 8 April 1923.

7. WL 7AMA/E/01. Letter from Adelaide Anderson to Mr Malan, 27 September 1922.

8. WL 7AMA/E/01. Letter from High Fowler to Adelaide Anderson. 12 December 1922.

9. Letter from Alexander Anderson to Ralf Anderson, 26 November 1922. Anderson family papers.

10. Vera Scantlebury-Brown Collection, Baillieu Library, University of Melbourne: Letter-Diaries from England, 1917–1919 (Acc 84/82), Vol. A2, 79.

11. Endell Street Hospital: A military hospital, established in Holborn, London, during the war by Drs Louisa Garrett Anderson and Flora Murray. It was the first hospital for male patients staffed entirely by women doctors.

12. Vera Scantlebury-Brown Collection.

13. Diary of Adelaide Anderson, 24 February 1923. Anderson family papers. LGA: Louisa Garrett Anderson; ED: Emily Davies.

14. Diary of Adelaide Anderson, 26 February 1923.

15. Diary of Adelaide Anderson, 28 March 1923.

16. Diary of Adelaide Anderson, 26 April 1923.

17. Diary of Adelaide Anderson, 15 May 1923.

18. Diary of Adelaide Anderson, 21 May 1923.

19. Diary of Adelaide Anderson, 8 May 1923.

20. Diary of Adelaide Anderson, 22 May 1923.

21. Letter from Adelaide Anderson to Mary Anderson, 17 June 1923. Anderson family papers.

22. The Marion Institute: this was established in 1918 by an Anglican Sister in Capetown. It was intended as a club offering singing, dancing and a night school to provide activities for young black women.

23. Harold Butler was formerly Deputy Permanent Secretary in the British Ministry of Labour.

24. WL 7AMA/D/01. Letter from Harold Butler to Adelaide Anderson, 6 March 1923.

25. Agatha Harrison was subsequently an activist for reform in India and a close associate of Mahatma Gandhi.

26. I. Harrison, *Agatha Harrison: An Impression by Her Sister* (London: George Allen & Unwin, 1956) 32. Quoted in K. Garner, *Precious Fire: Maud Russell and the Chinese Revolution* (Massachusetts: University of Massachusetts Press, 2003) 47.

27. WL 7AMA/D/01. Letter from Agatha Harrison to Adelaide Anderson, 10 May 1923.

28. B. Russell, *The Problem of China* (London: George Allen & Unwin, 1922, reprinted 2013 by Lightning Source, UK Ltd.)

29. The Treaty Ports was the name given to certain port cities in China, Japan, Taiwan, and Korea that were opened up to foreign trade and residence under the terms of what were known as Unequal Treaties. Shanghai was established by the British under the Treaty of Nanking in 1842 following their defeat of the Chinese in the First Opium War. It remained a Treaty Port for the next hundred years. The British occupied certain areas of the city and established 'extraterritoriality' meaning that British citizens residing in Shanghai were under the control of their own consul and judicial system and were not therefore subject to the laws of the land in which they were living.

30. Russell, *The Problem of China*, 31.

31. Russell, *The Problem of China*, 32.

32. Letter from Adelaide Anderson to Mary Anderson, 17 June 1923.

33. WL 7AMA/D/01. Letter from Adelaide Anderson to Bishop Logan Roots, 14 July 1923.

34. Diary of Adelaide Anderson, 20 June 1923.

35. Diary of Adelaide Anderson, 13 June 1923.

36. Letter from Adelaide Anderson to Mary Anderson, 17 June 1923.

37. Letter from Adelaide Anderson to Mary Anderson, 17 June 1923.

38. Letter from Adelaide Anderson to Mary Anderson, 17 June 1923.

39. Letter 'Dear Friends' from Adelaide Anderson, 5–27 November 1923, on board 'Tango Maru', Anderson family papers.

40. Letter, 'Dear Friends'. Extract from 'Melbourne' by Patrick Moloney.

41. Letter, 'Dear Friends'.

42. WL 7AMA/D/01. Letter from Agatha Harrison to Adelaide Anderson, 10 May 1923.

43. WL 7AMA/D/01. *North China Daily News*, 7 June 1922.

44. WL 7AMA/D/01. Note from Agatha Harrison to Adelaide Anderson, (undated).

45. Letter 'Dear Friends', 5–27 November 1923.

46. Diary of Adelaide Anderson, 26 July 1923.

47. Letter, 'Dear Friends', 5–27 November 1923.

48. WL 7AMA/D/01. Cable from Adelaide Anderson to Agatha Harrison, 14 July 1923.

49. Shanghailanders: contemporary name for Europeans who had settled in Shanghai.

50. The Bund: the waterfront area of Shanghai with its shops, restaurants and entertainments.

51. Letter 'Dear Friends', 5–27 November 1923.

52. Letter 'Dear Friends', 5–27 November 1923.

53. Letter 'Dear Friends', 5–27 November 1923.

54. WL 7AMA/D/01. Letter from Agatha Harrison to Adelaide Anderson, 8 October 1923.

55. WL 7AMA/D/01. Letter from Mary Dingman to Adelaide Anderson, 17 October 1923.

56. Spice Islands: Maluku Islands.

57. Letter 'Dear Friends', 5–27 November 1923.

58. Letter 'Dear Friends', 5–27 November 1923.

59. WL 7AMA/D/01. Letter from Adelaide Anderson to Agatha Harrison, 29 July 1923.

60. WL 7AMA/D/01. Letter from Adelaide Anderson, 29 July 1923.

61. Letter from Winifred Holtby to Vera Brittain. 14 October 1925. Hull History Centre.

62. WL 7AMA/D/01. Letters from Agatha Harrison to Adelaide Anderson, 9 November, 15 November 1923.

63. WL 7AMA/D/01. Letter from Agatha Harrison, 15 November 1923.

64. The Peak: the area of Hong Kong on 'The Mount' above the coastal area, populated by wealthy colonials who lived in luxurious villas. WL 7AMA/D/01. Letter from Agatha Harrison to Adelaide Anderson, 8 October 1923.

65. WL 7AMA/D/01. Letter from Adelaide Anderson to Harold Butler, 6 February 1924.

66. WL 7AMA/D/01. Letter from Agatha Harrison to Adelaide Anderson, 15 November 1923.

Chapter Fourteen

1. Anderson, *Humanity and Labour in China*, 79.

2. Anderson, *Humanity and Labour in China*, 80.

3. P. French, *The Old Shanghai A–Z* (Hong Kong: Hong Kong University Press, 2010) 150.

4. French, *The Old Shanghai A–Z*, 81.

5. Ningpo: Ningbo

6. WL 7AMA/ D01.Invitation, 15 January 1924.

7. WL 7AMA/D01. Speech of Welcome by Tao-Yin, 14 January 1924.

8. Tientsin: Tianjin

9. WL 7AMA/ D01. Letter from Lucy Ker to Adelaide Anderson, 18 March 1924.

10. WL 7AMA/D01. Letter from Adelaide Anderson to Harold Butler, 6 February 1924.

11. WL 7AMA/D01. Letter from Adelaide Anderson, 6 February 1924.

12. WL 7AMA/D01. Letter from Adelaide Anderson, 6 February 1924.

13. WL 7AMA/D01. Letter from Adelaide Anderson, 6 February 1924.

14. WL 7AMA/D01. Letter from Adelaide Anderson, 6 February 1924.

15. WL 7AMA/D01. Letter from Adelaide Anderson, 6 February 1924.

16. Filature: factory where silk is drawn from the cocoons (reeling) and twisted into a skein containing seven or eight filaments and spun into a silk thread (throwing).

17. WL 7AMA/D01. Letter from Adelaide Anderson, 6 February 1924.

18. WL 7AMA/D01. Letter from Adelaide Anderson, 6 February 1924.

19. WL 7AMA/D01. Letter from Adelaide Anderson, 6 February 1924.

20. Anderson, *Humanity and Labour in China*, 97.

21. Anderson, *Humanity and Labour in China*, 97.

22. WL 7AMA/D01. Letter from Adelaide Anderson, 6 February 1924.

23. The Factory Act of 1833 stipulated that children under the age of nine could not be employed in textile factories and between the ages of nine and thirteen they were required to have at least two hours schooling each day.

24. WL 7AMA/D01. Letter from Adelaide Anderson, 6 February 1924.

25. The National Christian Council of China

26. WL 7AMA/D01. Letter from Adelaide Anderson to Agatha Harrison, 11 June 1924. The Report was published in the Shanghai *Municipal Gazette*, 3 June, 1924.

27. WL 7AMA/D01. Letter from Adelaide Anderson, 11 June 1924.

28. WL 7AMA/Do1. Letter from Adelaide Anderson 11 June 1924.

29. WL 7AMA/ Do1. Letter from Agatha Harrison to Adelaide Anderson, 24 July 1924.

30. WL 7AMA/ Do1. Letter from Agatha Harrison, 24 July 1924.

31. Letter from Adelaide Anderson, 11 June 1924.

32. Letter from Adelaide Anderson, 11 June 1924.

33. Letter from Adelaide Anderson, 11 June 1924.

34. Bishop Roots had a house in the alpine village of Kuling in Jiangxi Province, a village settlement established in 1895 as a sanatorium and rest resort for European and American missionaries working in southern China.

35. Tuchun: military governor. Many provinces in China, including Hupeh (Hubei) Province, were effectively under military rule during this period with the government in Peking exercising only limited nominal control.

36. WL 7AMA/Do1. Letter from Adelaide Anderson to Bishop Roots, 11 August 1924.

37. WL 7AMA/E/o1. Letter from Adelaide Anderson to Zoe Walford, St Ebbs School, Madras. 28 September 1924.

38. WL 7AMA/Do1. Letter from Adelaide Anderson to Harold Butler, 5 February 1925.

39. WL 7AMA/Do1. Letter from Adelaide Anderson to Bishop Roots, 27 August 1924.

40. WL 7AMA/Do1. Letter from Adelaide Anderson to Harold Butler, 5 February 1925.

41. W. J. Young, 'William E. Soothill' in *Biographical Dictionary of Chinese Christianity*, http://www.bdcconline.net/en/stories (accessed 29 June 2015).

42. Chinese Indemnity (Application) Act 1925 (15 & 16 G5 c 41).

43. WL 7AMA/E/o3. Letter from Sir Courtney Ilbert to Adelaide Anderson (undated, but following the publication of Women in the Factory in October 1922 and preceding her second voyage which began in March 1923).

44. WL 7AMA/DO1. Letter from Harold Butler to Adelaide Anderson, 10 December 1925.

45. WL 7AMA/D/o3. Letter from Adelaide Anderson to Sir Christopher Needham, 15 January 1926.

46. WL 7AMA/D/o3. Letter from Adelaide Anderson to Humbert Wolfe, Ministry of Labour, 2 January 1926.

47. WL 7AMA/D/o1. Letter from Mary Dingman to Adelaide Anderson, 29 November 1926.

48. WL 7AMA/D/o3.Letter from Lily Hass to Adelaide Anderson, 19 February 1926, with a copy to Harold Butler.

49. WL 7AMA/D/o3. Letter to Adelaide Anderson from J. B. Taylor, Chairman of Commission on Rural Co-operation, 14 May 1926.

50. WL 7AMA/D/o3. Memorandum on the British Indemnity Funds presented to Dame Adelaide Anderson by the Chinese Women of Tientsin. 21 May 1926.

51. WL 7AMA/D/o3. Chinese Opinion Concerning the British Boxer Indemnity Funds, presented by Mrs Mei and Miss Ting on behalf of the YWCA of China, May 1926.

52. WL 7AMA/D/o3. Letter from Lily Hass to Harold Butler, 21 May 1926.

53. WL 7AMA/D/03. Letter from Adelaide Anderson to H W Lee, 14 June 1926.

54. WL 7AMA/D/03. Letter from Adelaide Anderson to Harold Butler, 17 June 1926.

55. WL 7AMA/D/03. Letter from Agatha Harrison to Adelaide Anderson, 28 July 1926.

56. WL 7AMA/D/03 Letter from Adelaide Anderson to Agatha Harrison, 14 January 1927.

57. WL 7AMA/D/03 Letter from Lord Buxton to Adelaide Anderson, 10 March 1931.

58. WL 7AMA/D/03. Letter from Adelaide Anderson to Lord Buxton, 5 March 1931.

Chapter Fifteen

1. WL 7AMA/E/04. Letter from William McKnight to Adelaide Anderson, 6 August 1929.

2. Cotton ginning: a process whereby cotton fibres were separated from their seeds. By the 1930s this was carried out using machines.

3. WL 7AMA/E/04. Letter from William McKnight, 6 August 1929.

4. Legge TM. *Industrial Maladies*, London: Oxford University Press; 1934, 9.

5. WL 7AMA/ C/08. Letter from Adelaide Anderson to John Murray, 18 February 1928.

6. TNA FO 164/4/30. Letter from J. W. Annulls to P. S. Scrivener, Egyptian Ministry of Interior, European Department, 18 January 1930.

7. TNA FO 141/658/5. Letter from J. Murray, Foreign Office, to Sir Percy Loraine, British High Commissioner to Egypt, 3 January 1930.

8. WL 7AMA/E/04. Letter from Constance Padwick to Mary Dingman, 24 October 1929.

9. WL 7AMA/E/04. Letter from Constance Padwick, 24 October 1929.

10. WL 7/AMA/E/04. Letter of introduction provided by the Earl of Lytton, January 1930.

11. WL 7AMA/E/04. Letter from Mary Dingman to Constance Padwick, 2 January 1930.

12. A. M. Anderson, 'The Employment of Children in Egyptian Industry', *International Labour Review*, December 1930; vol. xxii, no. 6; 655–81.

13. Anderson, 'The Employment of Children in Egyptian Industry'.

14. TNA FO 141/658/5. Memorandum from J. Dilke to Mr Stevenson at the Ministry of Interior, Egypt. 1 February 1930.

15. TNA FO 141/658/5. Memorandum from Mr Stevenson to J. Dilke, 4 February 1930.

16. TNA FO 141/658/5. Employment of Young Workers in Industrial Occupations in Egypt. Report by Adelaide M. Anderson, April 1930.

17. TNA FO 141/658/5. Employment of Young Workers.

18. WL 7AMA/E/04. Letter from Adelaide Anderson to M. R. K. Burge, 7 April 1930.

19. WL 7AMA/E/04. Letter from William McKnight to Adelaide Anderson, 6 October 1930.

20. TNA FO 164/21/30. Letter from Adelaide Anderson to Richard Turner, 29 March 1930.

21. TNA FO 164/21/30. Letter from Richard Turner to Adelaide Anderson, 12 June 1930.

22. WL 7AMA/E/04. Letter from William McKnight to Adelaide Anderson 22 August 1930.

23. WL 7AMA/E/04. Letter from M. R. K. Burge to Adelaide Anderson, 19 May 1931.

24. WL 7AMA/D/06. Letter from Adelaide Anderson to Lady Lyttelton, 18 April 1932.

25. Letter from Adelaide Anderson to Max Anderson, Dec 1931. Anderson family papers.

26. WL 7 AMA/D/O4. Letter from Adelaide Anderson to General MacNaughton, 20 October 1931.

27. WL 7 AMA/D/O4. Letter from General MacNaughton to Adelaide Anderson, 22 October 1931.

28. WL 7 AMA/D/O4. Letter from Adelaide Anderson to M. R. K. Burge, 18 November 1931.

29. WL 7 AMA/D/O4. Letter from Adelaide Anderson to Camille Pône, 15 December 1931.

30. WL 7 AMA/D/O4. Letter from Adelaide Anderson to Mr H. H. Kung, 23 November 1931.

31. WL 7 AMA/D/O4. Letter from Mr L. H. Fu to Adelaide Anderson, 30 November 1931.

32. WL 7 AMA/D/O4. Letter from Eleanor Hinder to Adelaide Anderson, 12 December 1931.

33. WL 7 AMA/D/O4. Letter from Chrystal Macmillan to Adelaide Anderson, 21 December 1932.

34. WL 7 AMA/D/O4. Letter from Adelaide Anderson to Camille Pône, 12 February 1932.

35. WL 7 AMA/D/O4. Letter from Adelaide Anderson to Camille Pône, 10 April 1932.

36. WL 7AMA/D/06. Letter from Adelaide Anderson to Kenneth Maclennan (Secretary of the Conference of Missionary Societies in Great Britain and Northern Ireland), 25 May 1932.

37. WL 7AMA/Do/4. Letter from Camille Pône to Adelaide Anderson 3 Oct 1932; letter from Adelaide Anderson to Camille Pône, 11 October 1932.

38. The League of Nations Union, founded in Britain in 1918, was an association formed to support and promote the work and principles of the League of Nations.

39. WL 7AMA/ D/04. Letter from Adelaide Anderson to Harold Butler, 23 June 1934.

40. WL 7AMA/ D/04. Letter from Adelaide Anderson, 23 June 1934.

41. WL 7AMA/ D/04. Letter from Adelaide Anderson, 23 June 1934.

42 WL 7AMA/ D/05. Letter from Camille Pône to Adelaide Anderson 25 April 1934.

Chapter Sixteen

1. WL 7AMA/ D/04. Letter from Sir John Simon to Adelaide Anderson, 19 July 1934.

2. WL 7AMA/D/04. Letter from assistant to Sir John Simon to Adelaide Anderson, 26 October 1934.

3. WL 7AMA/ F/04. Letter from Adelaide Anderson to J. C. Maxwell Garnet, Secretary of the League of Nations Union, 21 June 1932.

4   WL 7AMA/ F/04. Letter from Adelaide Anderson, 21 June 1932.

5. WL 7 AMA/F/ 09. Letter from Adelaide Anderson to Lord Buxton, 26 May 1935.

6. WL 7AMA/F/ 09. Letter from Lord Buxton to Adelaide Anderson, 29 May 1935.

7. Squire, *Thirty Years in Public Service*, 192.

8   WL 7AMA/F/10. Board to Promote Religious Training for Social Workers. Objective and Methods of Training (undated).

9. WL 7AMA/F/09. The Spiritual Basis of Social Work. Text of opening address given by Adelaide Anderson at the Health and Labour Exhibition, St Martin's High School for Girls, Tulse Hill. 17 May 1935.

10. Old English for 'peace movement'. Grith Fyrd survives in both Britain and America in the form of the 'Woodcraft Folk' which provides adults and children with opportunities for woodland camping with a focus on developing personal and social skills.

11 Walter Sickert's *Crucifixion*: None of Sickert's works bear this name, but Adelaide may have been referring to his painting of a street in Dieppe, a detail of which is thought by some art historians to have inspired later depictions of the Crucifixion.

12. WL 7AMA/F/07. 'The Experiment in Art Exhibitions for Small Towns'. Report on first phase by Adelaide Anderson (undated).

13. WL 7AMA/F/09. Letter from Adelaide Anderson to Mr Fuller, publicity secretary for Save the Children, 11 February 1934.

14. WL 7AMA/F/09. Letter from Adelaide Anderson, 11 February 1934.

15. WL 7AMA/F/12. Letter from Adelaide Anderson to the Vicar of Holy Trinity, Sloane Square, London, 26 June 1936.

16. Telegram from Alexander Anderson to Ralf and Margaret Anderson, 30 August 1936. Anderson family papers.

17. LSE PA 787 5/1. Letter from Constance Smith to Violet Markham, 30 January 1920.

BIBLIOGRAPHY

Anderson, A. M. *Women in the Factory: An Administrative Adventure, 1893–1921*. London: John Murray, 1922.

Anderson, A. M. *Humanity and Labour in China. An Industrial Visit and Its Sequel, 1923–1926*. London: Student Christian Movement, 1928.

Asquith, H. H. *Memories and Reflections, 1852–1927*. Vol. 1, Little Brown: Boston, 1928.

Bennett, A. *The Old Wives' Tale*. First published 1908, reprint by Loki publishing 2011.

Davey, E., A. Bolton, and M. Hogan. *Birkenhead High School: A History*. Birkenhead High School, 2002.

Drake B. *Women in Trade Unions*. London: Virago, 1920, republished 1984.

French P. *The Old Shanghai A–Z*. Hong Kong: Hong Kong University Press, 2010.

Garner K. *Precious Fire. Maud Russell and the Chinese Revolution*. Massachusetts: University of Massachusetts Press, 2003.

Geddes A. C. *The Forging of a Family*. London: Faber & Faber, 1952.

Groenewegen, P. *A Soaring Eagle: Alfred Marshall: 1842–1924*. Cheltenham: Edward Elgar Publishing, 1995.

Grylls, R. G. *Queen's College 1848–1948*. London: Routledge, 1948.

Hamilton, P. *Three Years or the Duration. The Memoirs of a Munition Worker, 1914–1918*. London: Peter Owen, 1978.

Harrison, I. *Agatha Harrison: An Impression by Her Sister*. London: George Allen & Unwin, 1956.

Hoskyn, E. L. *More Pictures of British History*. London: Adam & Charles Black, 1914.

Kaye, E. *A History of Queen's College, London, 1848–1972*. London: Chatto & Windus, 1972.

Lee, M., and C. Sutton. *From the Factories to the Front Line*. Smethwick: Smethwick Heritage Centre Publications, 2015.

Legge, T. M. *Industrial Maladies*. London: Oxford University Press, 1934.

Markham, V. R. *May Tennant, A Portrait*. London: Falcon Press, 1949.

Marshall, A. *Principles of Economics*. London: Macmillan (first published, 1890).

Martindale, H. *From One Generation to Another, 1839–1944*. London: George Allen & Unwin, 1944.

Martindale H. *Some Victorian Portraits and Others*. London: George Allen & Unwin Ltd, 1948.

Mumford, E. E. R. *Through Rose-coloured Spectacles: The Story of a Life*. Leicester: Edgar Backus, 1952.

Mohun, A. P. *Steam Laundries, Gender, Technology and Work in the United States and Great Britain, 1880–1940*. Baltimore: John Hopkins University Press, 1999.

Oliver, T. (ed.) *Dangerous Trades: The Historical, Social, and Legal Aspects of Industrial Occupations as Affecting Health, by a Number of Experts*. Bristol: First published 1902, Republished by Continuum, 2004.

Raw, L. *Striking a Light. The Bryant and May Matchwomen and their Place in History*. London: Continuum Books, 2009.

Routledge's Manual of Etiquette. London: Routledge, 1860.

Russell, B. *The Problem of China*. London: George Allen & Unwin, 1922.

Sharp, E. *Hertha Ayrton: A Memoir*. London: Edward Arnold & Co, 1926.

Sherard, R. H. *The White Slaves of England, Being True Pictures of Certain Social Conditions in the Kingdom of England in the Year 1897*. London: AC Fifield, 1910.

Shewan, A. *Spirat Adhuc Amor: The Record of the Gym*. (Chanonry House School) Old Aberdeen. Aberdeen: The Rosemount Press, 1923.

Squire, R. E. *Thirty Years in Public Service: An Industrial Retrospect*. London: Nisbet & Co Ltd, 1927.

Strachey, R. *The Cause*. London: Virgo, 1928, republished 1978.

Swanwick, H. M. *I Have Been Young*. London: Victor Gollancz Ltd, 1935.

Thom, D. *Nice Girls and Rude Girls: Women Workers in World War 1*. London: I B Taurus & Co. Ltd, 1998.

Thompson, G. S. *Mrs Arthur Strong: A Memoir*. London: Cohen & West Ltd, 1949.

Tuckwell, G. *Constance Smith: A Short Memoir*. London: Duckworth, 1931.

Whipp, R. *Patterns of Labour, Work and Social Change in the Pottery Industry*. London: Routledge, 1990.

Yeandle, S. *Women of Courage*. London: HMSO, 1993.

INDEX

About the Author

Anne Spurgeon was formerly a senior lecturer at the Institute
of Occupational Health, University of Birmingham. She now
carries out research in the field of labour history specialising
in the study of women's work and industrial health and safety.